# THE SUN
# CAME
# DOWN

# THE SUN CAME DOWN

## PERCY BULLCHILD

*1817*

**HARPER & ROW, PUBLISHERS**
**SAN FRANCISCO**

*Cambridge, Hagerstown, New York, Philadelphia*
*London, Mexico City, São Paulo, Singapore, Sydney*

FIRST EDITION

Design by Brad Greene

Library of Congress Cataloging in Publication Data

Bullchild, Percy.
  The sun came down.

  1. Siksika Indians—Religion and mythology.   2. Siksika Indians—Legends.   3. Indians of North America—Great Plains—Religion and mythology.   4. Indians of North America—Great Plains—Legends.
I. Title.
E99.S54B84      1985           398.2'08997           85-42771
ISBN 0-06-250107-0

85  86  87  88  89  RRD  10  9  8  7  6  5  4  3  2  1

# Dedication

I want to dedicate this book to my Indian faith and the prayers that went with it to the publishing company.

To all those that encouraged me to write this book. To the nurses at the Toppenish Hospital in 1969. To a dear friend Randy Croce of Minneapolis. To Darnell Doore and Patty Calling Last of our Blackfeet Tribal Media.

I want to especially thank everyone at Harper & Row, particularly Dessa Brashear and Bob San Souci for their help to get the book published.

I want to dedicate this book to my wife, Rose, for all the times she was beside me, helping me to remember things I'd lost from my mind.

Also, to my deceased son Bobby, who encouraged me so many times to stay with it until I completed the book. I am so sorry he didn't get to see it published.

And if I left anyone out who helped me in one way or another, don't feel bad, as I'm thanking you now and dedicating this book to all of you helpers.

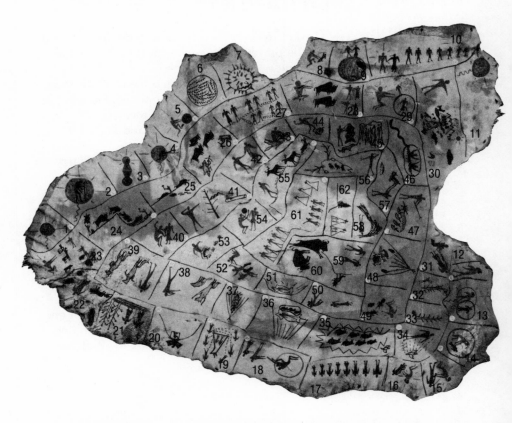

These illustrations, as drawn by the author on a cowhide, feature many of the Blackfeet legends retold in the book. The following numbered descriptions are keyed to numbers on the hide. A color version of this hide appears immediately inside the cover of the book on the endpapers.

1 Creator Sun
2 Spirit of the Sun
3 Creator Sun Is Everywhere
4 Creator Sun Becomes Lonely for Some Other Form of Life
5. Creating First Life
6 First Life of this World
7 The Natural Forces
8 The Moon Comes Into Being
9 Creator Sun and His New Mate
10 The Sun, the Moon and Their Seven Sons, the Big Dipper
11 First Life of the Heaven
12 Creator Sun
13 Snakeman Comes between Creator Sun and His Mate
14 Creator Sun Creating Man from Mud
15 Creating a Woman from the Man's Small Rib
16 Creating a Woman from the Man's Small Rib
17 The Children of Mudman and Ribwoman

*Creator Sun*
*The Only Being Before He Created This Universe*
*For Billions of Years He Was Alone*
*For He Alone Was the God*

# CONTENTS

# PREFACE

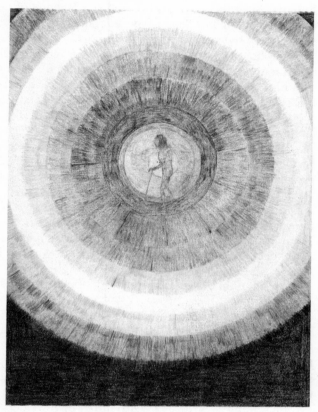

*Spirit of The Sun*

My name is Percy Bullchild, I'm sixty-seven years of age. I'm a Blackfeet Indian from Browning, Montana.

We are all of the former Tribe of the Piegans. Others of this former tribe are in Canada—the Kainais of the Bloods, the North Piegans, and North Blackfeet tribe or band, all in Alberta, Canada. Our four tribes were once one big Tribe of the Piegans. We were split by the coming of the whiteman and their international boundary that presently divides the United States and Canada.

I do not have a good education of the whiteman language, I cannot speak it fluently. Unfortunately, I only went to the sixth grade and I couldn't speak English before going to school. And so the whiteman language is still very foreign to me.

With what little education I have, I'm going to try to write the Indian version of our own true ways in our history and our legends.

Most written history of us Indians, the Natives of this North American continent, and the South American continent too, has been written by non-

Indians. But this is our history and our legends of our beginning, the very beginning of all life. Most of these are so false and smearing that it gets me mad. That's the very reason why I'm writing now.

I have done much research in the past several years. In my research I have asked many Indians from many tribes what they know of the Indians' past. The history and their legends. I have approached both young and old of these various tribes, both in the United States and Canada.

I have visited many historical Indian landmarks, and many legendary landmarks here in our area of the Piegans.

We Indians do not have written history like our white friends. Ours is handed down from generation to generation orally. In this way we have preserved our Indian history and our legends of the beginning of life.

All history the Native learns by heart, and must pass it on to the little ones as they grow up. This was very true up to my time. It's these days that the younger generation of every nationality do not have ears for such things. These young people are just too busy being smarties, radical, militant, with no respect for their elders. They just do not want to listen to anyone except themselves. They think they are always right.

From all of this, our oral prehistory of us Natives is dying away and being forgotten.

We don't tell of things that we hear from others, or recent happenings. These stories and other to follow were told to us from generation to generation as time went along. Even before the coming of the white people. Newcomers to Indian country did not teach us any of our history or how to tell a story. We do it ourselves. Things of the past are always in our minds, us old people. Our good old days that have gone by.

I, myself, must write as I heard it told by my elders and not what's written by whiteman or historians. They have a way of adding to their writings or leaving out things that may be important to the people being written about.

What of all the smear that is written about all the many Natives of all these Americas? Many things that are so untrue of the Native, things the white people done to us and say the Native done it. Examples: savagery, murdering, dirty, lust to kill, unclean, warlike, human sacrificing, lying, hatred, and many more. All of these things the Native never even heard of until the whiteman came here to teach us of them, even stealing was taught to us. So what you read of our prehistory legends, as I tell it, is just so very close to the actual truth, as we understand the stories.

My best informer of the past, both of history and the Indian legends, was my own paternal grandmother, Catches Last. She told me many things, many nights, when I was a very small boy.

My grandma, Catches Last, passed away in 1927. Since her death, many others have told me of our historic past and our legends. Those that I still remember are Yellow Kidney, Weaseltail, Herman Dusty Bull, Two Guns White Calf, Jim White Calf, Many Hides, Bear Medicine, Shortman, Lazy Boy, Shoots First, Little Plume, Percy Creighton, Heavy Breast, Calf Tail, Little Leaf, Yellow Horn, and many others. All of these men that I have named have all gone on to our Happy Hunting Grounds, where all Indians go after death.

This story is about a lone spirit that lived in this spiritual place before there was a world or any kind of life. As he lived on and on, at one time it dawned on him that there was something amiss from this lonely life of his. There was an emptiness in his heart. Somehow! He must fill that empty feeling.

This spirit was full of strange, mystic, and supernatural powers. He could do anything he wanted to do. He could transform into anything. There wasn't anything he couldn't do.

Death was nil to him, ever was his life. He has been alive from ever and will continue to live forever. Even to this day this supernatural and mystic being is still very much alive, and all of his mystic and supernatural powers are with us, among all of his creations of life. Life is given to all of us humans and to all of his creations on this earth and life is very abundant in Creator Sun's world today.

The sun came down and abided with his children in many instances to talk with them, to teach them certain things they must learn to use or do, and to give advice to them of how to survive the many treacherous things in this world he created for them.

All of this story is true, because we Natives preserved our history in our minds and handed it down from generation to generation, from time unknown, orally. From the time human life began. It isn't any different from the stories our white friends tell about such as King Arthur of the Round Table and Joan of Arc, there are many other stories of the white legends that are written too.

Some of these stories may sound a little foolish, but they are very true. And they have much influence over all of the people of this world, even now as we all live.

*Creator Sun is Everywhere*

# EARTH'S BEGINNING

## Earth's Beginning: A True Story to the Best of My Knowledge

All stories were handed down from generation to generation by the mouth, in words, which the whiteman calls orally.

I have listened to many wonderful stories that were told by the older men. At times, these storytellings went on for several days. The men told the stories while the womenfolk done the cooking for them. No one went to sleep until the wee hours of the morning, and every one awoke by sunrise to resume the storytelling.

The older men told this story of how the earth was made.

Creator Sun has lived from the beginning and he will live on forever. He can do all the impossible and more.

Creator Sun lived alone in a spiritual place for ages, no one else to be with, and naturally he got lonely for some kind of life to be with. One day he gathered the space dust and spit on it to make it into a clay. He had the future in his mind.

He could've shaped the mud into any form he wished, but thinking far ahead, made it into a round ball.

Creator Sun blew into this mud ball. The blow gave the ball life. It became suspended in mid air with air all around it to keep it in the air. There was nothing on it, it was plumb bare as it floated about in the vast void.

For the longest time he played with the ball as it floated about. He made himself small so he could play and romp on this ball of mud. For many eons of time, Creator Sun played and romped on this mud ball. But as time went along he got tired of it, he wasn't satisfied anymore. Again he began to think what else he should do to make things happier for himself.

"If only I can put something on it to make it look better," Creator Sun thought. Even then a plan was forming in his mind.

Creator Sun thought of another life besides his. Another life would surely fill in that empty place in his heart.

From the dirt of this mud ball, Creator Sun again gathered dust, because the mud ball had dried up already. From this dust he made mud again, by spitting on the dust. And with the mud of clay he made a long, slim form. This was to become the first living being on this mud ball. It was a snake. Creator Sun made the snakes to multiply, to make their own, so they would become many.

For many eons of time the snakes flourished, increasing by manyfold. In fact, they had filled this mud ball and they were still coming.

*First Life of This World*

There were certain commands given them by Creator Sun to follow. As time went on, the snakes forgot all about the command of their Maker. They went wild. Everything they did went against their Maker. They weren't listening, they took everything in their own way.

Creator Sun just couldn't stand anymore of this, he had to do something fast. The snakes were coming too fast now, and he had to stop this in some way.

Having mystical powers, Creator Sun thought of how he might destroy the snakes, the first life he made for this mud ball, which was the earth. With his power, he made this mud ball boil out from beneath. This way, the snake didn't have a chance to escape from this boiling dirt mixture. Creator Sun thought he got rid of all those snakes now. But, by a miracle, a very small female snake that was to have little ones escaped into a crevice—and for some reason, the boiling lava didn't ooze in this crevice. This small snake was saved, the rest were all boiled to destruction.

Some time after this destruction of the first life, the snakes, Creator Sun was walking around to see what had to be done to make up for this. As he walked along, he got a glimpse of the small female snake that was the only one to come out alive. Creator Sun only said, "From this small snake, let others come from her."

For the longest time again, there wasn't anything except the one snake that got away from all that boiling matter. Soon she had her little ones, and they

*Creating First Life*

were beginning to increase fast. Creator Sun, with his power, soon had them in control by using natural causes.

Creator Sun knew he was longing for something more than snakes, he just couldn't think of the right plan. One day, as he was playing and romping again in the dirt, he looked himself over. He was all dirty from the dust, and this got him to thinking about something else again—something soft to play on. It was then he invented the soft grass.

He made the grass so it would grow and grow, over and over. So the grass grew over and over—every time it got old and broken down, newer grass would grow in its place. Just like the snakes, it reproduced.

All over the ball of dirt, the grass grew as cushion or carpet for the ground. It gave the ball of dirt color, too—a beautiful, green carpet.

Creator Sun stood, admiring his work. It looked so pretty with the green now, and it was so soft to play on. But there was still something missing from this pretty ball of green.

Creator Sun again would stand around looking at his work, wondering what would make this green ball look even prettier. Thinking back to when he first destroyed the snakes, he remembered that after the mud ball was all boiled out, it got dry and hard. It dried into many pretty colors, but, of course, the green carpet was now almost all over, even covering most of the pretty color.

"I'll put pretty growth among the green, many pretty colors," Creator Sun thought. So the flower was invented to grow along with our green grass.

That first life, the snakes, had given Creator Sun many ideas of what to do to make this ball beautiful. Still, something was missing from all of this, but he just couldn't quite figure what was bothering him. He would look around, trying to pinpoint the missing something.

Creator Sun was playing and got very tired. He sat down, and almost at the same time he sat down, a thought came to him: "I must make something in my own way—something that will look like my image." He was also thinking about the snakes and how they had reproduced manyfold. He thought, "I must make my image in a way so it will reproduce like the snakes, who made themselves over and over again."

Creator Sun finally knew what he was yearning for.

# Moon and Big Dipper Come into Being

Creator Sun had a big plan for a special life to make for this ball of dirt he had made.

He, himself, was going to start this new, perfect life. But first he had to make a mate for himself.

From the dirt again, from his dirt ball, Creator Sun made mud by spitting on it. From this mud he made a figure exactly like his image, only he made it to bear fruit—to have little ones. He wanted it to multiply like the snake life.

Creator Sun was very happy after the image came to life. He had blown in the nostrils of the mud figure, which gave it life.

This was the part he had been missing all this time. Creator Sun was very contented now with this new life he was beginning for himself. He knew he would have many new images from this mate he had just made.

Being the only one on this dirt ball with his new mate, Creator Sun knew he was well on his way to bringing superior beings to this place of his. There couldn't be anything to go wrong with his plan now. He was a supreme being, all he had to do was command and he would get what he wanted.

This new life started out just as he had wanted. His mate, the Moon, bore him a little one. This little one looked exactly like he did, it was his very image and every bit like him. It was a male.

Creator Sun became a teacher now. He taught the mate what she had to do in her job as a maker of their place. He taught the little one to help the both of them in whatever the work was.

"This is the perfect way to live," Creator Sun thought to himself. He was just so well pleased for all of this.

Things went smoothly for a long time. One day, Creator Sun noticed his mate was already big again and he knew they were going to have another little one. Time flies by, as all time does. It was no time before the second little one came to Creator Sun's family.

The four of them lived very happy, because there wasn't anything dangerous to worry about. It was only the beginning of a long life for them.

For so long after this, Creator Sun's mate bore more little ones, between long intervals, until there were seven of them, the Big Dipper.

Mostly, he had to pull each one along and make motions to show it what it had to do, as there wasn't any language just at that particular time.

The time went by. Each time he was trying to show one what to do, he would be uttering a certain sound. And as this utterance of a sound went along, it became understandable to each one—our language was started now.

Time lengthened into time. Their ways became routine for all of them. They would rest for a time and begin their tasks again. The boys grew bigger and bigger, and wiser, too.

As time went along that one snake, who had escaped the destruction of her kind, also had many little ones. With each new snake that came into life, the mother snake would relate her story of how the snakes were killed off by Creator Sun's doings—the boiling of the earth.

These little snakes didn't pay much attention to the story, except for one male snake, who had already grown up into manhood. This snake wanted a revenge for his mother's sake.

At the time Creator Sun made the snakes, he had given them enough power to do certain things. Transforming themselves was one of those powers.

With what little power the male snake had, he was going to do Creator Sun as much harm as he could.

# The Natural Forces Are Created

The snakes had increased to many again. Creator Sun didn't let that worry him. He had made it so the snakes would be destroyed by natural causes.

The power Creator Sun had given them, the snakes still had that. In many ways they could use this power yet.

Creator Sun's family was getting along just so good. He was the one running this particular life of his wife, the Moon, and his seven sons, the Big Dipper. Each boy had a chore to do, their mother had hers too—taking care of their living place and going after food for them in the thickets of nature.

All of this was carried out as time went along. It was just a routine thing for them. They would rest after they got tired, lay down and sleep a while, eat after waking up, and go back to work at what was being done.

When all were at work, it was a routine thing for the woman to go off to herself to rustle what she needed for their camp.

It was one of these times the woman was alone. She was in a very high growth of shrubs, looking for food. It was there that she got very startled by the appearance of another being. A tall, slim man, and in the same manner the boys and their father, Creator Sun, were made. At that particular time, handsome or good-looking wasn't heard of. But for some reason, the woman seen something very extra special in this man's looks. She was completely overcome with surprise. She couldn't speak, she couldn't move, she just stood there and stared at this man.

Creator Sun hadn't mentioned any other beings around here. She wouldn't have been so surprised if he had said something about others being around here. She would've been expecting to see other beings like themselves.

For a long time they stood there staring at each other, probably waiting for each other to say the first word.

It was a funny thing, they understood one another when they did talk. This was very unusual. It would seem that only nine of them would know their words, the utterance they made to understand one another. But the woman was just so startled, she didn't notice.

The Snakeman was the first to break the silence. "Don't be so startled. I'm a being just like you."

The woman was still startled and couldn't quite find words to say. Finally finding words to use, she said, "You scared me very much. I didn't know there were others the same as we are around this place. My husband, Creator Sun, never mentioned others to be around here."

*First Life of the Heaven*

"He must've forgot to tell you about us," the Snakeman told the woman. "But don't be afraid of me, I won't hurt you."

By now the surprise was gone from them, they both began to talk earnestly, eventually sitting down to visit.

Both forgot time as they sat there visiting. All at once the woman jumped up, saying, "I'm supposed to be getting some things around here. I must hurry and get back, they will miss me if I do not get back to the camp."

The Snakeman jumped up too, saying, "I must be on my way, too. I have to get back to the others, before they miss me."

"Before you leave me," said the Snakeman to the woman, "I want to tell you not to mention our meeting here. If Creator Sun has forgotten about us and never mentioned our presence here, then he must find out for himself that we are still around yet. Just keep this to yourself."

The woman readily agreed to this. She was a little nervous about it herself, too.

The woman was a little late in getting home to her camp. There was no need to fear, no one was there yet.

Soon, though, each of the others began to come into camp for the meal and rest afterwards. For some reason, the woman felt quite uneasy. She really didn't have to worry, no one seen her with the strange man.

Creator Sun was always the last to come to the camp, he had quite a bit more to do than the rest of them. He came and sat down, he was quiet this time. For a long time he just sat there saying nothing. This made the woman that much more uneasy.

The woman too was unusually quiet, but she had to say something to break that awful silence. "What happened out there? Why is everyone so quiet? Maybe I can be of some help."

Creator Sun answered her, "Nothing happened. I was just wondering about a funny smell that's in the air. It's a wonder you and the boys don't smell it too."

Almost all at once, they answered, "We don't smell anything. It must be just a weed or something growing close by here, or maybe we went too close to some smelly weed."

All got quiet again. The incident was soon forgotten and all began to talk of something else. Talking of something funny for laughter, to forget the smelly incident.

At this particular time, day and night wasn't separated yet. Everyone ate and laid down for rest. All slept for some time before waking up and then went back to the chores they had to do all the time. It was just a routine thing for them.

Several times the woman went out to where she usually gathered things for their use in camp. Each time she went there, she had a secret hope of meeting the strange man she met there before.

The Snakeman bided his time. He was always around when the woman was there, but in hiding so she wouldn't see him. He didn't want to spoil things for himself. The right time would come sooner or later.

Time went on for the family of Creator Sun, each doing their part to occupy their time. Each would come to camp at a certain time for rest and food. One day the woman took her time getting out from camp. She always had other chores to do before leaving the camp area.

Once through with the camp work, she got ready to leave for her own particular area. Doing her usual thing among the growth, she had almost completely forgotten about the stranger she had met some time ago. Right at her busiest moment, she heard a noise just behind her that made her jump with fright. Again she was startled by the sight of that same strange man.

The Snakeman came again, and for some unknown reason the woman was very thrilled to see him. She wasn't afraid to see him this time. The woman even seemed very happy that this strange man came again, to talk with her again.

Right away they sat among the growth and began to talk of things that happened since their last meeting here.

The woman mentioned to the strange man that Creator Sun had some suspicion of their last meeting. Creator Sun said he smelled something peculiar. "We didn't know what it was, but I had a very good idea what it was. I never mentioned anything about our meeting. I was very near you the time we met, and I knew it had to come from you."

The Snakeman told the woman, "Just don't say anything about me yet, he will find out sooner or later. I like your company and I don't want to see it end so soon."

The woman and the Snakeman both agreed to this. They would never mention this to anyone. It would be their secret for the time being.

Meeting the strange man was like a magnetic force to the woman. She was being pulled more and more to this Snakeman, but she didn't know he was originally of the once great Snake family that overran this land before her time.

The woman went more and more to the meeting place among the high growth of bushes. She made many excuses to cover up her wrongdoings. This thing was deep in her heart, that magnetic pull was there, an urge to see that strange man all the time. The strange man seemed to be there more often, and their meetings got more and more cozy. The meetings had become more cuddly.

This went on for the longest time. Their secret meetings turned into very intimate doings.

Their meetings went on for a long time. And after all the intimate meetings between them, the Snakeman knew it was a very secure friendship, and there was nothing to come in between them from here on. So he told the woman of his true identity. He told her about himself and the snakes' previous existence. That they were the first life on Mother Earth and were put here by Creator Sun. It was all snake life then, there were tiny snakes, medium snakes, big snakes, and great big, big snakes. He told her of the destruction of them and how one female snake got away by hiding in a deep crevice. She was in family way and not too far from having her little ones. She alone survived that great destruction of the inferno. All the rest of that snake life was destroyed.

This stranger told a pitiful story, but he never mentioned why they were destroyed by Creator Sun. Naturally! The woman fell for the pitiful story. It was true to a certain extent, but the Snakeman made it so much more pitiful and worse. The woman felt awful sorry for that once great snake life and the way they were destroyed by Creator Sun. Maybe because of her feelings for this strange man, her feelings were now against her man, Creator Sun.

This woman of Creator Sun felt like she was the one to be responsible for what happened a long, long time ago.

By doing what she was doing, the meetings with the Snakeman, she had the idea she was paying for Creator Sun's wrongdoings. She really didn't have anything to do with it at all, it was a long time before her time.

This was the very thing the Snakeman was waiting for: to completely take the woman into his confidence.

He now had her where he wanted. She was on his side, it was very safe to tell her anything. He told her what to do if she wanted to get ahold of him. He took her to a very thick tangly brush not far from their meeting place. There, underneath the thick growth, where no one could see, was a den. The Snakeman told the woman to just stomp over the mouth of the den as hard as she could with her foot, and that would bring him out from his den.

It was this way for a very long time, she would stomp over the mouth of the den and he would come out to meet her. It was her now that was bothering the Snakeman, and that's just the way the Snakeman wanted it.

Many, many times she knew she was doing very wrong, but that strong magnetic force kept her coming back over and over again. She knew she shouldn't be doing this to her man, Creator Sun, and to her seven sons. It was many times she made up her mind that she would not meet the strange man anymore. But she couldn't resist that strange force of attraction.

Their meetings went on and on, and each time she left the Snakeman she wanted to go right back to him in a little while. One of the times of rest, she finally noticed that her man, Creator Sun, hadn't said much in many days—in fact, for a very long time. He was just always so very quiet now. She felt awful uneasy over this quietness. Creator Sun didn't come right out to accuse her, but that look in his eyes said enough for an accusation.

Creator Sun knew what was going on all this time, but, as always, he is so forgiving to all of his creations. He wanted her to overcome her wrongdoings by herself. This was his way of life.

Creator Sun is never the mean type, because he made all things of this Mother Earth. He loves us all. But no matter who sinned against him or his rules, they will surely pay for the sin in their life, not after, because the sin was made in this life we are living here on Mother Earth. It really is our bodies that make a sin, not our spirits, and so the body has to go through some sort of payment for those sins we commit. It may be a sickness or it may be a broken part of your body, even death or whatever is a befitting way to pay for a sin, and it all comes the way it's set for the seriousness of the sin. Nevertheless, all of us are to pay for whatever sins we commit and pay for them in this life we are living so the body will suffer for that particular sin.

Things went on as usual: the boys done their daily chores, the woman going to her usual place in the thickets to see her Snakeman almost every time she had that chance or her times in those thickets.

It was getting very close to where Creator Sun thought it should end, this wickedness of his woman. He knew of the Snakeman, because no one can hide anything from our Creator.

This time, all came in for their meal and rest. Everyone ate then laid down for their rest. After their rest, all got up to eat right after the meal, everyone left for their work area except the woman. She had to do her other chores around the camp area before she could leave for her own area of work.

Creator Sun left for his place of work, only this time he didn't go there. Creator Sun left, but went into the thickets to hide until his woman came out to her place of work. Creator Sun knew there was something going on. He knew it was her that the strange smell was coming from, he knew that no good was going on, but he must see it with his own eyes before he would believe it.

Creator Sun's woman was getting through with her camp chores and not hurrying much, she knew it wouldn't be too long before she would see her Snakeman friend. She got ready, and to the place of her work she went. She didn't even look to see if anyone was around, she went like nobody's business right to the den of her Snakeman friend.

This time, there was her own man, Creator Sun, spying on her as he waited in the thick bushes until she came. After passing him, he followed her to wherever she was going, but followed so she wouldn't see him.

The woman went right for the very thick bushes after reaching her work area, and right on to the den of her Snakeman friend. Without a bit of hesitation she went to where she usually stomped to attract her Snakeman friend in the den. In a moment, a tall, slim man emerged from the thickets. He had a slim face, his body was very tall and slim too. This! Creator Sun was taking all in from his hiding place, which wasn't too far from this very spot.

Creator Sun knew right away what it really was all about. He had recognized the strange man as one of those he had destroyed a long, long time ago.

Creator Sun didn't leave just yet, he wanted to find out firsthand what his woman was doing, why she smelled of that strange smell around the camp.

Creator Sun seen all that actually happened between the woman and her Snakeman friend. Creator Sun, after seeing what really happened between the two, hung his head in shame and sadness. His own woman was very bad.

Creator Sun, sneaking away from there, went to his place of work. He went along sadly and in a deep thought about what took place.

Creator Sun knew what he must do, but it was work first at all times.

After their work time, all had come to the camp area for their meal and rest time. Day and night wasn't divided yet, it was always bright out all the time. Each went to sleep for their rest except Creator Sun, he laid there thinking what should be done about his wife and her man friend, the Snake.

He knew the Snake family was after him for the destruction of them by him, and he must do something about them, so they would not again become many.

All refreshed from their rest after their sleep, everyone was to eat and go back to their chores again. Right after their meal, each one knew where their usual places were. The boys each went their separate ways and Creator Sun went his own way, but not to his accustomed place of work. He hid after he got out of sight of the camp and kept his eyes on the woman.

The woman always had chores to do around the camp area after everyone left. Once through with that chore, she would hurry to her usual place of work among the bushes.

Creator Sun made sure she had gone to her usual place of work before getting into action. Instead of going to his place of work, he followed his sons to their places of work, each one of them. Creator Sun brought all of the boys together in one place secretly, so the wife and mother of the boys wouldn't know of this meeting. This was a very important meeting between Creator Sun and his boys.

Creator Sun told his sons what was happening between their mother and her Snakeman friend. They were doing wicked things that was bad against his plans, and something must be done about it. He consulted his sons so they could help him decide what to do about all of this bad thing going on.

He told them all about the previous life of the Snakes and what they tried to do in this land. They had brought many evil things and wanted to run the land to their liking. How he destroyed them by a natural disaster—not by his hands, but by his power of destruction.

"After what happened to those snakes, I really didn't think I'd ever have any trouble by them. I know they want revenge for what happened to them. That revenge seems to be working, they have your mother in their confidence and can do almost anything with her now. I must put a stop to this in some way. I gave those snakes much power, which they are using against me. But I must overcome that power and stop them before they ruin this land and before they try to get you boys too into their confidence.

"From now on into the never-ending time ahead I shall destroy the power I gave them, as much of it as I can. I shall make it so even you boys will despise those snakes or any snake that is seen. From here on, all people shall go against all snakes for evilness. People shall kill them anytime they see a snake."

A plan had been made, each one knew what he must do. Creator Sun knew what was going to happen when the plan was put into effect. Creator

Sun knows all, but he is so compassionate to all of his creations, he has a big heart. All was ready, back to their place of work they all went.

At this particular time, the family didn't have names to be called by. Creator Sun and his wife, the Moon, began calling their youngest son after the way he arrived into this land through his mother. He was just so pink, he seemed to the two as if he was just raw. The two and even his brothers called him Rawman. This gave Creator Sun and his wife, the Moon, to name all of them by some sort of thing they done or built of their bodies.

Rawman being the youngest—they didn't get any more young ones after him—he became their favorite son. There was a special place in their hearts for Rawman. All of them loved him very, very much.

The boys didn't care much about their mother after hearing about her and the Snakeman. What might become of her, they didn't care, not even Rawman. They didn't want a mother like her. This was the very first experience about illicit behavior. To all of them it was the most wicked, the most evil thing that a woman could do, even if it was their own mother. All of the boys agreed with their father, Creator Sun, that the two should be punished— and for the rest of time—for their wrongdoings.

All came in for their rest and meal. The woman too came in a little earlier, for the first time since she had been meeting her Snakeman friend. After the meal all went to sleep as usual. The boys and their father, Creator Sun, were very quiet this time, no one saying much. This made the woman very nervous, she done this wrong and that, as she done her best to serve them their meals. She felt there was something awful wrong about all of this. Only the boys and their father, Creator Sun, knew they had condemned her.

Each of the boys got a special instruction for this coming period of work after their rest. Each knew what must be done in case of an emergency. This couldn't be rehearsed, and must know what must be done for their own safety. All of them were ready as they all fell asleep.

Waking up, all had their meal. No one didn't seem to want to eat, for some reason or another. The woman didn't eat much either. Getting up and leaving for their place of work as usual, none of the boys went to their usual area. Instead, after getting out of sight from the camp area, the seven boys met at a certain area preselected by their father, Creator Sun, and there they had to wait for whatever was going to happen next.

Creator Sun too left as the woman was busy with her chores. Creator Sun sneaked to the den of the woman's Snakeman friend. Before anything could go wrong—the woman just might accidentally hurry and get to her Snakeman friend's den—Creator Sun had to hurry to get there long before she might arrive.

Not hestitating for any reason, Creator Sun wanted to get this over fast. He went directly to the very spot he seen the woman stomping on. Creator Sun began stomping on the spot, and he didn't have long to wait. A commotion from within the den told him that the snake was coming out. Creator Sun was ready with a big, large flint knife in his hand and in a poise, ready to strike.

This strange Snakeman would transform into a snake as he got ready to go into his den, and he transforms into a man as he comes out all the way onto open ground.

In a poise, ready to strike just as the snake slithered to the open and his head emerged into sight, Creator Sun came down with all his might on the neck of the snake with the sharp flint knife.

The snake came slithering very fast to the surface, so when his head was chopped off, it fell to one side of the den. The snake's body kept a-coming until it was clear of the den before whipping around on the ground in its last throes of life. Creator Sun waited until the body of the snake laid still and in death before he ran for cover and to hide from the woman's view. Creator Sun had to wait to know what the woman was going to do about all of this.

It was a sad sight that Creator Sun saw of the snakes death. As the head of the snake stopped rolling, there was a surprised look in his eyes, his tongue was still a-spitting out of his mouth. Towards the last of what life was left in it, the eyes became very sad and never stopped blinking until it laid still. Its eyes stayed open as he died.

Hiding among the thick growth of bushes where the woman wouldn't be able to see him, Creator Sun waited for the woman.

The woman was getting through with her work around the camp area and biding her time so the menfolks would be far away at work before she went to the den of her Snakeman friend.

The woman didn't wait too long, probably anxious to see her Snakeman friend. She left the camp area and went to her Snakeman friend's den.

Creator Sun was very quiet as he waited there, hidden among the thick bushes. His ears were wide open for any kind of noise.

The woman came a-stealing through the bushes when Creator Sun heard the rustle of her feet in the dry growth. Creator Sun almost melted to the ground hiding, still, the woman almost brushed him as she went by. She must've been intent to get to the den, she didn't notice Creator Sun. Creator Sun, hiding there, felt very uneasy about all of this. He felt so lowly of himself, he felt ashamed, he felt guilty. After all, it was him that created these two that he was going to destroy. He already destroyed the whole snake population. He knew he should've done a good job of it the first time instead of letting that one female snake escape to bring in more trouble for him now.

The woman particularly he felt very bad about it, she was to be one of the perfect race of people he created for this earth, who he made after his own image, and now it has to be this way. It was a sad thought to Creator Sun as he waited for what was going to happen to the woman. He knew it must be done, because what the two done was very bad and shouldn't be an example for the boys in their future.

The boys had already gathered at the camp after they knew their mother had left for her place of work. They were all anxious, waiting for a word from their father, Creator Sun.

The woman passed by Creator Sun's hiding place so close, he seen a smile on her face, a smile of happiness. He knew the smile wouldn't last once she saw what became of her Snakeman friend.

In the next few steps she made, she came upon the remains of her Snakeman friend. The head was laying to one side and the body a little ways from the den. Her face turned to a horrified look as her eyes took in the whole situation. It was a pitiful sight to her. And the body, the head, looked so painful, he must've died an awful painful death.

The woman didn't know what to do. She froze in her tracks with fear and agony, slowly turning into rage and anger. For some reason, she knew it had to be Creator Sun that was to blame for this cruelty.

For the longest moment she stood there gazing on her Snakeman friend, still as a statue, frozen with dismay. All at once she got her senses back, her voice again, she let out a scream, a bloodcurdling scream. For a few moments she took the head of her Snakeman friend and sat by the body, holding the two pieces together as if that would mend them together again. She was crying, sobbing, and screaming all the time. All at once she jumped to her feet, as if she remembered something very important. She began to run for the camp area.

She ran with all her might as fast as she could go, and all the while she was screaming and crying at the top of her lungs. She was very, very hysterical, she was like a maniac.

The boys were all waiting at the camp for their next move, and all had their instructions given to them by their father, Creator Sun. Hearing their mother screaming and the sound coming closer and closer, the boys began to make a roundabout way from the camp so their mother wouldn't see them. They knew they must get to their father, he had told them where the den of the Snakeman was at.

The woman ran so fast that it didn't take long to get to the camp area. The boys had already left for the place shown to them by their father, Creator Sun.

As soon as the woman made for the camp area and away from the dead Snakeman friend of hers, Creator Sun got busy. He jumped here and there, gathering wood and piling it close by the Snakeman, who was in his snake form now. He gathered a lot of wood already before the boys came a-running to the spot. They too began to bring dry wood to the pile their father already had.

Creator Sun knew what the woman's next move would be, he made her from the dirt and should know her actions in every way. All of them were ready for the next move.

Finding the camp deserted, the woman didn't quite know what to do next. Without realizing what she was doing, she ran back towards the area where her Snakeman friend was slain. She was still a-screaming and crying hysterically. The boys and their father heard her awful screams, bloodcurdling, as loud as her lungs could sound. She was coming back to this place on a fast run.

As the woman was crying hysterically and screaming to the top of her lungs, at the same time she was calling her youngest son: *"Oo-ki-nah, Oo-ki-nah ki talk si-ni-tu, kahk sty in nah moo goo!* Rawman, Rawman, I'm going to kill you, no one will hold me from you!"

If the woman could get ahold of all of them, she wouldn't spare any of their lives, including Creator Sun's life, if she could overcome his strange powers.

Her power was almost equal with that of Creator Sun. He had given her almost all of his powers. He never once figured this life would turn out like it is going now. He was so very sure of the perfect beings he was going to have on this land, and it was to be through her too.

The boys and Creator Sun hid very near by, they were all ready for her soon as she got back here. She was coming back fast and still a-screaming, crying, and threatening them all. "I'll kill all of you soon as I get my hands on you."

Soon the woman came into sight of the hidden menfolks, they just got further down among the growth and bushes so she wouldn't see them. They waited, but kept their eyes on her.

The woman was so hysterical, she didn't notice the pile of dry wood not too far from her Snakeman friend's body. She came running into the area so fast too. She ran right straight for the body of that snake. She got on her knees and slowly laid on the snake body, she was still a-screaming, crying, and threatening the boys and their father, Creator Sun. As the woman laid across over her Snakeman friend's body, Creator Sun and his seven boys jumped out from the bushes they were hidden in and pounced on the woman. This was a complete surprise for the woman, she was overtaken by the whole ordeal. She didn't have time for any of her mysterious power that Creator Sun had given her to use for this purpose. Creator Sun and the boys didn't give her time for that. All this time she had thought they had left for places unknown.

Creator Sun and the boys, surprising her, jumped on her. With his big flint knife, Creator Sun stabbed her again and again until she laid still in death. His sons, all seven of them right alongside of him, helping him to do away with their wicked mother.

Creator Sun knew he had to make very sure the two bodies were very dead, he must make sure there weren't any parts or bits of the bodies left. He must completely destroy every bit of those two bodies. Otherwise, with the mysterious power he had given them, they could come at him and his seven sons somehow.

Telling the boys to gather more wood, he began to pile the dry wood, a good heap of dry wood, and on top of this he throwed the two bodies on. As the boys brought more wood, they piled those on top of the two bodies. Again and again the boys brought more wood to heap on top of those that were piled. It was a big heap of wood piled under and on top of the two bodies before Creator Sun was well satisfied.

He set the pile of wood on fire with his flint fire maker. The flames got bigger and bigger until the whole pile of wood was ablaze.

Creator Sun had told his sons before this to watch very closely for flying sparks from the big blaze of fire. To be sure to throw the spark of ash back into the fire. Not to let even one tiny spark go, but to be sure it was thrown back into the fire. This was very important—that Creator Sun knew alone.

Each one of the boys had a long stick to use for the sparks. Even Creator Sun had one in his hands to use to throw the sparks back into the fire.

The boys took turns in gathering more wood for the fire to make very sure that the two bodies burned to nothing, bones and all. The others, with their father, watched the fire very closely, almost non-stop, going around the fire watching for sparks. Each time a spark flew out of the fire, one of them would either use the stick or use their bare hands to throw it back into the fire. All of them trying to see every spark that might come out of the fire, they all gave that attention as close as can be done.

Every once in a while, Creator Sun would prod around in the fire and ashes to test the bodies of the two, to see if they have burned to soft ashes yet. He would stir the fire very thoroughly, the ashes, making sure the bodies were burning to nothing.

It took a long time, but the ashes burned to soft, white ashes, powdery, before Creator Sun thought it enough. The wood and the two bodies should be burned to powder. The eight of them stayed until that fireplace turned all into white powder and had cooled off before the boys and their father, Creator Sun, thought about going back to their camp area.

Creator Sun prodded around in the ashes, stirring it, making very sure there weren't any unburned particles in it. He finally thought it was good enough, telling his sons, "Come on, let us go back to our camp now and do the best we can without your mother, she is gone now and we must carry on without her somehow."

Going back towards the camp area, Creator Sun was advising the boys that all must stay together for some time, just in case of an emergency. He told them he didn't feel all that safe yet about the two they done away with. "We should know by the time we have our fourth rest or sleep."

There still was no division of night or day at this particular time. Whenever they got tired they rested and slept and ate, too. This routine often comes into a habit, work so long and rest and sleep so long.

It was a sad time at the camp, no mother to get the meals ready for them. They must take turns gathering food and preparing it—only the boys. Creator Sun had too much he had to take care of, so he was excluded from this work.

Going along and back at the camps, Creator Sun never hardly kept quiet. He talked away, giving his sons advice about what should be done in case something arises, an emergency.

"If anything happens within the next four rest periods, we must do our utmost to protect the youngest, which is Rawman. I will give each of you something to use in case of an emergency."

To Rawman, he gave a bladder of water and told him what he must do.

To the next oldest son he gave a beautiful bird, he told him what he must do if he called on him during such an emergency.

Creator Sun gave his third-oldest son a bladder that was blown up with air, and told him what must be done with it if an emergency arose within the next four rest periods. These bladders were made of roots and the leaves and barks of certain things, and made airtight by weaving them closely and tightly together. These bladders hold air and water, too, they were made as water containers. Up to this day, the Coastal Indians still weave things that are watertight and airtight, too.

To his fourth son he gave a short stick that he should carry. If needed, he would call on him for it.

To his fifth son Creator Sun gave a small rock to carry at all times until this state of emergency was called off, or until he would call on him for it.

The sixth son got instructions to use his fingers. Creator Sun told him what to do if such an emergency comes up.

The oldest and the seventh son also got a bladder full of water, which he must carry until he should be called on for it and told what to do with it.

Creator Sun would go back to check on that fireplace where the two were burnt after their return to the camp. Nothing happened before their first rest time. All ate and went to sleep, but with all the thought in them, they were lucky to sleep a few moments.

It was one of the times Creator Sun had just came back from that fireplace where the two were burnt, checking on it as usual, and so far nothing had happened. This was after their first rest.

All were sitting quietly, all sad over the recent events, waiting to see what would happen next. They heard a blood-chilling scream from the area of that fireplace. It made all of them jump to their feet.

Somehow, some way, a spark must've flew out of that fire undetected by any of them. This was what Creator Sun knew: if a spark came out of the fire, it could well mean a piece of the woman jumped out from the fire. Even a speck of her remains would bring her back to life and give her sons and her old man, Creator Sun, a bad time. Probably through her powers, a spark of her flew out of the fire undetected and here she is, screaming a blood-chilling sound. Her awful crying and those threats to all of them, especially to Rawman: "Oo-ki-nah, Oo-ki-nah, ki talk si nitu, kawk sty in na moo goo! Rawman, Rawman, I'll kill you, no one will hold me from you!"

From the sound of her, she was coming very fast, probably to check at the camp again for the menfolks. There wasn't any time for anything else but to leave in a hurry.

From the camp they all left in a hurry, on a fast run. Rawman was put in the lead, and from there all of them strung behind him. Creator Sun was the last of them all. He took the rear guard for the sake of his boys. He loved all of them, even this woman that he put to death and who was now chasing them.

They were far from the camp, they were running very fast from the woman. She would be quiet, then all of a sudden they would hear her terrible screams and cries, her threats to Rawman and all of them, and from the sound they knew she would come to the camp area soon.

The woman, coming to the area of the camp, tracked the boys and her old man, Creator Sun. It made her much madder than she already was, they left before she could get her hands on Rawman and them. She didn't realize the noise of her screams and the loud crying she was making. They would hear her coming in any direction.

It took no time for her to track them all, going from the camp on a run. All she had to do was to follow their tracks.

This was one of the things that was overlooked by Creator Sun—to cover up their tracks. Anyway! Things were happening too fast for them now.

All of the boys and their father knew she was a fast runner, they all seen her run. And as for wind, with the power that was given to her by Creator Sun, she could run forever, if she had to. So they must run fast, on and on, to try to get away from her.

This time she was hollering at the top of her lungs, "*Nook oose awk, kahk sty in nah moo goo wow, Nah-doo-si, Oo-ki-nah, ki dok si nit poo wow.* My children, no one will hold me from you all, Creator Sun, Rawman, I'm going to kill you all."

That awful-sounding screaming and the terrible cries she made were enough to make anyone run. It was bloodcurdling, blood-chilling to them all. This made them go that much faster.

They were running for their very lives now, away from their mother, and she was gaining fast on them. The woman hadn't lost all of the power Creator Sun had given her when they first got together. She was using what she had left of the power.

It wasn't too very long before she was breathing down their necks. She was right in back of them. A few more steps, she could easily catch one of them—and that would be Creator Sun. He was running last. She tried to put on more speed, which took all the power left in her. She almost was stepping on Creator Sun's heels.

Creator Sun hollered at the oldest son to throw the bladder up in the air towards his mother.

Creator Sun knew it wasn't any problem for him to get away from the woman, but it was for the boys' sake. He couldn't leave them behind and let the woman destroy the boys, especially Rawman. This was why he gave each of them something that would kind of help them in their getaway from the woman.

Creator Sun was hollering at the oldest son, "*I-stob-sks-spah-biks-it, ah-ni-yih, oi-ki-yi!* Throw the water bag up in the air towards her."

As soon as the oldest boy heard his father calling for him, for that mysterious help from the water bag, he didn't hesitate. He done what he was told. The water bag went into the air, towards the woman. And as it got just above her, for a very mysterious reason, it began to rain on the woman. It was pouring rain. This slowed her down, the ground got soaked and wet. It made it slippery for her to run very fast.

What was so mysterious about this, it only rained on the woman—which slowed her up. It gave Creator Sun and the boys time to get pretty far away from her again. In fact, they ran out of sight from her.

It took a little time for the woman to realize she had power to use for this rain. She was just so very mixed up from this ordeal she was going through. Too much thought of her Snakeman friend. It was a big loss for her.

Using that little power, the rain stopped, which put her on dry ground again. She picked up speed once on dry ground. Again she gained on those menfolks. She was catching up a little bit slowly this time.

There was no rest for all of them. Running and running for their lives. The woman running to catch them and to destroy their lives. She wasn't making any noise now—but not because she got wiser. She was very winded from that slippery ground she had to run on. She had to get her wind somehow, so she was very quiet now, but running as hard as she could go.

Creator Sun and the boys had let up on their running, too, to get their wind. They had been running very fast for quite some time now and were very winded. They thought they knew it would take the woman very long to get out from that mud, and she wouldn't be up with them for a long time yet. But all were fooled, they forgot she had some power left in her.

Without warning this time, and almost down their necks, the woman let out one of her chilling screams. She just couldn't help it. Every time she seen them all, she burnt up with fury, she must scream.

This screaming became a good warning for the boys and Creator Sun. But this first time, they almost didn't have time to get away from her.

If Creator Sun and the oldest boy hadn't jumped forward just in the nick of time, she could've grabbed one of them. It would've been the oldest boy. She knew too well that Creator Sun had too much power to be caught. That jump forward saved the oldest boy from being caught.

Again those cries, the bloodcurdling scream, and those threats to all of her sons, even to Creator Sun. "*Kawk sty in nah moo goo wow, nook oose awk!* No one will hold me from you, my children. It's just too bad when I do catch ahold of you boys and Creator Sun."

It was time to holler for help from those mystic powers, the woman was just too close for comfort. Creator Sun hollered out to the next-oldest son, "*Hi you, hi you, nu koo yi!* Urgent, urgent my son!" The three of them were about even as they ran alongside of one another. "Just in the back of you, make a mark in the dirt with your finger, across our trail." The second-oldest boy done it just so fast. They were just barely ahead of their mother. The mark in the dirt was made just a step or two before she got there. In a split moment, that finger mark became a canyon. The woman was caught on the other side of it. This mysterious canyon was very deep, with almost perpendicular walls on both sides of it.

It would be quite some time for the woman to get across this canyon, she would have to climb down and then climb back up the opposite side of it, and that would take a long time to do.

Once again, by Creator Sun's mysterious force of powers, he had saved his sons from the woman in the nick of time.

This gave the menfolks a little time for a breather. They slowed up to catch their wind. One thing, they must not stop for any reason or the woman would surely catch them. They did know it would take her quite a while to figure out how to go about getting across that deep canyon.

It was very slow going down the bank for the woman. She had to be very careful of her steps or she might fall and get hurt beyond walking again. It was a long slow descent from the top to the bottom, and the climbing was just as slow. Both sides of the canyon walls were very rugged.

At long last the woman finally made it across to the top of the other side. She didn't even take a breather after all the climbing. She went right back to her running and chasing the menfolks.

These mysterious happenings made her that much madder at Creator Sun and her sons. She could just twist their heads off if she could get ahold of them. These things made her scream and cry in fury.

They had done her mighty wrong, killing her Snakeman friend. Or probably it was vice-versa: that she had done them wrong was why this all began.

She was all-out determined to get those menfolks. She ran and ran faster than ever. She knew they were ahead quite far, her madness made her go much faster as she thought of the whole thing.

It seemed forever to catch up to them again. Her lungs were ready to burst, she was so winded now. But she didn't know the meaning of giving up.

As the boys with their father, Creator Sun, ran along, not very fast now, some distance back of them they heard that awful sound again—the cry of dismay, that blood-chilling scream, those threats to them all.

She had come up to them unexpectedly. Coming over a rise, she seen them not too far ahead. Anger seemed to make her scream something terrible.

That warning sound of her made the boys and their father, Creator Sun, come back to the realization that they were still running for their lives. Again the race was on, her trying to catch them and them trying their best to outrun her.

Again the woman was overtaking those menfolks. She was hoping against hope this time that she would catch one of them. She just had to catch one of them. She was wishing for Rawman, he could get out of all this misery, because she would kill him, do away with him.

They had destroyed something she really thought much of, the Snakeman she had intimate relations with. She must catch all of them sooner or later, whenever they got tired out.

Many thoughts entered their minds about all of this as they ran along as fast as they could go, either to catch up or to get away.

She was gaining on them very fast again. Those threats never forgotten, to be repeated every little while. "*Noo-coo-soki, noo-coo-soki, Oo-ki-nah, Nah-doo-si, kawk-sty-in-a-moo-tsi-poo-waw*. My children, my children, Rawman, Creator Sun, no one will hold me from all of you." (In my tribe of the Piegans, *kawk-sty-in-a-moo-goo-waw*, or finished off with just *moo-goo—moo-goo* means "one of them," *moo-goo-waw* means "more than one being.")

In just a few moments more the woman caught up to them, and this time she was almost in reach of the oldest boy again. Him and their father, Creator Sun, were running last, behind the rest, just for the others' safety, as they were the strongest of the group.

It was time for Creator Sun to holler for those mysterious powers again, as she was just too near for their comfort. *"Noo-koo-yi, noo-koo-yi, hah-you, hah-you, awb-aht-dob-igs-it, ah-ni-yih, o-koo-took-yi!* My son, my son, urgent, urgent, throw back that rock!"

Creator Sun no sooner said it, when the third of his sons throwed the rock he was carrying back towards his mother. Again that mysterious power worked to delay the woman so the boys and their father could rest a bit from her. As that little rock that was carried in the third boy's pouch hit the ground, a mighty mountain range sprang up. As far as the eyes could see in either direction, north and south, there seemed no end to this mysteriously placed mountain range. They were very rugged too. There were sheer walls, deep canyons, rivers and creeks, and jagged rocks throughout.

This jagged, rugged mountain terrain caught the woman again on the opposite side from the boys and their father, Creator Sun.

Once again, they knew the woman would take very long in finding a way through the rugged mountains. By Creator Sun's mystic powers the boys were saved once again from their wicked mother. Creator Sun had too much power for the woman to have her way. The woman was now facing and trying her best to overcome this mysterious force.

The woman was again burning with rage. She could eat them all if she could get her hands on them just now. All this madness didn't do her any good, just all confusion. She couldn't think straight while in a rage. She only went in circles.

She ran this way for a long time, along the foot of the rugged terrain. Looking ahead and seeing those rugged mountains endless in that way, she turned and went the opposite way along the foothills of these rugged things. That was also an endless sight of those mountains. As far as her eyes could see, she seen the mountains either way. She would have to find another way through them or over them.

The woman was still a-running along those foothills of these rugged mountains. All at once her bearings came back to her, her rage must've quieted down somewhat. A plan came to her. Why didn't she think of this in the first place?

Running along the foothills, she came to a canyon into the rugged mountains. Into this canyon she made her way, going as far as the canyon went. From there she took her own route, she scaled those walls and jagged peaks. She went up, up, and up. At long last she finally made it to the top of them. Now to get down on the other side and on to catch those boys and their father, Creator Sun.

Going down was just as hard a work as it was coming up those walls and peaks. But she had caught on to mountain climbing and she was going along much faster. It was long, hard work to get over these darn mountains Creator Sun put there as an obstacle for her, to slow her down.

Soon she was out in the open country. Away she went. If that climbing up and down those mountains made her tired, she didn't act it.

Running this way and that way, she soon found the trail of the menfolks. And from there she went as fast as her legs could carry her.

Creator Sun and the boys knew they were very far ahead of the woman. They knew when looking back to the mountains Creator Sun put in the woman's way—just by the sight of them—they would be a hard obstacle to get over. Almost impossible for anyone—but she wasn't anyone. She still had a little of the power left from Creator Sun. That! The menfolks always forgot.

Those boys and their father, Creator Sun, even stopped for a short rest. They thought the woman would have one hard time to get across the rugged walls and peaks. They were sitting there, it wasn't too long, when again from towards the mountain range came that terrible scream, the cry, and the threats to them all. She was coming fast again, it would not be very long before she caught up with them. This time they were almost taken by surprise.

Jumping up as fast as they could, the boys, with Rawman in the lead and Creator Sun with the oldest of the boys in the back, ran for dear life again. The woman was almost on top of them.

Those bloodcurdling screams, blood-chilling, enough to freeze one's spine. Them awful threats of hers to all of them. These things she hollered made them run that much more and faster.

In no time she was almost alongside of them. But the power from their father, Creator Sun, gave them a bit more power to get ahead of the woman.

At this instant Creator Sun hollered to his fourth son, "*Hah-you, noo-koo-yi, ni-tah-gaub-ot-obic-sit, ahn-ni-yi, miss-chis-yi!* Urgent my son, hurry, throw back that stick!" He didn't get through saying it when the fourth boy threw the stick back towards his mother. The stick landed right in front of the woman. The stick touched the ground, when instantly! A very large forest sprang up in front of her. It was also very thick, and one would have much trouble to get through it.

If cuss words were made then, how the woman could cuss her man, Creator Sun, and her seven sons. But it was only the beginning of time, no such words were used then.

Creator Sun, with his endless powers at work, kept the boys from their mother's harm. The woman had some of Creator Sun's powers yet, but mostly her power was no match for his.

The woman really never once really thought about that strange and powerful power of Creator Sun. She was only thinking of the kill in her mind, and not how it would be done by her.

Once again, the woman was delayed by that force of mystery, the mystic powers of Creator Sun. She didn't know how wide this forest would be or how large it was. She soon found out it was very thick in its growth. She could hardly get into it, she just about had to back out of it when she tried to go into it to find a way through it.

She ran this way and that way, looking for an opening through the tangly growth. Almost each time she tried, she had to back out of it.

For the longest time she tried to penetrate her way through the thick forest. She tried and tried again. After many, many tries, the woman finally got lucky and found a passage through this tangly growth of forest. It took her a long time, but she got through it to continue her chase of Creator Sun and her seven sons.

It was an awful job to get through the vast forest, especially the last few feet. It was squeeze through these trees, crawl under this bush or over that one. Getting scratched here and there, on her face, arms, and legs. Her hair all messed up by the limbs. She looked just so haggard, she looked awful when she emerged out on the other side of this vast forest. But again those powers left in her gave her the strength to get through it.

She was just so very tired after coming out into the open again, she could've just laid down and fell asleep to rest her tired, aching body. Creator Sun, her man, and her seven sons were just too much on her mind for even a little rest. She must run after them and catch them this time. They had given her too much trouble, killing her Snakeman friend.

Thinking back from their start after her snake boyfriend got killed, she finally realized that she had made those awful screams and the hysterical cries, along with the threats at the top of her voice. This was one reason the menfolks were well warned of her! She needed to sneak up on them without warning them with her bitter cries and agonizing screams.

She had been running for a very long way and it was a hard run, running with all of her might. One thing, she ran along very quietly this time. No more screams, no more cries, and no more threats out loud. All was under her breath this time as she ran along as fast as she could go. Trying to catch up to them all again.

Coming over a slight rise and some distance ahead of her, those menfolks were still a-running along, and not too fast. They thought the woman would take almost forever to get through that vast forest that was put in her way by the force of the mystery power. This made her go much faster on her feet.

Holding her temper, holding those cries, the screams, and those threats, the woman gained on them very fast. Just a little ways before she would be up with them, that anger began to build again. The rage in her began to boil again. She tried her best to keep quiet as she steadily gained on them. Just behind them now, only a very little gap between them.

The menfolks weren't running as fast as they should've been, they didn't have the idea the woman had come through that forest just yet, they thought she was probably still fighting to get through it.

That anger of hers, the rage that boiled up inside of her, that very thought of killing them just couldn't be held any longer. She was almost on top of them when that rage of hers came out in that bloodcurdling scream, a cry, and those threats of hers to kill them.

She gave herself away again just before she could've easily gotten ahold of one of them. It was that blood-chilling warning again for the boys and their father, Creator Sun.

They tried to pull away from her, their legs were doing all they could at this time. Only a few steps separated them now, and she was going stronger than them. She could almost easily reach out and touch the last one. This would be Creator Sun, and she was no match for him just yet. It had to be one of the boys. If only she could get ahold of Rawman.

That familiar cry for help from Creator Sun was directed at the fifth son: "*Hah-you, hah-you, noo-koo-yi, awb-aht-dob-igs-it, ah-ni-yih, koo-ma-paw-mah-ka-pi!* Urgent my son, throw it back, that you are running with!" No sooner said than done, the fifth boy threw an airtight bag of nothing but air in it. Of course, just before he threw it, he untied it. The bag landed right in front of their mother. As the bag hit the ground, a mighty wind came out of the bag. The forever mystery of Creator Sun's powers. This wind that came from the bag was so strong and mighty, it carried the woman back a ways before landing back on the ground. From there she began to bounce around in that terrible windstorm. She was being blown back where she came from.

As she blew along, bouncing, tumbling, and rolling along, she would get ahold of this and that, weeds and many kinds of growth. None would hold her, that wind was just too strong. Those things either pulled out or broke off by the force of that wind.

For a long ways, she was blown in the opposite direction from her man, Creator Sun, and her seven sons. They were headed the other way and on a faster run from her.

She blew this way and that way, grabbing ahold of this and that. Each one broke off or pulled out from the ground and still she was bouncing around by the force of this terrible wind.

She was still bouncing along by the force of the wind, when something stopped her. She had been blown against a tree, a strong one. This was a real luck for her—or was it one of the small powers that was left for her? She grabbed ahold of this tree before the wind could carry or tear her from it. With both hands and arms she hung on to the tree. The tree was rather large, with large roots into the ground. It held fast in the ground even as she whipped around it as her hands and arms held fast to it. The woman whipped this and that way by the tree, the wind wasn't strong enough to tear her hands away from it. It blew and it blew, but she hung on.

For the longest time she whipped around the tree. At last the strong wind abated.

At this same time, Creator Sun with his seven sons, had gone so very far from this area where the woman was stuck with that strong wind. They thought that the woman would never catch up to them again, no matter how fast she ran. They forgot about the little power she still had from Creator Sun's gift to her.

The woman let out a sigh of a great relief as that wind slowly quieted down. She knew she had been here for a long time and she also knew it would be hard to overtake the menfolks, she was so far behind them now. She wasn't going to give it up though, she must catch them somehow.

Letting the tree go, she ran this way and that way to find a faint track of them. Around in a circle she ran for some moments before coming onto a very faint track of one of them. She was back on their trail again, and now for a hot pursuit.

She must run all she had, she must wholly depend on her legs to overtake them. Those wicked boys and their wicked father, Creator Sun. She will still show them a thing or two about wickedness. She was getting mighty tired, but in her mind, was that thought to kill those cruel killers of her Snakeman friend. She must catch them and punish them for that cruel doing to her snake boyfriend.

Creator Sun with his seven sons were running along at a moderate speed, him and the oldest son tailing the others. Rawman in the lead of them. They were easing their lungs. Creator Sun, all at once remembering the little power of woman, hollered ahead to the boys that they must speed up now, as she might just get out of that windstorm that got in her way.

Somehow! Creator Sun knew he must get that little power from the woman if they were to be safe from her. With that little power of hers, the woman could always make it bad for them all. It would never be safe for the boys. No matter how long in the future. But at this time he couldn't possibly get at that power she had with her. He must wait for a better opportunity to get at it. It had to be done when she was helpless or when she wasn't aware of it.

Creator Sun never did fear for his own safety, it was his seven sons that he did fear that woman so much for. She could harm them all if she had that chance to do it. Creator Sun always knew he had a life that no other of this whole void, nor of this newly made place he created, or any other place, could have. His life was a never-ending one, he would live on and on forever. He was the sole owner of this void, no matter where one looked. His power of light reached out to as far as the eye can see and much.

The woman was again coming very fast, she had gained steadily since coming out of that terrible windstorm. It was always that little power she had left in her that was given to her by her man, Creator Sun, that she used to get out of these obstacles she ran up against.

Far, far ahead of her, she thought she seen specks a-moving. She wasn't so sure, she went into a deep ravine just as she spotted the specks. This made her go much faster again, although she was nearly falling from fatigue. She just had to catch them.

That rage in her, boiling mad, thinking about her Snakeman friend, killed by these men she was trying to catch. She'll show them yet. These things coming to her mind made her run much faster, as she would temporarily forget her tiredness. To catch them was all the serious thought she had in her.

Sure enough, as she came over another rise, those specks turned out to be them. More power, more power to her feet and legs to go much faster than they were doing. She again gained very fast on them. That thought of sneaking up to them again was in her mind. She mustn't make any kind of noise, not even with her running feet. Quietness, to sneak up to them before they notice her in back of them. She must control herself for sure this time. No screaming, no hollering, no crying in rage.

At this time the boys had slowed down very much. They had been running since their mother had found out about her Snakeman friend, and that had been very long now. Their father, Creator Sun, running along with them to protect them from their mother—he didn't seem to mind all of this running they were doing. There really was no soreness or tiredness in him. He was Creator Sun, Creator of all things.

This gave the woman a chance to catch up faster then she figured. It was almost a complete surprise when right in the back of them, when all were not watching or thinking of her, she again couldn't hold her rage any longer. That terrible scream, the horrible cry, and those awful threats to them all. She was almost on top of them. If she held her anger, she would've caught the oldest boy. But it was always her rage that she couldn't hold in, her screams and cries that saved the menfolks from her.

Creator Sun knew his sons were getting very tired from this long run, they just couldn't run any faster than they were going just now. He had to call on his sixth son to throw what he carried back towards his mother.

"*Hah-you, hah-you, noo-koo-yi, ishs-pobs-st-chis, ah-nah-yi, sits-si-wy!* Urgent, urgent my son, throw the bird up in the air towards your mother!" Only halfway through his father's talk, the sixth son threw a beautiful bird into the air towards his mother. It was a many-colored bird. No sooner had the bird gone into the air, when a very loud rumble was heard.

A streak of a light came from the rumble. Both the rumbling and the light seemed to come from a very dark cloud that formed instantly overhead. With this rumbling and the lightning, rain came also. All of this was taking place right in front of the woman. The streak of light was hitting the ground just in front of the woman, and that rumbling noise was ear-splitting, it sounded so loud and sharp. And with it, water seem to be pouring from above. This stopped the woman from going fast. She had to take her time, even stop at times to avoid getting hit by that streak of light coming from the dark clouds.

The woman didn't know what to make of all this, her first experience of thunder and lightning. The noise was so loud and sharp, she ducked around each time it thundered. And that lightning too, she had to duck from it or it would've struck her. But that little power she still had of Creator Sun's kept her from harm.

She had to stop under the covering of some trees, a bolt of the lightning came very close to her, it flung her for a ways in the air. She had to be extra careful about that streak of light, she found out the power of it.

Under the tree she waited and waited for this rain, the rumbling, and that powerful light that came out of those dark clouds.

It was a long time she stood under the tree, when almost just as suddenly as this storm came, it went away. It cleared up. The woman didn't wait much longer, she ran from the cover of the tree and out onto the flat again to look for those boys and Creator Sun's tracks.

It didn't take too long to find their faint tracks, but they were a little hard to follow, the rain almost washed them away.

It almost cost the boys their oldest brother the last time she caught up with them, because they had slowed down to catch a breather from all of the running. This time all of them tried their best to keep that speed up as they ran along. They were far ahead of the woman. It was that mystic power of their father, Creator Sun, that had been saving them from their mother's anger.

It could've been Oo-ki-nah, Rawman, their youngest brother, that she wanted to kill most. She knew he was loved by all of the older boys. Creator Sun, too, loved him very much. The woman loved this youngest too so very much. Probably a revenge for the killing of her Snakeman friend would be done if she could only get ahold of Rawman. They all loved him dearly.

Things flashing through her mind helped to make her go that much faster. She knew they were far ahead of her and she was beginning to get a little worried to catch up to them again, they were that far ahead. Somehow that power she had left in her still helped her to overcome all the obstacles in the way of her. It wasn't any different this time.

The boys were getting very tired from this running, it was so long ago that they were taking things easy around their peaceful camp. These thoughts were probably in all of their minds. Something must be done about this running from their mother. They just couldn't run for ever from her. Something has to happen soon.

Creator Sun's mind, too, was full. How to stop this nonsense? It shouldn't have to be like this. He made all of these things, the boys from their mother. The woman from mud made by him. He must control his own creations one way or another.

Coming over a rise again, and again, far ahead she seen those men as tiny specks, but they were moving fast yet. She was spurred on by the sight of them. Somehow, each time she seen them made her move that much faster. This time she will sneak up to them. No more yelling or screaming. She mustn't threaten them aloud as she ran along to overtake them. All that had to be done is to be very quiet and catch up to them. So on and on she went, gaining on them rapidly.

Right behind them once more, but not close enough yet to catch one. She was holding her anger very good this time. This time had to be that wish she was waiting for, to sneak up on them and get ahold of the one she wanted most, Oo-ki-nah. She still had a little of Creator Sun's power yet to depend on to get Oo-ki-nah this time. Easy, easy does it, as she started to close the gap between her and those wicked people she was trying so very hard to catch.

Creator Sun and his seven sons were running almost at their top speed.

Creator Sun and the oldest brother were still running at the rear so their mother wouldn't surprise them. All running as hard as they could go and not once looking back, because they all knew she was somewheres far back of them. The lightning and thunderstorm Creator Sun had brewed up would stop her for a very long time. That's what Creator Sun had in his mind as he ran along. It would be a long time before she could catch up with them this time, so it wasn't much use to be looking back to see if she were coming yet.

She meant to really surprise them and get ahold of Oo-ki-nah, Rawman, for sure this time. But for some reason—it could've been his mystic powers that warned him—Creator Sun sensed something in back of him. Almost alongside of him. Glancing to this movement, he noticed it was the woman. She was holding her cries of rage this time and she was upon them. She could've caught Creator Sun, but she knew better than to do that just yet. She would rather get ahold of Rawman. This would punish all of them. They all loved him so very much.

Without any hesitation, Creator Sun hollered out to the youngest, and the last one to be carrying something, to stop the woman again. All of these obstacles the woman went up against were still the creations of Creator Sun, and they were to become the natural forces of this Mother Earth.

"*Oo-ki-nah, Oo-ki-nah, hah-you, hah-you, ah-bah-da-soo-yin-it, ah-ni-yih, ow-ki-yih!* Rawman, Rawman, urgent, urgent, spill that water back towards your mother!"

As the first drop of water hit the ground in front of the woman, she disappeared from sight. In front of her was an endless body of water, and the woman was caught on the other side of this great body of water. She looked this way and the other way. There was no end to this water. How could she possibly get across this water to overtake those menfolks now? She started to scream again, cry again, those threatening rages. She was running back and forth along the shores of this great body of water.

As the first drop of water hit the ground in front of the woman, this water spread so fast that Creator Sun, with his mystic powers, floated up into the air with the boys. They went up and up to get away from the water and the woman too. She was all alone now, running this way and that way to find a way across this vast body of water. She hadn't seen the boys and their father floating up into the air yet.

As the boys and their father, Creator Sun, drifted further and further up into the void, they could see their mother running this way and that way to get to a place where one might be able to get across. It wasn't any use for her to even try any longer.

The woman got smaller and smaller until she disappeared from their view. But that huge body of water even seemed bigger from up here, there just wasn't any end to it.

The woman finally decided that it was no use to try and find a way to cross this big water. She sat down to think about it for awhile. She couldn't swim across or wade across. She didn't know where across was. She must find a way to overcome this obstacle.

The boys and Creator Sun drifted on ever upwards. As they drifted farther and farther away, knowing their mother was down there by the huge body of water, all of them began to beam with happiness. But that happiness was short-lived.

As the woman sat there by the shore of the big, big water, she was thinking what she should do. The power she had left of Creator Sun—why not try to use it some way? Whatever gift Creator Sun gives to his creations is always a mystery, because of its powers. The woman had a little of the sweet grass left. She took it and made a small fire. From this small fire she got some hot charcoals, and made incense from the sweet grass as she put some on the hot charcoals. She prayed as the sweet grass began to smoke, the smoke drifting upwards. By that mysterious power of the sweet grass smoke, as the woman stepped over it she became airborne. The mysterious smoke of the sweet grass lifted her up into the void. She found a way to overcome the water again and to keep on chasing those menfolks. For strange reasons that are unexplainable, the mysteries of our Creator Sun, the woman seemed to know which way those menfolks went or were drifting. She too went that way. She even found out she could go any way up there in the void. She could go fast or slow. It didn't take her long to find these things out. So again she began the chase.

Not knowing that their mother was able to overcome the vast body of water and was now drifting towards them again, chasing them, the boys were all very glad. Creator Sun knew the woman would be able to overcome the obstacle somehow, but he didn't know how soon she would find a way. But at this time he wasn't a bit worried about her.

Without any warning, the woman came up to them at a high speed. It almost cost one son's life. The woman used that mysterious power to her advantage wisely this time, but her power still wasn't any match with Creator Sun's powers.

She made for Rawman, she came so suddenly. Just before she got ahold of him, Creator Sun threw his flint hatchet at her. The sharp blade of the hatchet got the woman right square on the left knee. It was with such force that the hatchet cut her leg off. She went down as her leg came off, and Rawman was saved from his wicked mother once again.

This was a chance for Creator Sun to take back almost all of the powers he had given her. Running back to her and stopping by her, as she cursed them all. He didn't mind the talking now, she couldn't do anything because of her severed leg. Creator Sun touched her on the top of her head with both of his hands and then ran the hands along both sides of her head and down both arms, as he talked mysteriously.

All of this mysterious talk was the power of taking back those strange powers he had bestowed on the woman while they were together.

The woman wasn't giving up so easy, she was trying her best to jump up to Creator Sun as he stood by her. She still was full of fight, even with the pain of her severed leg. Creator Sun would touch her on the head every so often as he talked to her in a low tone.

She didn't want to listen to him, she had her own words, those threats and screams. But there wasn't any use to do all of this, she couldn't do anything because of her leg now. She just had to listen to the low-tone talk of Creator Sun, no one can shut their ears from the mysterious powers of our Creator Sun. This still is true, even now as we live in this twentieth century. We all have to listen to him at one time or another.

Because of her threats to continue her chase, Creator Sun had to create a thing to rest by, as the steady chase was just too tiresome. It was then that day and night were separated or created. Half of the time the Moon would see freely, and the other half she would not be able to see at all. This was to hide Creator Sun and the boys in the darkness while they rested.

For four days the woman sat where her leg was severed by Creator Sun's hatchet. As Creator Sun was talking to her, she took her severed leg and held it to her cut-off leg and held it there. Because the night and day was then separated, she sat for four nights and days and her leg healed together by the mysterious powers again. But she didn't hold it just right as it was healing. It healed a little off, and now both legs looked like they were both the same side, both right legs.

Because of the blood she lost from her leg and the big sin she had done to Creator Sun, he told the woman, "All women from now on must shed blood to commemorate the beginning of night and day and to remember the unfaithful woman who lost her leg for her sin, and the blood of life that was lost by her."

The women lose blood each month for their sins in these days, the set way, because of Severed Leg, the Moon. The precedents of life.

If only Creator Sun had done away with all of those snakes he created for that first life to exist—if he hadn't thought of compassion for that lone female snake he let escape—he would've had a perfect life started here.

Right at this moment, he was going through a revenge by those first snakes for what he done to them. So now he also put a curse on them, that for the rest of time they must face death from all life. They would be stepped on and killed on sight by the human race, their wicked doings to our Creator Sun revenged. No rest for them either, like the boys and their father, Creator Sun.

For the rest of the Moon's punishment, she was left completely bare of clothing. No growth on her of any kind to cover her, and no bearing any offspring. So today, the astronauts find the moon completely bare, even of air or wind. It doesn't get hot from the sun's heat, just completely bare of any form of life.

For four days and nights, no one sees the moon before she becomes visible again as a new moon.

# Earth Takes
# the Moon's Place

It was a torturous race for life, it was a long punishment for Creator Sun and his seven boys. No rest, no way to eat, a lot of sweating from the heat as they ran along. Even to the last of this chase blood was shed, blood from the woman's severed leg. This chase wasn't ending yet, not for eternity, but it was going to slow down at times. Severed Leg the Moon vowed, "I will not rest until I catch you all and kill you all, too, like you all did to my Snakeman friend."

Like our elders tell us, "This life we all have will then come to its end when Severed Leg the Moon catches Creator Sun and their seven sons, the Big Dipper."

This wasn't a happy ending, but a beginning for our kind of life. The Moon was Creator Sun's very first creation, and then his bride. For her wrongdoings to Creator Sun, she must be barren of all things, just as she is in these days—bare, but alive. Still trying to catch the menfolks as she had vowed.

A change came after Severed Leg ruined her try at having a perfect life in this world.

Creator Sun's second or standby wife, this Mother Earth, was producing many other forms of life for him. She was even suckling all that life for him. So she took the place of Severed Leg the Moon as his new bride.

At this time the Snake family still abounded on this land, the body of Mother Earth. These snakes were still trying their best to rule their own ways while Mother Earth was suckling them. From their wickedness, these snakes had become many—they were in many forms because of their crossbreeding with one another. Some were beginning to have legs, but they still looked like a snake. And because of no discipline or not wanting to listen, many of them became overgrown. Big, big in their form. Tall and long. The life of reptiles, dinosaurs. Again these reptiles reproduced many, manyfold. In fact, too many again roamed this land. So many of them again, they wouldn't listen to their Creator Sun's rules, but would rather have their own way.

After so long of this, Creator Sun couldn't stand them anymore. He done something about it all.

Up to that time our world was almost smooth surfaced. There weren't rolling hills or lowlands as we have now.

Again, with one of the natural forces he created for this place, he got rid of those snakes. Creator Sun made it rain. It rained and it rained. It rained so long, water was all over. Shallow and deep. And it rained so long, the water began to soak into the earth and the earth got soft and softer. After a time, it was a regular mudmire all over the surface of the land. There were places that crusted very hard on the surface, but most other places weren't that hard.

As it rained on and on, these heavy reptiles were sinking down into the soft mud-mire. All began to take refuge on these hard-surfaced places. They seemed to sense or see one another taking to these places for their safety, to keep from sinking in, so these heavy reptiles followed others to these places of survival.

It still rained on and on with no letup. These things kept on coming to these places for their survival. More and more of them. In the meantime, everything down under the surface was getting soaked, it was almost like running water down under there. While many of these heavy reptiles took refuge on these hard-surfaced places, others sank down into the mud-mire. Huge rivers were now being formed, running whichever way the land was low. And that begun to cut into the surface a channel for that water. The subterranean soil too was almost like a running water.

Too many of these reptiles would get on a hard surface, overweighing it. These places would tip over, dumping the heavy creatures into the mud-mire. This is very true. Look around anywhere you might drive and see the landscape. One can see clearly where the land tipped over or where it sank all together.

After a very long time the rain stopped. All of those bad, wicked lives that had abounded on the land were done away with. Creator Sun had done away with them through his created elements. There was no heavy reptiles left anyplace. But again the smaller snakes survived. Even to this day we see those snakes. But that curse on them remains, except for a few crazy people that probably are from that wicked life of that Snakeman.

When you are going through roadways, through some deep cuts of a sharp hill, look at the layers of the earth. One can readily see how the layer bent or how it slipped from the original surface. After the great rain, the land dried out on the top surface and it stayed that way. Except for natural erosion by Creator Sun's many created elements, the landscape further got out of shape. Those creatures of that prehistoric time were covered so fast—no air in those mud-mires—that they are found, in these days, intact.

Creator Sun and his seven sons became routine guards over their new Mother Earth. Severed Leg the Moon was still trying to catch them after her severed leg was healed, and she too became a routine sight as all circled the Mother Earth, far above her.

All of the attention now went to Mother Earth. From far above, Creator Sun took care of his new wife, Mother Earth. It was all spiritual contacts they made with one another to have many life forms again, and power for Mother Earth to give suck and life to all of their many children.

Today that spiritual power of both Creator Sun and Mother Earth combined can easily be seen or felt: the warmness of the rays of the sun, the many lives of this earth they have produced. Plants, insects, fowls, animals—so many different forms of life, we don't know all of them. Even the live elements for that life, or for the death to them—lightning, thunder, wind, the many kinds of storms. All of these bring life or death, as Creator Sun wants it to happen.

All of this became a routine way of life in those very young and early days of the beginning of time, which was several billion years ago. But only yesterday for Creator Sun and Mother Earth.

# Our Human Beginning

So that snake life was once again destroyed, except for the smaller ones that came out of that last destruction alive. These smaller snakes also made a vow to destroy Creator Sun's kind as long as they are around. Even in these days there are poisonous snakes that kill with their venom. Some of the harmless ones strike too. The larger ones of the warmer countries can strangle those they coil around on, and kill them that way. So the curses of those very early days go on.

Time went on ever forward, with the Moon or Severed Leg chasing after her seven sons and her man—Big Dipper and Creator Sun. Going forever around the new woman, Mother Earth.

Creator Sun came down to be with his new bride at times he had a chance to—when the Moon or Severed Leg was at rest for a four-day period and couldn't be seen. Each time he came down to be with her, he sensed something was amiss from their togetherness. He couldn't quite figure it out just yet.

Coming down to be with her again, she spoke of a little loneliness in her. She wanted company—life like her and Creator Sun. Before this, they had talked of more life for them on Mother Earth, but no certain kind.

When she spoke of a life like them, that settled that plan. It didn't take

**Creator Sun Creating Man From Mud**

long for Creator Sun to make his new woman happy. To the water's edge they went. From the mud Creator Sun molded a form in his own shape, his own image. The form completed, Creator Sun blew into its face and at the same time said, "Have the same kind of life we have and live to roam this land."

This mud figure came to life as Creator Sun blew into its nostrils. It got up from the ground where it laid and began to walk. Its first try was very wobbly. Almost each try, he fell back down, but each time he got up he became stronger. It wasn't too long before this Mudman began to get around like his counterpart, Creator Sun. Like his mother, Mother Earth. His mind wasn't too good to begin with. But as he got better at things, in all, his mind improved too.

As time went by, this new Mudman, their new baby in the shape they were in, got stronger and stronger. His mind was like that of his parents. It wasn't too very long before he done things just like his father and mother. He was a part of them.

As things got better for the new Mudman, Creator Sun took him out and began to teach him everything he knew of their own life and others. Creator Sun communicated with him in a way that he could understand clearly.

Creator Sun always remembered that perfect life he tried the first time, with this same image of himself and that of the woman, too, and how it was destroyed by those wicked snakes through their wickedness. A dream that came to a fast end. Hope against hope that this is the life, again in his own image, that would abound, live, and be every bit like him and his ways and that of Mother Earth too. Together they would try their best.

Day after day Creator Sun was with the new son, the Mudman. He was teaching him all necessary ways of life. This went on for a very long time.

Creator Sun worked with his new son each time he got to come down from his position far out in the void. They were all very close together, loved one another so very much.

Creator Sun sensed something wrong with the new son, Mudman. He wasn't so very happy with his time and the folks anymore.

Each time Creator Sun came down for his personal visits with the wife, Mother Earth, and the new son, Mudman, he tried to understand their personal needs or personal wants to keep them on the happy side of this life. He was studying Mudman's need. Mudman seemed so slow, no more interest in what was being taught to him. It had been a long time since his life came into existence.

On one of his visits with Mother Earth and Mudman, walking with the new son, Creator Sun heard him say, "If I only had someone like my mother to keep me company." This made Creator Sun realize the new son was very lonely being alone. He needed someone to play with, especially the kind his mother was made like, opposite from him.

Creator Sun remembered well how he began to yearn for something before he made the first woman, Severed Leg. How good it was to have someone different than you. Someone to develop a seed of you.

It had to be just as he made things to keep this place a-going for the right of things he made. Something opposite from the way he was made would keep his mind happy, and make them want to do more for their lives as they lived along.

Mudman had grown gaunt from that loneliness. Creator Sun had to do something for him in a hurry.

Before leaving again for that faraway place far out in the void, or nothingness, where they now were, Creator Sun talked it over with Mother Earth about their son, the Mudman.

Creator Sun told Mother Earth what he heard from their Mudman son. "Our new son needs someone made like you are to play with and keep him company. He is so all alone now and he is lonely for someone his own size to play with. We are so very busy all the time, we just don't have any time with him. He's lonely for company."

Creator Sun remembered when he created Severed Leg. How happy their lives were for so long. Then one day, wickedness struck. The very beginning of it. Those snakes he created as first life for his creation, and then destroyed, struck back in vengeance and ruined all of their plans for that perfect life he wanted for this land he created. Creator Sun was a little sorry for giving them so much power, power from his own. All he can do now is regret that time, long ago.

Thinking to himself, Creator Sun knew he shouldn't be thinking back of those times already past, he should be worrying about the Mudman now. He knew just how to go about the Mudman's needs.

Creator Sun waited for a real good time to put his plans to work. It was one of those tiring days. It had been a long day and all of them were dozing off where each one was sitting. Waking up kind of late, the three of them went to bed.

Creator Sun wasn't much of a sleeper. His mind was too full all the time. He thought about all of that life that was dependent on him, his personal touches to keep them alive. He was fathering and raising all the many different forms of life.

Up and around to care for all of that life, he went past the Mudman's bed. Mudman was fast asleep. This was the best time for that plan he had made in his mind.

It was now or never to do what he wanted to do for the Mudman son of theirs. Some way to help him overcome that loneliness. Using that strange power, Creator Sun put the Mudman into a deeper sleep so he wouldn't know what was going on.

Kneeling down beside him, Creator Sun took out the Mudman's lowest, smallest left rib. With this rib he made an image after the Mudman and himself, and Mother Earth too. The form was like all of them, except it was made after Mother Earth. To bear fruit, to bear offspring. Laying the figure down, Creator Sun blew on the figure's face and gave it breath. As he blew on the face of this figure, formed after the three of them, Creator Sun spoke to it. "Now you have a life as we have and you are made after our son, the

Mudman, to be his playmate. But you are made after your mother, Mother Earth, to bear others that will come from you and our Mudman son. You have breath like we have. The Mudman shall teach you what things you must learn to do. Most of all, be happy with your new mate or companion throughout time."

The Ribwoman too was very weak after she was created from the Mudman's rib. She too couldn't get up to walk soon after. It took several tries and many days to be able to walk around by herself.

Soon after the creation of the Ribwoman, before the Mudman woke up, the Ribwoman was squirming around, wriggling and struggling to get up or sit up. She woke up the Mudman as she fell against him several times. The Mudman was so very startled to see another beside him as he woke up. At this time, the sex made no difference to him because he wasn't aware of the opposite sex just then. The Mudman wasn't surprised too long. He knew for some strange reason that he had to help out the newcomer in some way, to make this new being comfortable. He also knew that he was to care for this new one the rest of time as they were together.

Jumping up on his feet, the Mudman gave this new one water and some food to give it a start in its life. He helped her to down all of this, it made the new one much better afterwards. From that time on, the Mudman became a steady servant to this newcomer.

This was the main reason for creating the two, the Mudman and the

*Creating a Woman from the Man's Small Rib*

Ribwoman: to become inseparable throughout time. To be mates and to bear others in their image and those of Creator Sun and Mother Earth. The very strange powers of our Creator Sun gave the two the idea of what should be done—especially Mudman, as he nursed the newcomer along.

As time went along, the newcomer got stronger and was able to do many of the things Mudman done. The two romped all through the fields, across the little running waters that were plenty all over. In short, they were having the time of their lives.

As all of this was going on, from the day the newcomer came about from Mudman's ribs, the two didn't have a stitch of clothing on to cover any parts of their bodies up. Neither of them was ashamed of the other. There wasn't any kind of sin between them, so they weren't aware of either's sex.

This is still so among the babies. All babies lay bare naked in their cribs and they do not even notice, no matter who is around them. They just aren't ashamed of themselves. Some of the strange precedents of our lives.

Day after day this running and romping went on. At night when they slept, the two laid down together to keep warm. There just wasn't any kind of shame between them. They never tried to find out about each other when either one woke up at night. There was no kind of sin between them just yet.

Creator Sun was always coming down to find out about all of his creations and to take care of them all, to keep them all alive. On these visits Creator Sun taught more and more to his Mudman son and to the Ribwoman. Many of these times, just him and his son went out for those strolls. Those we call "work house" nowadays. It was to teach him of self-survival and for his companion, the Ribwoman.

On one of these visits with his family, Creator Sun wanted to familiarize his son, the Mudman, with the companion that was given to him, the Ribwoman. They had been together for a very long time now and must know what this life was all about.

As they were walking along and Creator Sun was thinking about future beings, the people, he turned to his Mudman son and spoke to him about that future all of them were going forward to. He told the son, "My son, you have someone to be with you as you wanted, your wish as it is, the companion you have with you now is made after your mother, Mother Earth. She is made to reproduce whenever the time comes. Your woman is made to self-feed whatever she bears for you. Images of you and her shall come from this woman, providing you put the seeds of life in her. This new companion of yours is made exactly like Mother Earth, to reproduce life—but it has to come from you, the seed that will be planted in her. In her, that seed will turn into an image of both of you. All of this you do not know yet. There will be a time that will come when you will realize what I'm talking about and things will begin from there on."

The Mudman was listening very careful to his father, Creator Sun. After this very important lesson, the two went on to the camp, and soon after, Creator Sun departed for that new home far out in the emptiness. For awhile, the Mudman was thinking of what was told to him by his father. In a short while, it was all forgotten. He truly didn't understand it very much. And besides, he was so busy with his companion, playing and romping, there was no other worries in him just yet.

The two played at will all over the vast fields and hills, the creeks, and many places as they skipped, runned, and romped. No danger of any kind to be wary of. No sickness to think at that time. There just wasn't any kind of trouble to worry about as the two played on and on. Mudman and Ribwoman.

Since the making of the Ribwoman, it had been a long time now. All this time since the two were put together by Creator Sun, there wasn't a stitch of clothing on either one and the two didn't realize they were opposite from one another in their make, their sex. Without this thought between them, there just wasn't anything to notice about one another or to be ashamed of. The two played on in those fields of happiness, and for some time to come.

Around that time the weather was somewhat like the normal days of this time. There were times when the air was cold at nighttime, even in the daytimes too.

The two, Mudman and his Ribwoman, slept together to keep warm through the nights, especially during those cold nights that came every so often. It was one of these colder nights that it happened—what Creator Sun told his son, the Mudman. During this particular night, Mudman woke up late in the night from the cold. He felt as if he was freezing, so he cuddled up to the Ribwoman to get warmed up. And in order to get warmth, the Mudman had to put his arm around the body of the Ribwoman. When his arms went around the body of the Ribwoman, and as he cuddled his body to hers, there was an extra warmth that emanated from the Ribwoman's body. This warmth from her caused him to have a funny feeling all over his body. The Ribwoman was fast asleep as he laid by her, keeping warm, and this funny feeling in him.

Having his arm around her body and with this funny feeling he had towards her, he must explore further what it was all about and why. So while the Ribwoman was very fast asleep, Mudman explored the many parts of the woman's body. While doing this, something in him aroused from this hand exploration, especially when he touched the Ribwoman's private area. He had to find out further how different she was from him. His hands went all over her body, every inch of it. The Ribwoman woke up from all of this, the hands of Mudman feeling all parts of her body. She too got that feeling as she felt the hands of the Mudman going on all parts of her body. It was this time that they knew they weren't exactly the same as they had thought. What was being done now made their breathing much faster than usual. The Ribwoman just laid still as the Mudman's hands were feeling her body all over. For some strange reason, she felt ashamed, too ashamed to move or let the Mudman know she was aware of what was going on. Most probably, she must've liked it secretly. Anyway, it was something they found out about each other, the difference about them.

43

The Mudman came to realize what his father, Creator Sun, was talking about. For as they laid there, for those same strange reasons unexplainable to anyone, both him and her knew what else was to be done. Their first intimate relationship.

It still is this way in this life we are living. Young ones are born and they grow to just a few years old. No one tells them about sex, but they seem to always know what to do about it and how to go about it all the way. No one is the teacher for this, but it is always with the humans from the time they are born or soon after. Strange, but true. The precedents of life set by those first people.

This first sex act between them was very painful to the Ribwoman. But again, for strange reasons, she didn't seem to mind that pain very much, as she too had wanted to fulfill that yearning for one another that very night. And so it is, even in these days, that pain with the first one isn't minded so very much because of the fulfillment of that togetherness.

This act together made the Mudman realize this was what he really was yearning for. A fulfillment between the opposite sexes. Before this, he didn't really know what he was so lonely for. But now he understood what his father, Creator Sun, was talking about.

This was a true beginning of a man and a woman's true happiness and togetherness for the rest of their lives. At this time, it was to be a never-ending happiness and togetherness between the woman and the man. There wasn't anything to end one's life. No sickness to worry about, nothing to bring death. Life was forever. The two could now face anything that might come along, because their lives were like one.

Strange things happen from things that came into being. Before this sex act together, there wasn't anything to cover their bodies. The two were just completely naked. After their first sex act, it wasn't the same. For those same strange reasons, they couldn't look at one another's private areas anymore, they had to cover theirselves up with something. It was then that getting the shameful feeling came into existence. Shame of one another over the sex act and their first sin together.

Another of the precedents of life, embarrassment of being naked and to be seen by others in nakedness.

It was now altogether different in their living then at the beginning of the Mudman's life. Ribwoman and Mudman had to be covered at all times so they wouldn't be seeing one another's privates anymore. They were ashamed of themselves, embarrassed to be seen naked. Many things, both good and bad, were experienced by these two people that began the human life.

Creator Sun gave all of us a wonderful life of togetherness with the opposite sex, a life to fulfill both lives of the two sexes. Our Creator Sun, some time ago, away, way back, many, many years ago, went through what was being taught the Mudman and the Ribwoman. It took a seed to reproduce another in the exact image. Be it a plant life, any form of life. A seed planted in a female life would come out just the same image as the parent life.

All the male life, especially the human life—and this went for the other too, the female life—they were to honor each other throughout their lives. All of the life was given to find a companion of the opposite sex and the one chosen was to last for the rest of our days. We were to bear more of the same as we lived along with one another. Our seeds were to be just for the two of us, the chosen mate. This was a sacred commandment by our Creator Sun.

Our father, Creator Sun, gave all of us a commandment to live by. He is the only Creator of all life, one maker. There isn't another like him to exist anywhere, no matter how many million lightyears, as the astronomer talks, away from this earth or wherever. There is no one like our Creator Sun. He alone gave us a commandment that was to be used by all, especially the human beings. The commandment was just a plain, *"Be honest to life and to all life."* This one commandment covered everything: Be honest.

We have all lost that one lone commandment by our Creator Sun that covered all of our wrongs. Our Indian life had one of the truest form of religion before the coming of the Europeans. We led a life according to our Creator Sun's commandment, which all of us were given to live by. The other nationalities other then the Indian broke that one great commandment. They broke away from it for the want of riches, greed for power, and to be notable. This is still a-going in these days yet. Lust for power, lust for riches, and lust for women. Every day we hear of this. No matter how high up in politics they might be, that lust for sin is always there.

Those European newcomers shamed us Indians into following that corrupt way of life and belief. In many cases, their way of faith is still somewhat confusing to the Indian because of their persecution of one another. We were led astray from our true religion and faith by these newcomers. We were brainwashed by those so-called missions that once flourished on all Indian reservations, and by those non-Indians that operated them. The Indian learned many bad things from these mission schools. We foresaked our true Creator Sun over the coming of the whiteman.

All of our Indians have broken that one big and great commandment by our Creator Sun, one big commandment that covered all of their ten commandments. That one big great commandment was, Always be honest throughout your life. I truly do not think there is even one that is *honest* anywhere in this world. This is true, because we Indians have taken to the whiteman's religion and it leads us all into a very corrupt life.

If I'm not believed by anyone, just think of your presidents, congressmen, senators, and all the rest of them that has those high executive jobs.

What are they truly doing for anyone? Think of it.

The whiteman religion is foreign to the Indian, but we were forced into it. Also this whiteman religion is quite contrary to their coming to this land. They came for the freedom of religion, but it wasn't freedom for the Native of this land. They were brushed aside by those so-called missionaries and was replaced by that whiteman religion that was forced on them. They were told that they were devil-worshipers. Their own true Indian religion. How nervy can the whiteman be?

We—the Indian, as we were called recently by our supposed-to-be teachers of life—have forsaken that truest form of understanding taught to us by our Creator Sun. We were pushed from our culture, our traditions, and the truest form of religion—the laws of our Creator Sun, guidelines that we were to follow. Everyone in this world was given that guideline, the teachings all were to follow, by our great Creator Sun. This world wasn't given by two makers. Everything was given by only one Maker and that was Creator Sun. He is still alive and will be for the rest of time.

I for one will never accept another Maker or Creator. I truly know my Father, Creator Sun, made all of life as it is on Mother Earth. In many, many ways he reveals it to us people of Mother Earth.

The food we eat, the air we breathe are the works of the Sun. It is his elements that come forth from his powers of light, powers of life, for all life to exist. The Sun provides this life-giving element the world over as he goes around this planet, or as we go around him or whatever. As this Mother Earth turns towards the east, it also slowly turns to the sides where we get our turns of the heat it puts forth and those powerful elements to give growth and breath to his children. When our turn for the heat from his power comes to our side of Mother Earth, fresh food comes out from the body of Mother Earth. We, the many forms of life, readily take our suck from her body to make us grow, to get fat for the next coming cold as our Creator Sun goes to take care of the other side of Mother Earth. There isn't a place that our Creator Sun doesn't or cannot provide for. He takes good care of all of his creations. It is up to us to take and use that life-giving food they both put out for us all. Mother Earth and Creator Sun.

An example to consider: Our true Creator Sun isn't a whiteman Sun and it isn't only an Indian Sun. It isn't any one nationality Sun. No certain one of the many nationalities can claim our true Creator Sun. It's for all of us and it provides for all of us. We all breathe and all live by his elements of life. Creator Sun doesn't discriminate, he isn't prejudiced to anyone, but treats all the same. He isn't like some of our people that hasn't any respect for anyone except them and their kind. Creator Sun respects all of us, if we respect him.

This is the reason that I, probably alone, do not believe in any other Maker or Creator. Just the Creator Sun. He is my Father and Truest Maker of all life.

The Mudman and his woman, the Ribwoman, progressed as they went along in their lives. Routine things were learned by the two, and their happiness and togetherness got stronger and stronger. They had learned many things that must be learned of as people of togetherness, what we would call "love." Man and woman's way of life.

One day the two were walking and romping out in those vast fields the two had for a playground. Coming to a small creek, the Ribwoman told the Mudman, "Let's sit a while and rest. I'm just so very tired running and walking." Sitting down near the small creek, talking to one another in their happy ways and all about what they had done together so far. All at once the Ribwoman changed her talk, telling the Mudman, "I wonder what's wrong with me lately, I've been getting mighty tired and it seems that I'm carrying a heavy load for some reason."

Her words didn't surprise the Mudman. He knew from his father, Creator Sun, what there was to know about a man and woman's life together. How everything is planned out for the two of them, Mudman and his woman, the Ribwoman. The little ones that the Ribwoman was to bear for him as time went along to make more of them in their likeness. The planting of a seed into the woman, how it was to take root in her and grow in her belly for a short time and then one day it would come out from her. This would become a creation of their very own. Creator Sun told him how long it should be before all of this took place, when the Ribwoman should expect the little image to come from her. This would be a little painful to her, but Mudman would be there to comfort her through all of this time.

The Mudman sat a little more closely by his woman, the Ribwoman, to comfort her. Putting his arms around her, he told her all about what was wrong with her, saying, "From now on you will have to take it easy. You must be careful of what you do. Leave those that might be too heavy. You mustn't run much anymore. You'll have to learn to do things slower and easier. In you, you have a little one that's like us. But we won't know who this new one will be like, you or me, until the new one comes out of you. Don't be scared, I'll help all I can to make things easy for you."

The Ribwoman was a little puzzled over all of this, she couldn't quite understand it all. She never had any experience of any of this. A little one in my belly and it will be in the likeness of either one of us, how come I'm carrying it in my belly, why isn't he carrying one too? These were some of the questions in her mind.

This little talk was soon forgotten. Life went on as usual for the two. There were some instances when she would feel movements in her stomach not very long after their talk. Those movements in her got stronger as time went by, and it got that way both day and night now.

It was a lot of waiting now, as he said it would be. Anxiety, pains both day and night, but Mudman would soothe her with his kind words all the time.

The Ribwoman got bigger and bigger as those days went on, and the movements got stronger each day. Each day came with a new experience to both of them, and the Mudman kept his woman on a move slowly each day and even at nights. Just like his father told him to do, she has to move all the time or that life in her will get too big and she would have a harder time to make this new life come out from her. This was their life as they waited, moving about a little at a time. It became routine for them in the many days that followed.

Those pains came very frequently now as time went by. The Ribwoman was getting quite used to them by now. They would hurt her so much, but she would let them go by and bear them the best she could, especially with the Mudman's comforting words.

One night, late, both so tired from the previous day and as they slept quite heavy from this, the Ribwoman sat up moaning all of a sudden. Mudman woke up instantly, asking her what was wrong. He knew well enough what the wrong was, but he wanted to make sure. Asking her, "What's the matter with you, why are you moaning this way?"

"I'm having terrible pains in me. What's wrong with me?" The Mudman reassured her that everything would be all right soon, not to worry too much. That little image of theirs would be coming soon and those pains will stop when it came.

The night wore on, her pains became quite unbearable. She moaned, she hollered, even screamed at times. She would ask her man, "What is paining me so much?" The Mudman told her about Creator Sun's explanation. Those pains were for the sins they committed together, a payment for what happened by those two as they lived together. She was in a very physical severe pain and he was feeling those pains as if he were the one having them. They were both suffering so much for those sins they committed together.

The two couldn't sleep any longer, they were wide awake. Those pains were so close together, they felt as if one long pain. The Mudman couldn't help her in any way with those terrible pains except to talk to her and try to comfort her the best possible way. Rub her belly with his hands was the best he could do for her at this time.

All at once she let out a loud scream. She hollered to Mudman, "Help me, something is coming out of me, help me, help me!" Creator Sun had taught the Mudman all that he had to know about all of this. The Mudman didn't wait or get excited, he jumped to the woman's side, he threw all of his weight on the woman's belly and held her hands tightly. He told her to put her mouth against her shoulder and blow with all her might. She done what was asked of her. She wasn't making anymore noise, she was just busy doing what she was told to do. It was all over in a short while. The image of them came out of her. What a relief it was. Both done what had to be done to this new one that came from her belly.

He knew what else was to be done, and that was to feed that little one from the mother's breasts. Of course she had to be shown what to do by her man. It was him that was taught how to do things for the both of them. The new little one knew what must be done too. He went to work on his mother's breasts to fill himself with that fresh milk.

This was the first born in this world, Mother Earth's body. This particular one was just like its father, the Mudman. He was a boy.

Things happened and things were coming into place. A pattern of what was to come now and in the future. As each piece fell into place, and fitted into that pattern of life, those next things that were to come were much easier to absorb.

It had been a long time since his father, Creator Sun, had come to Mother Earth and to his family, the many different forms of life, to talk to them all. He was always so busy with Severed Leg the Moon, always running from her, that ex-woman of his that was threatening their lives, him and his seven sons, the Big Dipper. They were in that void, far from Mother Earth, all of them, the seven sons, Severed Leg the Moon, and him, Creator Sun. Forever being chased by Severed Leg the Moon. She made a committment to chase them all until some day that she will be able to catch them and destroy them as they done to her Snakeman friend. It would be then that all life will stop, except our Creator Sun's life and his woman, Mother Earth.

From where they were at now, it gave them a far better chance to look after their new mother, Mother Earth, and all of their brothers and sisters of the many forms of life.

Severed Leg still had to rest her leg four days and nights. It was one of these times that Creator Sun found time to come and have a visit with his son, the Mudman, and all of the family.

Creator Sun walked with the Mudman son and his wife, the Ribwoman. Even the newcomer, Mudman's and Ribwoman's creation, came along. It was a very happy life for all of them at that time. This was only the beginning of time for humans and there were only three of them here on Mother Earth.

As always, Creator Sun was the teacher for these children of his. As they walked along in those beautiful fields, he never ceased to teach them of new things they must learn. Things to do and things not to do. Creator Sun knew he had to teach them along as they went about their ways here on Mother Earth, for as long they were his children.

Not long after returning from this walk and teaching, Creator Sun knew he must take leave of them and go back out to his other children, the Big Dipper. He had to be up there to protect them from their mother, Severed Leg the Moon.

Many times the parents, Mother Earth, and Creator Sun would often get together to discuss the needs for their children. Foods, new and those that were already given them. Liquids, water, saps of the many different plants, juices too of the many plants that now grew on the land or body of Mother Earth.

Everything was going quite perfect. The three, Mudman and his family, had almost everything that would make their lives together a happy one. Plenty of food, plenty of liquids to drink, and the biggest of rooms to play in, the wide open fields. They were overjoyed with happiness, especially their togetherness.

All of them played together so much, never apart for very long, that the two, Mudman and Ribwoman, didn't notice their own boy was growing bigger and bigger. In no time at all the little one was running among them, playing along with them. It had been some time since this little one came.

One night as the three of them were in bed and ready to go to sleep, Ribwoman told Mudman, "I'm very sure that I'm on my way to have another of our own creations. But this time, I know we are ready for this one. We know just what to do when the time comes. We'll know how to care for the new one and me."

Of all the teachings that our father, Creator Sun, taught us, we should be able to take care of all things. We are well aware of the many things of our lives and we are well aware of all of our surroundings, which makes it easier to live.

It didn't seem too long of a wait this time before the Ribwoman had another child, their own creation again. That first one came the same as the Mudman. It was a boy. This second one came to them the exact image of the mother, Ribwoman. This one was a girl. It was now a boy and girl, son and daughter, that the two had.

To the two, Mudman and Ribwoman, time was slow. But their family seemed to be running away on them. Their family was getting larger and larger. It had been a very long time since the birth of the first little one.

There were several little ones now. Some were almost as tall as their parents, Mudman and Ribwoman. There were several girls and several boys of their own creation and all were very happy. Running and playing, as over those fields and hills they went.

As each day and night went by, these boys and girls of Mudman and Ribwoman grew older and bigger. Their knowledge of life grew with them. They played on together, hiking, swimming, hunting for small things. Gathering wood and doing chores for their parents. Things were done in a hurry, there were many of them doing those things for the parents.

Mudman and Ribwoman taught them almost from their birth how to find food and what is food for them. The vegetation, the roots, the berries, and the different kinds of barks. How to preserve this food for later use.

At this particular time of our beginning, there wasn't any kind of meat to use as food, so it was mostly vegetation that these first people ate.

While out doing these chores, the smaller children played a bit separate from the older boys and girls. They had their own way of fun and play. The older boys and girls played sort of away from those smaller children, but kept their eyes on them. There wasn't any danger of any kind at this time, not even wild animals or anything that would harm them.

We are still in the days no one has to teach us of all bad things. For the mystic reasons untold, or from those first snakes that has been taking revenge on Creator Sun—probably by these sinful snakes—we seem to know what should be done in all bad things.

Already, these boys and girls, the older ones of Mudman and Ribwoman knew all about adult life, without anyone teaching them. When out gathering food or doing chores, such as gathering wood, these children would go an extra distance from their camp. While out there, the play or games would take place. These older brothers and sisters would play together as a man and woman, just like their father and mother lived. Man and wife. A boy would pair off with one of his own sisters and play man and wife, far away from their camp where no one would come stealing upon them. No one was the wiser when they came home. Their parents didn't know this, just as many parents don't know about their children in these days we are living. This man and wife play was always very close to a real life.

It was one of these times they were all out to do their chores of getting food. This time, all of them went extra further, far over the hills and forest to find it. Again, after they had come to a place where there were many roots and berries to find, their games and play started. The little ones were put to playing games, while the older ones played their favorite pastime, man and wife. It was always the older brother and older sister that directed the younger ones in the games and plays. It was them that started this wife and husband play.

Each boy picked one of his sisters to be his wife for that time. There were several of them by now that had grown almost into manhood and woman-hood. These couples found a place behind bushes and in the deep grass to be their home. The boys would get together and play the part of out getting food for their wives and their family. Things went along fairly well, until they came to that part where it was played nighttime and time for a rest. Each of the pair went on behind those places they had picked for their home and where the others wouldn't see what was going on. There the man and wife play went on into the part of sleeping together. It was going fine for them all. But the very older ones had to make it so very real. They went all the way as a real man and wife, several of them. There wasn't anything wrong with it, although they knew it was not right for them to be doing this, which they found out some time after this.

Sex is something that doesn't have to be taught to kids. For some reason they know what to do. It is an instinct that we come into this world with. This learning of bad things is known from time untold and it is known among the many people that it's the bad things the little children learn first, almost every time. Sex seems to be always the first thing that is learned by these little ones. It is done in one way or another. It's an instinct by all the many forms of life.

So! Even in those very early days of Mudman and Ribwoman, in that young world, those very first children knew about sex and they knew it thoroughly. They had to play it among themselves, because then it was only them, all brothers and sisters that were brought into this world by their parents, Mudman and Ribwoman.

It was some time after this makebelieve as man and wife play that went on between the boy and his sister was easily seen. Some of girls got pregnant by their own brothers and there wasn't anything that the parents could do about this. Those girls were already getting big in their stomachs.

From all of this makebelieve of being man and wife among those first brothers and sisters, a new life was in the making. Those boys and the girls, true brothers and sisters, same father and same mother, remained with their parents until their little ones came. After all those babies were born safely, then came a punishment for them all. Their parents had taught them all of self-survival and so, in the trouble they were in, those boys were made to move away from their parent's camp with those sisters they got into trouble, those that had babies. Those boys had to provide for their sisters they got into trouble, and this was for the rest of their time. It really was this that helped spread human life a little more rapidly. Like our Creator Sun tells us, "All humans are related to one another, no matter what nationality you come from."

These few girls and boys that got into this mess were told by their parents,

"From now on, you children that done wrong will have to move other places where there is more food to provide for you all. If you all stay together in a group, things will be a bit easier for all of you. This is a punishment for what has happened among you. All of you may come to visit at times whenever you want or when in need of advice from your mother or father."

And so it was that the first group of people, directly from Mudman and Ribwoman, left in separate ways away from their parents, to provide for themselves.

After this happened, there just wasn't any way to control the relationships among them. Between the now two camps, those first humans spread their population much more rapidly.

Many more small groups went on their own when food got somewhat scarce, and they increased more and more.

More boys and girls got together, more babies were born, more men and women were now growing, and always more food was to be found for them all. More groups went their own way for the sake of food. In several more years, there were several camps spread all over the country within several miles of each other.

All of this life that came from Mudman and Ribwoman was now drifting further and further apart from one camp to another. They were still a-coming. Life increased manyfold. So whether we like it or not, we are all related, regardless.

# Creator Sun's Gift of Food to His Children

Legend has it that the many groups of children of Mudman and his wife, the Ribwoman, left their parents in the four cardinal directions: east, south, west, and north. From there on those children scattered the world over. Those children of those first two people, Mudman and Ribwoman, are us, the many people of this world today.

The people increased by manyfold as each group intermarried. And as they increased in a particular group, that group broke up into smaller groups to begin another camp of people somewhere else. These groups left the other groups because of the scarcity of food. If there were too many in one area, the food they ate became scarce. The search for food was always the main reason those people broke up into smaller groups. For many, many years our only food was berries, the roots or leaves of the many edible plants, or the barks of certain shrubs and trees.

Creator Sun, always his eyes on Mother Earth to see that their many children of the many different forms of life were being taken care of. His sons the seven stars, the Big Dipper, were always with him up there in the new place. And their mother, Severed Leg the Moon, was always behind them, chasing them and trying to kill them if ever she caught up with them.

One time, on one of his visits to his wife, Mother Earth, Creator Sun—always proud of his many forms of children—was looking them over. As he was looking them over he noticed they were all getting quite thin. He had given them food to grow on and to live on, and this food should be making them fill out on their bodies. Instead they seemed to all be getting thin. As he visited Mother Earth, he seen those children mostly all out looking for something to eat. There were too many of them to get their fill from those few berries they would find, or the other food too. Creator Sun knew right away from what he seen that they needed more food.

No matter how far they scattered to find the food, they weren't getting enough to eat. Enough to fatten them. Some days they found food very abundant, but it would only last for couple of days. All of the food that was given them was being depleted all around. The people were just getting too many. Further and further away they moved from one another to find more food for themselves. A day or two at the most in one place, then they would have to move to another to find more food. Too much moving around, not enough food found to supplement them all. Something had to be done by Creator Sun and his wife, Mother Earth, to help their children get enough for all of them—and soon.

Creator Sun thought very heavily, trying to find a way to get more abundant food for them all. In his mind he thought about creating some other kind of food that would come faster then those berries and those roots or barks.

With his mind on Severed Leg the Moon all the time, he must get back to his seven sons, the Big Dipper, before Severed Leg the Moon came back from her four-day rest. He must always protect the seven sons from their mother, or she wouldn't hesitate to harm them or kill all of them with what power she had left in her.

Again, Creator Sun had to wait for some time to get back down there to help Mother Earth's children. He would have to hurry whenever that time came. He always had only four days to do things for those children.

It didn't seem so long before the time came again for him to go visit the children on Mother Earth and try to help make more food for these children of his.

It was time for Severed Leg the Moon's rest. And Creator Sun, taking the opportunity and advantage of it, came down in a hurry to see about that shortage of food. Always, he had only four days to do things for all of his children. Down to Mother Earth he went for a visit and to add some other kind of food to those they already had. It was those images after him and Mother Earth that he had to take care of this time. Mudman's and Ribwoman's children.

It had been some time since Creator Sun had a good visit with his son, the Mudman, and all of the family. Mudman's family had been doing so good with everything that Creator Sun hadn't had a good visit with him for quite a while. Neither of the two, Mudman and Ribwoman, were getting any older, because it hadn't gotten to that appointed time for aging yet. Both were childish yet with their children.

Sickness was unheard of, life was just one long existence here on Mother Earth. At this particular time, it was only the shortage of their food. In time they would all get weaker and wouldn't be able to get around so good, but there wasn't any fear for them to die.

Creator Sun went directly to their place of camps and there he was welcomed by all of the children. He visited with all of them as soon as he arrived. Afterwards, he singled out his son, Mudman, and took a walk with him out into the open fields. He had to talk with him. He told his son, "Son! You have brought many children unto Mother Earth and they are also mine. They are getting too numerous for the food I have given you to eat. Those children of ours are coming so fast now and spreading all over this land that the food isn't ample anymore for all of you. I came for that reason especially. We will get you food that may be found most anyplace."

The two continued on their walk. Creator Sun kept on talking to his Mudman son. As the two got far away from the other people and out on the plains, Creator Sun stopped and both sat down besides a small running brook. Creator Sun took some of the mud again, as he had done when he made Mudman. And with his hands he molded a thing with four legs on it, a head and the body. The Mudman was astounded at his father's making. After this thing was shaped by Creator Sun's skilled hands, he made the thing's nostrils and held it up to his mouth. He blew very hard into this thing's nostrils. Creator Sun, as he blew into the thing, said to it, "Now breathe the air from me, my breath, and live with it like my children are now living with it. Eat the food of grass and foliage to fatten you and those in the same likeness as you are that will all roam this land sometime soon. Abound this land and become the food for my children."

As this new thing came to life from that blow into its nostrils, it got up on its feet, and it too was very wobbly on the legs as it tried to walk away from them. This new thing fell back down but kept on trying to stand up and walk. Creator Sun told his son, the Mudman, "This thing, we shall name it after how its going to be treated by you and the other children when you take it for food. We will call it *eye-i-in-nawhw*."

This new food fell back down, it was very exhausted from trying to stand and walk. It had to rest for awhile as it laid there. Creator Sun soon took the advantage of this. He told his son, the Mudman, "We will have to make them so they too will become many, just as you children are made, a place for a seed and come out as a growth, an image after its own kind. It will become many. It won't take them long to bring out their images so there will always be enough around for food." He knew he had given ample supply of food to those children of his this time by giving them flesh to eat along with the vegetation. That was his way of thinking.

As this thing laid there from exhaustion, it fell asleep. While it slept Creator Sun took out of it a rib bone, like he done to Mudman, and from this rib bone he made the female. Telling the Mudman, "This one shall be for the seed which will be planted in her by the first one I made and they will become many. You and all the other children shall use them for food."

This was the first flesh food given to Mudman and all of their children to supplement those roots, berries, and the barks of food, which they ate for a very long time.

This particular creature of flesh or the first flesh food became the food animal known as the buffalo. The word buffalo came from the first whiteman that came into this country. Probably named it after the water buffalo of Asia. The true name that was given them by Creator Sun was *eye-i-in-nawhw*, or as it's translated, "shall be peeled." All the killed buffalo were peeled or, as we know it, skinned, to get at the flesh for food.

As the two new food things got on their feet and got steady, they began to graze around. They were eating the grass and the many kinds of foliage growing all over. Creator Sun told his son, the Mudman, "Now leave them be for a while. I will let you know when to start using them for your food."

This was the original name given the buffalo by those first people, or directly by our Creator Sun: *eye-i-in-nawhw*, shall be peeled. In these days of misdoings this name of the buffalo, the original name, is wrongly pronounced. It is shortened and doesn't mean the same anymore. These people of today call them *ee-neew*, which is a shorter word than that original one, *eye-i-in-nawhw*. This new name means die, death, or deceased. This new version of the original name of the buffalo doesn't pertain to what has to be done to the buffalo after it is killed—the hide peeled off and then taking the flesh to eat.

The names of most of the many forms of creatures created by Creator

*Gift of Meat Food to His Children*

Sun—especially the animals and birds, even the many different kinds of growth—pertain to the way they look to one's eye, the way they taste, the way they act in their everyday life, or any of the things that they may resemble. With such a name they are easily identified. This was the true way each and all things were named.

After Creator Sun had made that first buffalo for food for his children on Mother Earth, he told Mudman to let the animal be for awhile until such time he told him he could begin to use it for food. Creator Sun bid them farewell for that time until he could come to visit with them again. He had only four days to do things, and so his visits were short with his family of Mother Earth. He had to watch Severed Leg the Moon close as he was taking care of his children of Mother Earth. Also, him and his seven sons can better aid their brothers and sisters of Mother Earth from away out here where all of them could be seen at all times.

It wasn't so very long when he gave word to his son, Mudman, and to all of his children on Mother Earth, that they may start using the new food, shall be peeled, the buffalo. It wasn't any time before those children of his had enough food from the new ones. Flesh food and not straight vegetation like before.

The Mudman and all of his children were doing good since this new food was created by his father. All of them began to fill out again from this flesh food, and it became plentiful.

After the children had more food, the children seem to increase much more rapidly, and probably from the richness in the new food of flesh. More and more they scattered, further and further out in all directions in this land.

Today the people call that land the Americas. North, Central, and South America. If measurement was known in those days by the mile, Mudman and Ribwoman would know their children had scattered out many hundreds of miles since Mudman and Ribwoman began to have little ones of their own. They were still having the little ones along with their children. From their very first child to this last one, there were many hundreds of them by now, even thousands.

Several hundred miles is nothing in these days, not with these automobile of today. But for those first people in that beginning, several hundred miles was to the end of the land. They were on foot. This is known among the elders and according to their stories: those first people that first moved away from their parents, Mudman and Ribwoman, never had any contact with these last few groups that left their parents, Mudman and Ribwoman. When neither one is in contact with the other, they forget each other. Relationship is forgotten, because we don't know who each one is.

Many, many more were born to them as the scattering of them went on. More and more miles between them were added as they steadily increased. As they went further apart, no contact between them, their language began to differ too. The first people that drifted away from their parents and those that left Mudman and Ribwoman, just recently—those two groups wouldn't understand each other if they would've met by chance at that time. Their language was already so different. Neither group knew it at the time, they never had the chance to ever meet those distant brothers and sisters. They were all too far apart from one another.

For a long time things were very rosy for all of the children of Mudman and Ribwoman. Especially their food. Each group seemed to have plenty since the animal, shall be peeled, came into existence.

But! Like always, good things never last. Once more that population increased, and even with the animal food, it began to diminish once again. There just wasn't enough vegetation and enough of the shall be peeled to supplement the children of Mudman and Ribwoman anymore. Too many of them again, once more. Again famine was there for all of them.

It got so bad, hardly any kind of food could be found, far or near. Mudman and Ribwoman felt so bad for their starving children, and thought that their father, Creator Sun, had abandoned them all. Early one morning Mudman went out on the plains, just before the sun came up. He waited until the sun just barely started to come into view. Mudman faced the sun and began to pray to him to come down and check on his children and all his creations here on Mother Earth. He prayed to him as if he was listening. He asked him for more food to use for all of the children. The food they had was almost all gone and could hardly be found anymore. He prayed to his father, Creator Sun, that he might hurry and help them all real soon, as hunger was everywhere.

Like always, Creator Sun had to wait for Severed Leg the Moon to go into her four days of rest, and out of sight of Mother Earth. Soon as this happened, Creator Sun soon took the advantage of it.

Creator Sun knew it all this time, he knew his children needed help. No matter how much compassion he had for all of his creations, somehow those creations had to be punished for what they were doing, being disobedient to him. Going against his rules at times. Not all of them, probably a few of them breaking the rules he set for all of them. It was these things that he hesitated a little to help them. He knew he couldn't punish them on and on. There were those that were always obedient to him. He must help all of them to find more food and for once and for all, to make the next food very abundant so that it would never run out any more.

As the chance came, he came down among those children once more. Again, right away, he sought out his son, Mudman, to consult with him about the famine that had again come to all of them. Creator Sun knew just what was to be done. He had been thinking about this as he was waiting for Severed Leg the Moon to disappear for those four days that had become routine for her and everyone else.

Finding Mudman, Creator Sun asked him to take a hike with him among the many fields. Getting him alone, he told him of his plan. "You have scattered in all directions. You have scattered far, far away from this original place I first brought you. The very first children you and your wife had left for want of more food. As more and more new children came about from you, they went further and further away until you all weren't able to see one another. Distance was getting too far between you all. Many of those children will never know one another, that they are full brothers and sisters with all of the others they left in other areas. They have their own areas in which they live and hunt now. There are many different conditions in the terrain of this land all over. I will try to give them the food best suited for the particular land."

Coming to a small running brook, the two sat down beside it. As they sat down and made themselves comfortable on the ground, Creator Sun dug into the mud along the water's edge. He molded this mud into another of his creatures with four legs. This one was smaller than shall be peeled, buffalo. It had split hooves like the buffalo. Creator Sun turned to Mudman and told him, "These creatures that I'm now making for you and all of the children to use as food, they shall all have split feet. These creatures with the split feet is the ones that will be used for food."

That first creature was a bit smaller than the buffalo. Creator Sun told Mudman, "We will know this one by its feet and legs. You will see why when you see this one run, in the fields or forests and mountains, through the heavy growth of trees. I'll name it *beek-si-gow*." This means mystic feet and legs, or magic feet and legs. Today we know this animal as the elk.

As it goes, this younger generation, since about 150 years ago they began to change that Native name of this elk into a faster pronunciation, easier to pronounce: *boo-noo-gaw*. And this name has stuck with the elk in our language.

Many, many people who I have asked what they knew about the elk and its original name have explained the word as it is pronounced in these days, *boo-noo-gaw*, that it is derived from a horse. They say the elk resembles a horse, and that was where the name came from. But through my research of our past, I came to my own conclusion about the name of the elk. The horse has only been in this country since the Spaniards brought it over from Europe, and the elk has been here from time untold. So it couldn't've been from the horse's name. But on the other hand, if one has seen an elk in motion through heavy timber or a moutainous terrain or no matter how rough an area it might be where its running, the way its feet and legs carry the elk, they are magic or mystic.

After the elk was made by Creator Sun, he blew his breath into the elk's nostrils to make it breathe and come alive. He didn't wait as long as he did when he made the buffalo to take a rib bone from its body to make the female. So there was male and female elk to begin the elk life and population.

Creator Sun took more mud from the brook's edge and molded a smaller one than the elk. He told Mudman, "We shall know this one from how it throws its legs as it's moving fast, running. We shall call it accordingly to those legs, *aw-wake-ausi*," this means throwing its hind legs and front legs criss-crossly fast. "This one too shall roam anywhere, be it the plains, the timber, the mountains, or the foothills. It will be just as sure-footed as the elk and fast for its own survival." These are today's deers, with white tails.

Creator Sun made them all the way things were made, a male first and then a bone from the male to make the female.

More mud from the water's edge to make more creatures for food for his children. He made another one about the same size as this last one, and as each one was molded, Creator Sun would blow into its nostrils to give them life. As each one came to life from his breath, Creator Sun would take a rib bone out from them to make the female, the one that would receive a planted seed. This was done when the first one fell asleep from exhaustion trying to stand on its feet and legs.

This was another one of those *aw-wake-ausi,* only the first pair were called *apu-du-yi,* meaning white tail which would roam the direct foothills of the mountains. This second pair of *aw-wake-ausi,* both a slightly different color, are to be known as *es-si-go-do-yi,* black tail. It would roam the mountain foothills and out on the plains. In these days the white tail deer got a second name from its actions. The Indian name is *ahwa-du-yi,* wiggly tail or shaky tail.

Creator Sun molded more animals for his children's food. He wanted to make very sure this time that all of the children would have enough food to last forever.

He molded the bighorn mountain sheep, taking a bone from it to make a female mountain sheep to bear little ones to increase as time went along. This one was to be known as the *oo-ma-kiki-ni,* big head. "This animal will be of the mountains," he said. This bighorn was named because of its large horns, which made them look like animals with extra-large heads.

Still another animal for the mountains was molded, a pair. This pair was also named after the way they were made to look. The name of them was *mi-stuk-si-sooy-ksi, apu-mah-ki-ki-nuy,* mountain shaggy white bighead. Today we know them as mountain goats.

Making more animals for the children to survive on, Creator Sun molded more from the mud. He told his son the Mudman he would make another almost the same size as the shall be peeled kind. Always making a pair of each, so all would multiply as they came along in the world. These were given the name of how they walked: *siki-chi-woo,* black walking proudly. Again, in these days, the new people has carried the original name of the moose a little differently. Instead of the original name, *siki-chi-woo,* these younger Indian people say *siks-chi-sew,* which means black going into village, town, or crowd. This animal shall hang around in swampy places, foothills, or any place where it might find food. Again a pair of them were made, just like the other animals. Today we find the moose most anywhere—near a lake, a river, or any wet area. Mostly in the low foothills.

Molding more from the mud, Creator Sun told his son, Mudman, "This one will be a bit smaller and will roam the prairies and shall be known among the people as *so-ki-ow-wake-ausi,* a flat place with no growth, or prairie, front legs and hind legs criss-crossing. We know this one as the antelope.

He molded more small animals for all parts of wherever the children had scattered to, and whatever animal was best suited for that particular place. Creator Sun made them for his children to survive on, to eat.

He made the rabbit, and the peccary as food for hunters, lunch food. The rabbit he named as it was to be eaten and cooked—*aug-ayes-chi-dud-dud-wa*, shall be roasted. Again, in this day we live, the younger people have changed that name of the rabbit to a simpler pronunciation, *awh-awh-chi-staw*.

The peccary was also called after what he did. It was *aak-si-niw*, it squeals or shrieks. This name seemed to stick, because it is easy to pronounce.

All of the food animals were made and given to Mudman. He was given a lesson in how to stalk them, how to kill them, and how to dress all of them out. He was taught how to cook them and how to preserve them for later use. How to preserve the hides for use as clothing and shelter. The smaller animals were for clothing mostly and the larger ones for shelter, but all of them were for food. Mudman was taught not to waste any part of the animals, even the bones were used for something. Every part of the animal was used for one thing or another.

After everything was taught to Mudman, Creator Sun told him, "I must leave now and I do not know if I shall ever come back in person to you and all of the children. If I must, it will have to be for something very important. You and the children have much food to find now, it will never run out as long as you do not waste the food. Now my son, I must leave. I have been gone almost four days and it's time that I should be getting back to your brothers up there before their mother, Severed Leg the Moon, comes back from her rest."

The food animals became many, much more than needed. In fact, too many now. Mudman had to call on his father, Creator Sun, once more for his help to solve this. Creator Sun again molded the mud into more animals, a little different then those first food animals he made. He made these with sharp claws on their feet and sharp teeth in their mouths. He told these animals to go and help eat those animals with split feet, the food kind. And so in these days we see the mountain lions, cougars, lynx, the bear, the wolverine, and all other predatory animals.

While he was at it, to make very sure that the people would never run out of food, Creator Sun made the edible birds. He also made all the rest of the animals to mingle with the food kind. This was to kind of confuse the people, to keep them guessing what animals should be for their food.

The edible birds were the prairie chicken, grouse, sage hen, pheasant, wild turkey, ducks, and geese, and again he made all the other birds to mingle with the edible ones for confusion.

He made other birds, birds of prey. Predatory birds that would keep the bird population down to what it should always be, a natural way of nature. Things wouldn't get out of hand like the first life of snake he put there.

Creator Sun always learned his lessons by his previous doings. He knew just what he was to do to make things just right for the distant future. In these days we are living, we see the birds prey on other birds in one way or another to keep the bird population down. We see the animals devour each other, a natural way to keep the animal population down.

After doing all of this for his children, Mudman and Ribwoman and their children, he took the Mudman out to teach him all about the ways to prepare the many different kinds of meat of birds for living and clothing. He showed him how to use some of this for the faith they were taught. As of yet there wasn't a set way of religion or faith, just what was taught them to do— which was mostly praying to their father, Creator Sun, and Mother Earth.

He told his son, the Mudman, "Now my son, go teach all of your children the many kinds of meat I have given you to eat. Teach them the ways I have taught you to preserve them, to prepare them, and to store them for use later on. With all of this meat food I have given you, you shall not run out and be without food anymore.

"I must tell you, do not ever waste food when you get it. When getting it do not overkill the birds or the animals, kill just enough for all those with you to use. If you waste food, food will become scarce for you. It will be very hard to come by anymore."

These very words of Creator Sun, not to waste food, were handed and passed on to generation after generation, right up to my time here on Mother Earth. My father and mother told me those same words too, which we all live by, the older of us Natives. Of course, the younger generation pays no heed to all of this that our father Creator Sun had taught us, and so many of us go hungry. Today, we older Indians see this to be very true, especially among our own people and maybe the other nationalities too.

All of his plans were coming into place for Creator Sun. It was getting to the time he had to return to that place far, far away from here to be by his other sons, the Big Dipper.

Creator Sun taught Mudman and all of the children how to get together and kill the buffalo by running them over a steep incline, the *pis-kun*. How to snare the antelope, the deer too. How to kill the elk in the thick forests. How to sneak up on the moose while it was feeding in the lake. Creator Sun taught Mudman all the ways and tricks to find food before he left again.

After this, Creator Sun came a few more times to visit his son, the Mudman, and the Ribwoman and all of the children that had now scattered to many parts of this land.

# Beginning of Many Different Dialects

Creator Sun was constantly watching over his creations, Mother Earth and all of his children of the many various lives, with his seven sons, the Big Dipper, forever helping him. Always behind all of them, Severed Leg the Moon. Always behind them except those four days and nights she rested her leg. The ever-increasing numbers of his children caused a shortage of food many times.

Creator Sun was always planning and thinking of the future for all of his children. An idea came to him about the way things were now a-going for these creations of his. This would be very good for all of them as time went along, for as long as life would go along in this place he made.

He always had to wait for Severed Leg the Moon to go into her rest before Creator Sun could come to the aid of his many children. Four days is a very short time for Creator Sun to do anything, but he didn't have much choice. He had to do what he could in these four days that he was able to come down. About this time Severed Leg went into another of her four-day rests, which gave Creator Sun the opportunity he needed to come down to his many children and put his new plan to work.

Immediately after getting down here, Creator Sun went to find his son, the Mudman, and his wife, the Ribwoman, to tell them of his new plan that might be just the thing that would be good for them all. He didn't have to look so very hard to find them, they were always near the place he created for them near the river. Losing no time, Creator Sun took them for a stroll into the fields and along the river. Coming to a nice green grass place along the river, he asked them to sit down with him. There Creator Sun told them about his new plan that would be wonders for them all here on Mother Earth.

Creator Sun began, "I'm happy to have created all of you and the many things that go along with it on this Mother Earth. It makes me happy to see all of the reproductions that each thing I made reproduces, the little ones of the many lives here. But it is so, those lives reproducing are coming a little too fast for the food that keeps them alive. Those lives must slow down a bit.

"A plan of mine we will try, and I know it will work. It is a little bit hard for those lives, those children of mine, but it will help their lives in time to come.

"This plan is the direct influence by Severed Leg the Moon. She disappears for four days and nights, at which time she has to rest her lame leg. No one can see her during that time from Mother Earth. During this time the women, all women of Mother Earth, shall become as Severed Leg the Moon. Whenever a girl becomes a woman, has direct contact with a man, she will have to lose her blood for the sin she committed. This will be during the time Severed Leg the Moon is visible to the human eye for four days and nights, just as Severed Leg has to rest for four days and nights. The pain of sin shall always accompany this four-day period.

"This four days of losing their blood, and the pain, should balance the birth of the humans. It would save much food for them. They would not have too many babies anymore. As long as the baby is suckling its mother, the mother will not become pregnant."

All of the children of Mudman and Ribwoman scattered ever so wide. Up to this time there wasn't any contact with those very first groups that left their parents. They had gone too far to be met again any time by their folks.

At the very beginning of the lives of Mudman and Ribwoman, when the few children born to Mudman and Ribwoman began this life we are in on Mother Earth, the words of their spoken language were very few. It was a real simple language. As the children of Mudman and Ribwoman scattered ever so far apart from one another, their languages changed more and more until none of them could understand the other. This happened to almost all of those small groups that had separated from one another. In time, none of those groups could even begin to understand the others.

Communication with one another was impossible. This language barrier existed between those first people until they learned to talk to one another with their hands. The Native sign language began over this language barrier in that beginning. Today, too, there are language barriers between all nations of this world. Translators or interpreters are needed to understand one another.

We are the people of the once mighty Piegan Nation that roamed the great plains and the foothills of these majestic Rocky Mountains. Our original hunting area covered many millions of acres of land: from the very beginning of the North Saskatchewan River far into the Rocky Mountains. It went east with the river to where the present town of Battleford, Saskatchewan, is located, then due south from there to the great Missouri River, up the Missouri River to the fork of the Yellowstone River. From there our area followed the Yellowstone River back into the Rocky Mountains, and half of the Rocky Mountains as they go northward back to the Saskatchewan River.

We are a tribe of Natives that are the direct descendants of that first being, Mudman, and his wife, the Ribwoman.

Nevertheless, no matter what your nationality might be, and regardless of whether you want to be or not, we are all descendants of these first humans of this Mother Earth.

I am sixty-six years old now. My paternal grandma died in 1926. She was approximately ninety-five years old at her death. That would put her date of birth about in the 1830s.

At the time of her death she had been adjusted to that era's language. Living with the environment and the people, language is no problem. It is learned as you grow along, and that was exactly as she was. She remembered well the language she used when she was very young, and she spoke to us in that language, which we just could not understand. That's how much and how fast language can be changed to a different dialect. It was all still the Piegan language, but the language changes in so many years and by the newer breeds that are born. It's mostly cut into shorter words so it wouldn't take so much breath out of one. Some in her age spoke the language they all used when they were all very young, and it was entirely different than that we speak today.

Even today, in some remote places, if for some reason the people split up for so many years, they differ in their language. And it's the same all over the world. The people who break away from their main body or group eventually speak a different language. An example is a breakaway tribe of the Assiniboines that are presently settled in the foothills of the Rockies near Banff, the Stony Band. Their language has differed since their breakaway, and today they can hardly understand one another. It's likewise with the

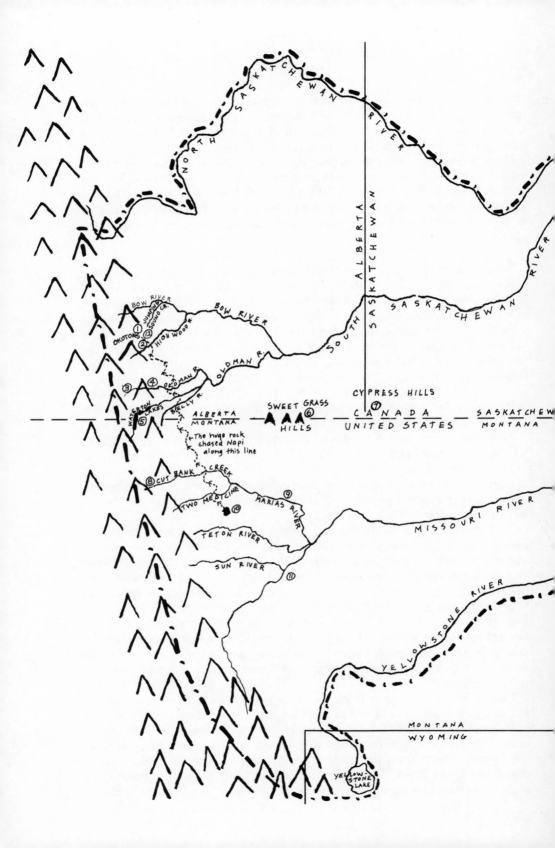

The broken border shows the Piegan-Blackfeet aboriginal hunting area. The province border lines and state lines, also the United States and Canadian boundary, are on this map, but of course there weren't any states or provinces or even an international boundary in the Piegan-Blackfeet aboriginal times. The locations of those prehistoric happenings mentioned in the book are numbered from north to south and explained on this page.

1 The place where Napi came to the Coyotes jumping on ice and Bellyfat came up through the ice as it cracked.

2 Where the women selecting husbands and Napi turned into a lone pine tree took place.

3 Where Napi and his sister originated the Oldman River.

4 Where I was born in 1916 along the Oldman River.

5 Where the Preserving Pelts Pipe Bundle began.

6 The most sacred hills of the Piegan Native or Blackfeet.

7 Cypress Hills are sacred too; this is where the young couple stole away from the main camp to go into the mountains and by mystery were given the Preserving Pelts Pipe Bundle.

8 The Cut Bank Canyon where Crowfeather Arrow hid all of the buffalo to starve the people.

9 Winter camping area of those aboriginal Natives or Piegans.

10 Lake Frances as it's called now, where Napi and the Rock began the chase, northward to Okotoks where it finally ended.

11 Great Falls, or as the Natives called it, "The Sound," in aboriginal time. The Natives would ford the Missouri above the falls.

12 Next to 1 in the north, here is Okotoks, where the huge rock was shattered by the nighthawks.

Arapahoe Tribe. The present-day Gros Ventre Tribe of Montana is a breakaway band from the Arapahoes of Wyoming many years ago. They too cannot
easily understand one another because of the change in their language.

Mudman and Ribwoman, being told to go spread the good news of more
variety of food for all by his father, Creator Sun, left the children they were
living with at that particular time. Telling them they were going to seek their
brothers and sisters that left a long time ago, to give them the good news
about more food for all.

Readying themselves the night before, the two left just before sunrise for
their long journey to find all of their children.

For many, many days they traveled, and always on foot, before they came
to the very first of their children's group. This group hadn't gone too far
away yet, it still knew the spoken language. They told them of the food
animals and fowls they were given to eat, and also more of the vegetation.
Not abiding too long in one place, they went on to find more of their children.

For many, many more days they went on before coming to more of their
children. As the two came within hearing distance of the camp, they heard
the children talking. The language these children were using differed somewhat from the language they spoke.

On and on the two went, Mudman and Ribwoman, trying to find all of
their children that had left them many, many years ago, to give them news
of the new food and what it was. As they went further and further away
from their camping area, the two learned of the different languages being
spoken by their very own children that had left them long ago. This different
language became stranger the further it got away from their home.

It was in this time that the hand language first came into existence, to
make their own children understand what they were talking about. With this
newer language with the hands, the sign language, the two told their children
about the food.

In sign language, the talker spoke out audibly, and at the same time made
signs with his hands of what was being said. For example, if the talk was
about a bear, he would be talking about the bear and at the same time making
like a bear, his fingers curled to his palms and hands held even with his
chest, and then a sign of the bear's teeth in its mouth. If it was a bird of
some sort, big or small, the sign of big or the sign of small would be used.
And then the hands and fingers to the shoulders and flapped like wings for
the bird sign.

So a new language was made by Mudman and Ribwoman to communicate
with their own children in that time. This hand sign language soon was used
by all of those that couldn't understand one another, and it still goes on
today among many Native Americans.

Although the many groups of children of Mudman and Ribwoman had
language difficulties, all of their children were just so happy to see the two
come to them, especially with the good news of more food. The hand sign

language was very new then, but it didn't take any time for those children of theirs to learn it.

Among the Native people, we have a tradition of love for one another, and it began almost the same time as the beginning of people. We give to one another gifts to show our love for the other and with no strings attached. We give our most valued possession as gifts to those we love, and this still goes on and on even in these days we are now living. Before leaving each group or camp, Mudman and Ribwoman were given presents by these children of theirs to take home, and to their brothers and sisters too.

It took the Mudman and his wife, Ribwoman, many, many moons to get the message of more food to all of their children. But nevertheless they covered the land as far as their children were scattered before returning to their own camp, and they were well satisfied with what they had done for all.

# The First Sickness and Death

Time flies by very fast. It had been a long, long, long time since Mudman was created by Creator Sun and put here on Mother Earth's body to become their very own son. To play, to roam on this body of Mother Earth.

In all of this time Mudman and the Ribwoman never grew, but stayed at the same age they were created. It had been many, many years since that time.

Their children had spread for many thousands of miles. Even their language differed among most of the groups, and most had forgotten their original language. But Mudman and Ribwoman lived on, and just as they were when first created.

This was the way Creator Sun wanted it to be for all of his children— never to grow old, never to die, but to live on and on forever. He wanted his images to be every bit like he was, never grow old and live on and on in an everlasting life, forever.

All of Mudman's and Ribwoman's children only grew to their parent's age. There growth seemed to stop. All stayed young no matter how old each one was. They were all full of life, always frisky and highly intelligent. It really didn't matter how old they might be. They were to resemble Creator Sun very closely. He was a man that looked to be around sixty years old when he walked the boy of his bride, Mother Earth, although it's been billions of years since he came into existence. There is just no one to say how really old Creator Sun is, or how long he has been in existence.

Whiteman's theory is six to seven billion years that the sun has been in existence. Our Indian faith tells us that our Creator Sun was always there and will always be there, no matter what might happen to all life. Creator

Sun will be here when all of the stars and planets are gone. This is the very true power of Creator Sun.

Everything was going very smoothly now. It had been a long time since Creator Sun had a good visit with his children here on Mother Earth, although he sees them day and night from away out there, where him and his seven other sons, the Big Dipper, are presently at.

Creator Sun was getting very lonesome for his wife, Mother Earth, and all of his children that were with Mother Earth. He wanted to pay them a good visit very soon. Always he had to wait until Severed Leg the Moon went into her four days of hiding. Creator Sun always took that advantage. As soon as she disappears, he comes down to Mother Earth and all of those that Mother Earth is taking care of. In no time he was by his son, the Mudman, and Ribwoman, telling them he didn't come for any certain reason, but that he was lonely for all of them and wanted a good visit with them.

It had been a long time since he was last down here with all of these children and Mother Earth, especially for a good visit with all of them. Not long after his arrival there, he told the two, "Let's go for a long walk, we can visit as we go along."

Walking and talking along leisurely. Talking about the beautiful place they had to live. Coming to a river, to its steep bank, somewhat like a cliff, the three of them sat down and hung their legs over the bank and looked down into the running water.

Just to do something while sitting there as they talked on and on, without noticing, they were picking small pebbles from the ground and throwing the pebbles into the river below. The pebbles hit the water with a small splash and then slowly sank down under. This they were doing, over and over, as they sat there visiting.

Ribwoman interrupted the friendly visit. Sitting up straight and with a very businesslike voice, she turned towards Creator Sun, saying as she turned, "Creator Sun, you are the most powerful being here, there isn't anything you couldn't do. No matter how impossible it may seem, you go ahead and do the impossible. You transform yourself into anything you want. You can make yourself small so you can hardly be seen or even not be seen. You can make yourself so large that you can be seen from anywhere. You can transform into an animal, a bird, a fish, a tree, or just anything you have in your mind. You're so highly intelligent, too, you control the wind, the weather, the days and nights. You are a very great supernatural being that controls all of this place, far up and down."

Ribwoman's turn of the leisurely conversation and visit made Creator Sun and Mudman sit up to listen to what she had to say. She continued, "Here we are, my man and I, we have come a long way to this present time. We have many, many children like you wanted us to have. Those children of ours and their children are having children too. Right down the line, children after children, and still many, many more to come.

"There are so many of us now that we are scattered out so very far and wide. Many of our children live many, many days away from here. We are so far apart that we do not meet our children anymore, we have lost contact with many of them. We have lost our language, too. Those first several groups that had moved away from us, they speak a far different language then the one we taught them all. We can't understand them anymore. The main things is, we just don't worry too much about one another. We don't worry of those in the camp, and so on to all of our children's camps.

"My Father, Creator Sun! Isn't there some way you can make it so we can really worry about one another? There must be something that can be done with us that we might worry much about each other. Our lives, our bodies, ourselves."

It took Creator Sun a very long, long time to find an answer for her. Creator Sun turned towards Ribwoman very slowly, as if he didn't want to answer the question, and was very much puzzled about the question.

Mudman was trying to cut in, saying, "We should let well enough alone. I'm satisfied with the way we are living now. Our Father, Creator Sun, knows what is best for us all." The two didn't even pay any attention to what he was saying. They weren't even listening to him.

Creator Sun's answer to Ribwoman was, "All of you are my own children that I dearly love with all of my heart. I love all the things that I created for all of us, Mother Earth, myself, and all. I love my wife Mother Earth and all that she beared for me. Ribwoman, my child! You do not understand what you are saying. What you just asked for is against all of my plans for all of you. You are asking about your life and your bodies and yourselves. If I affected your bodies in some way, it wouldn't be good for any of you and I really don't care to do anything like that. I made you all so that I would have something that I could love very, very much for time to come. I don't want to do anything to your bodies just to make all of you aware of each other."

Ribwoman wanted it her way. She begged Creator Sun and nagged him to do her bidding. It was a long argument. But like always, the woman won. She was just too set on something that was bad for them all. She didn't take no for an answer.

Creator Sun finally gave in to Ribwoman's asking, but not a total commitment. What Creator Sun told her was, "I'll make your bodies slow down with something that will make you feel bad in your bodies for a few days, then the body will come back to normal again."

Ribwoman argued, "That's not even anything to worry about. We'll know that the body will be all right in a few days, it's no worry at all. Why couldn't you make our body lay still and never move again, so we can cry for those bodies that are that way? We can really worry then, we wouldn't know who the next one would be to lay still and never move anymore."

Creator Sun never was a one that argued with his children, although he knew best. So once more he gave into Ribwoman, but still not a full commitment. "All right, I shall give you your asking, but the body will only lie still for four days and nights and it will come back as it was before then."

Ribwoman argued on, "How could we be lonely for one another if they are to be as they are in four days and nights? Its no worry or no loneliness for any of us."

All three of them were still sitting on the bank and throwing those small pebbles down into the water. Creator Sun, seeing those little pebbles hitting the water with a little splash and then slowly sinking down to the bottom. This gave Creator Sun an idea as they still argued on, over how it was to be for them all.

He told Ribwoman, "You have talked me into it, you argued me into it. Still, I won't entirely commit myself to it. We will decide by a stone about the size of your fist. I will throw the stone into the water below, and if it floats on the water without sinking down under, my plan of everlasting life will stand. If it sinks, then we will go with your idea of life."

Knowing that rocks are heavy and would easily sink down under, Ribwoman knew she had won the argument, although the rock wasn't thrown yet.

Ribwoman selected a good-sized rock and handed it to Creator Sun. Creator Sun held it for several moments. All at once, he threw it out to the middle of the river. The rock made a big splash as it hit the water. The three of them jumped up, their eyes on the rock as it hit the water with a splash. The splash of the water settled back to normal and to the uttermost amazement of Mudman and Ribwoman—especially Ribwoman—that rock she had selected her own self floated downstream with the current. Down, down the river it floated until it went out of their sight.

Creator Sun looked at the both of them with a smile on his face and, speaking to them at the same time, said he was very happy at that moment for what had happened to the rock, floating downstream. "There it is, both of you seen the rock floating downstream with your own eyes. Now we all know how we are to live our lives throughout our future, everlasting life."

Ribwoman wasn't at all satisfied with the outcome of this argument, she still wanted it her way. She began arguing with Creator Sun again. "This isn't a bit fair to me. We know that you are a being that can control all things of life, all elements we have on Mother Earth and even far out away from Mother Earth. This really isn't any surprise to me that the rock floated away with the current down the river. I'm the one that was to throw the rock into the river. I'm the one that is arguing with you about my idea of life here. We came from you, we should have some say about our own lives, especially our own future to come. At least a little say."

Creator Sun was very surprised at what Ribwoman said, he didn't care to have any further arguments with her. He was sad about this, but he must let his children decide their own fate. Creator Sun sadly told Ribwoman, "I shall have to let you have your own way about your future. After all, its yours to live. You know what you really want for all of your children that were born from you. I love all of you, because you're really all mine. I made you all, created you all for me to love you all. I will not affect the rock you are to throw into the water with any of my powers, it is all up to you now and all of the children and for the rest of time to come."

Picking up a good-size rock, about the size of his fist, Creator Sun handed it to Ribwoman, speaking to her at the same time. "Now my daughter, this is your own choice. It is the fate for all of you now and for all to come in the future, for as long as life may go on in this land of Mother Earth."

Ribwoman threw the rock as hard as she could upstream. The rock flew high and far out in the middle of the river. The rock made a big splash as it hit the water, it made a skip or two, then down under the water it slowly sank. Ribwoman was very gleeful over this, this was a fair throw and she had her way at the same time.

It was a sad thing for Creator Sun. He alone knew what sadness was all about, he had gone through it before.

Getting up from where he sat on the riverbank, with not very much to say anymore, he bid his children goodbye, the way to take leave. His head was stooped over as he slowly walked away from his children, Mudman and Ribwoman. He was very, very sad about all of this happening.

People say that from this unhappy change in his plans for all of his creations, as he left his children, the Mudman and Ribwoman, he walked ever so slowly away from them with his shoulders and head stooped over, he was so sad from all of this. And as far as anyone knows, he's still stooped.

Creator Sun very well knew what all his children faced. It was sickness and eventually death for all life, and he didn't want it that way. He wanted everlasting life for all of his creations so much.

Both Mudman and Ribwoman knew that Creator Sun was hurt very bad by what just happened, Ribwoman's fault. Creator Sun walked so slowly away from them, and he bade them goodbye with a barely audible voice, he spoke so low.

As Creator Sun slowly walked away, Mudman scolded his wife, Ribwoman. "I hope you are satisfied with your crazy askings. You have hurt our Father's feelings so much! He loved us all so very much, all of us and everything else he has put here with us. There is a time he will never come to us anymore to help us solve our problems. We should abide by his words. From here on, we will have to face your crazy idea of laying still, never to move our bodies any more for the rest of time. All of us, our children and all their children, have to face this. You have made a very foolish wish that has come true. I think you are selfish for what you have done."

Creator Sun hadn't gone too far yet. Mudman got up and chased his father, catching up with him. He tried to cheer him up. Mudman was talking about other things, trying to get that sad thought away from his father's mind. "When will you be able to come to visit us again, Father?"

Creator Sun didn't cheer that easy. His mind was just too heavy at this moment as he kept on a-going. He hardly spoke to Mudman, but nodded his head silently several times.

Creator Sun finally broke his silence, and with a voice so serious and very decisive said, "I'm leaving you all, you children and the other lives that are here with Mother Earth. I'll be there with the others, your seven other brothers, the Big Dipper. I am not coming just for visits anymore. I'm not coming unless it's something very important that you children have to see me about personally. I want you all to call on me all the time. I will still hear all of you. My power is of such to hear the distant calls of help, and I shall always be ready to help everything I have created with Mother Earth."

Mudman and Ribwoman were just so happy in the days after their meeting with Creator Sun. The smallest of their children were still with them, several of them, and all were happy. But their happiness didn't last too long after that one meeting. Ribwoman had made a choice between happiness for eternity or part loneliness throughout life. Loneliness had won.

One day one of their favorite young ones didn't seem as lively as it usually was. All that day that young one seemed to be more quiet and not able to move much, inactive. The child was complaining of his feelings in his body. Towards evening, the child lay very still, just barely breathing. Late that night, things for the child seem to get much worse. As the light began to show in the east, the little one had become very still. No more breathing, he laid limp. He was dead.

Both Ribwoman and Mudman jumped to him, picking him up and trying to make him breathe again. Taking him from one another and doing different things to bring him back to life, but to no avail. The two got very hysterical, running around inside of their tipi hollering, and Ribwoman screaming to the top of her lungs for someone to help them with the little one, to bring the child back to life.

All of a sudden, Mudman seem to get his sense back to normal. The woman had the little child in her arms at that moment and was still running around, screaming wildly. Mudman was at the doorway just then, and as the woman ran past him, he grabbed her arm and pulled her towards him, stopped her. She was still screaming for some help. Mudman had to holler at her to make her shut up so she would listen to him, to stop this foolish cry for help.

It took a long time for Ribwoman to quiet down to listen to Mudman. Mudman was talking soothingly to her. "You asked for this and now it's happened. Our Father, Creator Sun, told you and argued with you about the sadness this would cause any of us, including the children, all of life. Now we have our first one of the many heartaches and sadnesses you have asked for."

Ribwoman was sobbing as Mudman held her to him, comforting her the best he could. She was now able to talk a little. She asked Mudman to call for Creator Sun, if he could come back to them right now. "He said he would hear our calls for his help." Ribwoman was very sorry now for what she had caused, and now she was going to ask Creator Sun to change her wrongful doing to the way Creator Sun had wanted it. She wanted to get another chance to throw that rock into the river so all would have that everlasting life. She wanted to amend things she had so selfishly and wrongfully done.

Mudman was now calling out to his father, Creator Sun, to come just once more and to help them with this new happening that had befallen them. He was begging for him, crying for him to come to their side once more.

Creator Sun, having such a great compassion for his children here on Mother Earth, and all the rest of his creations, really didn't have to be begged. He was already on his way to them, to be by their side.

In no time at all, Creator Sun appeared before them. Ribwoman was still crying and sobbing and Mudman was rubbing his hands together thinking of what just happened,. They had laid the little one down on their bed and just stood by that still body, looking at it and crying. Both were just so very sorrowful.

Creator Sun felt very sorry for them, but things had already come to pass as it was wished. There wouldn't be another chance, and nothing could be done for that still body now. All Creator Sun could do at the moment was to comfort both of them and then have a good talk with them. Make them understand that once words were complied with, there could be no other way to right them or revoke them. Time couldn't be reversed, it couldn't be redone in any way. What's done is done, and that would be for the rest of time here on Mother Earth.

It was very hard for Creator Sun to stand fast on his words, but his ways must be carried as he puts them and let them be for that everlasting life here on Mother Earth. His compassion for his children was great. He did almost anything his children asked for. But once his words were out from his mouth, those words became law for those children and all of the rest of his creations. There was nothing that could change them words once they were out.

This first death of this young one was a punishment for Ribwoman, for those wicked thoughts of hers and that wicked wish of hers not to have everlasting life for all of them, the children of Creator Sun. She got her wish of dying. It must be this way for the rest of time.

Creator Sun was very quiet for a long time as he stood by Mudman and Ribwoman, waiting for them to quiet down from their crying and sobbing, to calm down enough to listen and understand their father.

Ribwoman was taking this happening very hard, she was all to blame for this. It had come to pass as she wished it would. Both quieted down, but still sobbing a little, eager to hear what their father, Creator Sun, was going to say.

Creator Sun's voice was barely audible to the two as he began to speak to them. "Both of you have taken what happened very hard. Don't once think that just the two of you are the only ones hurt by all of this. My heart is hurt more then either one of you. I'm the one that made life, I created it for all things that are here on Mother Earth. The child was one of the many that I own, regardless of who beared it for me. What we see all around us, everything, those are all I have made for Mother Earth, for her to love. To destroy any of them is not what I want for them. I wanted to see everything as it came to life and to leave it as it came throughout time.

"But now! That wish of yours shall have to be, my words can never be taken back and done over again. You wished it and it must stay as it is now throughout time to come. The only thing I can do now is to take the dead body of the little one back and return it to Mother Earth's body and leave the spirit of the body go as it wishes to. That spirit will live on. You will not see that spirit until you have gone to that same place it is now gone to. The body shall be as Mother Earth's body again. Mother Earth will take care of them that leaves their bodies with her, and their spirits go on.

"I want you two to wrap the body of the little one, our beloved child, in a tanned hide and bundle the hide and the body with a rawhide thong as tight as you possibly can. Take the bundled body into the woods and find a large tree with a large branch that protrudes to the east, and high enough so wild animals will not get at that body. On that branch, tie the body as secure as you can so it will stay there for years to come. The face upwards and facing the east. This will be the symbol of giving me back that body of the one that passed on from this land. Together, I and Mother Earth shall take the still body back into the land of spirits. If ever you happen by this place where that body is tied to the branch in several years, check it and you will see that we have taken the body back as we have promised. You won't find a body, but you might find nothing but dust then and a few bones."

It was a long talk with the two as Creator Sun explained the consequence of Ribwoman's awful wish of still bodies, or death, as it finally became known. Ribwoman wished for a short life and it came to pass as she wanted it.

The two had listened very well and seem to understand Creator Sun's words and explanation. But of course! The little one was their favorite and the two would never forget that child for many years to come. Because of this, Mudman and Ribwoman came to love their children so much more, more then ever.

After the tree burial Creator Sun again left the two, telling them, "You must be very careful from now on, there are many things that will make your bodies slow down and not feel good. Things that you might eat or drink will affect your bodies. Some of these things that are bad will eventually cause your bodies to lay still like this little child you have just put away. So from here on, take good care of yourselves and warn all of your children to do the same. Everyone that is alive. Spread the word to all and soon."

Creator Sun left for his abode near his other sons, the Big Dipper, far away from here. Mudman and Ribwoman were in a deep sorrow, heavy hearts. Their other children couldn't fill that empty place of their favorite child that they had lost to that terrible wish of Ribwoman.

Today, we live with the fact that we all must face death eventually, a foolish wish made by Ribwoman, sickness and on to death. But it still was a benefit for Mother Earth, a balance of nature, not to overpopulate.

Mudman and Ribwoman eventually died after living for many, many hundreds of years, probably thousands of years. They left many children scattered out in these lands of North America and South America, and we are all still coming and a-going yet. It will be so until Creator Sun says otherwise. Today, we are faced with more troubles than that time. We have the nuclear power, many, many strange sicknesses, guns, knives, cars, airplanes, and wars. We face much more then just plain sickness, and we will be lucky if we survive the next hundred years. And that's the world over.

# Medicine, Power to Heal and Prolong Life

Sickness and almost sure death came to the children of Creator Sun and Mother Earth, all of the children of Mudman and Ribwoman. These children of the powers didn't know how to fight the sickness that prevailed among them now.

A person got sick and died because there wasn't any kind of medicine to combat the sickness. It wasn't a bad sickness, either. Just a bad case of a cold could kill them off. At that time there wasn't any strange disease like the ones we know of today. Death from the bad common cold, which generally turns into lung disease or pneumonia (which was known among the Piegans as "the yellowspit") was a dreaded disease throughout the Native past, right up to the time penicillin came into existance. Pneumonia was combated with pure kerosene before penicillin, among my tribe of the Piegans. If the kerosene wasn't given in time—and it had to be taken internally to get at the lungs and cause sweat—it was sure death.

Mudman's and Ribwoman's children were now dying off very fast because of sickness, and this sickness was among all of the children throughout the land. Almost nothing could be done about this.

Each day the people woke up to a new day of the now dreaded sickness then death. In the woods, mourning was done near the big trees or on high hills, which also became a burial place.

Creator Sun kept his eyes on his children, nothing but sorrow in his heart now as his children returned their spirits to him after death. He also knew that the children were going too fast in death, there had to be something done to slow it up. He thought about the wish of Ribwoman, for sickness and death. If it weren't for that wish, people would all be happy now, as there would be nothing known about this bad turn.

It had been a long time now that sickness and death had prevailed among the children of Creator Sun and Mother Earth. Always looking down on them, Creator Sun took pity on them. They had enough punishment and they should be helped in some way.

As much as Creator Sun hated to go back among his children, he just had to, to help them once more. Of course he told Mudman and Ribwoman he would not come any more among them, unless it was very important. But this was an important part of the children's lives and he had to come to their help.

Waiting again for that right time to come among them, when once more Severed Leg the Moon went into her rest period, Creator Sun immediately took the advantage, coming directly to Mudman to tell him what could be done about the sickness and death.

Taking Mudman out into the countryside and into the woods, Creator Sun told Mudman to watch closely at what he done. Out around the countryside, Creator Sun uprooted several kinds of plants. And as he pulled each one out, he named it and told Mudman what it was for, what sickness it would heal.

Into the woods he took Mudman. He showed him some barks of certain trees, the sap part of some of the bushes, and certain berries that were for medical use. After he had shown him all the many different leaves, barks, roots, saps, berries, and certain weeds, and told him what sickness they were good for, he then taught Mudman how to apply them to the one that was being doctored. Some were for internal use and some were for external medication.

The person who applies the Native medicine externally, be it root, leave, stalk, or bark, must first chew the thing soft and mushy. Then he either applies it with his hand, or direct from his mouth, a-spraying or squirting it from the lips on the affected part of the body.

For internal medication, any one of nature's medicines are given just the way they are. The sick person chews them and swallows the juice. To mix them or make them stronger, they are brewed in water and the liquid is then taken.

Many of these Native medicines were very good for many diseases. Even to this day much of the Native medicine is used among many Native tribes of this country.

Sickness and death was the wish of Ribwoman, and it had prevailed from that time on, among all of their children. Creator Sun and Mother Earth gave nature's medicine for the several sicknesses among the people, and help saved many from death.

Now! There were more causes for that sickness and death. It wasn't disease this time, it was injury to one's body, such as cuts of the flesh, broken bones, eye injuries, cases of poison, the try at suicide, and so on.

Many of these afflictions to the body began to kill many of the people once more—gangrene, blood poisoning from infection to the wounds. The people didn't know how to combat this trouble, and it was taking its toll on the children of Mudman and Ribwoman. There was nothing that could be done about this, the herb medicine that was given the people by Creator Sun and Mother Earth to use for sickness wasn't working good for the injuries to the body. There had to be another way to overcome these injuries that many of the people were dying from.

Once more Creator Sun seen that his children could use his help again. It was very important to slow the death rate of his children, so he decided to come to their aid once more.

Like always, he had to wait a certain time before he could come to the children's side. Severed Leg the Moon again disappeared from sight to rest her injured leg, and right away Creator Sun took that advantage to come to Mother Earth where his children abided.

Coming to the side of his children, Mudman and Ribwoman, Creator Sun immediately came to the point. "I see from where I'm at the things that befall all of you, all of my children of Mother Earth. I have come to help you overcome much of the trouble that you are facing these days, and what I have to teach you will help in many ways towards the health of our children, particularly the bodily injuries they cause themselves.

"I must take you alone into the mountains, my son, and there I will teach you a way to overcome many of the deaths caused from those bodily injuries. We will have to go to a high hill."

Creator Sun and Mudman, leaving Ribwoman, set out for the high country. It took quite some time to get there.

Creator Sun wasn't wasting any time. As soon as they arrived there he took Mudman to the highest place, and there they both sat down. "Now, my son, I'll give you some of my power that can cure anything if you use it the way I teach you. Listen good, this is a song that goes with my power." Creator Sun sang a song and, being a song by a supernatural being like Creator Sun, Mudman didn't have any trouble learning the song. It stuck with him.

"Also, here is a feather that goes with the power. It is a feather of a red-winged woodpecker, for that particular bird is mine. It works for me. That is why the colors are the same as my color at times. You shall use this red earth paint that I use all over my body, which is the same color of me at times too. The song, the feather of the red-winged woodpecker, and the red earth paint, along with a prayer to me, will help the sick or the injured get well, especially if you use the red earth paint to annoint their face. This is my power that you shall use for the good of the children.

"Furthermore, I shall give anyone powers if they seek it. To find the power is a little hard to do. First the one to seek power shall have to have a sweat bath to cleanse his or her body. One has to do this four consecutive days and nights, praying all the time.

"After the completion of this sweat bath, he then must leave the camps alone and go away out where no one else is around. No matter where you go, there is a power spirit there. Of course not all spirits are that all-powerful, but they are good for something. Spirits are up in the high hills, mountains, trees, rivers. All animals have supernatural spirits, the birds too. There is no shortage in the spirit world, but one shall have to seek them to find one. Once you get a spirit to like your way of reverence to seek it, then it will come to you. From there on it will teach you what it expects of you and how you have to treat it. It may have some restrictions that one must follow to keep the spirit. Many spirits have such restrictions that they give along with the power. This is to keep the receiver of the power obedient to the spirit's wishes.

"When in seek of the spirit, one must pray at all times. Before leaving,

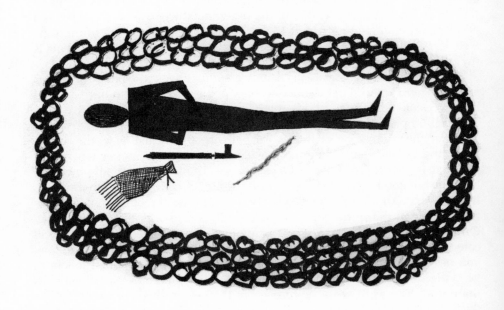

*A Vision Quest*

one must have these things that are necessary to bring along on a seek for the spirit. It is a quest for a vision. The necessary things are a pipe, tobacco, your flint and striker, the dry moss, and, most of all, the incense. There are six different kinds: the cedar bows, sweet grass, sweet pine, juniper bows, sage, and the pine moss that hangs from the limbs of the pines. It looks like hair, either black or greenish gray. These you shall try. A spirit likes either one of them, or it goes with the power the spirit is giving you.

"The quest for vision or seeking a power is no easy task. A spirit just doesn't come up to you and say, 'Here! take my power to use.' No! It's a hard task to receive a vision or to achieve a supernatural power.

"Even after one finds the right location for the quest, which has to be several days away from any other human being, one must be alone. In this way the supernatural spirit shall test you for your bravery, and if you stand the test, then shall you receive that power.

"You are a way out from nowhere, no food for you to eat, because one has to be humble and act pitiful. You shall have no food for four days. If a spirit comes and gives you the power within the four days that are required, then food and water can be had. Remember! Only four days for one try, no food or water in those four days, just your smoking, your burning of the incense, and your prayers. If the vision is achieved within the four required days, then you could eat, but only after you have taken four more sweat baths to purify the body.

"In these four required days for seeking vision and power, you will be all alone. No one else will be around. Most often, a spirit will not bother you the very first night. Probably the spirit will be checking you over, so the first night is usually an empty night. The second night is usually the time when the spirit will begin his test for your bravery. Away in the dead of the night, when everything else is still, a spirit will come to try and scare you away from your spot. A spirit will not stop short to scare you away, a spirit will do anything to scare you—throw you around, drag you by your feet, pull your hair, anything short of killing. Maybe this will happen one night if luck is with you, but mostly this goes on for two nights or even right up to the fourth night. And if you stay with it and are not scared away from this spot, then the spirit shall give you his powers.

"A spirit shall put you into a trance or a deep sleep after you have proven your bravery. And while you are in this trance or deep sleep, the spirit will teach you what to do. And if there is a song that goes with the power, which there usually is, you shall learn every bit of what he has to offer you in power. It's funny how those powers work. After the trance or deep sleep that the spirit power is given to you, you will remember everything. Most all powers from the spirit world come with something that goes with the power— it might be a bone of some certain animal or bird, a certain kind of stick, maybe a rock, a feather, it might be a skin of some animal, a skin of some bird, most all of the powers given by the spirits must have with it the earth paint of a special color, which there are several colors. Also the pipe and tobacco comes with the power, these things you will have to get and keep on your person after you return from the vision quest.

"Everything you see around you on this Mother Earth—the growth, the air you breath, the water you drink, the small stones, rocks, right to the big mountains, animals and birds, creatures of the waters, trees, bushes, just everything and anything of Mother Earth has a life and some of my powers to keep it alive. So there is no shortage of supernatural powers.

"Even within yourself this power exists. If you combine it with another source of power, it become supernatural. A human being can have several powers from the different spirits, and with the several powers, it would even be more powerful.

"All of the supernatural powers that are given are for the existence of our human life. The receiver of the power must use such power for the good of human life. They must help those that are afflicted by injury or sickness, anyone in need of medical help.

"Anyone that uses this strange power for the good of himself or for bad purposes, such as to destroy the life of another, to cheat someone or cause any type of harm to anyone, his or her bad wishes shall come back unto them and the power shall be taken away from them."

All of this, the strange powers that were given to certain individuals, a woman or a man, were very unbelievable. He or she could do miracles with such power—mending broken bones, stopping a severe nosebleed or hemorrhage, stopping blood flow from injury to main arteries without surgical tools, even deaths. This power is used to revive a dead being as long as two days after death. If the one with power is gotten in time, can save people who are choking on food. This supernatural power can save a life if the one with power can be gotten in time.

All of these emergencies that would cause death for sure, most lives were saved by this supernatural medical power, even up to the last part of the 1800s. All of this achievement of the supernatural powers were direct from our Creator Sun, a gift for use against death.

This wasn't a form of witchcraft, like our white neighbors or the priests and preachers claim. If our Native powers are of witchcraft, then! What the white man teaches us through the school system or through the many kinds of churches is more a witchcraft then what we did to save lives. Their teachings cause more destruction and taking of human lives then I ever knew.

After coming back from a vision quest, if one had luck and received a power from some sort of spirit, he or she will make a debut to let people know of their power achievement. He or she will offer their knowledge of power to the one in need of medical help. For a medicine man to help, the medical need has to be something very serious, that a common herb or Native medicine couldn't cure.

A new finder of the supernatural powers often waits for the most severe cases, where several medicine men had failed. And if he has that particular power to surely arrest the trouble, then he makes a great debut of his powers.

In most all doctoring of a patient, several Native doctors are called in to help the sick. The doctor usually has a certain song to go with his power, and most have their own hand drums, made of rawhide, that are used to beat on while he is doctoring a patient. The doctor's song of his spirit helper is sung, and the doctor calls on one of the other attending doctors to drum for him and help him sing the song while he does the doctoring.

Most all doctors use the hot rock. This is made ready by the patient's family. A hot fire is made, in those days it was an open fire. The rocks are closely fitted together in a close pile, wood is then piled over the rocks and fired up. Wood is kept constantly on the fire to keep it hot, and when the rocks are ready, red-hot, then the fire is fed slowly to keep the rocks red-hot for use by the attending doctors. The rocks are kept in a rawhide bowl.

A doctor has by him an eagle wing fan to fan himself when it gets too hot from the steam of the hot rocks in the rawhide bowl. The doctor uses his bare hands, to heat the affected part of the patient's body. Immediately after the red-hot rock is dropped into the rawhide bowl, and the water is boiling hot, the doctor with his power will dip all of his fingers into the boiling hot water and touch the patient with his hot fingers. When the affected part of the body is very pink or red from heat of the hot water, the doctor applies the root or herb medicine. Immediately he takes his eagle-wing-bone tube and blows the medicated area so the medicine will penetrate the patient's skin.

By the time the doctor has done what he can and is all hot and sweaty from the hot rocks he used, he would call another doctor to take his place. In this way, each doctor had a rest. As another doctor take his place at the patient's side, a new batch of red-hot rocks are made ready for him to use for his try at the patient. This Native doctoring would take time, probably an hour and a half to each doctor, according to our time of today.

The family of the sick person must have a stone bowl to burn incense in. Incense had to be used in mostly all Native doctorings. Most Native doctors are given them by the spirits that gave them power.

All families of the Plains Natives have at all times a forked stick, made either from wild chokecherry bush or the sarvis berry bush. The bark is peeled at the forked end of the stick, which is about thirty inches long, according to the measurements of today. The opposite end of this stick is then peeled fancy, mostly in designs. This end is the handle part of this stick. The fork end is used to pick up hot charcoal from the open fire. The wood for the fire is quaking aspen or, as the people call it, cotton wood. This wood holds a hot spark for quite a while, which is needed for the burning of incense.

The pipe is another necessary thing that must always be on hand for the doctors of the Natives of our Great Plains. The pipe and tobacco were given to us by our father, Creator Sun, and it is used for reverence and faith, to ask the Creator for his help while the pipe and tobacco are smoking. As the smoke drifts upward, a prayer is being said. This smoke is the carrier of our prayers as it goes drifting upward and slowly disappears before your eyes, like that of a spirit. The smoke that's drifting upwards is the carrier of the prayer that is being said when a pipe and tobacco are burning.

About one out of thirty ill persons in those days might lose their life because of an advanced stage of their illness. Mostly all sick people are saved by this power doctoring and by herbs. Faith too.

When the patient is well, all of the doctors hang on for a while, making sure there is no relapse of the illness. In a day or so, the doctors that stayed to make sure the patient is well will then take leave to go home.

Before the doctors leave, the patient's family cooks up a special good meal, which is a thanksgiving meal for the doctors. When the food is ready all will sit on the floor where a hide rug is spread out, and on this rug the meal is served.

Everyone sits down and waits. No one must touch the food. The oldest of the place, one of the attending doctors, is appointed to give a thanksgiving prayer. He will break a piece off of the choicest piece of meat or tongue, which usually is a sacred food. The others follow suit. When all have a piece in their hands, the prayer is said. At the end of prayer, all of those pieces that were broken off—just a pinch of the choicest food—are then stuck into the dirt or ground and each one must say, under his or her breath, "Here's eating with you holy spirits."

The meal is quite noisy, everyone is talking about the happiness that had come back to the particular home. Some are talking of their buffalo hunts, or something of interest to the others. The noise goes all the way through the meal.

Immediately after the meal, all of the attending doctors will take their leave and head for home to sleep. They probably had stayed up for several nights without much rest.

The family gives each of the doctors something of value, something that he probably needs as pay for help getting the sick person well. Each doctor, even those that had gone before the recovery of the patient, gets their pay too.

In the very early days riches were in the line of furs, soft-tanned hide garments, specially made strong bows and arrows, tipis, and good dogs. Dogs were used for moving around from place to place, and they were truly valuable to the people.

In those early days, wasn't no such a thing as a horse, cow, money, nor any precious stone or metal jewelry. No such jewelry or riches as they have in these days.

All Native jewelry was a nature's riches and from birds of the air, the animals of the land, the many various growth of the land, and the shells of the waters. These were made into jewelry. The claws of the different animals were made into bracelets or necklaces, the shells were made in the same ways, and a lot of the fur was worn with the garments.

Elk teeth were the most valuable of all the animals, concha shells too were most valuable, whenever they could be traded for. They also had perfume that was very valuable, made from the gland of the beaver, which was a hard animal to trap in those days. The otter was a valuable animal too, which made the otter fur very valuable.

The Native doctor never asks for the pay. We have much compassion for one another, we have love for our fellow Natives, the love that our Creator Sun bestowed on everyone to use throughout life for all of the things he created for his wife Mother Earth and himself. Love and honesty are his commandments.

A payment from the family of a sick person is not payment for doctoring, but a gift for their love for a doctor to come and spend time with their sick. It is a way of buying and paying for the prayers, the power that was used by the attending doctors.

If the sick person is lost to death, those attending doctors still get the valuable gifts from the family. Love is what life is about.

Our love for others still exists among most people, those that aren't influenced by the white race. Among all of the Native tribes, both in the United States and Canada, and I'm very sure it still exists in South America too, share our love for one another.

If you haven't attended a Native *pow-wow*, the intertribal dances, you missed something that would show this love for their fellow Natives and from many tribes. During the *pow-wow* a special time is called for a deceased member of a family, or a noted leader of a certain tribe, or it might be a serviceman home on a furlough. An honoring of someone who is special to someone in a *pow-wow*. A special song is song for them, an honor song, that special party or group will get up and dance and all of their relations get up to help them. After their dance, they all gather in the center of the arena and there an announcer will call mostly visiting tribespeople to come to the family, and all of those called get a gift from that special group.

Today there aren't any Native doctors like there was in the early years, up to about the 1940s. From there on the Native doctors disappeared, because to get their kind of power was too much for the modern Native, who was scared to go alone to seek the vision, too used to crowds. The modern Native is too lazy to spend time for the Native tradition. Too much alcohol, drugs, and things to keep them in the crowd.

I'm up in years, as I was born in 1916. So I was around and knew quite a bit of life towards the last of the twenties. It was then that I actually seen these things happen, the Native doctoring.

I seen Two Guns White Calf, Jim White Calf, Sr., and Herman Dusty Bull use that supernatural power. I actually seen each of these men take a red-hot rock from the wood kitchen stove and walk to the other room where the very sick woman laid. Their bare hands, their wet hands were just a-sizzling, but they weren't burnt or even harmed. Many strange ways of power I seen in those few days they were doctoring the woman.

There must've been about eight Native doctors that were there for the few days the woman was awful sick. She even stopped breathing for a few seconds, but Jim White Calf brought her back to breathing with his mystic powers and his doctoring. Two Guns White Calf was the father of the sick woman, and the other Native doctors were Herman Dusty Bull, Yellow Kidney, Manyhides, Victor Chief Coward, Home Guns, and Pete Redhorn. Each of these men had their own supernatural powers that was used for the good of other Natives. The sick woman being my cousin, I was there to assist in anyway I could to help, getting firewood and water from the small creek was mostly my help.

The medicine and the supernatural power has been around for many, many hundreds of years, since Creator Sun gave it for the good of his creations. For several years it was lost with much of the native culture. From around the 1880s up to just a few years ago, much of our culture was forbidden to use by our friends the paleface, who wanted to rule the Native people. Many Catholic missionaries came into these Native domains to influence them into their way of Christianity, which to me is full of corruption.

The last of the 1930s brought back some of the culture the Native lost. But in the many years previous, we weren't allowed to use our own culture, which was several generations. Most of it was outright lost to our younger people that tried to reorganize for the lost culture. Most of the people that had lived with the Native culture were already gone by then. There weren't no others to turn to, to get the information from, because we never write things down as history or otherwise.

Today we the Natives of these United States are trying to pick up our Native customs and cultures, seeking to find the lost part of that once precious way of our ancestors. We find pieces, those we are fitting like a jigsaw puzzle, because our young people hunger for that great culture. And as the Native goes along in life, we piece together those lost parts of our great culture of life and once more live like those precious days of yesteryear.

I have read many books on the Native of these countries. Our white friends done much smearing in those books. In most cases we were called almost everything except our true name, Natives. So with this book I am trying to right the wrongs. All of the books written about the Native is done for money and for recognition, so there is much added or taken out about our true ways.

We were called witch doctors, savages, cannibals, dirty filthy people, and most of all, we were the dumb people.

Comparing this country with the way the first white people found our land and that of today, who would be the filthiest, the dirtiest, the most savage, the witch doctor, and cannibal? I'm sure everyone knows the answer, as much as the guilty party hates to admit this.

In the times before the coming of the white people, our lands were pure, all water anyplace in this country was pure, we had more then surplus of all food animals, all of the food fowls, all of the water food, the land itself was pure, and most of all, we had pure sunshine from our Creator.

All of the existing lives of Mother Earth, Mother Nature—the dirt, grass, weeds, brush, trees, rivers, creeks, springs, brooks, and the great bodies of water, mountains, and so on—to me, these things of life are the ones that give power to people, every one. Even the white people live by the power of these things created by Creator Sun. So to me, these aren't the works of Satan, the Devil, or hell, the power from them isn't satanic like the white people like to call it. It isn't even witch power either, but the great power of Creator Sun. If it's what the white people call it, witch power, then I don't see how the white people can be something else then a witch too, because they too live by the powers of our Creator Sun.

All food has the poison in it today, because our white farmers use a chemical fertilizer that is full of poison, just to grow a bigger and heavier yield of their crop, and all for the money they want to make from this. Not one thought about the poison that the consumer will be eating along with that certain food. That's how much we think of one another. Life isn't worth nothing to those that are growing all of our food, because of this poison fertilizer.

Money is the main thing, money is the white people's God. The more money the less friends you have. The hell with life, as long as I have lots of money, is their attitude. So more poison and bigger, heavier crops to make it.

# A Disciple of Creator Sun

Many, many hundreds of years went by. And all this time Mudman and his wife Ribwoman were alive and well, teaching their children what they had been taught by Creator Sun.

The two had many children, those children had many too, their children and their children having many more. As the population of Mudman got too numerous, the people broke up into small groups and left for their own place to live. Now the population of the two was so broad that it must've spread out into most of the land, which today we know as the North American continent and South America too.

When Mudman and his wife created from his own ribs, the Ribwoman, passed away, the people didn't have anyone to teach them what to do anymore, and all were taking things into their own way. Things were getting bad among the children of Mudman and Ribwoman, getting out of hand, no one around to correct them or teach them the dos and don'ts.

Creator Sun was in a deep sorrow again for the way the children of his were doing since their parents, Mudman and Ribwoman, had passed on to that beautiful place of Happy Hunting Grounds, where all spirits of his children to go after death.

Creator Sun had to get someone to lead the people on Mother Earth. With his great supernatural powers that no one could surpass, he thought of a way. He must be with his seven sons, the Big Dipper, most of the time because of the threat of their mother, Severed Leg the Moon. Creator Sun must be ready for her at all times, so he must have someone else look after his children of Mother Earth. He just couldn't be two places at once.

The idea he had was to send a small part of himself to watch over his children and to teach them to come out of the bad ways they had been doing now since the death of their parents, Mudman and Ribwoman.

One day Creator Sun took a small part of this great supernatural spirit and it become himself all over again. He made it to be in the same form like the people of Mother Earth, his children.

To this day, of all the legends of the Natives, our history, all the way back to time beginning, no story teller has ever mentioned when or where or how Oldman, Napi, came about. But this is the way through my research I found it to begin.

He made this being from part of his spirit into a solid form like his children of Mother Earth. Creator Sun gave this being much of his powers and taught him what to teach those brothers and sisters of Mother Earth. Knowing this job as he learned it from the Creator Sun, Creator Sun put Oldman on Mother Earth with the rest of his children to lead them on into more learning from him this time. Teaching them all the ways to better living and better ways of life to lead to satisfy their father, Creator Sun. To be obedient, to be faithful, to revere him in every way, to hold sacred his ways, to be devoted to him.

Oldman came to take charge of the people here on Mother Earth, stealing in where no one noticed where he came from or how he came. Without a question from the people, he became one of them.

Everyone thought he was just another one of their own people and someone's relation. What was noted about him was his attire and his build, his age, which people thought was somewhere around middle age, a slight stoop of his shoulders and the graying hair, the eagle feathers and eagle plume that he wore on his head. He seemed to the people an outstanding being.

He was just a good-looking man. There was something very outstanding about him. He looked to be a prominent being, a proud look about him. His leggings were fringed with the red-winged woodpecker feathers, his shirt was also fringed with them. A tobacco and pipe pouch was tied down on his right side. In his left hand he held a staff, a long stick that he used for a cane. To the people he was probably one of the chiefs of the camp.

None of the people knew that he really was put here on Mother Earth by Creator Sun, an exact image of himself. That was Napi, Oldman.

Things had gone astray after Mudman and Ribwoman passed away, their children went into a corrupt life, a bad life for most of them. Creator Sun was always worrying about the life of his children, a good life he wanted them to lead. Creator Sun sent a disciple among them to lead them into a better way of living, out of corruption. That was Napi. Oldman was to live exactly the way Creator Sun lived. He was to teach and set an example for the people to live by. Napi was to do all things as if Creator Sun was doing them himself, Napi was Creator Sun, a part of his spirit, only in a solid form.

*Creator Sun's Disciple Napi Put on Mother Earth*

Napi, the Oldman, didn't spend too long in any one Native village. He was teaching the ways of Creator Sun, so constantly he traveled from Native camp to Native camp teaching and teaching the right ways of Creator Sun.

Napi never had the difficulty of understanding the many dialects the now many groups were speaking. Creator Sun made him understand everything here on Mother Earth. Napi was part of Creator Sun, so he thought like him and done many miracles like him. He had much of his power to use for the good of Creator Suns children.

Among the many tribes of the American Natives, this Napi, Oldman, was known in many ways and names. He was Coyote to many Western Natives and to some of the many bands of Crees too. He was Raven to many Coastal Tribes. To some he was *Sayn Day.* Oldman was known throughout the two continents, North and South America and all in between, and is named many ways.

Oldman's power was almost as great as his counterpart, Creator Sun. He could do almost anything Creator Sun does. He could transform himself into many things, all of the things his counterpart created. Transform into coyote, raven, bear, eagle, just anything of the many things of Mother Earth.

Napi, Oldman, could do the opposite too. He could change anyone into anything he wanted them to be and still talk like a human being in any dialect.

Of all the many dialects of the now many tribes or groups in all parts of these countries, Napi never had any problems. He spoke all of them without a hitch.

After a time on Mother Earth with the rest of the human beings, people began to realize the power of Napi. His ways were so perfect, his knowledge was so superior, he knew more then anyone else. Being told of the description of Creator Sun, the people began to suspect Napi as being him to teach them. Almost everyone took to him and followed his ways and teachings. He was Creator Sun, a part of him, and was sent down by him to lead the children of his, only in an earthly form like his sisters and brothers of the human race.

For many years after he came down here to help straighten out the children of Mother Earth and Creator Sun, Napi went from camp to camp, over and over again, teaching, giving advice on honest living for all of the people. Napi, Oldman, meant real well, he was doing his job very well. Creator Sun was very pleased with Napi's teachings and what he was doing for the people here on Mother Earth. Creator Sun was very much pleased.

As Napi went around to all the people of these lands, he used his Maker's power to influence the people with his teachings, which were very good. At times he used the magic power to put something over in the minds of the people, other times he used the miracle power to heal an impossible case of illness or to bring a dead being back to life. These were all for a point, a point that would bring to the minds of the people that he, Napi, was the great one.

This went on for a very long time. Napi was getting used to the magic power that he possessed, that Creator Sun trusted him with, a power to use for the good of the people, Creator Sun's and Mother Earth's children.

Because of all of his good deeds for his sisters and brothers, the teachings and everything that he'd been doing for them, the miracle healings, the magic he used on them for the good of it, all of the people were looking up to him, he was their big brother, their savior. In time the people began to call him *nin-ah*, which meant father. It was because of all the magic he was doing with the power given to him, for the people. There really wasn't anything wrong in that, it was given him by Creator Sun, as long as he used it right.

Being called like the great one that put him here on Mother Earth and with the power he had, well, things kind of went to his head. All the power he had and all the magic he used it for, why couldn't he use some of it for himself? This was an idea that went around in his mind as he went about his way to all of the camps.

Napi had been with the people for many years now and he had the people pretty well reformed to Creator Sun's liking. That title everyone was calling him, Napi, he even resembled the great one. And most of all, he had that power from him. Everything pointed to a certain greatness for him, he's done his job as an instructor, a teacher, an advisor, he had done many magic things for the people in curing sickness, he's even brought back several lives for those people. Maybe! Just a tiny use of this power for himself to further influence the people that he was truly a great being. Creator Sun wouldn't know.

It wasn't much to begin with, but Napi used a little of the power that was entrusted to him for a little mischievous doing. Creator Sun was always so busy that he didn't have his mind on Napi. Napi was doing so great that he didn't need watching over, so the little mischief went unnoticed at this time and for more times that he done more mischief.

As time went on, that power that was entrusted to him got the better of him. He began to use it a little more for himself. He was taking more and more advantage of that power Creator Sun entrusted to him.

As time went on, those mischiefs Napi was doing were becoming more out in the open. Creator Sun, turning his attention on him, found out what Napi was doing. He didn't bother to stop him, the things he was doing weren't bad, they were only to make the people think of him as a great being. Creator Sun was going to keep him in sight at all times so he wouldn't do anything seriously wrong with that power he had.

As time went by Napi's doings began to get a little crazy, and they were being done almost openly now.

Napi, Oldman, was getting into more and more mischief, nonsense after nonsense he done using the power of Creator Sun.

The thought in him was that while Creator Sun was busy way up there, he wouldn't know what Oldman was doing to make himself great among the people here on Mother Earth. He really wanted to make himself great to his subjects. They'd love him more for his greatness.

They'd love him more for those great deeds and miracle doings he was doing for his subjects. Those crazy things he done were only to make them have more and more respect for him, because most of those crazy things were done magically, with that power he had of Creator Sun.

Napi was getting older, and the older he was getting the more those crazy doings were becoming routine. They still weren't bad, as Creator Sun was watching him closely all the time now.

A few more years went on by and Napi got a little older and more crazy. His respect for Creator Sun was getting weaker, he began thinking of himself a little more with the power that he posessed of his master, Creator Sun. In fact, he was admiring himself for his doings, even if they were crazy doings. He was showing the people he was a great one and that he should be respected just as well.

Not many years after this, Napi completely broke away from his duties as a leader put here on Mother Earth to lead the children of Creator Sun and Mother Earth to righteousness. He was the great one in his own mind, he could do anything with that power he had of Creator Sun. So now he was running his own life as well as that of the children of the great ones, Mother Earth and Creator Sun.

Napi, here on the earth, took his own way to run his own life and the others that were followers of him. Not all of them became followers, some or maybe most thought of him as a foolish man and didn't want any part of him.

# Oo-chi-scub-pah-pah, Dragging Entrails Full of Dirt

Napi lost himself in the multitude of Creator Sun's and Mother Earth's children, living among this group and that group, up and down the country, criss-crossing.

He was mostly welcomed as a great one, and that covered the two continents of the Americas. He was just getting more foolish as time went on. The greatness was completely in his head.

Creator Sun hesitated to put a stop to this nonsense that Napi was doing. It wasn't bad, it was just foolishness. After all, he put him here to do good for his children, to lead them to righteousness, and he had done his work very good. So why should he take away that little fun Napi was having. Napi thought his Creator didn't know what he was doing, he thought he was pulling the wool over Creator Sun's eyes.

As time went on, the people kind of forgot Napi. He was just one of them now. The things he was doing were getting too foolish, they were beyond what the real Creator would do. But nevertheless, Napi still had those features of Creator Sun, even that proud look with the slight stoop of the shoulders.

At times Napi would become absent from all of the people and things went on without him. It was during one of these times that this story happened.

All living creatures and the living things of the creations of Creator Sun were flourishing and bursting with that small but strong power they had been given by the Maker. Many strange happenings were taking place all over the land. It was done by the power in their own selves combined with the achieving of a vision quest. Some people had much more strange powers then others, and it was one of these that came into existence while Napi was some other place.

At this time some individuals realized it was nothing but trouble living close to other people or in groups. Still others went to remote places because of jealousy over their wives.

Whatever the case may be, a man and his wife moved away from their camp. In those days there wasn't horses nor any kind of transportation for the people. They had to depend on their legs. And for their burdens or belongings, a small travois was hitched up to a dog—dogs were the only domestic animals back in those days. Whoever had many dogs was rated rich, because many dogs can carry many belongings.

The couple only had only two dogs to depend on to carry their few belongings. They moved towards the foothills of the mountains. For several days they were on the move. They could only cover a few miles a day, so it took them several days to get to the foothills and a few more days to find the right place for their camp.

It was nothing but happiness after they settled down. They were very young and full of life, ready to take on the impossible.

The man no more than got settled at the new place when he decided to hunt and trap for the fur-bearing animals that were abundant all over. Furs in those days were riches to the many people of the country.

First he went on the hunt, killing enough animals so that he could dry the meat and preserve it for their use. He would cut the meat into a thin slice, hang it over a tripod with crossed sticks on the side, then build a fire under the meat to let it be in the smoke. This was smoke-drying meat. This meat could then be kept for several years in a parfleche case without spoiling. Their food was more important then anything else. The more food they stored, the longer he could hunt and trap without having to bother about food.

The couple must've hit it just right. Berries were ripe and the many different root foods also. They picked berries and dug roots, which were all dried for long keeping. In those days, everything was plentiful, all things were abundant, no problem to get, so it took no time to accumulate all of the food.

Everything was done to almost perfectness, the couple meant to stay awhile here. Winters were very severe along the mountains, so everything must be done before winter set in.

Already they had a tipi set up and well lined with animal robes. All of the food that could be stored for the long cold winter was ready, all of their clothing made warm. They even had an arbor close by their tipi which was made extra-warm inside—it was lined with fur of the larger animals. This was just in case an extra-hard cold weather hit them. The arbor was smaller then the tipi, so it had to be warm to withstand any cold day.

Now it was all set for the fun of trapping for the fur-bearing animals. The man got his traps made and ready to set, a regular trap line for the winter. Those days steel traps were unheard of, everything was improvisation. Traps were made according to the size of the animal you are trapping for.

Traps were made somewhat like the log-type houses. The logs for the large animals, or sticks for small animals, were stacked on top of one another in a small square with a cover, the trap part. The tripper was the parts of the cover. This was baited with whatever food the animal you are trapping liked. A little stick held the cover open to let the animal into the trap, and the bait was rigged to the trip with small sticks to make that cover close on the animal. A slick substance, like tallow, was also used for the trip.

It was several days preparing the necessary things for the many different sizes of traps, but the man was young, it was no problem to him to get what was needed.

When all of the necessary pieces were prepared, it took several more days to get all of the pieces to the different locations. It was a trap line for the whole winter, so they had to be made right for long winter use, and this takes time.

In our area, the Montana plains, fur-bearing animals became very good from the middle or the last part of October. This month was known by the Natives as Turning White Moon. It is the month the weasel and the plains rabbit turned from a brown color to pure white. The two seasons of summer and winter these two animals of the plains camouflage themselves—a brownish tint for the summer and pure white for the winter snows. So the last of October was a good time to start trapping for the fur-bearing animals.

The couple weren't only ready for the coming winter, they were ready for a long, long time to come. They were set on staying here away from other people, and probably would start another group here along the mountains.

Winter came and gone. Summer was a busy time again for the couple— the job of gathering food and processing it for the winter, storing it in the parfleche cases took time too.

Another winter went by again. The summer moons brought the easier time around for the two, only this beginning of the summer was a happier one for the two. The Maker gave them something to be happy about, something that will keep them company and a start for the next tribe. The woman had become pregnant and would soon be having her little one. The two were just so happy for all of this, their living and now an addition to the two.

They had been here going on three years, and the game was now being scared farther away from the local area. The man took from one day to three days now to come back from a hunt, to kill enough for them.

The woman was getting bigger and bigger as the days grew warmer. "It might be this fall when the leaves begin to fall before I have my little one," she was thinking.

The man had quit trapping for the summer, fur wasn't any good in the summer moons. Hunting for the animals for food, trapping the grouse, pheasant, and the prairie chicken to dry for food, even fishing, which was done with a net of the roots of certain trees. Buckskin was interwoven with the roots or strips of roots to make a net or fish trap. The fish too was dried for future use.

The man had his hands full this year, because his wife couldn't do too much work. Women in those days, because of the lack of doctors, must have the baby only with the help of their husband or a midwife, if they lived anywhere near anyone else.

It was a known fact among the Native people, especially the women, that when in family way, pregnant, a woman must work as hard as she could until she felt her birth pains starting. And also, she must continue to have intercourse almost up to the last few days. This was to ensure an easy birth, because the hard work kept the baby from growing big in the womb, getting fat while still in her mother. The intercourse was done almost throughout the pregnancy, and that was like a lubricant to the passage way for the coming baby. Without this knowledge by the women, many would die while in childbirth, because of no doctors or medicine, nor any of the present-day pain killers and methods. In these days of the twentieth century, many doctors tell pregnant women that it's a no-no for intercourse while they are pregnant, that it would cause blood poisoning. But in the days of unwritten history, way, way back, all things were so pure—the food we ate, the water we drank, the air we breathed, and the pure way we lived—there wasn't any way we could cause blood poisoning, if the two bloods are of the same type.

The man had to return real soon each time he went hunting. But as it was now, the animals were on the move away from their camp, they weren't as numerous as they were when the two first came to this place. So most of the time he at least took overnight, and once in a while he took about three days to return to his camp.

Each time he went on a hunting trip, he would warn his wife not to let anyone in their tipi. They had lived here for going on three years and there must be someone that knew they lived here. He tells the wife to be sure to use the dried-hard stiff rawhide that was put across the doorway on the inside of the tipi, between the poles and the tanned-hide tipi. This served as an indoor lock when tied in place.

This stiff rawhide piece kept the wild mean animals out of the tipi, and people too. Tipis in those days were made from the heavy hides of the moose, elk, and buffalo. The hair was scraped off and processed with the brain of the animal, then soaked in a water until soaked through. Then it was worked back and forth across a rough edge of a rock, or something with a sharp edge. This was a continual work to the finish, because the hide had to be dry and soft while you're working on it. If one quits work on it without the continual work, the hide will dry hard and stiff. It is important to stay with the work until the hide is soft and dry.

The man always had to rush home when he was on a hunt. Most of the time he would be away for three days before he could kill anything for their food. He must kill an animal, the food animal, otherwise they would have to go without eating.

In these days, all we have to do to get something to eat is to have money. We just have to step outside and walk to a store or a café to buy food. If it's a little ways, we jump into our car and go get something to eat.

All the time the man was gone he would be just so worried about his pregnant wife. She was so big and most anytime she would be having the little ones. The man just had to be there when that time came, he had to help his wife at childbirth. He was the only one to help her.

Staying around the camp was getting very monotonous for the man, he was just so used to walking, looking after his traps, or being out on a hunt. But he had to be around for the coming baby.

Each time he was leaving on a hunt, he'd tell his wife, "Be sure to keep that doorway closed with the rawhide doorpiece so no one can come in." This was a must for the woman, to ensure her safety from unwanted intruders.

It was time again for stocking up on meat. Berries were starting to come off the bushes, a few leaves were turning yellow, the storm that turned leaves yellow will be coming soon, the two must have enough dried meat for their winter use.

As much as he didn't want to leave his wife alone at this time, her time to have the little one was so close. There wasn't any choice, he just had to go hunt for the winter supply of dried meat.

He was leaving early, the eastern sky was just graying as the man got up to go hunt again. He wanted to return as early as he could, his wife's time was getting very close.

As he was getting ready, he reminded his wife about the stiff rawhide doorpiece, to be sure and keep it in place so no one would come in, and always to stay quiet while alone.

He was ready to go now. As he left, the same words was for the rawhide doorpiece, to have it ready for use at a split second. With all of the last-minute warnings, the man left for his hunt.

Going farther and farther away from the camp, the man was thinking about his wife, hoping she didn't start laboring while he was gone. He must hurry and get back. But that meat was almost as important. If no meat now, the winter will set in, then they will never be able to get meat while the snow is flying and it would be starvation for them.

He was just so sure he would scare up an elk or deer close by, maybe a moose, then he wouldn't be gone too long. These were all hopes in his mind as he got farther away from the camp.

There is always fate to deal with. His luck wasn't any too good this day. On and on he walked, no game to be seen, he just had to keep on a-going until he could spot one or two. Something has to happen soon, he was already far away from their camp.

On and on he trudged, keeping his sharp eyes on everything all around him. Still no luck. It was getting too dark now, he couldn't see anymore, he must bed down for the night, must eat something and rest.

The early people carried lunch, too, whenever necessary. A trip that might take a few days, a lunch is carried. The lunch might consist of dried meat and dried back fat, *oo-suc*. Most generally, the liver of a large animal, such as an elk, a moose, or a buffalo, was cooked right in the hot coals of an open fire. While cooking, the top part of the liver hardens into a crust and burns almost total black, but the inside of it is cooked nice, juicy and soft. This liver keeps for several days without spoiling. With it, there's always the juicy back fat of the buffalo that goes very good with that liver or any lean meat. A few bites of the roasted liver, will last for many hours without one getting hungry. Try it, the way it should be cooked sometimes.

The man woke up just as the eastern sky was graying. He took a couple of bites from his lunch of liver and away he went, all the time expecting to scare up some kind of meat animal.

All that day he walked again, not seeing anything to shoot at for food. Night found him farther away from camp. He ate on the liver again then went to sleep and rest for the night.

The sky was graying in the east again when he got up and got underway. This time, just as it got light enough and just head of him in the brush, several head of elk were grazing. Already going along as stealthy as a cat, the man sneaking so close to the elk herd, it wasn't any problem to kill a few of them.

In those early days, a hunter could sneak almost alongside of the game he was hunting for. A good hunter is just as quiet as a mouse or a cat. In them days, game weren't scared off by gunfire, the bow and arrows didn't make noise. The hunter could kill several in a herd of any game before the kill is noticed by the rest of the herd.

A hunter is a fast butcher, too. He can skin out several carcasses in just a few minutes, and only with a flint knife. It took no time for the man to dress out his kill. One of the elk, a whole one, he cut up. That one he will take home on his shoulders, the rest of the meat hung on trees for safety.

Them Natives were very strong and tough, they could carry a whole dressed-out elk, almost a whole moose, or almost a whole buffalo on their backs for many miles, to their camps.

It was still early as the man got underway for his camp. He had to go slow with the pack on his back, a whole elk.

On and on he went, cutting the distance to his camp. It was well in the afternoon when he came to the last little hill before he could reach his camp. He was anxious to get over this little hill to get a glimpse of his camp. Slowly coming over this little rise and seeing ahead to his camp. The doorway was open, but there wasn't any smoke coming from the fireplace.

He hurried his footsteps with the heavy load on his back. He wanted to find out what could be wrong, why no smoke was coming from their fireplace.

He just knew there was something very wrong at his camp. He hurried on to the camp. All his dogs were very glad to see him, they came back to meet him as he approached the camp. But no wife to come running out to meet him this time. Getting to the doorway he dropped his load of meat on the ground and rushed inside. Right away he seen his wife laying there with her belly wide open, cut open by someone. He was just too stunned to cry or to do anything right at that moment. Sitting quietly by the body of his wife, his head hanging low from the awful feeling of losing his wife, everything so still, when he heard the cry of a newborn baby. The cry came from back of the tipi wall liner, from the south side of the tipi. Forgetting for an instant about his hard luck, the man jumped to the sound. Reaching back of the wall liner he felt the body of a tiny being. He pulled the baby out from the back of tipi wall liner, it was a little boy. He immediately wrapped it up in one of the robes and held him in his arms.

The man no sooner sat back down when he heard another cry. This time the cry came from near the fireplace. Dropping the first baby down, he jumped to the other sound of a baby. This baby was covered with the soft ashes of the fireplace.

He took the little baby from the ashes. It was another boy, it was a set of twin boys for him. At least his wife left him with couple of lovely boys that he must think very much of because of his wife.

He didn't have much time for bereavement, his hands were full now with his twin boys. He must take good care of them, he was alone with them.

This is what happened during the man's hunt:

The man had been away from his camp for one day. As his woman sat alone in her tipi, from somewhere far, far away, she heard a cry. It was a strange sort of cry, it sounded like someone talking and hollering at the same time. She couldn't make out what the words were, but the sound was coming closer to their tipi.

The woman jumped up as fast as she could, sliding the heavy, stiff rawhide into place, closing the doorway to the tipi and tying it fast with buckskin thongs from the inside, then covering up with a robe so whomever it may be couldn't hear her breath. The thing might go away if it knows no one is there.

Whatever the thing was, it was coming closer to the camp. She heard the words clearly now, the thing was saying, "*Nuh-tsi-skay, nuh-tsi-skay, ni-stu-wok-oke, Oo-chi-scub-pah-pah.* Which way, which way, I am Dragging Entrails Full of Dirt."

Whatever was talking kept on coming towards the tipi, it was getting closer and closer. Whatever it was, the thing was coming very slow. The thing took time to get close to the camp. He was now just back of the tipi among the trees, but steadily coming towards the tipi.

Over and over he repeated the cry and words, coming closer and closer to the tipi. The woman just huddled up in the thick robes, hardly daring to breathe for fear the thing might hear her. Still as a mouse she lay under those robes.

The cry was coming near the doorway, soon it sounded past the doorway. The thing was talking and hollering as it walked along. It was going around the tipi, repeating his cry and talking. Around and around the tipi the thing went.

After a while, the thing changed the words. It was now saying, *"Nuh-tsi-skay, nuh-tsi-skay, tsah ki-tsi-ma, tsah ki-tsi-ma.* Which way, which way, where's the door, where's the door?"

The woman laid there as still as could be and the thing kept on with his hollering and talking, over and over, around the tipi he went. It must've been late in the afternoon and there was no let-up from that thing.

The woman had a soft place in her heart, and at the same time she was getting mighty tired of the noise the thing was making, that hollering and that talking. The woman began to pity the thing, he must be getting tired with all that hollering and talking.

"I should let the poor man in," she thought. The thing had a masculine voice, she knew the thing was some sort of a man. "He must be very hungry, he's been going around this tipi for a long time. He just might go away if I feed him, maybe that's all it wants is something to eat. I pity the poor fellow."

The woman, hoping her husband would come back from the hunt, had boiled his favorite part of the meat just in case he comes home hungry, which he usually was.

"I'll just let him in. My husband wouldn't know about it, the poor man will be gone after he eats a good meal. I'll feed him the meat and food I cooked for my husband."

She got up from under all of those robes she covered herself up with. She was still very quiet yet as she went to the door of the tipi. She untied the rawhide thongs that held the rawhide in place. About that time the hollering man was nearing the back of the tipi once more. She slid the rawhide doorpiece out of the way and waited for the man to come again to the entrance of the tipi.

Whatever kind of a man it was, it sure took long to make one round. Around the tipi each time, it took several moments for the hollering man to come back around to the doorway. She was still there waiting for the man.

This strange man appeared, coming around the tipi. As the woman laid her eyes on him, she almost fell backwards.

It was something she had never hoped to see in her life. She didn't know if she should get sick from him, to vomit, throw up, or just plain faint from the sight of him.

It was a half man. Just half of its body was there, he didn't have any legs. It was walking on its bottom rib cage with the help from his long and strong arms. They were well-developed arms. With these arms and the hands the man swung himself along, using the bottom ribs to stand on.

He was dragging along part of his insides or entrails, and they were full of dirt. Some of his lungs were showing too, partly on the ground all dirty.

The woman didn't know what to make of him, she didn't know how anyone could live in his condition. But he was alive and getting along, it seemed.

As the strange man came to the doorway, the woman had it open now. She was so taken aback and hadn't recovered from the shock, she didn't shut the doorway. It was too late now, he had come to the doorway already and she still held it open, her eyes still bugged out and mouth wide open, looking down at the half-bodied man.

The woman didn't have to say anything, this strange man came right in to the tipi as he got to the doorway and made himself right at home. He went to the very opposite side of the doorway and sat where the chief of the tipi usually sits, the man of the tipi.

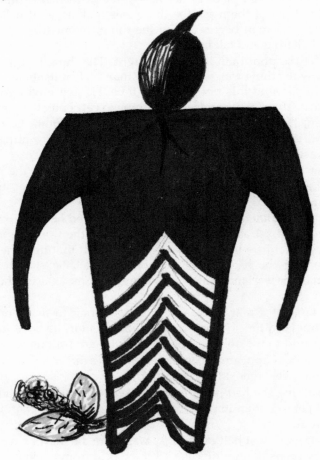

*Oo-chi-scub-pah-pah, Dragging Entrails Full of Dirt*

As the strange man made himself comfortable on the couple's bed, he asked the woman for a drink of water. She was already so very nervous from the first sight of him, she was still very jumpy over him. Keeping her eyes on him she handed him a wooden bowl full of water, which he drank. As he drank it, just in a few seconds, the water came through right onto the couple's bedding. The water seemed to wash away much of that dirt that stuck to his dragging guts, and now those insides looked just bloody after all the dirt washed away.

Never taking her eyes off of him, the woman was getting sick in her stomach now from the sight of those entrails. She jumped to the food and prepared a dish for this strange man, thinking he would leave as soon as he had something to eat. She set a willow mat before him and placed the wooden dish full of the delicious choicy meat and roots upon the mat before the strange man.

"*Suh-uh, ma-tsi-daa-su-da-pa, ah-nits-ka.*" "No! I don't use those for a plate," the strange man told the woman.

She took the plate of food back and put them on a clean buckskin and again set them before him to eat. He said the same thing to her, "No! I don't use those for a plate."

The woman tried something else for a plate, but it was the same answer. Something else she used, but the strange man always gave her the same answer, "I don't use those for a plate."

Thing after thing she tried for a plate, soon she just couldn't think of anything else to try to use as a plate for that strange man.

She had even tried to use the clothing she had on her, which wasn't very much, just her tanned-hide dress. The woman even tried her breechclout but it was still no. (Panties, bikinis, and bloomers were all unheard of in those days, just a narrow strip of buckskin was worn for a breechclout to cover the private parts of a woman.)

She tried her hair to feed him on, but it was that same no. As she sat there, she was trying to think of something else she might've forgotten to try to use as a plate for this man.

She thought and thought, she had tried everything she could think of. All of a sudden she sat up. "There is one more that I could try as a plate for this darn man," she thought.

She got up off of the floor and moved to the willow mat, she laid on her back on the willow mat and put the food on her big stomach. Her stomach was very big, she was very close to have her baby. She was completely naked as she laid down and put the food on her stomach.

This darn old Oo-chi-scub-pah-pah got very gleeful when the woman offered her body as a plate for him.

"*Ah-ah, ki-uhn-nits-kai, jit-aa-sui-ta.* Yes, yes, that's the kind I use for a plate." The dirty old man, Oo-chi-scub-pah-pah, was now a happy man as he took his big flint knife out of its sheath. With his other hand he got himself a tender-looking choicy meat, he bit the one end of the meat and with his other hand he cut it off close to his mouth and began chewing on it. This he done several times as he ate away on the delicious food.

He had just about eaten all of the food on his human plate. In fact, it was the last piece of meat that he had to cut into a bite size as the woman laid there very still, anxiously waiting for this darn man to get through with that darn food.

Up went the man's knife to his mouth to lop off the meat, down it came right on through the meat and on down to the woman's stomach. The knife cut into her stomach and across it.

She tried to jump up, but the darn old man, Oo-chi-scub-pah-pah, pushed her back on her back. She was already helpless because of her bigness of her stomach. As he pushed her back down, this caused a lot of pressure in her middle, and squeezed the baby out of its womb—not only one baby, but two!

From this, the woman lost her strength and into a coma she went, eventually dying from the loss of blood and laying there as the dirty old man left her on that willow mat at the head of the tipi.

Oo-chi-sub-pah-pah stuck one of the twins back of the tipi wall liner, and the other little baby boy he stuck under the ashes alongside the fireplace. Then on his way Dragging Entrails Full of Dirt, Oo-chi-scub-pah-pah, went slowly but surely.

That was the way the man found his camp from the return of his hunt. He had taken care of the twin boys as best he could, but they must have milk food soon in order to live and grow big.

As he recovered from all that surprise, the way he found his camp, the man took his twin sons in his arms and went down to the creek. Going upstream he went to a beaver dam that he knew was there all this time, he knew right where the beaver hut was near the bank. To this he took his twin boys. Coming to the hut of the beavers he found the entrance to it. One at a time he stuck the twin boys of his into the beaver hut, and as he stuck each one in, he prayed to the beavers to raise his twin sons for him.

Both of the twins were inside of the beaver hut in the creek. Standing up, the man prayed very hard to his Creator and the beavers to care for the twin sons of his until they are old enough to take care of themselves, then he would take over on them.

Coming back to the tipi and fully recovered from all of the shock he just went through, he picked up his bow and arrows and went out looking on the ground for Oo-chi-scub-pah-pah's trail. This strange man left a trail that was easy to find and follow, because of his dragging entrails.

The man was very mad when he set out to find this thing who done him so much heartache. He followed the tracks of Oo-chi-scub-pah-pah. Dragging Entrails had gone quite far already, it took the man a long time to overtake this strange man.

He was just coming over this little rise and through the timber, but straight ahead of him, in a small opening among the trees, he seen the man thing moving along very slow. The man quickened his walk almost to a run to overtake this man.

Coming around a bend in the thickets and walking fast, he almost fell backwards when he came upon the man that left those tracks. The strangest man he had ever seen. This thing didn't have legs to walk on, his guts were on the ground in the dirt dragging behind him, he was walking on his ribs with the help of his strong, brawny arms. His arms swung out ahead of him, then he swung forward on them, while his insides were dragging along. This thing was a pitiful-looking sight. Even to the man, as mad as he was, seeing him was different, he was a pitiful being. He meant to kill him on sight when he caught up with him. But after seeing this strange man it was a different story, his compassion for him overcame him.

But he was still mad at him for killing his wife, he must punish him. Catching up with him, the man didn't speak to the half-man, Oo-chi-scub-pah-pah. The anger coming back on him, he grabbed the strange man. Carrying him to a fairly good size stump of a tree, he lifted him high in the air and brought him down over the tree stump, his rib cage sliding down over it.

Walking away from him, leaving him on the tree stump, the man turned his head back towards him, saying, "From now on you can look like this to people."

He wiggled to free himself from the tree stump, back and forth, to and fro. But his rib cage was down over the tree stump, trapping the body there. The remains of Oo-chi-scub-pah-pah slowly rotted back into dirt.

Today, people wherever you may go, there are always posts or other things that resemble a tree stump along roadways, trails, mostly anywhere you travel. Look at them some distance ahead of you, maybe half a mile or so. I bet you can swear that it moved. That was what the man made of Dragging Entrails Full of Dirt or, as the Natives call him, Oo-chi-scub-pah-pah.

The man slowly made his way back to their camp, no happy feelings in him. The wife was dead, and all because of this half-made man, Oo-chi-scub-pah-pah.

He had taken care of his twin sons, they were safely with those beavers nearby their camp.

Coming back to their tipi, the man went on inside and stood for a long time looking at the remains of his dear wife, softly crying, tears running down his cheeks. After a long moment of this, he finally got ahold of himself and took a good big buffalo robe, covering his wife's remains very carefully, right where he found her. He made sure the robe was tucked in all around her body. He then went back out of that tipi, sliding the stiff rawhide across the doorway and weighing the tipi down with heavy stones all around so nothing could enter it.

A ways from this tipi, the man made himself a temporary place to live, a small arbor. There he slept and ate.

He didn't stay home very much anymore. He was out trapping as the winter set in, hunting occasionally for fresh meat. They had stored much dried food for their winter use, so there was plenty food for him. But just to be doing something to keep his lonely mind occupied, he occasionally went hunting for fresh meat.

That first year alone was quite an experience for the man. He was all alone in the arbor, while in their tipi laid his dead wife. He didn't look in on her body at all, he just made sure nothing went inside of that tipi. It was too much for him to look in on a place that once was a happy tipi for them all. He would only go to pieces if he seen the body of his wife so soon again.

Time seemed so short, but already four years had gone by since that old half man Oo-chi-scub-pah-pah, Dragging Entrails Full of Dirt, had paid that tragic visit to this camp. It was a lonely camp now, even after four years. The man was all alone, hanging on, just over his twin sons that the beavers were raising for him.

Most of the time the man was out hunting, staying away from his camp as much as he could, but there was always that feeling a part of him was there at that camp. His wife's body laid there and those twin boys were there too, with the beavers of the small creek. So no matter how long he was gone he would always return to that once happy camp.

One day, as he sat in front of his little arbor repairing arrows, he heard laughter and screaming down towards the small creek. Glancing down there, he seen these two little boys playing around, chasing one another through the bushes near their beaver hut home. Right away he knew it was his twin sons that were raised by the beaver family of the creek.

Just the glimpse of them made his heart race. He was already in love with them, they were what was left of his wife. He must speak to them soon. Leaving his work, the man went down where the boys were playing.

It was harder than it looked, for no sooner he got down there near them, they ran away. The twin boys soon sensed him close by. They were raised by animals, so they had animal instinct, a keen sense of hearing, smelling, and seeing. They took off for their beaver hut out in that small creek, and in they went. They were afraid to come back out, they didn't know their father.

The father tried again and he tried again, time after time and day after day. It was no use, he just couldn't coax them to him. They got very wild, even wilder then the beavers themselves.

The father tried many ways to catch them, but it was still no use. One day he tried so hard, he didn't know that one of his arrows dropped out of his quiver not too far from the beaver hut. Not knowing this, he went into the thickets to hide from the two sons of his so he could just look at them and admire his sons from a distance like he'd done so many times now since he seen them come from the creek and the beaver hut.

After a very long wait in those thickets, the two boys, thinking everything was clear, came out from that beaver hut out in the creek. First they looked out from the entrance, then their heads came out little at a time, further and further, and when they think the coast is clear, then they came all the way out. They don't just rush out into the thickets, but go just so far and stop, look, listen. After they made double sure that no one's around, then a little at a time they went out into the woods and not too far from the creek. Just a little noise made them streak back to the hut.

It was a long wait. The boys began to come out again from that beaver hut, a little at a time. Finally they came across into the thickets, but only a few steps at a time, until they knew for sure no one was around to try and catch them.

As they came out into the brush further, one of them found the arrow that dropped from his father's quiver and he made a jump for it. When the other twin seen it too, he made a grab for his twin brother and caught him just as he jumped, and pulled him back. He spoke to him. Whatever he said, the father didn't hear, he was out of hearing range.

The twin boys stood there for a long time, undecided about the arrow. They both wanted it, it was something they didn't know anything about. They hadn't ever seen an arrow, they were only about four years old now and were raised by the beaver family, but they were very curious. They wanted it, but were afraid to pick it up now—it was their animal instinct.

For the longest time they went around the arrow. They would go near it, then jump back from it, around and around it until they were very, very sure it wouldn't do anything to them. One of them finally got the courage to pick it up. After he touched it, the other twin boy jumped to his brother and wrassled his brother for that arrow. They almost forgot about being afraid, they were so busy trying to take the arrow from one another.

The man was watching all this time and seen what the twin boys of his were doing. He knew they were very interested in the arrow, which made him think of a good plan to catch his sons.

He sat in those bushes for the longest time watching his twin sons playing around, his heart aching for the touch of those twin boys.

It was getting quite late when he finally went to his arbor home near their original tipi. He made himself something to eat and went to bed for the night.

Just at the graying of dawn, the get up time for all of those long gone Natives of the past, the man got up and ate his breakfast. He went to the wild cherry bushes that grew along the small creek, he got himself many straight, wild chokecherry shoots, took these to his arbor home, cleaned them, peeled the bark off of them, straightened them, then hung them to dry. It takes a few days to dry and cure the chokecherry bushes before they can be made into arrows.

A few days gone by. The man didn't go to the creek to watch his twin sons playing, he was just busy with the arrows. About three days he took to make the arrows, until they were well cured and dry.

The next morning, just as gray of dawn, he stole down to the creek while everything was still asleep. Finding the twin boys' favorite beaver slide, where they got up on the bank or back into the creek, the man stuck an arrow very near the bank, then another one just a short ways from the first one, then another one, then another one, not too close to one another and leading straight out from the creek into the thickest part of the bushes. He had made many of them, so they went a long ways out into the thickets.

When all of the arrows were stuck into the ground, the man went into a good hiding place where he could see all of the arrows and be close to them and the bank of the river. His plan was to intercept the boys before they made it to the bank.

From graying of dawn he waited for the twin boys to come out. At last, about midday, they came peeking out from the beaver hut. Further and further they came out. Then, making sure no one was around, across to the bank they went.

Again they hesitated for the longest time, making sure no one was around to interfere with their play.

One of the twins went out a ways from the bank. He spotted the arrow sticking out of the ground and made a dash for it. The other one seen it at the same time, He tried to beat his brother to it, but then he seen another arrow just a ways from the first one, so he made a dash for that one.

From these arrows, they seen the long line of them in the ground. Running along, trying to beat one another to the line of arrows, they were making it to every other one. About four or five arrows were picked by the boys, when all of a sudden they stopped, they listened, they looked all around them to see if anyone was around. Satisfying their senses, they went on to try to beat one another to as many arrows as they could get their hands on.

Every once in a while they stopped to check the area for others to be present, always ready to run for their beaver hut for safety.

On and on they raced to the arrows. They were quite a ways from the creek now when the man jumped up and ran in between them and the creek. They didn't realize they were cut off from their sanctuary. It was too late when they seen this man in between them and their beaver hut home, which was safety for them.

The first one came charging to get past his father, but this time the man was ready for them. He quickly caught the first boy, then the other twin came running to get past the man—their father, and they didn't know it. He caught him also, there they were, the twin boys in their father's hands, both jumping around to free themselves. It was no use, he was much stronger than them.

As he held them, he was talking to them, telling them he was their father. They weren't talking, but they seemed to understand him a little—after all, they were raised by the wild beaver family. He kept on talking to them, trying to quiet them down some.

After a long wrestling match with them, the twins finally begin to tire out, they weren't jumping around too much anymore now.

The man kept on talking to them, soothing them with kind, low words of love. They finally realized they weren't going to get away from this man. They went limp, and as they did, the man told them, "Taste my arms, I am your father."

At first the twin boys didn't want to taste the flesh of their father, he had to force them to do this. As they licked their father's arm, that same animal instinct they were raised with soon let the two boys know that this was their true father.

That fear of their father immediately left their minds and they took to him like they had always been around him.

The man took the twins up to the camp. He brought them into the small arbor living place of his, and there they made themselves at home, just as if they always lived there.

For several days, for quite some time, the father was just so glad to have his twin sons with him that he couldn't leave them to go hunting, and they were a little too young to go with him. He was with them constantly since he took them back from those beavers. He loved them much, they were the only parts of their mother that was left of her.

The original tipi was still standing up through all the worse weather in those last four years, since the death of their mother that was killed by terrible old Oo-chi-scub-pah-pah, Dragging Entrails Full of Dirt.

The skeleton of the mother was laying just as this Oo-chi-scub-pah-pah left it. The man took care of the tipi around the outside and the body of his wife. Well, he knew it was covered up very good with the thickest of the robes, about three of them.

Everything came back to normal. The twin boys already got acquainted with their father's way of life and things got into a routine way.

The man's love for his twins got greater as time went by. How he wished his wife was alive to share this love for these twin sons of theirs.

Occasionally, the man went hunting for food and left the little boys to take care of the camp. One day when the man came back to the camp with his kill, he seen his twin boys come out from the original tipi, where their mother's body, her remains, was laying. The man was just coming over the little rise before coming into camp. He seen the little boys close the doorway just as good as they found it.

The twin boys seen their father approaching the camp with much fresh meat, and ran back to meet him. Their curiosity was killing them. Soon as they got by the father, the question came out from both of them, "What is that in that other place near our camp?"

The man acted like he didn't hear them. He went on walking towards the camp, the twin boys alongside of him.

Coming to camp, the man dropped his fresh meat on the ground near the outside fireplace. He went on in to the arbor, the little ones followed.

He still didn't answer them yet, and they were just so curious to find out what was inside of the other place.

Coming back outside, the little twin boys still behind him, he sat down close to the outside fireplace, by the fresh meat he just brought home. He lit the fire and cut some of the fresh meat up into thin slices. He cooked the fresh meat on the open fire, which was the way our ancestors cooked their food, and a much healthier way too.

When the meat was cooked, he told the boys to sit good and eat their nice fresh meat. This the boys did, and it quieted them down.

As the boys started to eat their food, their father began to tell them what had happened to their mother. That thing covered up with the robes in the other place was what was left of their mother that the old wicked Oo-chi-scub-pah-pah done. How he killed their mother, and just before she died, the twin boys were born. He told them how he found them—one of them in the ashes near the fireplace, the other one behind the tipi wall liner.

Now it was time for them to receive a Native name. He told his twin sons, "I'm giving you boys these names, because of how your mother died when you were born, the two happenings at the same time."

He called the boy he found behind the tipi wall liner to him first, stood him in the front of him, his hands on the boy's shoulders. "You shall be known to us and to others that may come around us sometime in the future by the name of Oo-si-stucks-cah-staa-nah, Behind the Tipi Wall Liner Man."

The other twin stood in front of his dad, both hands on the boy's shoulders. The father pushed the boy away from him, just as he did with the first boy. "You'll be known by the name of Iss-sooks-kit-si-nah, Ashes Near the Fireplace Man."

It was a task for the man to teach the twin boys and at the same time provide food for them and make their home. He loved the boys and he loved life itself. He loved his wife, after four long years. The man spoke of his wife to his twin boys very much.

With this love for them and other things, the man never tired out, but always found time to do this and that, especially teaching his twin sons all of the Native crafts he knew and that were necessary to their living.

When the man was away from home, out trapping or hunting, the twins practiced making things of what was taught to them by their father, they were very bright, they understood whatever their father talked of or taught them.

One of their favorite pastimes was making bows and arrows, each one made was better than the last one. The more bows and arrows they made, the stronger and much better they were. Other things too. They would do it better next time, that was their motto.

The man and the boys had tanned many hides of the larger animals, they had many more than enough to make a new tipi. The boys were growing up and they must have a tipi to live in now, not this arbor home the man used as his home these last few years, since the tragic day Oo-chi-scub-pah-pah done his wicked deed.

Each time the man stayed around the camp, him and the twins were busy making a new tipi. It was several days when they finally finished the tipi. It didn't take them long to put it up, right near the original one, which was still up with everything intact, even the body, the skeleton of the twins' mother and still covered with those thick buffalo robes. The tipi was just the same as when the man came home that unforgettable day.

It was a few days after the new tipi was set up and moved into that the man decided on going after fresh meat. He got ready, told the boys he was going to hunt for fresh meat, they must watch the home and be good while he was away.

For the twin boys, it was getting routine with them to go into the original tipi and look at their mother's skeletal remains, they even uncovered the skeleton of their mother, looked at it longingly, wishing their mother was alive and living happily with them.

It was a lovely morning when their father left them to go hunting for fresh meat. Soon as he left, the boys got busy and made a rawhide pot. Then, taking their bows and arrows, they went to the original tipi. The boys made a fire in front of the original tipi where the remains of their mother was lying, and set up the rawhide pot. The twin boys brought a freshly tanned hide and laid it out near the fire they built. Going into the original tipi, the twins gathered all of the bones of their mother, which they pieced together on the freshly tanned hide they brought out from their new tipi. It was quite a job to find the right places for all of those pieces of bones.

At last the bones were all pieced together, hopefully all in the right place. More wood was thrown on the fire, four rocks were also put on the fire to heat. Waiting until all of the rocks were red hot, they poured water into the rawhide pot. Everything was all set.

The twin boys received a lot of power from their foster parents, the beavers that raised them, and now that power was being tested on a very important part of their future life. This test of power meant either a happy life for them, or a life they'd been living since they were born. This was an important meaning to the twin boys.

There were four rocks in the fire and they were just so red-hot, one could almost see through them. Behind the Tipi Wall Liner Man got the first rock with the forked stick. He put it into the rawhide pot, while Ashes Near the Fireplace Man got his bow and arrow ready.

The red-hot rock hit the water in the rawhide pot and, as it touched the water, the water immediately went into a boil. As it did, Ashes Near the Fireplace Man shot his bow and arrow straight up into the air. He watched the arrow, and as it started back down, about halfway down to the ground, he hollered loud and very excitedly, "*Nu-waug-aug, nu-waug-aug, na-ah, goo-ca, awk-saug-su-yi!* Excuse me, excuse me, mother, your pot is going to boil over!"

The arrow hit the ground, nothing happened. Now it was Ashes Near the Fireplace Man that got the next red-hot rock, which he put into the rawhide pot. It was Behind the Tipi Wall Liner Man's turn to shoot an arrow up into the air just as the water boiled in the rawhide pot.

The arrow was coming back to the ground, about halfway back down. Hollering excitedly, Ashes Near the Fireplace Man said the same thing, "*Nu-waug-aug, nu-waug-aug, na-ah, goo-ca, awk-saug-su-yi!* Excuse me, excuse me, mother, your pot is going to boil over!"

This time the twins thought they seen one of her feet twitch a little, they weren't quite sure.

The twins stood around for a moment, praying as they were taught by their foster parents, the beaver family.

It was time to try again. Behind the Tipi Wall Liner Man got the next red-hot rock from the fire, while Ashes Near the Fireplace Man got his bow and arrow ready again. The rock hit the water again and immediately boiled. At the same time Ashes Near the Fireplace Man hollered loud and as excitedly as he could, "*Nu-waug-aug, nu-waug-aug, na-ah, goo-ca, awk-saug-su-yi!* Excuse me, excuse me, mother, your pot is going to boil over!"

Just as the arrow hit the ground the mother's both legs bent at the knees. They straightened back out again after the arrow was in the ground.

The twins said to one another, "Let's cover our mother's skeleton with one of the big robes, because this is the last chance to bring her back to life and we must use all of our power to do it if we can."

A big buffalo robe was used to cover the skeleton of the mother. Now it was Ashes Near the Fireplace Man's turn to get a red-hot rock to put into the rawhide pot, while Behind the Tipi Wall Liner Man got ready with the bow and arrow.

Ashes Near the Fireplace Man got a good hold of the last rock of the four they had put into the fire to heat, and it was the last hope of their future life. It must work! They must have that power to bring their mother back to life.

Ashes Near the Fireplace Man brought the red-hot rock to the rawhide pot. Into the pot went the red-hot rock. As the red-hot rock hit the water, the water immediately boiled and Behind the Tipi Wall Liner Man shot his bow and arrow straight up into the air with all of his might. The arrow went far up into air then almost straight back down it came. About one-third of the way back down Ashes Near the Fireplace Man hollered, "*Nu-waug-aug, nu-waug-aug, na-ah, iss-som-iss, goo-ca, ugh-ass-saug-soo-yi!* Excuse me, excuse me, mother, look at your pot, it has boiled over!" He hollered this out so excitedly he could've scared any spirit back to life.

At the same time the arrow was on its way down, Behind the Tipi Wall Liner Man was hollering just as excited as his brother, both of them at the same time, only Behind the Tipi Wall Liner Man was hollering something else. He was hollering, "*Nu-waug, nu-waug, na-ah, ah-ni-stub-ist-stob-iks-it, ka-coo-stis-si-toke-oo-wa, ohnii, obb-si-yi!* Excuse, excuse mother, duck out of the way, it might hit you, that arrow!"

While both hollering, their eyes were on the covered skeleton of their mother. Just before the end of their holler, from under that big buffalo robe their mother kicked it out of the way as she jumped up and right to her pot. She grabbed a stick and began stirring it, she was whole again and alive.

After four long years dead and even becoming a skeleton, the twin boys had brought their mother back to life. The only trouble was putting the skeleton back in place, to fit all of the bones in the right place. The twins placed the shin bones on the wrong leg, the left on the right, the right on the left. In today's time, we see that wrong fitting at times on some people, they seem to walk with criss-cross legs.

The boys were silent as their mother jumped from one chore to another.

They were just watching her, she acted like she had never left this place at any time, in fact she didn't know she was dead for four years.

Doing everything that was to be done at that moment, she had time to talk with the twins, saying, "I must have fallen asleep for a long time. I wasn't aware of you boys growing, you have both grown so big, it's like I was gone for awhile, that old Oo-chi-scub-pah-pah must've used something on me to forget the time, he must've been wicked."

The boys didn't say anything, they only listened to her. They talked of other things, like the fresh meat that had to be taken care of. The mother soon took care of that too. Then she began to cook, saying her husband might be coming home soon from his hunt, the boy's dad.

It may have been an omen, because the man soon came over that little rise just before the camp. The load on his back was big, lots of meat that he was bringing home for the boys.

Looking ahead towards his camp, he seen the boys busy around there, but there was someone else too. "Maybe a visitor," the man thought, "but then no one knows our whereabouts. It might be a stranger that got lost hunting or wanting something to eat." The man quickened his pace, wanting to find out who this other person would be.

Coming closer to the camp and still his eyes on the three people, two of them he knew was his own sons, the twins, but the third person was dressed like a woman. Now he was more curious then ever and wondering who this woman might be.

Not letting the mother know or hear him, one of the twin boys went running back to his dad. Soon as he caught his wind upon reaching his dad, the boy told his father everything about what had happened since he left for his hunt a few days ago. "I must tell you all of this so you will not be too surprised or say something out of the way. And be sure you don't act like you haven't seen her for four long years, act like she has always been home."

It was a very hard thing to do, to act natural when you haven't seen or been near someone that you have missed for four long years, and especially when they weren't supposed to come back to life from death.

It was all he could bear to stay away from her, his dead wife who was now resurrected by the twins' power from the beaver family, but he had to act natural until he was made whole after taking four separate sweat baths. These he knew would be ready—those twin sons of theirs were very bright for their age, they knew just what to do.

Dropping the meat in front of her, he told her, "I must go get a sweat bath as I'm very sore from that load of meat I just brought in, and from walking up and down the hills these last few days."

Down to the little creek he and twin boys went, right among the thick brush into a little opening. Four neat sweat huts were already to go into. In our Native religion, given to us by our Maker, Creator Sun, four is always a charm. The rocks were nice and hot at the first one, because the boys seen to it that it was ready for their father.

The twins took turns to sweat with their father and anoint him in the special way that they both received from the beaver family. First it was Behind the Tipi Wall Liner Man's turn, then it was Ashes Near the Fireplace Man's turn to go into the first sweat hut with their dad. If timed right it would take about one hour to get through in there, about fifteen minutes apart of letting the air in by throwing the doorway open. The fourth time it was opened, out they would come and go on into the second one of the sweat huts. This was repeated until all four sweat huts were used, a good five hours from the beginning.

Now they could go to the tipi, the man was all cleansed and this time ready to touch his wife. But he must still act natural, and that went for always, until either one of them passed on to Happy Hunting Grounds. That was a restriction that he must follow if he wanted to keep his wife.

The man was just so very happy to see his wife again, but he must act natural to her, as they didn't want her to find out that she had died by the hands of Dragging Entrails Full of Dirt, had been brought back to life after four years of death. The three wanted her to be happy and not know what grief she had caused them all.

The man acted as natural as he could. Coming into the tipi, he asked his wife if the meal was ready. He was very hungry, he had not eaten much since he left on this last hunt. It was true, the man hadn't eaten much since the death of his wife, he was very gaunt. Just seeing his wife made him so very hungry all of a sudden.

He sat down at his usual place in the tipi, and the boys sat near their mother. The food was served and everybody sat quiet as they ate. It was nearly dark when finally the last food was downed. The man kept on asking for refills of his plate and his horn cup with broth of the fresh meat.

It was a fresh start for all of them, only the woman didn't know this. But she was very happy with her little family now.

Things went along very smoothly for a long time, their life was very happy with all of them together again. The twin boys got older and eventually they took turns going with their father on a hunt, while the other remained at the camp with the mother. They didn't want her out of their sight any more.

The boys grew old enough to know better. When the father was home the boys would go out alone and hunt around the nearby area.

One day the father heard them talking about going to a south creek which was quite someway from the camp. The father called them in, and as they sat down, he told them about a strange bird that lurked around in that area. They must be very careful of this bird. The bird had very pretty color feathers on it, no ordinary bird had those colors, it was very easy to distinguish this bird even the first time you see it. If bothered, very bad consequences would follow. "I am not going to stop you boys from this venture, just be careful and don't bother that particular bird if you see it."

The boys went out to the south creek to hunt around for small game, and came back home without incident. They had promised their dad that they would not bother anything to get them in trouble, so this first hunt to the south creek was all right.

A few days went by, and they were still taking turns going out with their father to hunt for fresh meat. One day nothing was taking place, so again the boys decided on going to that south creek again to hunt, and again their father told them to leave that particular bird alone, not to bother it. Again they promised not to, and they returned safely.

Each time there was an idle time, the boys would go hunting in that south area, and always their father would tell them not to bother the particular bird. It was the third time they had come to this area and each time the twins would see the very pretty bird fluttering around among the trees and brush and each time it would seem prettier to them. The looking and seeing got a little longer too. This time too the boys came home without incident.

It was time to go hunting for fresh meat now. The man and one twin went, the other stayed with his mother. It was several days before the two came back from the hunt, game was going farther away because of feed and them being around here all the time. They had lots of fresh meat, enough to last for several days, and this gave the twin boys more chance to themselves, to do what they wanted to do.

Again it was to that south area they wanted to go, and again the father told the twins not to bother that pretty bird, no matter how much it tempted them.

It was always Ashes Near the Fireplace Man that was a foolish boy. He wanted to try this and that, to do this and that, but Behind the Tipi Wall Liner Man always tried talking him out of mischief. He had more sense.

The twin boys got to the south area and began hunting, in through the brush, this and that way, behind this bush and the other, and always quiet as a couple of mice. They knew their business about hunting, as young as they were. Their father taught them all of the hunting tricks and, to top this off, they used their own weapons, the bow and arrows they made with their hands, the flint knives they carried on their sides in a sheath.

They were stealing along, when right above them they heard a beautiful sound. Looking up into the tree, just above them sat that pretty bird, almost close enough to reach with the hand. He looked very tempting to catch or shoot at with an arrow, just like their father had said it would be.

Three times before the twin boys had encountered this pretty bird and they had come away from the bird without trying to do anything to it. They had stuck with their promise to their father. But this time it was like a magnetic force, they were being drawn to it, especially Ashes Near the Fireplace Man, who of the two was the crazy one, foolhardy. He was telling Behind the Tipi Wall Liner Man that he should jump up to it and catch the bird with his bare hands. It was all Behind the Tipi Wall Liner Man could do to keep him from jumping at the bird.

Ashes Near the Fireplace Man just couldn't let this swell opportunity to catch the bird or shoot an arrow at it go by, he was just itching to find out what would happen if he did bother the bird. He thought his father was just saying things to keep them from harming the bird. "I'm going to shoot it or catch this pretty bird. If I do that, I think Father will think I'm great for doing it. I know there is no harm in doing this, he just don't want us to get it first, he wants those pretty feathers on it for himself."

Behind the Tipi Wall Liner Man was arguing to keep his twin brother from doing this, he must keep in line of the promise they made to their father. Ashes Near the Fireplace Man kept at it to shoot at the pretty bird or try to catch it, they were still standing under the tree and the bird was still overhead, just barely out of reach. It wasn't making any attempt to fly away or move to another branch, it was just making very pretty sounds which made it that much harder for Ashes Near the Fireplace Man to keep away from it. He was begging his twin brother with all of his might to shoot at it just once or try and catch it just once, then he would never try again. Over and over again he begged his twin brother, but Behind the Tipi Wall Liner Man just wouldn't give in to his twin brother. Still he begged on and on.

The two had stood there a very long time arguing to shoot or not to shoot. The sun was getting low in the west when finally Behind the Tipi Wall Liner Man gave in to Ashes Near the Fireplace Man, to shoot just one arrow at the pretty bird, saying, "I don't think our father would find out about one arrow being shot at this pretty bird."

The bird was still overhead and just out of their reach. Ashes Near the Fireplace Man fitted an arrow to his bow. He took a careful aim at the bird, and let go of the arrow. It flew straight at the bird. The arrow just missed the head of this pretty bird and went just behind the bird in some tangled branches. The darn arrow for some strange reason stuck up there among those branches, it didn't come falling back down like they had expected it to.

Behind the Tipi Wall Liner Man told his brother Ashes Near the Fireplace Man that they had many arrows, to leave this one. They had better be starting home, it was getting dark, the sun was almost down.

Ashes Near the Fireplace Man said, "*Kik-ah, jik-sti-mits-keep, nu-psi-sis, nah-kip-oots-ip.* Wait, I don't want to leave my arrow, let me get it."

Behind the Tipi Wall Liner Man was arguing with his twin brother to just leave this one arrow and they better start home or they might get lost in the dark. Ashes Near the Fireplace Man was foolhardy and stubborn, he wanted it his way, he had to get that lone arrow before they went home. Behind the Tipi Wall Liner Man finally gave in. He told Ashes Near the Fireplace Man to get up into that tree and hurry up, get the arrow, so we can start home.

Ashes Near the Fireplace Man was kind of smiling as he got next to the tree, putting his leg up into a branch to begin the climb. He said to his twin brother, "I will only take a moment to get it, then we are on our way home." He lifted himself up towards the arrow. The pretty bird hopped up to another branch just above the arrow. Just before Ashes Near the Fireplace Man could put his outreaching hand on the arrow, for some mysterious reason, from the slight touch of his hand, the arrow slipped upward into the next branch where it got caught again. It was still just out of Ashes Near the Fireplace Man's reach.

"*Kik-ah nah-bi, daa-saun-ooch-eep.* Wait pardner, I just barely miss it."

Behind the Tipi Wall Liner Man started to beg his brother to give up on the arrow. They had a lot more than the one. "It's getting dark fast we must get home soon."

Ashes Near the Fireplace Man just wouldn't give up. He had to get the arrow before he went home. So onward he climbed after the arrow, almost getting ahold of it. But then the pretty bird would get above the arrow, which seemed to draw the arrow ever upward and just barely out of Ashes Near the Fireplace Man's reach. Each time he missed, he would holler down at his brother, "*Kik-ah nah-bi, dot-dah-mauk-iss-si-note-seep.* Wait pardner, I'm almost catching it."

Behind the Tipi Wall Liner Man kept on begging his twin brother to come back down. It was dark already, they must get home. But Ashes Near the Fireplace Man was set on getting his arrow back. Up, up he went, his voice was getting fainter to Behind the Tipi Wall Liner Man's ears. He couldn't see him anymore, it was dark, but he could still hear his voice, but ever fainter each time until he could hear it no more.

It was dark. Behind the Tipi Wall Liner Man laid down at the foot of the tree, crying for his brother, Ashes Near the Fireplace Man, to come back to him. He didn't hear him anymore and it was dark. He just laid there crying and crying for him.

Morning came. Looking up into that tree, Behind the Tipi Wall Liner Man seen nothing but the blue sky above the tree, no brother Ashes Near the Fireplace Man. That beautiful pretty bird had taken him away for trying to hurt it.

Behind the Tipi Wall Liner Man was too grief-stricken to move from under that tree, he just laid there crying and crying for his brother. For many, many days after he cried, not eating anything, just laying under that tree crying until he had shrunk from his cries, he had cried himself back into an infant, still he laid there crying.

Their father and mother were never heard from again. I don't know whether they had come looking for them or not, or just given the twin boys up. Probably they were eaten by wild animals. Anyway, there was no contact between them and Behind the Tipi Wall Liner Man, the survivor of the two.

# *Awk-waa-suh-wah, Bellyfat*

Behind the Tipi Wall Liner Man was still crying for his twin brother. It had been many, many days since that happened and he had shrunk back into an infant, he even lost his speech. He became almost completely helpless again, just like a newborn baby. He was laying in his own stool there under the tree, still crying for Ashes Near the Fireplace Man.

It happened that not too far away a group of people, probably from his own tribe of people, had just moved into the area not far from where Behind the Tipi Wall Liner Man was laying under the tree and still a-crying.

An old widow and her little granddaughter got their tipi up and all straightened out, ready to move into. There wasn't any wood to burn, to cook with, so she told her little granddaughter, *"Oo-ki un-coon-ohp-oo-doo-dah-cope.* Come on, let's get firewood."

This old lady had four daughters. Three of them were too lazy and acted too dainty to do any strenuous work or a job that might be on the dirty side, but this one, the youngest, would do anything for her. In fact, she didn't have to do anything while she was around, so the little granddaughter just stayed with her all the time. (In the Native way—and it is still that way among our people—your own children and those you might have raised, or your grandchildren, aren't thought of as different from your own family. All of the children, even those, the older and a little younger than owners of the home, were called as their own children. The older Natives of these days are that way—men staying with them even at the age of forty, older too, we still call them as our own.)

The two left the camp and went into the woods to gather firewood. They piled wood here and over there. The little girl was full of life, she ran ahead looking for a pile of dry wood. Coming to a place far into the woods, still gathering dry wood for their fireplace, the little girl was way ahead of her grandma. She stopped among a pile of dry wood and stooped over to pick some up and to pile for her grandma. She was quiet as she done this. Just to the southwest of her and not too far, she thought she heard a faint cry. She straightened out, standing upright now, listening for that sound. Sure

*Finding Bellyfat*

enough, there it was again, she could just barely hear it. She made her way towards it, walking very slow so she could hear again that noise or cry. There! Just off to her left was where that cry came from. She slowly went in that direction. There was a big tree and lot of high grass around it. In the high grass was a baby crying. But oh my, it was filthy!

The little girl hollered at her grandma to come in a hurry and see what she had found.

Slowly making her way towards her granddaughter, the old woman came to the big tree. As she got there, the little girl pointed down to where the baby was laying, the baby was still a-crying, although it couldn't be heard too much—his vocal cord was giving out because of the long cry, since his twin brother disappeared up in that tree a very long time ago, many, many days ago.

The grandmother said, "According to his own filth he was laying in and the lay of the area he was laying in, I'd say this baby was here for a long time, this baby is left here, abandoned by its folks, we will take it to our tipi and take care of it."

The little girl didn't know anything about acting too good for anything, she had never hesitated to handle all, no matter how dirty it may seem. She jumped to the little baby as soon as her grandma said they would take the baby home with them, saying, "*Soo-gop-pi nis-stu-wah dok-aa-sin-oss-sah-dow.* Good, me I'll take care of him."

The little girl picked the baby up from all of that filth and took him to some nice fresh green grass and some cool spring water, where she gave him a good bath and cleaning. The baby was still crying as they went on their way home. The old woman carried a big bundle of wood home on her back for their fireplace.

Right away, as soon as they came into the tipi, the old woman made a fire, threw the rocks in to heat up, and got her rawhide pot ready. She cut some nice fatty meat up and put it in the rawhide pot. The little girl was all ready coming back from a nearby spring with a bladder full of good, cool spring water. Coming into the tipi, she poured some in the rawhide pot. Now they only would have to wait for the rocks to get red-hot.

The rocks didn't take so long to get red-hot. Immediately the old woman took her forked stick she always used for her cooking, got hold of one of the red-hot rocks, and into the pot the rock went, making the water come to an immediate boil. This was almost an instant food of that time—soon as the hot rock touches the water, it comes to an immediate boil. About four or five rocks, one at a time, would cook the food tender.

It was just a little while before they had the food cooked and a nice broth from the fatty meat was ready. Right away the little girl fed the newcomer, the baby they found away out in the woods.

After having something in its stomach, the baby quit crying. The little girl was busy with the new addition, playing with it and cleaning him every so often. From crying so long, this baby must have cried his bowels very loose too, for every little while he would let go with his insides and mess himself, every few moments he dirtied. The little girl didn't mind it, she just cleaned him each time he messed.

After the excitement for the two, bringing the baby home with them, the two settled down with their newcomer by them. But oh my, how he stooled, and so often!

The little girl had so much to do, so the old woman went to her oldest daughter and asked her if she wouldn't take care of a newcomer to the family, a little baby they had found while getting firewood.

"A new boy baby, he must be cute," said the oldest daughter. "I'll take care of him for you until he is old enough to watch for himself."

The baby was brought to her. The little girl brought him to the oldest daughter's tipi. After giving him to her, the little girl went on back to her grandma's tipi. She hadn't come back very long when they heard the oldest daughter. She sounded like she was going to vomit, she got sick to her stomach about the third time the baby ran out on the bowels, and it was just one right after the other. Running to her mother's tipi gagging, holding her mouth, she told the mother, "Take that dirty nasty baby back, he is just too nasty for me, he runs out just too fast for me. I can't stand him dirtying so often." She ran back to her tipi.

The youngest girl being there always near her grandmother, always ready to give her a helping hand, ran out after the oldest girl, followed her to her tipi and brought the new baby boy back to their tipi. She really pitied the poor little boy they had found in the woods, she didn't want harm to come to this baby boy.

Back in their own tipi again, the youngest girl took care of the dirtied baby boy. She loved the little nasty boy and showed it.

Her grandma, realizing all of the work her youngest daughter tried to do all the time, told her, "Take the baby to your other aunt, to your other sister, and tell her to take care of him until we catch up with our own work."

The baby boy was as clean as can be again, and the little girl took him to the other aunt or sister's tipi. Coming in there, she repeated what the mother said. This one too readily took the baby boy.

It wasn't too long after the baby was brought to her that she too came running over with the baby boy in her arms very close to vomiting, gagging as she came running and holdering her head away from the little boy. She put the baby just in the doorway, turned around, and started to run back to her tipi, as she turned, she said, "The baby is just too dirty for me, he poops too much. You folks take care of him."

The mother told the little girl, "Clean him up again and take him to the last of the girls, maybe she will take care of him for us for a while."

The little girl done what she was told to do, only to find out that this daughter was also too good for the new baby boy they found in the woods. The two of them must look after the baby boy themselves, they must take turns watching him and that they did, the youngest girl taking most of the responsibility on her.

This little girl of the old lady never complained, she done her work for their home and took care of the new baby boy too. She had much compassion for others.

The people moved from place to place, always in seek of fresh meat and other food. The baby boy was growing bigger and bigger again. Late that fall, the little baby boy was almost back to original size, the size he was when his twin brother mysteriously disappeared in that tree, following an arrow and a very pretty bird.

He never spoke of the other twin nor any of his past, he either forgot all about it when he shrank back into a little baby, or something put a spell on him, probably the pretty bird they were after. Not even his parents were in his mind. No one knew of him of this group, so he was just a mysterious newcomer to this camp and that's the way he remained to them all.

Winter was now approaching. They had got all the meat for their winter's need, and they must move to their wintering area.

One morning a camp crier went around crying out the message from their chief, "No one leaves the camp anymore today, everyone must get ready for moving. We are moving to the river bottom, our wintering campground, we shall leave here before the sun rises and try to go as far as we can go from here. We will move before the sun rises and try to go as far as we can go from here. We will move before the sun rises each morning until we have reached our destination, the river bottom, our winter camping ground."

Everyone gave their dogs a nice extra-big portion of food before going to bed, it was the dogs that carried on their backs or pulled in a travois most of the heavier bundles on every moving time. Every one, children, women, and the men, had a job to do when on the move. Still, the men have time to hunt a little, the women visit as they move along, the children running and playing on either side of the procession. This was their life, it was fun at times and heartbreaking at times. As the group moved along, it wasn't just a solemn procession. They had to have fun along with the move.

The Native American has always been on the bright side of life. They were highly emotional whenever there was something to get emotional about, but always and always they mixed seriousness with fun. They made light of things.

So even on these long moving times, there had to be pleasure along the way to keep worry away. They played games, the young and old alike, at the overnight rest stops.

One of the most popular games of the Plains Native was the rawhide wheel game. The wheel was made about six inches in diameter, wrapped with rawhide, and the rawhide was criss-crossed to a smaller circle in the center. This made it look like the horse-drawn wagon wheel with spokes.

One way to appoint someone to roll the rawhide wheel was to have all of the players shoot their arrows at some target. The one whose arrow went the farthest from the target was usually the first one to roll the wheel.

To play this rawhide wheel game, all of the players formed an aisle about ten feet wide. The roller of the wheel then took his position at one end of the aisle, approximately twenty feet from the players. The wheel in his hands, he rolls the wheel down the center of the aisle of the players. As the wheel rolled by each one, an arrow was shot from a bow aiming to shoot into the center ring of the wheel, which is probably about an inch and a half in diameter, or to shoot through one of the spokes, a good point for the player.

Another favorite game was spear throwing. A hoop about thirty inches in diameter was laid down. A player stepped fifty steps away from this hoop and marked the place with a stick or something. From this mark each player throwed a spear of his own, trying to stick the spear in that hoop. This is played until someone's spear actually sticks into the ground within the hoop and becomes a winner. Then a new mark is counted away from the first one, another twenty-five steps farther. Then, when there's another winner the throwing mark goes farther away from the hoop. This is played until the players are unable to reach the hoop. Most often the players wager a bet between them at each mark.

Another game is the larger hoop rolling. A plain hoop about two feet in diameter without any spokes on it was rolled. The players all stand in a neat line about twenty-five yards away from the path of the wheel or hoop their spears ready. The hoop is rolled along a certain path. The player must be fast. As the wheel or hoop comes by about twenty-five yards away, he must throw his spear and try to throw through the hoop. Whoever throws a spear through the hoop first is the winner, and must go back to the last place in line, while another takes the first place in line.

After dark, or later in the evening, a mystic game might be in progress. Today we know this game as the bone game or stick game. This is an ancient game and is still played in these days, but a little differently then those ancient Natives played it. It was called a mystic game because it was a serious game, and many valuables were wagered—valuable furs, or whatever their most prized possession might be.

It took many days to get to the destined place to winter, along the present-day Marias River or the great Missouri River. It always was some place in the southern part of our aboriginal territory, because it was a little milder than the northern part. There was more game for fresh meat there, more small creeks to catch the native trout.

When they reached their destination, everyone selected a good place among the cottonwood trees and quaking aspens to set their camp, a good shelter from the wind and storms. Blizzards were the worst to fear.

Once settled down to routine living everyone then gathers wood, it was mostly the women and children's work. All of the able-bodied men are still out hunting while the weather was still good. Whenever the men are available, they too help their womenfolk to gather more and more wood, great big piles of wood near each tipi.

Most of the longer wood that had been gathered were erected into a tipi-like structure so it wouldn't be buried in the deep snow, and also to keep the wet off of the wood. All tipis were made of tanned hide. They weren't made as big as the tipis of today, otherwise they would be too heavy to carry from one place to another as they moved about. They had to be light enough to carry on backs or be pulled by a dog travois.

The tipis were made warm inside, too. A wall liner was tied to each pole on the inside of the tipi and inside of the tipi poles, which left a space between the pole and wall liner. This space was like a draft to carry the smoke upwards to the smoke vent at the top of the tipi. As the tipi was pegged down, the women seen to it there was a slight opening in the bottom about two or three inches above the ground, between each peg. This was the ventilation for the air to come through to carry the smoke upwards. The tipi wall liner was weighed down with stones on the inside of the tipi to keep that incoming air around the bottom from coming into the living room of the tipi. This liner was also made of tanned hide. It reached almost halfway up the tipi walls. This made a double wall or insulation, and acted as an air vent, too.

As the meat was brought in by the hunters each day, it was smoke-dried fast and stored in the dried rawhide cases. A layer of dry meat was sprinkled with dried wild peppermint, then a layer of back fat, and that too was sprinkled with peppermint. Each layer was sprinkled with peppermint, then stored away. This wild peppermint was a preservative for the dried meat.

Roots were not forgotten, as they too were food for the Native. Much sarvis berries and wild chokecherries were already dried during the Berry-Ripening Moon.

Winter was now approaching fast. Soon there was clouds coming in from the north, geese were flying very high, seeming to go nonstop to the south. One old man looking at a flock of geese going south said, "Its going to be a mighty long cold winter this year, so everyone try to get more wood and tan more hides and go easy with your food. We will be needing it all before the winter is over with. The muskrat huts are out in the middle of lakes and rivers, the beaver cuttings are very deep in the water, and now those geese are flying so high and fast, it points to a very cold, long winter."

All of the Natives of this country are very active, always busy on something or other or playing games through the winter. Never was many obese Natives. An obese Native was either too darn lazy or sick—obesity among our Native people came with the coming of the white people, corralling us into the Reservations, where we couldn't do anything very much for a long time, and it still is about the same today.

The day came when the snow began to fly. It came from the north, the coldest of the four cardinal directions. Everyone settled down for the winter, everyone had stored enough food to last them until the warmer weather comes again.

The storm lasts for several days, then a break comes. It turns warm for a while, all of the summer leaves are on the ground over this first storm. Indian summer was now on, about a two- or three-week break to hunt again at their buffalo runs or their *pis-kuns*.

It was very nice for several days, but now storm clouds are again forming in the west. It will be the real beginning of winter, but no worry, everyone is well prepared for the long, cold winter.

The snow falls and it falls again and again, more snow on top of the other, around four or five feet of snow. The weather lets up for a spell, the sun comes out, but not for long. More storms. The wind begins to blow from the west only to switch to the north. It gets stronger and stronger until a blizzard is in progress. Everyone stays inside. Once in a while the woman of the tipi has to get out to bring in more wood to burn.

Whenever the weather permitted, the men would go out and set their traps for the many fur-bearing animals. This trapping season began in about the month of November when the fur turns prime, and it lasts until about the month of April, when the summer hair starts to grow on the animal.

The Native American knew all about the effect of the stars, the moon, the sun too. Weather could be known in advance by observing these, the color of the morning or the color of the evening twilight could tell you if it's going to be a slight breeze or a very windy day.

All of the months of the year had names. Rightfully, it was each moon that had a name. Beginning with the month of January, the Natives call it the Moon of Big Smoke, the Moon That Helps Eat. That's because in January, when the air is very still, the smoke from the tipis go straight upward, and for some reason it comes very big in size from the tipi. "Helps eat" is because the weather is so cold, no one could get out to do anything outside, everyone just about has to stay inside of the tipi. When one is always near the food, it's always tempting to eat, and naturally the food goes faster. So January is the Help Eat Moon.

February is the Moon of the Eagle, when the eagle returns from the winter migration. Also it is known as the Hatching Time of the Owl. The owl takes time to grow, he is awful slow. So to be ready for the spring months and able to fly, the owl hatches in February. This is true for other predatory animals or birds. The owl must be able to fly when all of the summer birds and hibernating animals come out for the warmer months. February is also the moon of the dreaded northern blizzard. The natives call it Taking Orderly Position for the Attack.

March is the Geese Arrive Moon. It is also known as the time Napi Comes Running Down Off of the Mountains, the Moon of the Warm Chinook Winds. It is the moon for gophers, too.

April is the Moon of the Frogs. April is the moon the frogs come and begin their noisemaking, croaking. It is also the Moon of the Returning Bluebirds. April is also the moon when the thunder returns and all the holy bundles that pertain to the thunder are taken out to honor the return of the thunder.

May is the Moon of the Green Grass. It begins to grow, comes out of the ground, it also is the moon of leaves, when the leaf begins to appear on the growth. It is also the moon that changes the color on some certain animals, the summer color comes on. It is known too for the pretty flowers blooming.

June is the Moon of Hatching, most birds eggs hatch. It is also the Moon of High Waters, the moon when the sarvis berry begins to ripen.

July is the Moon of Ripe Berries, the gathering of the holy encampment that comes annually, midsummer time.

August is the moon that ends the summer holy encampment, the crows begin to gather or bunch up, the moon to move back to their hunting areas to stock up on meat for their winter use.

September is the moon when the long time rain comes, the departing of the thunder for that year, the yellowing of the leaves, the gathering of the white fish or sharpface fish, the moon that dries the berries up. The moon to move to their wintering areas. To bless all holy bundles and put away for winter.

October is the Geese Go South Moon. Certain animals such as the plains rabbit and the weasel begin to turn white for their winter coat.

November is the moon to knock bullberries off of their thornie bushes, cold and frost really turns them on for the sweetness. All animal hair is prime in November, trapping begins for those early ancestors of ours. The eagle goes on its southern migration. Ice covers most waters.

December is the Moon of Winter Cold. It's also the Moon That Parts Her Hair Right Square in the Middle. This is because of the days, the shortest day and the beginning of the longer days.

There were times when the weather got warmer during the winter months. It was one of these times that the Chief of the camp wanted his daughter to get married.

One evening he had his camp crier go around to announce a meeting for him at his own tipi. He invited all the men of the camp. The meeting began as he got through feeding all of them. When all were seated, he began, "It has come to the time when my daughter should get married. I called this meeting to tell all of you to pass the word around to the eligible bachelors, young and old alike.

"Looks isn't what we are going to select on. My daughter wants a manly husband, a man that can do almost anything. She will be the judge herself, she will call a contest between all of the men, young and old, all those that are eligible singles. We think this is fair to all of these men."

After the meeting the men all left the Chief's tipi and went on their way to their own tipis for their night's rest.

Next morning, all of the men that had attended the Chief's meeting went around getting in touch with all of the slickerfoots, or eligible bachelors, to let all of them know of the selecting of a husband by the Chief's daughter. Whoever wins the contest or game wins the Chief's daughter too.

The day came when the Chief's daughter was going to select a winning man. All of the slickerfoots or eligible bachelors gathered in the middle of the camps, young and old alike. Even some of the married men came for the great contest, expecting to win her too, to add to their other wives.

When all that were to come had gathered, the Chief and his daughter came out to the group, to the midst of them they went. Many women came out too, to see what was going on or how the contest was going to be had.

The Chief held his hands up for quiet. The many bachelors and the women that were present all quieted down, the Chief had something to say. He began, "My daughter wants to select a husband for herself, she will be the judge to see who wins her as a wife. To make it a fair competition and to find the right man for herself, a man that can do anything, that knows what life is, is what she wants.

"Tonight, I want all of you that are in this selecting contest to go and set your traps for a black fox that comes around. Whoever catches it in his traps shall be my daughter's husband. That is all. Now get a-going, as it takes time to set a trap."

All of the men dispersed and immediately went to get their traps ready for that *sig-o-dot-oyyi*, black fox.

Among them all was Bellyfat, him and his sister or adopted mother, the young girl that found him in the woods. All of the single men were making fun of him, telling him, "You will surely dirty the Chief's daughter with your bowel movements if you win her." Bellyfat didn't pay any attention to them all, not even listening to them. He was asking the girl to help him set the trap, he was trying for the black fox too.

Bellyfat was the name given to this little boy found in the woods by the old lady and her little daughter as they were gathering wood for their tipi. Belly fat is the fat that surrounds the stomach of the buffalo and is on the outside of this stomach paunch. Usually when the Native kills a buffalo, the belly fat is taken off first when the carcass is cut open. It is washed off in water to clean it, as most generally it is almost covered with the manure within the belly of the animal.

This belly fat is white in color, but if one is not careful about the cutting of the paunch, all of the manure comes out and covers the belly fat. It doesn't smell very good either. This was why he was named Bellyfat, the little boy that was found in the woods. He dirtied so much and he smelled like it too.

About this time there was also another being that was very jealous of Bellyfat, the way Bellyfat was being treated by his adopted people, treated good. His name was My-stu-bun, Crowfeather Arrow.

Crowfeather Arrow was a mysterious being too. He was a real crow. He would transform himself into a human being, a man, and come among the people to steal from them. At this time all crows were white in color, there weren't any black crows. They were all beautiful white.

Crowfeather Arrow kept an eye on Bellyfat. He knew there was some sort of luck or power behind this fellow, Bellyfat, otherwise he wouldn't've lived through what he went through, he would've died by that tree.

Bellyfat and the young girl went down along the small creek not very far from the camps. There among the birch he set his traps. He just told the young girl what to do as he sat by the place. Every once in a while he would dirty his breechclout, still running out on his bowels. But the young girl had lots of patience with Bellyfat, she just cleaned him up each time.

My-stu-bun, Crowfeather Arrow, was close by watching from his hiding place among the patch of willows. He waited until Bellyfat and the young girl had set the trap and left for the camps, then My-stu-bun, Crowfeather Arrow, came out of hiding. He went right to the exact place where Bellyfat had set his trap. There My-stu-bun, Crowfeather Arrow, also set his trap, right close by Bellyfat's trap. There was a fishy look on his face. He had a crooked plan to win this contest tomorrow morning.

All of the contestants for the Chief's daughter probably never slept a wink, all were too nervous and anxious to win the beautiful girl. Every one of them got up just as the eastern sky was getting grey, and it was a cold winter morning too, but no one cared about the cold as all were anxious to go look at their traps.

Among all of the contestants, there was one that got up extra early, it wasn't even getting gray in the east when he crept out of his warm bed. It was My-stu-bun, Crowfeather Arrow. He got up before anyone else and stole down to his trap. Sure enough, there in Bellyfat's trap was the *sig-o-dot-oyyi*, the black fox.

He had to be fast, this Crowfeather Arrow. He grabbed the black fox and put the fox into his own trap. Then back to the camps he ran where no one would see him, back into his tipi he went and waited for a while.

It was daylight now. The sun was coming up slowly and all of the men were gathered again for the contest.

The Chief and his daughter came out to judge. Coming among them, the Chief told them to go and check the traps. All of the bachelors were a little rushy to get to their traps, some of them actually ran.

It wasn't long after that the contestants began to return to the camp, their heads bowed. No black fox was in their traps.

Bellyfat was one of the last to go check his trap. Crowfeather Arrow went too, right behind Bellyfat.

Bellyfat and the young girl reached their trap just ahead of Crowfeather Arrow. Crowfeather Arrow gave a great big holler as he said in the loudest voice he could, "I've got the black fox. I have won the Chief's daughter fair and square!"

Bellyfat and the young girl were standing beside their trap, examining it. The girl ran back up to the camp while Bellyfat waited by the trap, examining it at the same time. It wasn't long before the girl brought the Chief and his daughter back with her to their trap.

The young girl told the Chief and the daughter, "I want you two to see for yourselves what has taken place. My brother, Bellyfat, really caught the black fox, but someone stole it out of the trap and put it into his own trap. You both can tell by the fresh tracks, there was a trace of new snow last night and the tracks of someone tells the story."

Crowfeather Arrow was already at the camps with the black fox, really bragging himself up and talking of the bride he won. One thing he didn't do, he forgot to cover up his tracks. He was in too much of a hurry, and besides it was still very dark when he stole the fox from Bellyfat's trap.

Every one of the contestants were back to the camp by now and all were wishing they could be Crowfeather Arrow. He won the Chief's daughter and all the riches that went with her, too.

The Chief, still being an honest man, was among them with the daughter. Again he was speaking with kind words to them all, "We have a mix-up among the contestants. We will have to do this over again, we shall have to make an entirely different contest for all of those that want my daughter for a wife." All of the men were very disappointed, especially Crowfeather Arrow.

Again the Chief cried out, "In the morning, there is a white prairie chicken that roosts on the birch over there, in that clump of birch trees. The white prairie chicken will be there before the sun rises. Now whoever shoots this pure white prairie chicken down with their own bow and arrow shall be the winner this time. My daughter and I shall be watching you to judge the winner."

There are still times when we see these albino prairie chickens among the ordinary ones.

All of the eligible bachelors went home, and so did the married men who were in this contest for the Chief's daughter, to get more wives or a young one. Again all of the men were very excited. Crowfeather Arrow didn't sleep too much, he was busy trying to find a way to cheat so he could win the Chief's daughter and so he could harass the men too.

It was still a little dark out when all of the contestants began to arise for the next chance at the Chief's daughter, especially Crowfeather Arrow. He had gotten out of bed long before all of them, checking his bow and arrows.

Just at daylight, all of the men had gathered close to the clump of birch near the camp. It was here the white prairie chicken was to be on one of the trees.

Bellyfat was about the last to come, and with him the young girl that was so very close to him. It was about this time when the white prairie chicken was spotted among the birch trees, right away all of the men got ready for the shoot.

Because Bellyfat lost the last contest to a thief, he was given the first chance to shoot. Without anyone seeing him, Crowfeather Arrow got ready too, he knew Bellyfat wouldn't miss his mark, he had that power to be lucky.

Crowfeather Arrow was to shoot second after Bellyfat. This made his plan to win a little easier.

All eyes were on Bellyfat as he aimed his bow for the white prairie chicken. No one looked at Crowfeather Arrow. He aimed too, and shot just as Bellyfat shot his bow and arrow. Crowfeather Arrow didn't wait, he ran to where the white prairie chicken had fallen, an arrow went right through the middle of the prairie chicken's heart. Crowfeather Arrow was hollering again as he ran, "I hit him, I killed him, again I win the daughter of the Chief!"

Crowfeather Arrow was fast on his feet, he beat everyone to the fallen white prairie chicken and was fast enough to change his arrow in place of Bellyfat's arrow. He came running back to the crowd with the white prairie chicken in his hands, hollering that he had killed the prairie chicken.

The Chief, being in the lead of the men, met Crowfeather Arrow first. He took the chicken from him and sized the chicken up very closely. He didn't like the looks of it. He held his hands up and told the men, "Wait here, my daughter and I shall take a look where the white prairie chicken fell."

Coming to where the white prairie chicken had fallen from the tree, the Chief and his daughter examined it very closely. They found an arrow, it was broken and still had fresh blood on it. Picking it up, the two went back to the contestants with the arrow they found.

The Chief again announced his disapproval of this contest. The men must have another contest to win the beautiful daughter of the Chief.

The Chief announced the new contest for the next day. "This time I have a foolproof way to hold this contest. Among a particular herd of buffalo, there is one young buffalo with hair like a beaver's pelt. Whoever brings this robe into me shall be declared the winner. All of you contestants must be out hunting before daylight."

As all of the bachelors were very anxious for the outcome of this game, everyone was out before daylight, even Crowfeather Arrow. Like always, he was trying to scheme around some way to win this one, so he stayed very close to Bellyfat and the young girl.

By midday, most of the contestants were trickling back into camp with what they thought was the beaver-furred buffalo hide. As each one was seen by the Chief, he shook his head, "*Sahh-uh, mah-dom-mi-wahts.* No, it's not the one."

Although Crowfeather Arrow tried very hard to come up with an idea, he just couldn't think up a good one. He finally gave it up. By that time, Bellyfat had gotten his buffalo.

All dressed out, Bellyfat and the young girl loaded the meat on their backs and their dog travois, bringing the hide with them. As you can guess, Crowfeather Arrow wasn't too far behind them.

They went right to the Chief's tipi. Seeing the hide, the Chief hollered out, "Bellyfat is the winner, he brought the beaver-furred buffalo hide!"

The Chief sent his beautiful daughter home with Bellyfat. Bellyfat was very happy about all of this, so was the Chief's daughter.

No one seen where Crowfeather Arrow went to, he seem to have disappeared into thin air. He alone knew where he was and what revenge he was planning for all of them.

The young girl that was constantly with Bellyfat was gone too, brokenhearted over losing Bellyfat.

The excitement was just too much for Bellyfat. When they took over one of the Chief's tipis, he began to come out on his bowels one right after the other. His new wife just couldn't stand this, "Aaawk, aaawk," she went, gagging over the filth of Bellyfat. She couldn't stand it very long, it was too much for a Chief's daughter, she ran home to her parents.

"I just can't stand the filth of Bellyfat, it's too dirty. I'm not going to marry him."

Bellyfat wasn't even married for a half a day, his wife left him over his bowel movements. But then it must not have been meant to be, because soon as the young girl that had found him in the first place out in the woods heard what happened, she immediately ran to his side to take care of him.

As she was cleaning him up, she told him, "Bellyfat, people think they are too good for you because of your bowel movements. I'm different from them, I love you no matter what. I'll marry you myself and be with you always."

Bellyfat became a great man. It was just one way to find out who really cared for him, running out on his bowels all the time.

Bellyfat wanted to show his appreciation to the people of this camp. After everything was over with and things were looking good all around, Bellyfat took out his arrow feathers, which were all eagle feathers and plumes. They were all wrapped up in his robe. This robe he took to the center of the camp, held the robe up very high and shook all of the eagle feathers and plumes off of the robe. All of the people, knowing what a great person Bellyfat got to be, ran to where the feathers and plumes fell to the ground. Not one of them was left. All of the feathers and eagle plumes were taken as tokens of good luck.

Seeing how the people went for Bellyfat's feathers and plumes, old Crowfeather Arrow thought he would do better with his feathers that were left over from his arrow makings. He took his robe with the feathers and plumes in it to the center of the camps too, and dumped them all on the ground, hollering at the same time, "Here's my arrow feathers, which are better than Bellyfat's. Take them all for your souvenir or your next arrows. These feathers and plumes will give all of you good luck."

It was sorrowful, no one came running or breaking their necks, to get any of Crowfeather Arrow's plumes and feathers like they did with Bellyfat's eagle feathers and plumes.

This made Crowfeather Arrow all the more angry, and gave him reason for a big revenge to the people of this camp, and all of the people any place else, too.

# NAPI TALES

## *My-stu-bun, Crowfeather Arrow's Revenge*

My-stu-bun came mysteriously. No one knew where he had come from, just himself knew who he really was. He knew he had transformed himself into another being. Crowfeather Arrow was really Oldman, Napi. He was put here on Mother Earth to teach the children of Creator Sun and Mother Earth how to live like them, a sinless life. But he had made a few mistakes with the people already, so now he was trying to break away from Creator Sun's rulings. He was tempted to live like his subjects, the people of Mother Earth, and at the same time to retain the power that was entrusted to him by Creator Sun. He was also stealing that power entrusted to him by Creator Sun to gain himself a wife. But wrong never holds up no matter what, and no matter how much power is entrusted to you, that power never works when you are using it for the wrong purpose.

My-stu-bun, Crowfeather Arrow, was very embarrassed over what he had done, cheating to get a wife for himself. At the same time he was mad at all of the people, they were all against him for what he had done, or so he thought.

My-stu-bun was going to show them a lesson they must learn, not to make fun of anyone. He was going to have revenge and make them suffer for what they had done to him, belittling him, making fun of him, harassing him. This wasn't all that true, but that's what Crowfeather Arrow had in his mind, that all were against him and making fun of him for what he had tried to do.

Crowfeather Arrow bided his time, waiting for the best time to get revenge on the people. It had to be something to affect all of the people, the children of Mother Earth and Creator Sun.

It was a very long time after his defeat at the contest of the Chief's daughter that his chance for revenge came at last. The people were getting very hungry. The buffalo was on the move and it was hard for them to keep up with the herds of buffalo. Being on foot wasn't easy, their leg power was the only thing that got them places.

Crowfeather Arrow, seeing the people moving here and there about every other day looking for the buffalo, got an idea to get that revenge he wanted. He must hide the buffalo so the people wouldn't find them at all.

Using that supernatural power entrusted to him by Creator Sun, he rounded up all of the buffalo and hid them all in a mountain canyon. This particular canyon was at the head of the present-day Cut Bank Creek and Cut Bank Canyon, to the south of Saint Mary Lake. The people were camped just east of there in the hills, still looking for the buffalo.

All of the men of the camp and other camps all over were out in mass to find the herds of buffalo. The deer and the antelope, the elk, moose, and

*Crowfeather Arrow Hides the Buffalo*

other game, even the fowls that were food to the people were just too hard to get—they were so much faster than the buffalo and so much harder to kill. It was easier to kill a lot of buffalo. They were stampeded over high steep places in herds. Many are killed in the fall, and those that might be still alive are trampled to death by others falling on them. There, enough meat was gotten for even a big camp of people to last them for quite a while.

Even the dried meat that was stored away was eaten up, some of the older people were beginning to get weak from the lack of fresh meat as every one of the Plains people depend on the meat as the main source of energy and vitamins.

All of the people seemed to be starving from the lack of fresh meat—except Crowfeather Arrow. For some reason he still had lot of energy, even some to spare. This, Bellyfat had observed of him. Bellyfat was now watching Crowfeather Arrow very close, from the time Crowfeather Arrow got up out of bed until he retired for the night.

Bellyfat was up way before daylight and was hiding up on a little knoll that was thick with quaking aspens. From this clump of quaking aspens where he hid, he had a good observation of almost everything surrounding the place.

Just at daylight, it was no problem for Bellyfat to see from his hiding place all those that got out of their tipis and went for their usual morning strolls. He kept his eyes on Crowfeather Arrow's tipi. Crowfeather Arrow also got up before the other people got up, and right away went sneaking out of camp right to a thick clump of quaking aspens not far from where Bellyfat was hiding. Bellyfat seen him disappear into the quaking aspens. A little while after, a beautiful white crow came up out of the thickets. Bellyfat wasn't a type to be fooled easily, he knew right away what it was all about. He kept his eyes on this white crow, he knew that it was no other than Crowfeather Arrow.

Crowfeather Arrow was on his way to eat. He knew where the herds of buffalos were, where he hid them. Crowfeather Arrow was getting his fill each day and letting the rest go hungry. He was very wise, but not as wise as Bellyfat. For some reason he had a feeling someone was watching him this one morning. Flying up out of the thick quaking aspens, he watched very close down on ground. He circled around and around, that feeling of someone watching his every movement. He went into bigger circles and was quite high in the air, he was trying very hard to see who was watching him. Bellyfat was too well hidden to be seen, especially from the air. He just kept his eyes on Crowfeather Arrow, the white crow that was flying.

After he made very sure no one was watching, he flew to the north. He was trying to fool whoever might be watching him, he thought whoever was doing the watching might come out and follow him to the north.

Bellyfat was just too smart for that. He didn't move, he just kept his eyes glued on the white crow flying north.

Crowfeather Arrow, the flying crow, was tricky this morning. As he flew, his eyes were looking back and all over to see if someone was watching where he flew to.

He flew a long ways north before he was very sure that no one was watching him or following him north.

Bellyfat just kept frozen to the spot where he was hiding, but his eyes were on the white flying crow. He knew it was Crowfeather Arrow.

Crowfeather Arrow, the white crow, finally sure of himself, turned and came flying back towards the camps. It took time to get back to where the camps were, but reaching them, he didn't come down. He went on flying to the south now. His worries were all for nothing, it was just his imagination that he thought someone was watching him. He flew on towards Cut Bank Canyon, and there he circled for awhile to make very sure again no one was watching him.

Bellyfat just laid there, taking it all in with his eyes. He seen every move the white crow made from the time he came flying out of the quaking aspens, and now he had seen where the white crow had disappeared to. Bellyfat wanted to make very sure before he made a move. He didn't want to get his hopes up too much, but he thought he had it solved, the disappearance of the herds of buffalo. He just laid there. The sun was way up, almost midday, before he seen the white crow come flying out of the head of this canyon.

Bellyfat seen the crow fly along the mountain side, far west of the camps. He flew again far to the north of the camps—just to throw everyone that may have seen him as the crow off-guard, so he wouldn't be suspected of any wrongdoing. He was flying around like he was looking for food, looking like a plain old crow.

Bellyfat was never anyone to be fooled by such as Crowfeather Arrow. He knew that it was Crowfeather Arrow, transformed into a crow and flying around. He also knew that this crow came from where the buffalo were, all of the herds bunched together. Bellyfat also knew that this Crowfeather Arrow, this crow flying around, was getting his fill of fresh meat while the others, all of the other people, were almost starved. Bellyfat just laid still and kept his eyes on that crow.

Before the crow came back, while it was still flying out of sight far, far to the north, Bellyfat made a dash for the clump of quaking aspens that Crowfeather Arrow had disappeared into. Sure enough, there in the center of this thicket, laid in a heap, was Crowfeather Arrow's clothing—his breechclout, his leggings, his buckskin shirt, everything he owned. Being very sure of this, Bellyfat ran back to his hiding place not too far away, and hid again.

Bellyfat just made it back to his hiding place when the crow came flying back from that north side, zigzagging towards the camps, just trying to make sure no one seen him. Coming closer to the camps, the crow went way down low, just above the treetops where hardly anyone would notice him.

The crow flew to the clump of quaking aspens to the west of them, and went right down into the thicket where his clothing laid. It wasn't long after this that Crowfeather Arrow came walking out of the thickets and hurried down to his tipi.

Bellyfat came out from his hiding place after making very sure that Crow-feather Arrow wasn't going to come back out of his tipi. "That crow, that Crowfeather Arrow, must be very tired now," he thought. "He's been on the go since just getting daylight. I'll go check on him to make sure he does know something about the herds of buffalo that disappeared."

As he came out from his hiding place, Bellyfat took his time making his way to Crowfeather Arrow's tipi. He stole very quietly to the tipi. Being just so quiet, he slowly opened the doorway and peeked in. Sure enough, Crow-feather Arrow was already asleep. He was very tired.

Opening the doorway wider, Bellyfat went sneaking in there, crawling to the side of Crowfeather Arrow near his head.

Crowfeather Arrow was so very tired, he was sleeping very soundly, just dead to the world. Bellyfat was right by his head, looking into the wide-open mouth of Crowfeather Arrow as he slept square on his back. Sure enough between some of his teeth was pieces of fresh meat. This Crowfeather Arrow really was starving the people all over the country. He must be stopped.

For a couple of days Crowfeather Arrow didn't make much of a move, he walked mostly around the camps. All of the time, Bellyfat's eyes were on him, waiting for his next move to the herds of buffalo. Bellyfat had told the Chief of this camp to wait a while, that he was onto the disappearance of the buffalo, that soon they might have fresh meat.

Crowfeather Arrow's hunger got the best of him again. He must go and fill his greedy stomach up. He got up very early again, just getting daylight, and to the thickets again he went. But there was always one that got up before him, and that was Bellyfat. Bellyfat was already watching this Crow-feather Arrow's tipi soon as he got up, long before daylight.

It wasn't too long after daylight that Crowfeather Arrow got busy. He got up out of bed and right away went to the quaking aspen patch. Not long after this, a white crow came flying out from the thickets again. Bellyfat watched his every move.

The crow flew this way and that way. Several times it flew north then south, and it would circle around for awhile. For a long time he flew around. If anyone was looking, he might've thrown them off by confusing them with his flight.

All this time Bellyfat laid there. He finally seen the crow take a roundabout course towards the south. The crow disappeared far to the south. Bellyfat jumped from his hiding place and ran with all his might southward to Cut Bank Canyon, where the crow had disappeared again.

Bellyfat, coming into the canyon, followed the creek up as far as he dared to go. He hid himself very near a small park, an opening in the timber where the creek ran through. Over this area, the crow had to fly over. Right near the creek's edge, Bellyfat transformed himself into a dead beaver lying on its back.

Bellyfat didn't have too long to wait. As he laid there in the form of a dead beaver, with his eyes open to observe everything around him, he seen the crow as it came flying out of the thickets quite a ways to the west. The crow had to fly this way to go north. The dead beaver just laid very still now.

Crowfeather Arrow, the flying crow, wasn't flying very high. He was keeping his eyes open for anything that looked suspicious. Coming over the small park, the opening in the timber where the creek ran through, his gazing eyes seen a dead beaver laying there. A beaver was a tender morsel for a crow, a treat that couldn't be passed up. But for some reason it was sort of suspicious. "Anyway," he thought to himself, "I'll come down and test this dead beaver that was sprawled square on its back." The dead beaver had one eye barely open to see what was going on as he kept his eye on this crow.

The crow lit a little ways from the dead beaver. He stood very still, his eyes were fastened on the dead beaver. He walked all around this dead thing for the longest time. After making a few rounds around the dead beaver, the crow finally came a little closer. Again he walked all around it, then he went a little closer to it. The crow checked every bit of the beaver's body with his eyes, testing for signs of life in the beaver, a little quiver of the muscles, a blinking of the eyes, any slight movement. Being very sure there wasn't any kind of movement, he went for the most vulnerable place of the beaver, to the head. There again the crow paused for the longest time, rechecking for the sign of life.

The crow must've known what its next move would be. All at once he jumped towards the head of the beaver and he pecked at the slightly open eye of this dead beaver, which the beaver didn't expect. The dead beaver winced at this eye-pecking.

The crow flew instantly, and to the north he went. He knew this was a trick. He wanted to throw whoever it was that tried to trick him into confusion.

As the crow flew out of sight, Bellyfat transformed himself back into his real self and slowly walked back towards the camps, his eye hurting quite a bit from that good peck the crow had done to him. He knew he had to try harder to catch that Crowfeather Arrow so he could find out about all of the buffalo.

It was several days before Crowfeather Arrow attempted to go and get something to eat, this time getting up extra early. It was still a little dark out when he got out of bed to sneak away to his stash of all the buffalo, and he was mighty hungry, he hadn't had anything to eat all these days that he held back for fear of someone catching on to what he was doing.

Bellyfat never had lost track of Crowfeather Arrow since he first suspected him for the disappearance of the buffalo herds. It was no different this morning. Bellyfat had his eyes on Crowfeather Arrow's tipi. He was about before Crowfeather Arrow even stirred in his bed. He seen him sneaking out before daylight, sneaking right close in behind him as Crowfeather Arrow left the camp and went right back to his favorite spot for his transformation.

Bellyfat didn't waste any time this morning, he left the area before Crowfeather Arrow transformed into a white crow. Bellyfat knew where the white crow would fly to. Very sure all of the buffalo herds were in those mountains somewhere, he must find out for sure where they were hidden. He knew Crowfeather Arrow hid them for some reason.

All of the people of this area were very hungry, they must have their main food back, the buffalo meat. Some were very near death from hunger, the root food wasn't nourishing enough to keep them a-going in their strenuous life.

Bellyfat didn't get to the head of Cut Bank Creek any too soon. He just made it there and hid, when there came that white crow flying proudly, coming over the north ridge of Cut Bank Creek. It was daylight already, the sun hadn't come out of the east horizon. The crow didn't waste any time along the way. He was mighty hungry this morning, he hadn't had anything to eat the last few days. In fact, his stomach was just roaring from the lack of food.

With Bellyfat's eyes on him, the crow flew right over Bellyfat's hiding place. The crow wasn't even gazing around like the last time, he knew that he had left those camps extra early this time, and there wouldn't be anyone around to see him leave camp. He was very sure of himself. But those eyes of Bellyfat weren't to be fooled anytime.

The crow flew on up the canyon and disappeared somewhere wrong those several canyons that come into Cut Bank Canyon. It was a long time when he reappeared in Bellyfat's view, coming out from one of the several canyons. Bellyfat wanted to find out what canyon it was, so he could get the buffalo back out into the plains for the people to hunt and kill for food.

Just as the crow reappeared, Bellyfat made his way again to the creek. It was in a very small park in this timber, but near the creek. He knew that this crow had to fly over this spot, and the crow's keen eyes wouldn't miss anything. It was there Bellyfat transformed himself into a deer.

This time Bellyfat laid himself down where he could protect his eyes from the crow, but in a position to see what was going on as he transformed into a dead deer.

Crows are foolish when it comes to food, even in these days, so it wasn't any different with Crowfeather Arrow as a crow.

Crowfeather Arrow just loved deer meat when it was fresh, like a person does. That was the reason Bellyfat transformed himself into a dead deer. He knew it wouldn't be any different with Crowfeather Arrow even as a crow.

Before the coming of the whiteman, those early natives didn't have any kinds of sweets. So for the sweet tooth there were wild berries of the many different edible types that grew in the summertime. But wintertime was different, there weren't any berries growing. That's where the deer came in. The deer tasted sweet to those oldtimers, and they just loved the deer meat when it was fresh. The antelope was even sweeter, but it was too fast to kill most of time. Those natives had more of a chance on the deer than the antelope, which was out in the open plains—a hard place to even sneak up to them. The deer lived mostly in the timber and it was easy for hunters to sneak in among the trees and stalk them for the kill. This gave them more deer meat for their sweets.

The deer was in plain sight in the little park, the opening in this timber. It wasn't too long before the crow came flying overhead, its sharp, beady eyes peeled for observation. Crows have very sharp eyes. They can spot food from way up in the air, even if it's quite a distance. It was nothing for this crow to spot a dead deer from where it was flying. Even with his full stomach it was so tempting to the crow he couldn't resist this tender sweet morsel. He had to get a taste of it. He even momentarily forgot about the tricks.

Coming down fast to where the dead deer laid, he almost lit on him, when it dawned on him that this may be a trick too. So he skipped the deer and lit on the growd not too far from it. The crow would hop on the dead deer every once in a while, it would peck at the most tender places of the animal, places where he knew it would hurt if he were alive. Pecking now, then jumping off of the carcass fast, he would walk around for a while then try again. The crow done this for a while, then he finally got a taste of that tender fresh morsel, the flesh. This made that crow somewhat careless. He jumped on the deer carcass more often now and pecked several times before he jumped back off. Those pecks by the crow hurt very much, especially when the crow tore a little of the flesh.

After several more peckings, the crow got careless. This sweet flesh of the fresh deer meat was just too tasty. He didn't jump off the deer carcass any more, he was just pecking away, trying to tear more meat off to eat.

Under the crow and in the form of a dead deer laid Bellyfat. He was almost jumping up from the pain that the crow was causing to his body. But he thought about the people all near starving, so he tried his best not to give up so easily.

The crow was now jumping around like nobody's business, no more fear in him. This fresh deer meat was just too delicious to waste time in eating it. He jumped here and there on the carcass, but not in the right spot for Bellyfat to carry out his plan. All at once the crow made its wrong move, hopping to the middle of the deer's front legs. That was it. The deer made a fast grab for the crow as he transformed quickly back into his rightful origin, Bellyfat, a human. It was a lucky grab, he caught the crow by its legs and held it.

The crow was jumping around very much to get free from Bellyfat, but he held on. The crow couldn't transform into his original self, back into Crowfeather Arrow. His power couldn't work with someone around, he had to stay as a crow until he got alone.

In those early days animals and birds could talk, even rocks and trees could talk, everything talked, anything with life's spirit could talk. Right now the crow could only talk, but couldn't transform back into his original self. He had to stay a crow until he could get alone, or when Bellyfat turned him loose to freedom.

Bellyfat asked the crow where all of the herds of buffalo had disappeared. Bellyfat was quizzing the crow very close, shooting question after question to him, asking why all the buffalo herds had disappeared.

The crow didn't know anything about all of the buffalo disappearing from the plains. Every question he answered with, "I don't know where they are."

Bellyfat was getting mighty angry with this crow. He knew who this crow really was, My-stu-bun himself, Crowfeather Arrow, and he knew the place the buffalo were. Bellyfat told him, "We shall see about all of this that you don't know when I get you to the camp."

Getting back to the camps near Saint Mary's Lake, Bellyfat got himself a piece of rawhide rope while he held on to the crow with the other hand. With this rawhide rope Bellyfat tied the crow's legs together very tight so the rope wouldn't slip off. He then ran the rope over one of the tipi poles at the very top inside of this tipi, right where the smoke vent was, where all of the smoke went when the fire was a-going. The crow hung down from the tipi poles, head down.

Bellyfat was still asking him where the people could find the herds of buffalo that had all disappeared from the plains. The crow didn't know anything about them.

"We shall see about this. Everything I ask you, you don't know. But you are the only one that isn't starving of all these people. Looking at your teeth while you were asleep one morning, between your teeth was fresh meat. How do you account for that? And how come you transform into a crow? I know who you really are—My-stu-bun, Crowfeather Arrow!

"All right! Since you won't tell me where the buffalo are, I'll keep you hanging down from there until you tell me about the buffalo." Not very long after, Bellyfat asked the crow where the buffalo were, still the answer was he didn't know.

Bellyfat told the crow, "I'm going out for a while, and if you don't tell me where the buffalo are, I think I have a way to make you talk."

Before Bellyfat left the tipi, the crow was pleading with Bellyfat to free him from that place so he could sit upright. But Bellyfat didn't even pay attention to him. He went out of his tipi and on out to the open, away from the camp. There he picked an armful of sage. To the tipi he took it, then after some wood he went. A big armful he brought back to the tipi. A pile of sage and a pile of wood. Bellyfat took both piles inside of his tipi. He make a fire, and as the fire started to burn good, Bellyfat piled the sage on top of the dry wood. Right away it started a thick smoke, and right away the crow began to plead with Bellyfat to put the fire out so it wouldn't smoke anymore. Bellyfat only piled some more sage on the fire again. The crow was screaming his plea out, but Bellyfat didn't have ears, he wasn't listening, he only closed the doorway tighter.

Bellyfat was standing just outside of his doorway, listening to the crow's pleadings. But he was waiting for the right words. All this time the crow was pleading to be let down from that awful smoke, Bellyfat only waited more.

It wasn't too long in the thick smoke when the crow said he would tell where the buffalo were. He was gagging from the smoke, almost suffocating from the thick black smoke. Bellyfat wanted to hear more, so he waited as the smoke came up in thick black clouds. The crow was now crying, pleading with Bellyfat, he would tell him where the buffalo were. Bellyfat stood there still waiting, but this time he was waiting for the smoke to clear. He knew the fire had burned out, but the smoke hadn't cleared just yet. Not knowing this, the crow was pleading with all his might, saying that he would let the people know the whereabouts of the buffalo.

Bellyfat went in after he knew the smoke had cleared from the inside, and what he seen made him laugh and laugh. From above, the crow was hanging down head first. He was burnt black and his eyes were just red. Bellyfat was very wise. He didn't untie the crow, he asked him, "Now tell me where all of the buffalo are. If you don't, I can always get more wood and sagebrush to burn and make more smoke for you. Just tell me where to go to find them, because I am not going to let you go until you tell me where they are. I shall keep you tied up there with your head down until you tell me."

Crowfeather Arrow, the now black crow, wanted freedom. He didn't want to spend much more time up there, he must tell the truth. The black crow told Bellyfat where to go and how to get there. "Up there in that canyon," which is the present-day Cut Bank Canyon.

Bellyfat didn't waste any time. The people were very hungry, very near starvation. If it weren't for the roots and edible leaves, they would have already starved. Right to the canyon he went, found the place where he was told to go, and sure enough, up one of the blind canyons with a lot of fresh green grass and fresh water were the thousands of buffalo. Bellyfat made his way around the back of them. He spooked them to the entrance of this long large canyon of Cut Bank Creek. Running back to this entrance, Bellyfat stood there with his bow and arrows and killed many of the buffalo as they came running out.

Bellyfat butchered all of the buffalo he had killed, dressed them all out, and hung them up on the limbs all over the place. Some he piled up where it was cool, then back to the camps he went with the good news and what he could carry of the entrails of the buffalo. Seeing the tasty entrails in his arms, the people lost no time to get a-going to where he had hung all of the fresh meat.

As for him, he went back to his tipi and told the now black crow to promise never to try to starve his people again. If he didn't promise, Bellyfat was going to leave the crow up there tied to the poles and make more smokey fire. The crow readily promised never to do that again, so Bellyfat untied him and let him down off of the poles. As he let him loose to fly away, Bellyfat hollered after him, "All of the crows to come, after this, shall all be black like you are now, to remember never to try to starve the people again."

As the crow flew away, he was readily agreeing to what Bellyfat was talking about—"*aw, aw, aw, aw.*" In our Piegan language, *aw* or *ah* means yes, agreeing to. To this day, you can hear the crow still agreeing to that promise as they say "*aw, aw, aw,*" and they are still black.

# Second Revenge of My-stu-bun, Crowfeather Arrow

Bellyfat had become one of the most noted Chiefs of his time. He had overcome that loose bowel movement that he had when the girl, now his wife, first found him in those woods after his twin brother had disappeared into the air as he climbed after that beautiful bird, and Bellyfat had cried himself back into a newborn child.

Things had come back to normal since Crowfeather Arrow had hidden the buffalo in Cut Bank Canyon. Crowfeather Arrow had never forgotten the embarrassment he went through when Bellyfat had won the Chief's daughter, and when he had to give up those herds of buffalo that he hid in Cut Bank Canyon. All of this he blamed Bellyfat for. He must get some kind of revenge on him, even if he had to hurt all of the people too.

After the Cut Bank Canyon incident, My-stu-bun, Crowfeather Arrow, was so embarrassed. Not too long after that he moved away alone with his family. He wanted to find a way to pay those people back for that embarrassment he went through, especially Bellyfat. He must get even with him.

Crowfeather Arrow camped far to the north country, many, many days away from the main camp. There he was alone with his wife and one baby boy that they had since the buffalo incident. Alone he hunted out on the Great Plains. His camp was located at what is now the Porcupine Hills, just north of Brocket, Alberta, Canada.

Each day Crowfeather Arrow, brought home much fresh meat for his family. They had lots of dried meat stored for their winter use.

One day, coming home from a hunt, Crowfeather Arrow stumbled onto a very large cave far into the Porcupine Hills. He stopped to look it over, he was much amazed over such a large cave. Venturing on into the cave, he walked very far and didn't come to the end of it. He also found a small lake just inside of the cave, not far from the entrance.

Sizing it up as he came walking back out of the cave, he thought to himself, "There must be some use for such a big cave." With this in his mind, Crowfeather Arrow picked up his load of meat and started back to his camp. The large cave just couldn't leave his mind.

Coming home, he yelled at his wife to take care of all the fresh meat he brought this time, and he went on into the tipi and sat down. Crowfeather Arrow was most unusually quiet this evening. The cave, he keeps on thinking of it. There must be some way to use it.

When everything was done for the day and it was getting dark out, and his woman and child had already gone to bed, Crowfeather Arrow was sitting up on his bed thinking. All of a sudden! He jumped up, and his wife jumped up in fright when he done this. She thought something had happened to him. Crowfeather Arrow talked very excitedly, very fast to his wife, telling her about the large cave he found and what he thought to do with it. His wife told him to calm down a little so she could understand his jumble. He began all over again, this time more slowly. "I can run all of the buffalo in there and no one will be the wiser. I must have my revenge. I'll work it so no one will think I'm to blame for the disappearance of the buffalo this time."

His wife tried to argue with him, that he got caught trying to take revenge on the people and he was so embarrassed. This was where they are over that incident, alone, far from anyone else. "Don't try it again, you will be caught again and be further embarrassed. You will never be able to face our people again. It is enough what you have already done to them." But Crowfeather Arrow didn't have ears, he was a stubborn fool. He had his mind made up already, a plan had been formed in his mind.

From that time one, as he went out on each hunt, Crowfeather Arrow would round up a large herd of buffalo and chase them into the large cave. As time went by, the buffalo herds were dwindling down again. This was noticed by people other than Crowfeather Arrow, especially by Bellyfat. Crowfeather Arrow went hunting quite often, just to bring more of the buffalo herds into the cave.

This went on a long time, and the buffalo were again disappearing from the Great Plains very rapidly. There was no end to this, and no one seemed to know anything about it. Although his eyes were on Crowfeather Arrow, Bellyfat couldn't see anything wrong with his doings. He was out there hunting with the rest of the people, looking for more buffalo. Crowfeather Arrow didn't let anyone see him at what he was doing again—he made very sure of this, this time.

It was several days now that no one had seen any buffalo out in those plains, again those vast herds of buffalo had disappeared mysteriously. Who was to blame this time? It couldn't be Crowfeather Arrow, he's been out just the same as everyone else, to find the buffalo. Where could the buffalo be? For sure they aren't all killed off, there's too many of them.

In the meantime, Crowfeather Arrow was well satisfied that all of the buffalo were now gone from the Great Plains. Not one was left. Now it was his sweet revenge on Bellyfat and the people that made fun of him.

When all of the buffalo were in that huge cave, Crowfeather Arrow moved his tipi on top of the huge cave, over the entrance of it. His tipi was up over this entrance, and there straight across from the doorway was the entrance to the cave. Laying sticks across the opening of the cave, Crowfeather Arrow had his wife make their bed over the cave entrance. With the bed made on the entrance, there wasn't any sign of the cave or the entrance. The tipi was covering the cave, and Crowfeather Arrow's bed covered the entrance to the cave. He was all set.

Bellyfat was always suspicious of My-stu-bun. He knew that Crowfeather Arrow was very cunning, he beared close watching all the time. Even this time, he knew Crowfeather Arrow had something to do with the disappearance of the buffalo again, he was involved somehow, he knew the answer. There was no way that Bellyfat could prove his suspicion, unless he actually seen what Crowfeather Arrow was doing, and that was hard to do. He had to be in the tipi of Crowfeather Arrow, to know all of this, he didn't even know the whereabouts of Crowfeather Arrow, much less where his camp was or what part of the country he was hunting.

Through Bellyfat's mind these thoughts were going around. Somehow he must find a way to catch Crowfeather Arrow with the goods. He must do something right away, for the people are already getting short of fresh meat.

As a human being, Bellyfat knew he just couldn't cover very much territory to find where Crowfeather Arrow was hanging out. He must do the next best thing, he must transform into something fast. "I'll fool that Crowfeather Arrow with a disguise that he used once," thought Bellyfat. "I'll transform into a crow and have a good look at the countryside, maybe I'll find that Crowfeather Arrow faster that way."

Bellyfat wasn't the type that lets the grass grow under his feet, he put physical action behind his plans. He transformed into a crow and was on his way in no time. First he went south, zigzagging as he went about, west then east, back and forth. Zigzagging as he went about, he went south for a long, long ways. Bellyfat knew he wouldn't find his camp this way, "That guy Crowfeather Arrow must be in the north area. I'll go take a look that way and see if he might be there." Bellyfat turned to the north, the same thing. He went east then west, still working northward, zigzagging as he went along.

Bellyfat was a crow as he was looking for the camp of Crowfeather Arrow. He could fly right along as fast as he could and still see everything below him. Crows have sharp eyes, never miss much.

All morning he flew and part of the afternoon. He was already flying over the south part of the Porcupine Hills and hadn't seen anything yet. This Bellyfat was getting kind of tired, and he was getting mighty hungry too. Not only that, but he was beginning to think that Crowfeather Arrow must've left this part of the country and gone into another's hunting territory. Bellyfat was about ready to give up as he was flying westward again, when all of a sudden, with the right corner of his right eye, he seen something white in the hilly timber down one of the many coulees. He turned and took a second look. There, to the north of him, stood a lone tipi.

Bellyfat, in a crow form, flew directly to this lone tipi and circled it a few times. There were real crows down there pecking around for food near the tipi. Bellyfat flew down to join them, he wasn't any different from them. Pecking around for food too, like the other crows, he had to work his way closer and closer to the tipi. The doorway was open and he wanted to see inside of it to make sure he wasn't making a mistake. It could well be someone else other than Crowfeather Arrow.

Bellyfat pecked here, then over there, but all the time he was working towards the doorway of this tipi. Closer and closer he got, pecking at this and that as he went along. He finally made it to the doorway of the tipi. He was still a-pecking away, but each time he raised his head he glanced inside. He seen what he wanted to see.

All of a sudden, without any warning, this man, Crowfeather Arrow, My-stu-bun, throwed a stick at the crow that was pecking around the doorway. He was talking at the same time, saying, "Yeah, this is a real crow, he wants to take a good look inside of our tipi." The crow flew away as the stick landed almost too close to him. He was still Bellyfat in a crow disguise. No mistake, this was Crowfeather Arrow's camp and he had lots of dry meat hanging down inside of his tipi. Bellyfat was right, Crowfeather Arrow has something to do with the disappearance of the buffalo again.

As Bellyfat flew away from the tipi, still in a crow form, he was thinking how he could get closer to those people inside of that tipi. Once out of sight of the tipi, Bellyfat came down among the trees and transformed back into his original self, back into Bellyfat as a human being. He laid around for a while trying to think up a good way to get closer, even inside of Crowfeather Arrow's tipi.

Darkness came, and Bellyfat laid down for the night. He needed some rest after all of this searching for this man Crowfeather Arrow. Now he found him, he must find a way to make him tell where the buffalo had disappeared to again.

Laying there in that timber, Bellyfat couldn't sleep for quite a while. Those coyotes were something else, all that noise they were making, he could even hear the yelp of the coyote puppies. All at once he sat up, coyote puppies was in his mind. That gave him an idea of how to get closer to the tipi of Crowfeather Arrow. Bellyfat definitely seen a small boy inside of that tipi. A boy and a puppy, that tied in together very good.

Very early in the morning, before daylight, Bellyfat went nearer to the tipi of Crowfeather Arrow. But in the woods, he transformed himself into a cute little puppy. Right away he began to cry and whimper like a real one, acting like it was lost, strayed from its mother.

The little boy of the tipi woke from all that whimpering and crying of the little puppy. The little boy got up out of bed and walked out to find the little puppy that was making all of the noise. "He must be cold, he must be hungry, that little lost puppy. I wonder how he strayed here?" thought the little boy. It didn't make much difference, though, he's here now, "I'll take him home and warm him up and then feed him." The little boy took the puppy home while his parents were still asleep.

Crowfeather Arrow woke up over the noise of the little puppy as he was playing with the little boy, barking and growling in play like all little pups. "Where did you get that puppy?" Crowfeather Arrow asked his son. The little boy told his father, "Right over there in those trees, it must've got there by straying from its mother. It was crying, so I went after it while you were asleep. I fed him and he's feeling much happier now."

"Take that puppy back to where you found him, he is not a real puppy. Go on, take him back among those trees now, I don't want him or anything else around here where we are camping." The boy was crying. This woke the mother up. She asked the little boy why he was crying, and the little boy said, "My father said for me to take this little puppy I found in the woods back out where I found it. He said it wasn't a real puppy and I want to keep him. I don't have anything to play with. I like the puppy."

The boy's mother got up talking. She was just like any other woman, getting up out of bed on the wrong side. She was scolding her man, Crowfeather Arrow, about making their son cry just over a little pup, saying, "How could a small thing like this pup find out what you are doing? In the first place, you just don't have any business to do what you are doing to our own people, hiding all of the buffalo, so they can starve. Just to pay them for what they done to you. It was all your fault, you put it on yourself. That little puppy won't do any harm. You took our boy away from the friends he would have to play with, and now you won't let him have one little puppy to play with. What kind of man are you?"

My-stu-bun, Crowfeather Arrow, hung his head down, feeling kind of ashamed of himself over this incident. Slowly, he spoke. "The boy can have that little puppy, but I want him to keep it by him all the time, never to let it out of his sight. I still don't think it's a real puppy."

The little boy and the little puppy had a very good time together for the next few days. The little puppy got enough to eat from the little boy. The food he was getting was mostly fresh meat, but he didn't know where it was coming from. The little puppy must find out, because he was none other than Bellyfat.

One early morning Crowfeather Arrow left the tipi. As close as the puppy could understand, Crowfeather Arrow was on an all-day trip. He would be out scouting around for strangers in these hills, or see if he had overlooked a herd of buffalo. This was a good chance for Bellyfat, him as a puppy. Before Crowfeather Arrow left the tipi, he told his wife, "You are the cause of the boy to keep that little puppy around. I want you to help look after that little puppy. I'll never believe he is a real pup. Be sure now and do what I told you."

Crowfeather Arrow left. The boy and the little pup played and played outside in the open. And all this time the little pup was taking in everything he seen and heard. As the day wore on, the little pup's curiosity was even more aroused, especially to know all about the inside of Crowfeather Arrow's tipi. As they played, the little boy and the pup were chasing one another more than anything else. The little pup ran from the little boy, the little boy chased the pup this way and that way. The little pup was running inside quite often, tiring for both of them, and the little boy took the little pup inside to rest awhile. Inside they both played a while on the boy's bed.

Not too long after the two went inside of the tipi, the woman must've forgot her watch over the boy and the pup. She got ready, told the boy she was going to go get firewood, and out she went.

The two sat on the bed and played for a long time after the woman left, playing quietly. The little boy all at once jumped up from the bed. Going to the door and looking out, there wasn't anyone around. Coming back in, he went directly to his folks' bed and called the pup over to him. The pup jumped up and ran to the little boy. As the pup got to him, the little boy lifted the robes that made up the bed while the little pup's ears perked up, eyes wide open. Under this bed was a large cave with poles laid across it so the bedding wouldn't fall through. As the bedding was lifted out of the way, the pup, very close by, heard all the rumbling down in this cave. At the same time, the little boy told the pup, "Down in here is a large cave. My father hid all of the buffalo down in there."

The little boy was still talking when all of a sudden the pup broke away from the boy's hold around his neck, and down into the cave he ran. The little boy was crying after him, "Don't go down in there. My folks told me not to show anyone this cave. They will be very mad at me. Come back here puppy!" The pup was already far into the cave, he wasn't even listening anyway.

About the same time, Crowfeather Arrow was returning to his camp as the pup was running into the cave. He caught his son by surprise, he was still a-hollering down into the cave after the pup, "Come back here, come back here," when his father came inside and spoke to him. "What's going on here? What happened here? Why are you holding the bedding up over the cave?" Coming nearer to the boy and the cave, Crowfeather Arrow heard the faint barking of the pup, far down in the cave. He heard the bellow of the buffalo, they were stirring around far back inside of the cave. There wasn't anything he could do but wait for the buffalo to come stampeding out, there were thousands of them down in there.

About this time, the little pup, who was Bellyfat in disguise, had gotten back of the buffalo that were the furthest in the cave. He was barking hard and loud. It was even louder in the cave, and it didn't take much to stampede the mighty herd of buffalo.

The buffalo was on a dead run, stampeding to the entrance of this cave. The leaders of this mighty herd went past Crowfeather Arrow, narrowly missing him as they shot past him. Crowfeather Arrow stepped aside, his spear ready for instant use. In his mind he had it made up, he was going to kill that little puppy. He very well knew it wasn't a real puppy, but Bellyfat in disguise. What a dirty rotten luck, this Bellyfat had shown him up again. He must kill him for sure as he came out past him by this cave entrance, whether he came out as the puppy or in his own human form as Bellyfat, he'll kill him.

The many, many buffalo sped by him as he stood there waiting. They ran past him and ran past him, thousands upon thousands of them. He had hid them all down in this cave. He stood waiting for Bellyfat to come by, his spear ready to come down on the puppy or Bellyfat in his human form, the herd still running by him. After a long time, the sun was almost setting. This mighty herd of buffalo began to dwindle down, just the stragglers, the older ones coming last.

Bellyfat was always a step ahead of Crowfeather Arrow. He didn't survive his younger life ordeal for nothing, he knew what it was all about. Something, probably his power, told him what side of the entrance of the cave Crowfeather Arrow was waiting. He was still disguised as a puppy and running after the last of the buffalos. Knowing it was the last three head running to their freedom, the exit of this cave, and they didn't need anyone to push them along as the last three were following the main herd. Bellyfat, still as a pup, caught up with the first of these three head that were the last of the great herd of hidden buffalo. Bellyfat overtook this buffalo on its right side. He jumped for the long hair of the old buffalo just back of its right foreleg. Bellyfat hung on to this buffalo with his teeth, hidden from view among the long hair.

At the entrance, Crowfeather Arrow waited for the last of the buffalo and Bellyfat to appear from the great cave. He waited as the last three of the buffalo went by him. No Bellyfat come out. "What's holding him back in the cave?" he wondered. Those last three head were about gone behind all the timber, when he heard hollering behind the herd of buffalo. Turning around fast to see who was doing the hollering, Crowfeather Arrow got a glimpse of Bellyfat as he rounded the corner and went behind the timber. Bellyfat was in his original form, a human being again.

Once again, Bellyfat got the best of Crowfeather Arrow. Crowfeather Arrow was standing there, all puzzled about Bellyfat getting out and free of the cave. He was further embarrassed by this man, now!

# Napi and the Coyotes Jumping on Ice

Crowfeather Arrow was very embarrassed. He couldn't face his people, he must become someone else if he was to go near the people that knew him. He was still the disciple that Creator Sun had put here on Earth to teach the people all about living, survival on Mother Earth, but he had gone wrong. That power that was entrusted to him by Creator Sun, he was using it for his own benefit, to make a name for himself, and it wasn't working out as he planned.

Instead of being someone else, he must be that disciple again to once more go among his people. He must be Napi again and leave Crowfeather Arrow where it made the last embarrassment for him. Since he became Crowfeather Arrow, it was nothing but embarrassment after embarrassment.

Back to his natural self as Napi, he moved away from the cave that he hid the buffalo in. This huge cave still stands among the Porcupine Hills to this day. At least some of it remains and probably the most part of this cave has caved in. This is presently located north of Brocket, Alberta, Canada, in the Porcupine Hills.

Napi slowly moved towards the people. He didn't want to face them just yet, he was still a-feeling the embarrassment Bellyfat had caused him. The cold winter overtook him as he moved along. He had camped along a small creek with much windbreak, and there he had to stay for that winter. The days wore on, and as they went by, his food was also being used up. It was one of those extra-hard winters, he couldn't hardly get out to rustle for food most of the time, because of the cold and deep snow.

All that dried meat he had stored for his winter use, was going fast because of the weather. He just couldn't get out to replenish the larder.

The day came when the weather broke. It cleared up for a change and Napi took the advantage fast, because his food was getting very small and he must in some way supplement what he had left. Not having much to eat, he didn't want to short-change the family by taking a little of it along for lunch. He figured he might get lucky and kill some kind of game along the way. He left without taking lunch.

It was grueling for him to walk in the snow, it had not gone down very much. He took to the creek which had thick ice on it, and the wind had blown off most of the snow. It was better walking, but not too good for hunting.

All day long he walked and walked. Winter days are very short, he didn't have too much time to hunt. He was getting mighty hungry, his stomach was growling from hunger, but he didn't want to give up. He must try to get more food for the family.

He went farther along the ice and he was just so very hungry, there wasn't anything that he could nibble on, not in the coldest of the winters. No berries of any kind, they were all off of the bushes. He just had to stay hungry. Up ahead of him, he thought he heard a faint noise, it sounded like a group or someone singing or having a good time. He went on slowly, listening at the same time. Yeah, yeah, ahead of him. He could hear them better, but he couldn't make out what they were saying or if they were singing. He must get closer.

Slowly coming around a bend, he seen these coyotes jumping up and down in the middle of this small creek, on the ice. He heard them, too, very distinctly. They were singing and jumping at the same time. Every once in a while the coyotes would bend down to pick up something and eat it. Napi had to find out what they were doing and what they were eating. He was very, very hungry.

Slowly going towards them, Napi began to cry, "*Aye, aye, aye niss-gah-nuk, ah-ni, nah-goo-kah-wahn-ists, ah-hey.* Aye, aye, aye, that my little brothers I'd like to do too."

Napi was close enough now to see what they were eating. As the coyotes jumped on the ice, pieces of belly fat would come out through the ice. Their jumping was squeezing that fat out, and as it came up through the ice, they ate it.

The coyotes kept on jumping, telling each other that it was only their big brother Napi coming and asking to join them. The coyotes let Napi join them in their jumping on the ice for food. "Before you start to jump, we must let you know the restrictions to this dance on ice. You must not do this all the time, this kind of ice dance is only for very, very hard times, when you are on the verge of starvation. If you do this dance often, it's no good, it backfires."

The coyotes gave him the high sign to dance and to sing that same song they were singing. "Don't try to change the song or it won't work for you." Up and down, up and down, Napi danced, while at his feet belly fat would come out from beneath the ice. He would bend over pick it up and eat it. He was very hungry and it was getting late in the day. The coyotes had enough, they left but Napi was still a-going, trying to fill himself up with the belly fat.

After a long go at the ice dance, Napi finally decided he had enough. Back towards his camp he went along the ice, but every once in a while he stopped to dance to get more to eat of the belly fat, he was hungry. He would fill up, but a little while after he would get hungry again, so he would stop and do the ice dance again. Again and again he stopped to do the ice dance those coyotes taught him.

Before he ever reached home, his camp, he had done the ice dance over and over again, eating as he danced it.

It was just before he reached his camp when he decided he must have his final ice dance for the day and to fill up for the night. He stopped again in the middle of the ice and began the singing again and his dancing up and down, jumping hard to get that belly fat a-coming and singing harder. Napi jumped up and down. At last things began to come up out of the ice. He stooped over to pick up what came out. To his utmost surprise, the stuff he picked up oozed all over his hands. It was soft coyote droppings, and not the belly fat that usually came up out of the ice.

*Coyotes Dancing on Ice*

This taught Napi another important lesson: never to do more then the restriction requires.

# Napi Doctors
# A Girl He Killed

Napi had been on the go since he got himself into trouble over the coyotes' ice dance, many days ago. In those very early days, the many camps of the Natives were many days apart, because of the scarce population. So Napi had a long way to go.

Napi was going along one of the many streams that were very abundant at the time. Many red willows, the diamond willow, birch and cottonwood trees grew along all rivers and waterways. As he came over a little rise, he seen far ahead of him, a very large encampment. It was even larger than the one he just left in a hurry. Many, many tipis were in the circle encampment.

The people of those very early days moved around constantly, always after their main food source, the buffalo. They moved from one *pis-kun* to another to be near these buffalo jumps that were so important to their way of mass killing of the buffalo.

These *pis-kuns* or buffalo jumps were built at the bottom of a low-cut bank or a low cliff, and most generally these slaughtering places had to be near a lake or a running creek, near some water where they could wash the meat and the entrails off. At times when the butchering was being done, the manure of the carcass gets all over these edible parts and has to be washed off.

The Natives of these countries never waste an edible part of all they kill or dig for food. About the only thing that is not used too much are the bones of the buffalo, but even those bones are trimmed and soft boiled for soup. The flesh is all eaten off, and some of the smaller pieces of bones are used for such things as necklaces, bracelets, or just plain tipi ornaments. The spinal bones are the decoration for the Native bedstead, and these butterfly-shaped bones are also used to ward off the bad sleeping spirits of the night. These butterfly-shaped bones are also hung up near the top of a tipi for the same purpose, to ward off bad night spirits. On painted tipis one can see this butterfly painting near the top at the back. These are called sleeping spirits. They are to give the owners a good night's sleep, no nightmares or having a hard time to go to sleep. They worked if you have faith in them.

The buffalo horns are for the different types of headdresses the Native wore, and were also used for drinking cups and spoons and for water or soup. In the very early days, the larger of the buffalo horns was made to be airtight, a cover was fitted on the open end. These large horns were used to carry live charcoal from one camp as they moved to another camping place. Of course, in a long distance, the carrier of the live charcoal had to stop several places to remake a large charcoal from making another fire along the way. This was done until they had reached their next camping place. Then from one fire, other fires were lit.

The hide was used for the dwelling or tipi, and it was used also for their bedding, the tipi lining, and the rugs for the bare floor. To cover whatever sacred things the owner might have. Some of the hide isn't tanned. This raw hide is semi-tanned, between hard and soft, and used for storage of clothing and food, especially dried meat and pemmican.

The hoofs were used as bells. They too were soft boiled, and cleaned out. Oh yes! All that soft part of the inside of the hoof was very delicious. If you haven't tasted a soft-boiled hoof, you don't know what you're missing. Maybe you have eaten pig's knuckles or pig's feet, it's all the same, only the larger hoof has a better flavor.

The *pis-kun* was built at the end of a long, flat land that ended with a steep bank at a creek canyon, or just a bluff. The buffalo are kept within a wide, V-shaped pile of rocks, with the point of the V ending at the cliff. A man hides behind about every third or fourth pile of these rocks, to scare the lead buffalo on into a faster run. If the buffalo runs to the other side of the V, the man on that side jumps up to scare the lead buffalo on. As the man jumps, he has both hands on a large robe, waving it up and down before him to scare the buffalo. The stampeding herd of buffalo goes faster and faster. As the leaders reach the edge of the cliff, they are unable to stop. Even if they did, the herd in back would push them on over to their deaths. Those in the rear of the buffalo herd follow them on over to their death.

At the base of this *pis-kun* or buffalo jump, the men build an enclosure or a corral of piled logs with all the branches intact and high enough that the buffalo couldn't jump over the corral, and thickly laid so they couldn't crawl through. These logs are laid against the cliff on one side of the *pis-kun* and away from the cliff in a big half-circle to the other side of the *pis-kun*. Large enough logs are also tied down from the cliff near the bottom and across from one end of the corral to the other end. This was to ensure that the buffalo couldn't try to escape by climbing back up the bank or cliff.

Not all of the buffalo get killed as they fall over the cliff. Many of them survive the fall, because those that went over before them cushion their fall. Those that aren't hurt or crippled from the fall, but are unable to run much, are killed with stone mallets or the Native large hammer (but only after the uncrippled buffalo are shot and killed with the bow and arrow). After all buffalo are killed, then the women and children come into the corral to help dress out the kill.

This method of slaughtering buffalo in herds was used many, many years before the coming of horses and the whiteman. Where there wasn't a buffalo jump, another method was used to kill the buffalo. This method is used as it is getting light enough to see in the early morning, or about twilight of the evening, just as the shadows get deeper. The native men surround the herd of buffalo some time in the afternoon and follow them to wherever the buffalo may bed down. When all or most of the buffalo bed down for the night, these men then get their coyote outfits on them. A coyote outfit is only a tanned coyote hide with the head intact and mounted, like the present-day taxidermists do. These coyote hides are put over the men's upper torso and the head. They then crawl out among the buffalo herd with their bow and arrows and kill the buffalo at will until they have their want of the herd. Signals are given among the men to let each other know that all have killed plenty for their use.

Of course, in those early days, all animals were very plentiful. The buffalo is never afraid of the coyote, and many coyotes each day comes among the herd, so what's to scare the buffalo when many coyotes come among them from all sides? But they are surprised as the coyotes start their kill with their bow and arrows.

These ways of killing buffalo was mostly done away with when horses came into the country, about the last of the 1600s or the first part of the 1700s. When the horse came in to the hands of the Native, it was used to chase the buffalo and shoot off the horse's back only with those bow and arrows. After the gun came into the hands of the Natives, chasing and killing the buffalo became very simple for them, because of the gun's power.

Napi was very hungry, he hadn't eaten all day. It had been several days like this. His stomach was just so empty that his stomach walls seemed like they were rubbing against one another.

The people of this camp had just gotten through with their almost daily killing of the buffalo at the *pis-kun*. Out in front of mostly all of the tipis fresh meat was hanging from the drying racks that were always part of the camp. Some were even still carrying fresh meat from this *pis-kun*, while other women were still washing the meat and entrails at the river's edge. Much smoke was in the air from the many fireplaces being lit at almost every camp or tipi.

Napi's mouth was watering so much from seeing all the fresh meat and those delicious sights of the entrails, the tripe, the brisket, the liver, the kidneys, and all of the other delicacies that were for raw eating.

To the Native of these Americas, eating raw food—especially those insides of the buffalo, and even in these days the insides of the cattle that took the place of our once great herds of buffalo, our main source of food—was for building the body and for purification of one's blood system. In those days of the buffalo there was no garbage strewn all over the countryside, like today. The buffalo fed on pure, clean healthy hay, wild grass, no chemicals to poison that grass. The buffalo was a very clean animal, and from what it eats everyday, the buffalo was the healthiest animal throughout its whole body. Therefore, when eaten raw, some parts of it (and mostly those entrails or insides of the buffalo), the raw intake was like getting pure vitamins right from the source it comes from. Those Natives of them days are so healthy, their lifespan averaged about one hundred and twenty years of age. It wasn't until the coming of the whiteman and his food that my ancestor's lifespan dropped to about thirty years of age. It was from the intake of foreign food and how it was grown. The lifespan of the Native came back up again as they got used to the food of the whiteman, which today is right around seventy years old.

As Napi came walking into the circle of this very large camp, without hesitation he walked right to the first tipi that was nearest to him. Without stopping he made the entering sound as he got to the doorway and went right on in to the tipi, right to the visitor's side inside of the tipi, Napi made his way. And without waiting for approval from the owners of this tipi, Napi sat down and made himself comfortable.

Napi finally took notice of the three old women that were in this tipi. He didn't wait for any word from them. Napi asked them if they wouldn't be kind enough to feed him, as he was starving, he had traveled a long way and for many days. One of the old women jumped up, and from the rawhide pot she got a piece of gristly meat. It was more of a muscle then meat. From her parfleche food case, she took out a dried belly fat. These she served to Napi. There wasn't a strip of fresh meat to hang from their meat hanger within the tipi, nor was there any fresh meat hanging out on their drying racks outside of the tipi. Napi noticed this as he sat there, wondering why these old women didn't have any fresh meat to dry. Everyone else in this camp was bringing in fresh meat and entrails, and these poor old women are just sitting in here when they should be bringing in their fresh meat too.

Napi didn't ask questions right then, he was very hungry. He didn't care what kind of food they fed him, as long as it filled him to satisfy that hunger. Between mouthfuls, Napi asked the old women why they fed him like this when everyone else was bringing fresh meat to their tipis.

One of the old ladies answered him "*Kuy-yo,*" an expression of resignation by older women. "We are made to wait until everyone has gone from the *pis-kun*, then we get to go there to take what's left over, if any. Most of the time it's only the gristle parts of the necks and pieces of belly fat that are unwanted by the people left in the *pis-kun*. Those we get.

"We are helpless to go out for our own, and we don't have anyone to go out for us to help in getting fresh meat. So we are a burden to the people here. We haven't any place to go, we just have to suffer along the best we could and always get what's left over."

"*Huh-ah-yah, mah-gop-yiw,*" said Napi. This is an expression by older men meaning "all is not well, it's bad." "After I get through eating I'll go to the *pis-kun* and see if I can't pick up a few pieces of fresh meat for you women," said Napi.

Getting up after his meal, Napi asked the old women if he couldn't sleep here for the night. The old ladies readily agreed. Napi took leave of them. As he left out of the doorway, he said he would go to the *pis-kun* and would be back. Coming to the *pis-kun* and looking around for fresh meat, he just couldn't find any to bring to the old ladies.

Coming back to the old ladies' tipi, Napi went inside again to let the old ladies know that there wasn't any fresh meat to be found at the *pis-kun*. They must wait until tomorrow, as all of the hunters were going out again to bring more buffalo to the *pis-kun*. Then we will have fresh meat and lots of entrails too, even back fat that the old ladies hadn't a taste of for so long.

Everyone in those very early days went to bed with the birds. Birds roost right after the sun sets, and it was likewise for the Native. Probably a few of the chiefs are up a little bit late, because of visitors invited for an evening meal and for a smoke too.

Napi was very tired, he went to sleep right away. He must've slept sound, the old ladies had to wake him up as it was getting daylight. Food was all ready for him. Right after his meal, Napi left the tipi and walked around the camps. He wasn't one of the hunters today. Anyway, this gave him a good chance to throughly look this camp over.

It was after midday when the first of the buffalo stampeded into the *pis-kun*. It wasn't long after this that the whole herd was piled up down below the bluf and in the *pis-kun*. The men were now killing the live ones, those that were still able to run and those that were crippled. Shooting them with bow and arrows and clubbing them over the head with stone mallets to make sure none was alive when the women and children came into this *pis-kun*.

The women and children were called in, and they all came scrambling into the corral to start dressing the animals out. Their rawhide toboggans were left outside of the corral, and so were the dogs and travois.

Napi ran to the three old ladies' tipi and told them, *"Oki neet-ah-kik no-coo-dah-coo-sik.* Come, hurry, go hold your hands out" This means to go and fetch the food, or whatever is given you.

Napi walked ahead of the three old women, knives out as they all walked to the *pis-kun*. Without hesitation, Napi went right into the *pis-kun* and up to the first buffalo laying there. He took his knife out and went to work on it. He bared the brisket of the buffalo. Cutting some of that fresh brisket, he hollered at the three old women to come in so they could eat some nice fresh brisket. The three old women came in almost running, so happy to come into this *pis-kun*, which they hadn't seen for so many years now, at the same time bringing back those memories of their husbands that had long time ago passed on to Happy Hunting Grounds. The three old women readily ate the brisket Napi gave them. Napi opened up the buffalo, telling the three old women to help him get the entrails out so they could better work on them. The three old women readily jumped from one place to another to help out as much as they could. They enjoyed it so much, it had been long ago since they done this. As they took each delicious morsel out of the carcass, the ones that are for raw eating, the three would take a break and munch on the delicious bit. Napi skinned out about four of these dead buffalos for the three poor old women.

It was pretty well after midday when finally the four got through with their butchering and began to take the meat to the tipi. Once again the three old women had their drying racks filled. After all the meat was brought to the tipi, Napi asked the old ladies, *"Kik-ka-doke-kib-sca-pah ka-coo-kid-ose-poo-wow ah-boe-oh-si?* Did any of you get some of the blood so you could make a blood berry soup?'' The three old women almost spoke up at the same time to answer Napi that there wasn't a thing they had forgotten about dressing out a buffalo, they would be making berry soup with the blood they got. All four of them forgot their troubles and were very happy as they worked on the fresh meat.

Napi had to go back to the *pis-kun* to find his knife. It was so warm this mid-afternoon that some of the tipis had their doors wide open, right where Napi had to come through. Going to the *pis-kun*, Napi hadn't noticed this one tipi that had its doorway wide open. But coming back, this same doorway was facing him and he couldn't miss it. As he came towards the tipi he just couldn't help but see inside of it, and right in plain view on the bed was a girl laying there sleeping. She was covered with a robe on her upper body, but from the waist down she had kicked off the covers and, to make it worse, her dress was kicked way up too. Her legs from the thighs on down were bare, and for a teenage girl, a young girl, she looked so good to Napi that he stopped to gaze on here, his sex organs all worked up as he stood staring at her. Napi glanced all over, all around, and not a soul was around at this time. Most of the people were still down by the river washing the meat and fresh entrails.

Seeing no one in sight, Napi didn't hesitate no longer, he went inside and raped the teenage girl as she lay sleeping. It was very surprising to the teenage girl to be rudely awakened by someone on top of her and raping her. She started screaming and hollering for help, but Napi didn't give her much chance to be heard by other people. He clamped his hands down over her mouth and held them there. By her jumping around under him, Napi climaxed and was through. He was trying to talk her out of her hollering and screaming, but wouldn't listen to Napi. She just didn't care for his nearness, and besides he had already raped her.

Napi took his knife out and killed the poor girl by stabbing her to death. Napi took off after making sure the girl was dead, and he made his way to the three old women's tipi. Napi felt very sick over what he had done, killing a young girl just for his satisfaction wasn't one of his ways.

The three old women set a plate of food in front of Napi, all those delicious entrails and fresh meat they had just got that day. It looked good, but Napi hardly touched the food, he was feeling so bad about his bad deed. He felt sick in his stomach.

The three old women noticed right away that Napi didn't eat very hearty, and asked him what was wrong, why he didn't eat much. He said he just felt sick all of a sudden.

One of the old ladies took out her medicine bag and brewed some herbs for Napi. He was thought of very much in this old lady tipi, he had done a lot for these old women in the past few days, and now they wanted to return the good in some way to show their appreciation.

In the meantime, all of the people that were busy washing their meat and entrails were coming back to their tipis as they got through. One of them was the teenage girl's mother. She brought the washed meat to their tipi. She was going right back to fetch more when she thought she would ask the girl if she couldn't help with some of the meat and entrails. The mother turned to the bed and,as she did, her eyes seen blood all over the bed. She jumped to the girl's side, but it was too late, she was dead already. The woman began to scream and cry. She called her husband to come, he came in a hurry. All of their next-door neighbors, hearing about the girl getting killed by some one that raped her, were all feeling bad. Even in a camp like this, a great big camp, news gets around fast. In no time the news was heard by most of the camp, and Napi too, which made him all the sicker. It was a sad day for everyone. This was a rare doing among the Natives.

As the father came to see what had happened, he didn't say much. Tears came to his eyes, silently he stood there for a long time. After his moment of that long silence and tears, he called a camp crier to his side and talked to him. The camp crier went around the camps crying out the message of the slain girl. "We have ways to find out things like this, bad things, tonight we are going to find out what happened here while everyone was busy with the fresh meat that was gotten this day. Furthermore, don't anyone try to leave camp at any time. If anyone does, this will mean that they have something to do with today's killing." This was the message the father of the slain girl had the camp crier convey to the people of this camp.

Napi didn't have much of a choice. He couldn't leave the camp or he'd be the main suspect, and they would hunt him down no matter where he might hide. He just had to stay put.

Napi got sicker as things progressed about the slain girl. The old ladies gave him more of the brewed herbs to make him feel better, and they were very concerned over him. He was their only way of getting fresh meat for their camp.

During the night the dead girl's parents had a meeting with their close relations, about how to find the guilty person. They decided on a trick that might solve it in fast order. A plan was then adopted for the next day.

Very early the next morning all of the men, old and young, were called out by the camp crier to come to a certain brook not far from this camp. Even the very young boys that may have learned about sex were called along with the rest of the men of the camp. The men were all eager to get this over with, as none of them had guilty feelings about what had happened to the girl. Even the curious women of the camp came too, just to see who was guilty or who had done this dirty cruel deed. Everyone came except Napi.

The slain girl's father soon sent his closer men to go fetch Napi so he could show he too wasn't guilty of the crime that was committed in this camp.

The message was forwarded to him by the men that were sent for him. The three old women told the men that Napi wouldn't have had anything to do with the happening as he was sick all day long yesterday and is still sick. The men insisted on him being there to show his guiltlessness before all of these people.

"I'm very sick right now, but I'll be there to do what the rest of the men are going to do to show the people that I'm not to blame either."

Napi took his good old time as he got ready to go to the brook where all the people were congregating. He went along very slowly as he started out from the tipi. It happened that a friend of his, a close friend, was at the same time leaving for the brook for their trial. Napi met up with his friend and right away asked him if he couldn't help him out, as he was a very sick man at this moment. "In what way do you need help?" asked his friend. Napi said to him, "I need some of your power of flight. I'm weak from this sickness I have and I know I won't be able to jump the brook in this weak condition. Your power will help me jump safely across the creek."

Napi had found out about what was to take place from the men that had come to get him at the old women's tipi. He knew all the men had to jump the brook to prove they were not guilty. He passed this on to his friend.

After hearing his friend Napi was a sick man, the friend of Napis didn't hesitate to help Napi with his power of birds, flight power. In return, Napi put his knuckle-bone necklace around his friend's neck to show his appreciation for the power that was loaned to him. Almost there now, the two livened up their walk.

Everyone had now come to the place of trial. The dead girl's father told the crowd, "All of the men must jump this brook where I have marked it. Safely jumping it will mean you are not guilty of what happened to my daughter."

The men lined up in a single file away from the brook. The first man was given a signal to run and jump the brook. Away he went to the bank of the brook, running with all his might that he may jump the brook with ease. Up in the air he went, sailing smoothly across the brook and onto the opposite bank. The man on trial was given the signal to do his jump. He too made a remarkable jump across the brook, which was a sign of innocence. One by one the rest of the men jumped the brook to get them off of the suspicion list.

The trial was getting very close to Napi's turn. There was only one ahead of him, his friend that loaned him some power, and the one also wearing his necklace of knucklebones. His friend was called to show his innocence or guilt. Backing away from the brook to get a good run, Napi's friend ran with all his might. At the bank he sailed up in the air and over the water of the brook, saying, "*Huh-ah-yah*," a grunt or word for failure or mistake. Napi's friend landed short of the opposite bank and went into the water. Right then and there, the power that was loaned to Napi was taken back by his friend. His friend knew right away it was the knuckle-bone necklace that shortened his jump, and now he was the suspect of the girl's death.

Even then, Napi knew he had to either show his innocence or the guilt that's been with him all this time. Just before he was told to jump the brook too, Napi made a suggestion to the father of the slain girl. If Napi were to bring the girl back to life, the men shall all be innocent. Napi had a daring plan. He knew he would never be able to jump the brook without power of some sort, his friend had already taken back the power he had loaned him. So now other plans had to be followed.

The father of the slain girl readily agreed to Napi's suggestion. He knew it was better to have his daughter come back to life then to punish whoever had done this awful deed.

The plan was announced to the people as they stood by the brook. Everybody was anxious to see the girl brought back to life, and Napi seen that all of these people were just as interested in the outcome of this doctoring by Napi. All went to the camp of the dead girl. She was laying there in her tipi as the people began to gather around it.

Napi was a little nervous as he came along with the last of the men. Beside him was the slain girl's father, watching Napi very closely so he wouldn't try to run out. Slowly coming to the tipi of the slain girl, Napi gave a glance all around him, probably seeking out the best avenue for escape.

Coming into the tipi and placing himself by the side of the dead girl in kneeling position, Napi cleared his throat and spoke to all of the people in this tipi and also to the people on the outside of the tipi, loud enough for everyone to hear him.

"First, before I start doctoring this girl, I must say that I have much supernatural power to help me, and I have a few strange restrictions for all of you, inside and outside of this tipi. The first is, I need a big hot fire inside here that I have to use in my doctoring. Next! I need a very large piece of belly fat. Next! I want all of the women to go home and fetch their stone hammers, bring them back here with you. The men must all go to their tipis and bring their spears with them here. If either you women or men don't want to bring your stone hammer or your spear, you must stay inside your tipis until my doctoring is done. I'll give the word."

Everyone was anxious to get this doctoring underway. All the women and men hurried to their tipis to get their stone hammers and spears. Those that didn't want to be bothered about this doctoring stayed put in their tipis. The rest, which weren't too many, returned to the dead girl's tipi. Mostly everyone that had returned with their stone hammers and spears fitted into this tipi.

After all had returned and no one else was coming, Napi spoke again. "This belly fat I shall spread upright near the hot fire to get it melting hot between those two stakes driven in the ground. I want the women all on one side of this tipi, the south side, and all the men on the north side. I want you all to face one another, every two face each other. You women, hold you stone hammers up in the air as if ready to strike one another. The men too, hold your spears up as if ready to spear one another when I start singing my doctoring song. And as you all sit there as if ready to attack one another, sway your bodies and your arms, your head too, with the time of my song's rhythm. All of you do this with your eyes tightly closed, and if there's anyone outside, they must also keep to the time of my music with their eyes closed tightly.

"Anyone here doesn't comply with the restrictions, something very bad shall happen to him or her, so beware and do what I say."

A very hot fire was a-going now, and the belly fat was hanging near the fire between two stakes that were driven into the ground. It was very hot and beginning to melt, as it was near the fire. The women were all set, every two were facing one another with their stone hammers up in the air as if ready to strike each other. The men too were ready with their spears up in the air and facing one another, as if ready to spear each other.

Everything in order, Napi began his doctoring. As he sang his power song, the people began to sway back and forth to the time of Napi's music. Their arms and heads too were in time with the music, and all had their eyes very tightly closed. Napi seen this, as he would glance all around him every once in a while. As he sang along he began to speed it up more and more. "*Ki-ahk-si-ki-wahts-ah, ki-ahk-ki-si-wahts-ah, ki-ahk-si-ki-wahts-ah.* I wonder what's going to happen to her." All of the people went right along with this song and its rhythm. Faster and faster everyone went swaying back and forth.

"*Kik-ah kik-ah.* Wait, wait." All stopped and waited to hear Napi speak. "Now all listen well with your ears. My spirit helper is now going to come in as soon as we start my song again. All close your eyes as tight as you all can and sing to the top of your voices. If anyone tries to see my spirit helper, my spirit helper will not do its work and the girl must go on to Happy Hunting Grounds."

The girl's folks pleaded with the crowd to do what Napi said, to keep the eyes closed tightly and sing as loud as they can.

The doctoring continued, everyone done what was to be done. The music went faster and faster, louder and louder, their body rhythm and arms went faster and faster along with their heads. All were going fast, when without anyone expecting such a thing, Napi jumped up. No one saw him, as everyone's eyes were tightly closed, and they were hollering to the top of their lungs. Napi jumped to the center of the tipi near the fire and the hot melting belly fat, which was just dripping hot. He grabbed it and swung it around the tipi. The hot grease splattered all over the people inside. Getting burnt from the hot grease made them strike one another with their stone hammers and their spears.

Almost everyone killed one another inside of this tipi, and at the same time Napi made a break for it. He ran and ran, away and away from it all, never to come back to this camp anymore.

# Napi and
# The Chickadees

Napi, as the disciple of Creator Sun, done a good job. But as time went on he overdone things, and besides he was using that power of Creator Sun that was entrusted to him for his own good, and not for the good of the people or the Creator. In other words, he was getting crazy over the power he had.

The weather was beginning to warm up. It was nearing spring and at times the sun would get very warm in the daytime. The ice was still on the small creek that he had wintered along. As it got to be spring-like weather, Napi would go out quite often now along this small creek on the ice, always in need of food and looking for it.

It was one of those days that he got up fairly early in the morning and got out to take a walk along the ice and hunt for food to supplement what he had in his parfleche cases, which had dwindled almost to nothing. Along the ice he went, hunting for bush rabbits or prairie chickens that roost on the trees. Slowly he went along, looking here and there for anything that was edible to him and his family.

Napi was a cunning being. He was very playful too, he loved games very much. At the same time, if he could use a game to his benefit, he wouldn't hesitate, even if it meant the life of another one, especially if he needed food.

He was going along the ice very slowly so he wouldn't scare the game up if there were any along this ice in the bushes. He had gone along quite far from his camp and it was just so nice and sunny along the creek that the ice was kind of thawing in places. Where it was a good windbreak, the sun got very warm.

Going along very quietly, some place ahead of him, Napi heard someone talking. It had a small voice. Stealing more quietly along the ice, Napi wanted to see who it was before he was seen by whoever was talking. Getting closer to the sound of talking, he now knew it was more then one doing the talking, and they all had small voices. They seemed to be having the time of their lives, they were laughing and sometimes hollering a little.

Coming around a bend along this little creek, and in a good warm place where the sun was shining, there on a low limb of a tree sat in a neat row several chickadees. They were all busy talking happily and excitedly.

Sneaking closer and closer, Napi wanted to see what they were so happy about. Going along under the cover of the bushes, Napi got very close, but he still couldn't see what it was all about. He decided to put on his usual act, cry and go towards them, begging them to let him in on the game. He knew it was some sort of a game they were playing. He didn't know if it meant food too, and that was the main thing he wanted to find out about.

Towards them Napi went, crying as he went towards them, "*Aye, aye, aye niss-gah-nuk, ah-ni nah-goo-kah-wahn-ists-ah-hey.* My little brothers, I too would like to do what you are doing." The chickadees didn't fly away, they told one another, "Its only our big brother, Napi, let him come on over to join us in our happy game."

The leader of this small group of chickadees met Napi as he came to them. Right away the leader told Napi, "We chickadees are playing a game we usually play as it gets close to springtime, the warmer days. It's a happy game for us, we feel very happy when the sun is getting warmer and the days get longer, because then food will be more plentiful and it will be warm too.

"Now, come to the limb of the tree and I'll show you what to do to play the happy game. Climb up here alongside of me on this limb and sit with us up here." Napi went along with the leader. He climbed up on the tree limb and sat with the rest of the chickadees.

Again the leader of the chickadees spoke to him. "This game is only when you are happy for good things, especially for food and warm days. You must not overdo it or you will surely feel the consequence of it. Just when you are very happy in the warmth of the day and your belly is full. This is what you do. You see that log over there laying in the sun? It's a dry, dry log that looks white from the sun's bleach. You are sitting here and the log is over there. What you do is look straight at the log and say, 'Nee-boo-muk.' This word will let your eyeballs fly out of the sockets to the tree I showed you. There they will stick until you say another word, 'Mut-ski-sub-ahk-goo-kii-nuk-im,' your eyeballs will fly back into their sockets. About four times you do this, not anymore then the four times. Now go ahead and play and be very careful and don't overdo it."

Napi up there on the limb with the chickadees said the word and his eyeballs flew out of their sockets. Right to the tree they flew and stuck on the side of it. For a brief moment he was silent, then those other words he said, his eyeballs flew from the log and back into their sockets they went. Four times he done this in short intervals. About that time the chickadees were through playing for the day. Again before they departed from Napi, the leader of them told Napi never to play it often. "Beware, beware," he told him. They left Napi to himself.

Napi was alone again and started back towards his camp. But along the way towards the camp, he would stop and climb a limb to play the eye game of happiness. Napi was just one of those people that listens, but never uses what he hears. Again and again he climbed on a limb to play.

Very near his camp, he thought to himself he would play the happy game once more before he reached the camp. He climbed up on a tree that had a

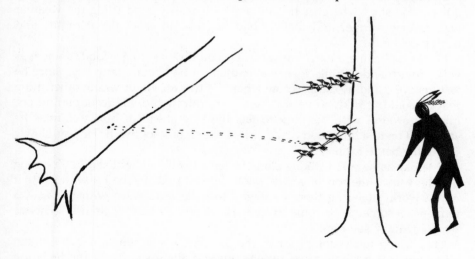

**Chickadees Playing the Eye Game**

very good dry log not far from it. The sun was getting very low, but it didn't make any difference to Napi. "*Nee-boo-muk*. Make summer," said Napi. Waiting for a moment, he said the words that brought the eyeballs back into the sockets, "*Mut-ski-sub-ahk-goo-ki-nuk-im*. Back into the eyesockets healed." Napi waited, but no eyeballs came back into place. Again he repeated the words, but still no eyeballs came back in.

Over and over he said the word to get his eyeballs back, but no such luck. He had overdone it again and now he was a blind man. He never uses the advice he hears, again the consequences of his foolishness.

# Napi and the Compassionate Woman

Live and learn was Napi's moto. He lived and he learned the hard way many times throughout his time here on Mother Earth.

He was a disciple of Creator Sun, sent to teach the people how to abide by the Creator's ways here on Mother Earth. But he wanted a name for himself, so he used that power to make name for himself. He did make a great name for himself, but all of the children of Creator Sun are influenced by that foolish life of Napi.

There he was, blind! No place to go, no one to guide him around, he was just plumb blind. He groped around on the ground. Finding a long stick to hold on to, he used it for a guide. He hit around in front of himself to find out if he was clear of all obstacles that he might trip on or run into.

For many days and nights he went around blind, and from his own foolish doings. He slept wherever he got sleepy. It was a good thing the weather was getting warmer and that he had his robe to cover up at nights and during cold days.

Napi was having a hard time of it. He couldn't see to get food, so he was very hungry and getting close to starvation. It had been many days since he lost his eyes, and he didn't know where he was at. Water was another thing that he couldn't find, so he was very, very thirsty too. He went on and on, groping around with his stick to feel the way ahead of him. At times he stumbled on to a little food or a drink of water, but not much. He was slowly losing the battle for life.

One day as he was walking along he felt a climb, a slight climb. Guessing that he was at the top of a little knoll, he stopped. He had a big idea that might work. Standing there be began to holler and wave with his arm, a motion for someone to come to him. He done this just by chance someone would actually see him.

That was a lucky doing, for in the distance a lone woman was walking along towards a small creek. As she walked along she heard the hollering from someone quite far. Looking all around, she seen this lone person on a small knoll waving at her, or so she thought. Making her way to this person, she saw he was a man. Right away she knew who he was, it was none other then Napi. Reaching him, right away she asked him why he was waving at her.

Napi was always ready with a good answer. He told her, "A few days ago it snowed a little and the sun was very bright as I was going along. I got snow blinded, but I heard faint footsteps in the distance so I waved to attract your attention so you could help me along until I'm able to see again."

The woman readily agreed to Napi's words. "I'll be glad to help you along until you are able to see again, then I'll go my way again."

The two of them got together, the woman became a seeing eye for Napi. The woman made a small arbor shelter for them near the woods where firewood was plentiful, and the creek was close by to use for drinking and cooking. There they were very happy, as they lived there while Napi was recuperating from snow blindness. The woman was getting enough food to live on, snaring small game and fowl, gathering some roots and barks to eat.

One day as the two were sitting outside of their little arbor shelter, the woman seen a big herd of buffalo going down towards the creek to quench their thirst. Right away she got very excited about them. "Come on, come on, let's try to kill some of those buffalo that are down there getting a drink of water." Leading Napi down with her, the woman worked as close as she could to the herd of buffalo without being seen. She was about ready to shoot, but was not too sure of herself, afraid she would miss a good chance and scare off the big herd of buffalo, which would leave them without fresh meat. Aloud she said, "I might just miss the shot and scare the buffalo off, then we will not have another chance like this for a long time or none at all."

Napi, jumping up to her side, told her, "Just aim the bow and arrow good and straight for me, I'll pull it and shoot it. If all is well, just keep aiming it for me while I do the pulling and shooting."

This they did. The woman aimed the bow and the arrow for Napi, and at her command Napi released the string to the bow and the arrow went straight and true, found the mark, and down went one buffalo. "Aim it for me again, aim it for me again. Hurry, hurry before the buffalo starts to running. We must kill more so it will last for a long time." Aim after aim, shot after shot, went straight and true, finding the mark and knocking the buffalo down one right after another. Many of them were killed by Napi's straight shots that day, before the big buffalo herd recovered from the surprise of being shot at.

Napi and the woman had already gotten together as man and wife long before this herd of buffalo came along, not long after the woman found him. Both of them got down to business to skin the buffalo and dress them out. Nothing was spared of all the killed buffalo, everything on them was either eaten or put to some use. This was the way of all the Natives of this country, never waste anything.

The two were almost through with their skinning when the woman told Napi, "We are just about through dressing out the buffalo. Go on ahead to that quaking aspen patch and build an arbor for us and make it large enough for our meat and for us to live in. Now go and hurry with it."

Napi, still blind from the chickadees' eye game, did not know if he ever would actually see again. He got busy to get to the quaking aspen patch, asking his wife to turn him towards the patch. The woman turned Napi, and told him to go straight ahead, he'd run into that patch. Going straight ahead, Napi went along for quite a ways before he bumped into the trees of the quaking aspen patch.

He just couldn't see a darn thing, but he was trying to act natural, like he could see a little. He went on into the bushes and, with his flint knife, cut enough small quaking aspen trees to make an arbor. Right along the patch of trees he built one. He had it almost done when he found out he was a little short of small trees to complete the arbor. He had to go and get more small trees to use. But on returning to the spot, he just couldn't find the arbor he was working on. So, instead of trying to find it, he went and got more small trees to use for a new arbor, only to lose this one too when he had to go after more small trees.

Arbor after arbor he built, only to lose them because he couldn't find them. He couldn't even run into any of them. About this time the woman got through with her chore of cutting the meat. She brought the first load of meat to the arbor she thought was ready by now, but to her surprise she seen all of the arbors that he had started on next to the quaking aspen patch. She dropped her load down by the first one she came to and hollered at Napi, "What are you doing with all of these partly built arbors?" Napi answered her, "I built several, I thought you would take your pick of them. We will finish the best one of them with the hides you are bringing up. I'll help you carry the meat up here now, but you will have to guide me back and forth."

The two of them hauled all the fresh meat to the new camp, they had all the meat they could use for a long time. The two settled down for a good living now with all the food that they needed.

There wasn't anything to do but eat and sleep, even love too, while he was snow blind. The woman was getting very suspicious of Napi. It had been a very long time since they got together, and through her experience with snow blindness, she thought he was taking a long time for his recovery.

During this time, when there were many buffalo hoofs around, Napi made a belt for the woman. This belt was made with hoof bells, and these hoof bells hung all the way around the belt.

He asked the woman to come to him, and he tied the bells on her. She asked Napi what the reason was for tying those bells on her. Answering her, he said, "I put those bells on you because you have done many things for me since we met, I couldn't see, you were my eyes. I had to repay you in some way and show my love for you at the same time, and besides, those bells will sound so cute on you while you are walking around." Wherever the woman went, Napi heard the sound of those bells and knew where she was at, at all times when she was near. He was always so afraid she would sneak out on him and leave him for good.

The love and happiness went on for some time, and the two lived among all the food for time to come. It was a leisurely life, not much to do but lay around. In those days there wasn't a modern way to clean the hair and head, but to wash it with some roots and clean water. If there was any vermin on it, mostly it was hand-cleaned by the woman. So most leisure times, this head cleaning by hand was done, feeling around for the nits or eggs of the vermin or just plain looking for the vermin itself.

The two were very used to one another, they were inseparable by now. This time of leisure had to come at the time Napi was lying about his blindness. It was in the midday that Napi laid his head on his woman's lap and asked if she could look for vermin, his head was itching very much. Like most lovestruck people, she helped him to lay on his back so she could look very good for vermin.

Laying in a comfortable position, Napi laid his head on the woman's lap and she began to look through his head, fooling around with it made Napi very drowsy, which made him forget his guard about his eyes. Before this, he kept those eyelids closed when around the woman, for fear she might find out he didn't have any eyeballs in his sockets.

Napi was almost falling asleep when he forgot to keep those eyelids shut. He was drowsy and ready to fall asleep, and the woman was looking right down into his face. She seen his eye sockets for the first time up close. "This man doesn't have any eyeballs in his eye sockets. He's been lying to me all this time, he's been using me, he'll never be able to see again, I'm stuck with him unless I run away from him, and now. I'll just be a slave to him and a seeing eye for him the rest of my life. I'm young yet, I must go and leave him now."

Napi was almost asleep, when all of a sudden the woman jerked Napi's head off of her lap. She jumped up and hollered at him, "You are totally blind, you've been lying to me, you will never see again." She took off away from him and their camp. Napi didn't hesitate one second, he jumped up and after her he went. For some strange reason he was right behind her as she tried to get away. He was right on her heels running, at times just barely missing her dress as he would grab for it. She didn't notice, but as he chased her, they were close to the creek.

All at once, as she was running along and with him right behind her, she thought about those hoof bells around her middle. It was them he heard and was following all this time while she was trying to get away. She must get rid of the bells in hurry before he catches her.

She was untying those bells as she was running towards the creek. Any bend in any waterway or river is usually quite deep, and it was this bend in the small creek she was running for. By the time she reached the bend she had the bells free from her waist. As she ran past the bend, the woman took the bells and rattled them as she threw them into the creek, where she knew it was quite deep. Napi, running after the sound of the bells, kept right on a-going as the woman turned and ran from the creek. Into the deep part of the bend Napi landed in the water. This was quite a surprise for him, landing in the water. He didn't know what to do right then, but to flounder around in the water until he got his bearings again.

Napi stood up in the water. It was almost up to his neck, but he was touching bottom, which was quite a relief to him. First he went this way, then that way, feeling around for the shore of this small creek. He was going around and around, feeling and groping with hands and feet, trying to get out of the water. Finally, after a long while, he got into shallow water. And the shallower the water got, the closer he knew he was getting to dry land. At last out on the dry land once more, Napi laid down to rest and think what to do next. After a long while he got up and groped around for a long slim stick to use as a feeler to guide him. Finding one he could use and handle, Napi went very easy and away from the sound of the running water. Straight away from the water he walked, feeling ahead with the stick he had in his hands.

Away and away from the sound of the creek he went. All at once he knew he was climbing a very steep incline, the bank of the creek. It was a long steep climb, at times he would slide almost all the way back down this bank. At last he was on top of this darn bank where people could see him from a distance.

# Napi and the Coyote

Napi was still very blind yet. He never did get his eyes back. They were still stuck to that bleached dry log, laying wherever it was along the creek.

Napi couldn't even find his own little arbor home where he knew there was a lot of food, all of that meat. The woman ran away already, so if he could find the location he'd be all right for awhile. But falling into the running water and groping around to get out of it turned him all around. He didn't even have a faint recollection where it was at.

He was very glad that he got up this bank where it was higher, and now anyone passing by could see him a little easier up here. He walked along slowly, feeling ahead with his long stick. He would notice when he walked up a little high place or go downhill a little. Even the big steep places he felt more as he walked up and down those hills, wherever it was he was going.

It's been several days since he lost his woman, he was surviving on the wild growth of weeds and barks of certain trees that he came upon by chance. Napi was getting awful hungry for meat, meat was the Plains people's main nourishment.

One day as he was walking along, several days after the woman took off from him, he noticed he had begun to climb again and it was a very steep climb. It took quite a while to get to the top of this hill, and by the feel of his legs, the hill was high. He felt around when he reached the top of the hill, he tried all different directions till he came to where it began to go down again. He found a rock large enough to sit on, and there he sat down to rest a while, and most of all to attract attention again.

Sitting there thinking things over, he didn't know whether to feel sorry for himself or to be thankful he was alive. With his wild ideas again, he began to wave his arm as if he was waving at someone to come to him, as he did before when the woman came to him.

It happened that a coyote was going by away off from this hill. The coyotes are very sharp-eyed and have shifty eyes, taking in everything that comes into their view. So it was nothing for the coyote to see Napi up there on the hill, waving wildly to the coyote—that's what the coyote thought.

Coyotes are very cunning, and this coyote wasn't any different. Right away he didn't trust what he seen, he must go a roundabout way to find out why this man was waving so wildly. Instead of going right towards the man on the hill, the coyote went around in a circle-about way and kept his eyes on him as he did this. The coyote soon found out that this man waving frantically wasn't even looking at him, the man was still there waving towards the other way. The coyote thought he would go up a little closer to the man. Getting as close as he could without him noticing, the coyote stopped almost directly in front of the man, a little to the side. This man didn't even look towards him and, to make things more uncertain, this man was none other then Napi, the big brother of everyone of life. The coyote's suspicion was confirmed by what he done. The man Napi was blind.

Napi was always playing tricks on people or his animal and bird brothers. The coyote thought it wouldn't do any harm to play a trick on Napi for a while. Stealing up to him, no sound coming from his soft-stepping feet, the coyote got up to Napi, almost touching distance. Still he didn't notice the coyote. The coyote felt more secure now that he knew Napi was really blind.

This coyote had a very bad sore foot on one side of his fore feet, it was so bad that it had begun to smell, getting to stink, and he knew it. As Napi sat on the rock waving his arm for someone to come to him, the coyote stole up very close to him. Just as Napi came down with the waving arm, the coyote quickly moved closer to Napi and held his smelly foot to Napi's nose. Napi got a quick whiff of that smelly foot. He jerked his head back and said, "*Huh ah-mouhk?* What's this?" The coyote quickly got back away from Napi and stood still while he watched him trying to figure out the smell he had a whiff of. Every time Napi waved and then stopped, the coyote was right there to give him a whiff of that smelly foot.

After a few whiffs of the coyote's smelly foot, Napi said, "*Huh-ah-yuh goke-pis-kaa-stoo-dids-imoo, nis-sta-moo-wah, oo-gaa-bis-kuni.* Oh my, oh gosh, it smells just like my brother-in-law's old buffalo jump." An old buffalo jump was a smelly place where many unused parts of the buffalo piled up and rotted.

The coyote, hearing this, was quite amused over it, smiling about the words Napi just said. So again and again the coyote would hold his rotten foot to Napi's nose and give him a whiff of that smelly foot.

Napi didn't mind one bit. But deep in his cunning mind, he had it figured out that was someone playing tricks on him, and he had sensed just about how the trickster would stand. In his mind he had it that this trickster wasn't going to be laughing very long if his plan worked.

Napi was waving again and the coyote stole to his side and again held his paw under Napi's nose. Napi didn't wait, no hesitation this time, he made a wild grab for the body of whoever it was that was playing tricks on him. It was a big surprise to the coyote as Napi grabbed him around his body and hung onto him, talking as he wrestled the coyote down and got on top of him. *"Ah un-nah-yi das-sim-atch-oo-ga cuh-sty-in-amoo-goo.* Yeah, you giving me a smell, no one will hold for you." Napi sat on the coyote. And with one hand holding the coyote's head, the other hand was digging into the coyote's eyes, pulling them out of the coyote's eye sockets. The coyote was begging with all his might, *"Nis-ah, nis-ah nuwk-pi-kim-oo-kit doo-ksgum-ah nu-wub-spah mah-duse doo-skum-ah.* Big brother, big brother take pity on me with one eye, take one eye and leave me with one eye." Napi didn't listen to this plea, he took both eyes out and put them into his own eye sockets, which gave him something to see with again.

This is the true reason why some people have coyote eyes, very light grayish-bluish eyes.

Once more Napi had his vision. No one knows the coyote's fate, what became of the one that lost his eyes to Napi.

Probably this was the very first transplant of eyes in this place of Mother Earth we live in.

*Napi Plucks Out the Coyote's Eye*

# Napi and the Big Prairie Chicken

The human race is influenced by this Creator Sun's disciple, Napi, in many ways by his teachings to the children of Creator Sun and Mother Earth. Many of our learnings are very foolish, and many are the way our Creator Sun wanted us to follow.

Whether we like it or not, we act very foolish many times. About half of the time, we act the way we should in the first place. For this is the true way we were taught by Creator Sun's disciple, Napi. These are the precedents he taught to live by.

There were no horses in the days of Napi, people were dependent on their feet to take them from one place to another and to move their belongings. The huge dogs of those very early days were used to haul a travois that was attached to the dog's back with a harness made of tanned buffalo hide. On this early day transport, belongings of the people were hauled as they moved about. People with many dogs were wealthy. With many dogs, many things could be transported from one place to another without the owners having to carry any burden on their backs.

Napi wasn't any different, he was always foot and going from one place to another, probably seeking more adventure. This day wasn't unusual for Napi as he went along out in the great prairies. This day was one of the most beautiful days that ever happened, and Napi was taking the full advantage of it. For once he wasn't hungry or tired like he always was. Going along leisurely with not a worry in his mind, feeling as free as the wind, not a thing to be afraid of.

Birds, animals, and life itself was abundant everywhere he gazed. Food was everywhere—all of the game fowls, game animals, and wild edible growth, sustenance to people and all life. There were many prairie chickens along with everything else. Napi was getting a little mad over those prairie chickens. Each time he came a little close to one, it would fly away. He either made a very loud frightening noise as he walked along, or they were just naturally afraid of him. He didn't like that one bit. As he went along, the prairie chickens still a-flying off as he came too close to them, Napi began to boil a little inside of him. Further along and just in front of him, a big prairie chicken took off as Napi got too close again. This time he didn't wait. Napi hollered after him, "Yeah! You big cowards, you! You are always so afraid and ready to fly away from just a little noise. Why couldn't you be brave like I am?"

Napi went about his ways and the prairie chickens flew away as they heard his footsteps coming. Napi repeated those words he told all of those prairie chickens that flew off in fright of him. As he went along, an extra big prairie chicken flew away as he got too near it. Napi immediately hollered after him,

"Coward, coward you fly off like something was after you. Why couldn't you be brave like I am?"

When the big prairie chicken heard Napi say what he said, he made a big circle in his flight and came flying back to Napi, landing close by him. The big prairie chicken didn't hesitate one bit to tell Napi, "I've heard you every day calling us prairie chickens cowards. I want you to know that we are not the cowards you think we are, we just naturally get out of people's way. Not because we fear them, but they may not see us and will step on us, which would kill us. To make this strong of my words, I'll play a game with you,

*The Prairie Chicken Frightens Napi*
*and Wins a Bet*

Napi. You say you are brave and I'm a coward, but we shall continue to go about our ways each day and in time we shall find out who is the true coward."

Napi, knowing he had more brains and a better knowledge of things, readily consented to play the game. He'll teach these prairie chickens a thing or two about cowardice, he'll show them who the bravest is. The game was on.

The test of cowardice was to come any time. There wasn't any specified time. Both were alert as they went about their ways each day. Many days elapsed and the game was a little overlooked by Napi, but the big prairie chicken never did get it off of his mind.

Napi had almost completely forgotten about that game he was playing with the prairie chicken. He had so many other things in his mind each day.

Napi was going someplace in a fast walk, and not a thing was on his mind, not even the game he was playing with the prairie chicken. All of a sudden, just before his foot touched the ground, from under that foot shot the big prairie chicken, and with as much wing noise as he could make as he flew away. Napi was so frightened from this sudden noise that he fell on his back as he jumped in fright. He had fainted, and to make it worse, Napi messed in his breechclout. Napi had to go to the nearest water and wash himself off. While Napi was sitting in the water taking a bath, the big prairie chicken came to Napi and laughed in his face, saying, "Now who is the bravest of us two?" Napi was too embarrassed to reply, he knew he was beat by a small bird. Napi could only say, "Life shall be this way for the future."

This was another precedent set by Napi.

# Napi and the Rock

Napi, as the Disciple of Creator Sun, is known by many names among the many different nationalities. If you were to dig back in the past, our legends are the same, and they are still very similar to one another.

It had been thousands of years since human beings were put here on Mother Earth to live and appear as the image of Creator Sun. Scattered all over Mother Earth, they lost contact with one another. Their language changed to where they had different languages and couldn't understand one another, and their customs were changed too. But if you give these customs and languages a closer look, they're not as strange as they seem. Because some time ago, those many different people had almost identical customs and languages.

The only major difference about the people of this world is their ways and dress in the many different climates this world has. Other then that, we are the same people Creator Sun put here on Mother Earth to live as he does— and most of all, to love one another and all life of Creator Sun and Mother Earth. It is the wonderful work of our Creator that we don't all speak the same language or have all the same customs. If we did, we wouldn't've lasted long here on Mother Earth, because all things would be the same.

Napi was a very good disciple, a good teacher, and the people of Mother Earth learned many things from him. Respect to our Creator Sun and to one another was of great importance, to acquire food was great too. Getting well from using roots, barks, and weeds was a wonderful gift also—of course, sickness was unheard of in those earlier days. We Natives of this North American continent never had more then a severe cold or the likes until the whiteman came to our country.

At this time, Napi's power was almost equal with Creator Sun's power. And with all the things Napi done for the world and people, he was getting kind of bored. For some reason the power he had was always there nagging him to use it for himself. Maybe by getting older here on Mother Earth, Napi was getting astray of the progress that he had already achieved for the Mother Earth and its children. Maybe tiredness done it. Anyway, Napi was getting reckless with the power entrusted to him, and he was restless too. He was doing some crazy things now.

One day, while hurrying along with his coyote pet, the sun got very, very hot and the heat just beat down on them as they went along. Napi had his

*The Rock Chases Napi with the Robe*

old faithful robe with him in his arms. In this heat, the robe was getting mighty heavy for Napi. Stopping by a very large rock, spread his robe over it, telling the rock, *"Oogi ahm-ooy nu-gahts-iss*. All right, this robe you can have."

Back on their way they went, him and his coyote pet. They hadn't gone too far from the great rock when the clouds started to form right above the two. It got blacker and blacker up there, soon there was lightning and thunder. The two didn't go very far when the rain began to come down, and it wasn't long before the rain seemed to be just pouring down.

Napi told his coyote pet, "Run back to the rock and ask him if I could borrow the robe until this rain blows over." The coyote, being very fleet on its legs, soon got back to the great rock and repeated what Napi said. Hearing the message, the great rock spoke with a roar, *"Huh-ah-yah! Awk-skin-neek ahm-oo-yi ook-koo-took ace-ki-boh-doo-moo-wah*. By gosh! I haven't ever known anyone to take something back from a rock." The coyote pet ran back to Napi and told him the rock's answer. Right away, Napi flared up. He was angry, probably from the scorching heat and then the rain that was now coming down on them. He needed the robe right now, it was his in the first place. Turning sharply in his tracks, Napi started back towards the great rock, his

coyote pet right on his heels. It wasn't very long to get back to the great rock, and Napi was very angry with the rock. Walking right up to it, he jerked the robe off of the great rock and said these words: "*Ah! Ah-ny-yi is-ston-si-ki-mim-ii naa-yi.* Yeah! You just kind of got stingy with my own robe." Taking the robe, Napi walked away from the great rock and went back on his way, the coyote pet right behind him.

The two hadn't gone very far when, just as sudden as it came, the rain stopped and the sun came out again to beat down on them as they went along. They were going happily along in the sun, drying out at the same time, when all of a sudden the coyote jumped away from Napi, talking excitedly at the same time. "*New-waug, new-waug, ah-naw-goke ah-nauk ook-koo-too-cuk.* Watch out, watch out, here comes that rock." Napi jumped out of the way just in time as the rock rolled by. It didn't take long for the rock to make a circle and head back for Napi and his coyote pet. Napi and his coyote pet made a wild dash for it—to where, they didn't know. They ran this way and that way, the rock just barely missing them each time it rolled by. The great rock was very angry, because Napi had taken back the robe, and now he was ready to kill for that robe he lost.

The coyote pet was right at his heels, trying its darndest to stay out of the rock's way. Finally the coyote realized that it wasn't him the rock was after, it was Napi. The coyote ran one way and, with the rock right behind him, Napi ran the other way. Napi was getting very winded and tired too, he was just barely jumping out of the rock's way. This had gone on for quite awhile already, and Napi had to run fast and jump fast, which was very tiring.

On and on the rock chased Napi around, while his coyote pet looked on. There was nothing he could do to help Napi, his friend. Further and further the chase went on, over the hill, across rivers and creeks, and Napi was all in. It was getting late in the day. He was about ready to give up and let the rock roll over him to be done with everything, when from nowhere some nighthawks came to Napi's rescue.

These nighthawks dive bombed the rock with the gas in their stomachs. Each time they came down on that rock and let go with their gas, large pieces of the rock would fall away and roll another way to a standstill. Soon there was no more rock big enough to roll over Napi. The rock gave up, it was just too small to do harm.

Napi was very thankful to the nighthawks—in fact, he didn't know how to thank them for saving his life. He took his robe and went on his way. He hadn't gone very far when he came across the baby nighthawks in their nests. But instead of loving them up because of their parents' help, Napi took the baby nighthawks one by one and, as he took each one in his hands, he tore the mouth of these baby nighthawks a little wider for them. As he tore each mouth, he told each one, "*Ah! Ah-neeks-ah-yi oots-ii-dup-eem-oo-waks nit-si-gum-oots-ii buke-ow. Ah-ny-yi nis-staa-nuk.* Yeah! You, your folks saved me, now you must have this appearance always." All of the little one's mouths torn wider left blood at the corner of their mouths and to this day they still appear like they still have a little blood at the corners of their mouths.

When all of the little nighthawks mouths were torn wider, Napi went on his way. By this time, the nighthawk parents came back to their nests. At the first glance at their little ones, the parent nighthawks thought someone had fed these little ones raw entrails. It wasn't unusual to feed others, especially the little ones. The nighthawks said to those little ones, *"Huh, gahk-go-couk-si-ou-poe-waw.* Huh, someone must've fed you all entrails." The little nighthawks answered, *"Suh-ah, Napi-wah dass-stut-doo-yoot-oo-kin-oun.* No, it was Napi tearing our mouths wider."

"We will see about that Napi," all of the nighthawks said as they flew away to find that ungrateful Napi.

Napi was quite a ways by this time. Without warning, as he was going along, those nighthawks swooped down on Napi and with all their might they blasted him with all the gas they had. It was very powerful. It didn't take them very long to blow his clothes to shreds, especially his robe. There was nothing left of it, because it was the robe that started all of this trouble in the first place, and now those nighthawks done away with it.

Napi was left so tired from all of that dive bombing by those nighthawks, and nothing was left of his clothes or robe. He was plumb covered over with the nighthawks' droppings. He fell and laid there a while before getting up to go look for a creek to bathe in, and he was stark naked as he went along.

This particular happening of the Rock and Napi happened from Lake Francis in Montana at Valier to the present day site of Oka-toks, Alberta, Canada, west of the town. It ended where you could see the rock that chased Napi.

# The Making of Oldman River

It was in the Rocky Mountains, as they are called today, and this particualr river flows eastward from just south of Frank Slide, in the Province of Alberta, Canada.

In those early days, a small group of the people would have some sort of trouble among the large camp of people. These small groups, not wanting trouble, would then leave the main camp to go find another area where they might find a good place to hunt and live for the time being.

This small group of people left the main camp to go find themselves a good hunting area because of a little trouble arising between them and another clan. This was before the Oldman River came to be, many hundreds of years ago, and this group camped right up in the mountains just south of Frank Slide (it wasn't a slide then). The camp consisted of about six or seven tipis and only a handful of people. Napi was among them with his sister.

For many happy days this group of people lived happily in those foothills of the Rockies. They hunted each day, everything was plentiful here. The root food, the smaller game of the mountains, many fowls that were edible. They were a happy bunch of people.

The small group had been there for several months, and there were only a very few grown boys and girls among them. In fact, there was only Napi as a very young man and there were only about four or five girls, including Napi's sister. These were the teenagers of the camp, and they were in the age to know love with the opposite sex. But with only one young man and five girls, this was a problem for them.

Being no other young men around, the four girls besides Napi's sister began to make plans who would be the first one to get Napi. Napi's sister overheard this and she made her own plans, but she didn't let the other girls in on her plans.

Before the other girls got to Napi, she must put her plans into action. The only way she knew how to do it was to work at nights when it was just so dark and nothing could be seen. That very night, Napi's sister waited until she knew everyone must be asleep. She got up out of her bed and went sneaking to her brother's bed. She woke him up without talking, only hand language to make him understand that she was crawling in bed with him. Napi knew the other girls were after him, and he took it for granted this was one of those other girls. He never once thought it was his own sister that came crawling in bed with him.

It was well toward morning when the girl left Napi's bed, but it was still very dark, nothing could be seen yet. So she was safe.

From then on Napi had company almost every night, only he didn't know who this secret lover was. Thinking it was one of these other girls, Napi would flirt with them all. For several months this went on.

One day as Napi was walking around in the forest, he began to think about who this secret lover of his could be. The more he thought about her, the more he decided to find out somehow. Right away, he began to make a plan. After many plans, Napi finally decided on one good plan. It would take several days of hard work, but he must do it to find out who this girl was.

Whenever the hunters—and Napi was one of them—brought in a big load of fresh meat, all of the women and the girls and children would go down to a nearby lake and wash off the meat and the entrails. It was one of these days that Napi would sneak away from the group and go to his tipi to work on this plan. It took several days like this to complete what he was doing.

Directly under his bed he dug a pit, a deep one that no one could get out of without the help from someone above, on the surface. Napi hid all the telltale dirt in the nearby trees, and whenever the group would come, Napi would fix his bed over this pit and no one was the wiser. Rigged with a rawhide rope trip, he could just pull a little on this rawhide rope and the bed would tip into the deep pit. Everything was ready to catch this secret lover of his.

Napi wasn't one to put things off. That very night he had the chance to put his trap into action. Not very long after everyone had gone to bed, that secret lover came crawling in bed with Napi again. Through the night they laid there making love. The girl must've had a way to know when it was getting towards morning, she made motions with her hands on Napi's hands to let him know she was leaving. There never were any words from this girl. Napi would talk to her in a very low whisper so no one could hear, but she only answered with her hand language. She was starting to get out of Napi's bed when Napi tripped the trap and down into the pit they both fell. There was no way out for the girl, she had to stay put.

Slowly daylight came, and as it got lighter the girl tried to hide herself with a buffalo robe. Napi let her be until it was light enough to see all over. The girl had the buffalo robe over her, but Napi wanted to know who she was. Slowly he pulled the robe off of her and, to his biggest surprise, he seen the face and body of his sister. He couldn't get mad at her, but he just felt so very cheap. The girl too felt it was so cheap to be with her own brother, making love with each other all this time. Both felt so low, cheap, and dirty that, without knowing it, both were urinating as they stood there gazing at each other.

They urinated and urinated. The pit filled up and the urination began to run down the low spots, and the two still urinated. The urination began to run first as a brook, then a creek, and finally into a river, which channeled down through southern Alberta and became known as the Oldman River, or as the Natives know it, Napi's River.

This was their punishment for knowing each other, Napi and his sister. And the Oldman River is there to remember that a sister and a brother shouldn't get together as lovers.

# *Napi and the Gophers*

Napi was always on the hungry side of life. He didn't stay in one place very long, he was always on the move for more adventure, showing off to be recognized. Napi was always traveling—he got used to it when he was doing good for the people, teaching and talking to all of the people of Creator Sun from village to village. But now it was mostly for foolishness that he traveled and starved over.

The weather had been very warm in these last few days. Animals running all over the place, playing games and eating the fresh growth of nature. They all were having the time of their life here on Mother Earth. Old Napi's mouth would water, drooling for the taste of these tender morsels running all over the place. He went slowly along, his stomach growling for want of food. Water would help a little when he drank it, filling his empty stomach for a little while but as it came out again, his hunger would be that much worse.

Getting kind of weak from his hunger, staggering a little now and then,

Napi was beginning to worry how he was to get something in his stomach to ease the hunger pain.

As usual, he was walking along a little creek on this warm day—but oh so hungry!—when a faint, shrill whistle came to his ears from up ahead, somewhere in the bushes. Napi went sneaking along, temporarily forgetting his hunger, wanting to find out what it was that was making the shrill whistling sounds. Napi was a very nosy person, he wanted to find out about everything he seen or heard. And if it were a game he wanted to get in it.

Slowly coming around a bend in the bushes, straight ahead of him he saw several gophers doing something. He didn't come right out to them, he hid from their sight until he seen what they were doing. The gophers didn't sense his coming, they were too busy playing a game among themselves.

These gophers were playing a roasting game among themselves. They had built a very hot fire. As the fire began to cool off, but while those ashes were still red hot, the gophers would clear a place among those red-hot ashes down to the ground and one of them would lie down in the cleared spot, while the rest of them covered this one with the live red-hot ashes. When the covered one blew a shrill whistle, they would uncover him in hurry and get away from those red-hot ashes. The one that stayed under those red-hot ashes the longest was the winner.

Napi came around the bed crying *"Aye aye aye, niss-gah-nuk ahni nah-goo-kah-wahn-ists ah-hey. Aye aye aye, my little brothers, let me do what you are doing."*

The gophers said, *"Ah-nah-goke geese-in-own-ah Napi-wa.* Yeah, that's our big brother Napi coming. Let him join us like he wants." Napi's stomach was a-growling and his mouth watering as he really seen what was going on. He was very anxious and a little excited over this, a little nervous.

Napi could hardly wait for the plan that he had already formed in his mind. He told the gophers, "Why not let me do it now, clear a place for me and let me get covered up with those red-hot ashes. I just can't wait for my turn to come, I think it's so much fun to do this game with all of you." Napi was laughing and giggling.

The gophers thought Napi's wanting to play with them was genuine, not once thinking that this was a trick he was doing to them. The gophers cleared a place in those ashes large enough for Napi to lie down in. In went Napi and was covered up with the hot charcoals by the gophers. He didn't even stay under to lose a breath, when he made the shrill whistle to be let out. The gophers jumped to his side and uncovered him in a hurry. Napi, jumping up, was all gleeful and very happy, telling the gophers how much fun it was to be covered up with the live ashes.

Napi was jumping around for happiness and hollering about the game's fun, telling the gophers that he couldn't wait his turn to come again, but he didn't want all the fun for himself. "You! My little brothers you must take your turn too, which makes this game that much more fun. But one thing, I'd sure like my turn to come again soon. So I'll tell you, my little brothers. For my turn to come again soon, I'll clear a place for all of you in one spot and cover you all at one time. This will save time and my turn will come soon again."

Not once suspecting their big brother Napi of anything, the gophers agreed to Napi's plan. Napi was happy all right, but not about the game—it was for the plan he had in his mind. He was laughing and jumping around as he cleared a big placed for his little brothers, the gophers. "All right, the place is cleared for you all. You will have to get very close to one another, as tight as you can squeeze together so you will all have room in that one clearing."

All of the gophers were laughing too, just so happy with this game of theirs. They took turns jumping into those hot ashes, as close together as they could squeeze—every one of them except a female gopher that didn't want to be hurt by the tight squeeze. She went away from the game, not once trusting Napi, and saying as she want, "*Owk-tsi-gee-stub-op-oam-coo-ka-daas-koup*. This will give more gophers again."

Napi was already covering those little gopher brothers of his as the female gopher ran away, she was in family way and about ready to have her little ones.

Napi covered all of the others up with hotter ashes than they were using for their game, he piled it on them very thick. For a while he stood guard over them with a stick. They were whistling with all their might. Many shrill whistles were coming from those pile of ashes, but Napi didn't pay any attention to all that noise that came from those roasting gophers.

Soon that shrill whistling quieted down to stillness, it was quiet now except for Napi's stomach that was growling all this time. He went into the willow patch and cut himself several small pieces of the willows. With these he made a large plate for himself. Taking time to make the plate, thinking to himself, "About the time I finish this willow plate, those gophers should be

**Napi Roasts the Gophers**

well done and ready to eat." The plate was finally finished to use. To the fire and the pile of ashes went Napi.

Uncovering the gophers, they were well done and they smelled so delicious to Napi, he couldn't wait to get his teeth on them. Napi ate and ate, it was a feast he had with those roasted gophers. He ate his fill and there were a lot more that he didn't eat, he got too full. Those he didn't eat, he saved for his next meal. Left them on a huge rock sticking up a little above ground. Eating so much got him quite drowsy, so he laid down by the fire and before he went to sleep, he gave his rectum, his butt, orders to wake him up if anyone came near the roast gophers.

Going to sleep and depending on his butt to wake him up by making noise from releasing gas from his stomach, Napi wasn't worried at all. He was just dozing off when one right after another, his butt made several loud noises. Glancing up from his pillow, Napi seen several crows flying by. He told his butt, "Those are only crows flying by. I mean if someone comes very near or towards those roasted gophers. Now be quiet while I sleep for a while." It wasn't too long after that his butt made an excited noise again, but again it was only birds flying by.

All at once Napi fell into a deep sleep. On he slept. He was tired to begin with, and on top of it all, that bed of hot charcoals got at him too, got him very sleepy. But his lookout—his butt—was wide awake.

A hungry bobcat was coming along this same creek. He was also very hungry, and with his keen sense of smell, this bobcat smelled the roasted gophers somewhere down the creek. He sniffed along on the ground and in the air until he knew what direction to go. That sweet aroma of the roasted gophers he couldn't stand. It didn't take the bobcat long to get to the spot where Napi was sleeping by the fire and those delicious roasted gophers of his, his butt was on guard for him as he slept.

In those days animals had a different apperance. This bobcat's face was of the regular length, not a short stubby face as it is today. And all animals talked, too.

The bobcat stalked along towards the smell of that sweet aroma. Getting close to the spot, he slowed down to sneak up to whatever it was that smelled so good. Sneaking along just so slowly, he came in sight of the fire and those luscious, delicious-smelling morsels of roasted gophers. He couldn't wait. His fear of Napi was overcome by that delicious sight and smell. Up on a rock he got and ate and ate until all of those delicious roasted gophers were all gone. He ate them all up. Off he went.

As he was coming, the butt of Napi was just playing tunes with its gas from his stomach full of roast gophers, trying to wake Napi up before the bobcat got to eating, but to no avail. Phooot, phooot, phoot, put, put, put, it was just no use to wake Napi up, he was dead to the world with the deep sleep. The butt didn't give up until the bobcat ate all of the roasted gophers up.

The bobcat didn't go very far either. He really ate, and all of those leftover roasted gophers he cleaned. He could hardly walk or breathe he ate so much, he must lie down and digest the food. Finding a flat rock under the hot sun, the bobact laid down on his stomach to digest its food. Drowsy from the heat and the full stomach, he too went to sleep, and a very deep sleep.

It was getting a little late in the day when Napi woke up. Without opening his eyes, Napi reached up to where he had his leftover roasted gophers. He felt all over, and not finding what he was feeling for, Napi slowly opened his eyes and looked to where the roasted gophers were supposed to be. Nothing, just his empty willow plate. Quickly he said to his butt, "I told you to keep a sharp lookout for anyone that was coming." "I did," the butt said. "I made all the noise I could to wake you up, over and over again. I didn't give up trying until the bobact ate all of the gopher up and left."

Again Napi asked his butt, "Where did he go? Which way did he go?" His butt answered, "He went that way." Napi jumped up and soon was following the bobcat. He didn't have to go very far when he came upon that bobcat fast asleep on the flat rock, snoring away.

Grabbing the bobcat by its hind legs, Napi was saying, "*Ah, ah-nom-ah-yi, aa-bok-scaa-say-dah-mi-tsi.* Yeah, you there, kind of snoring away." Napi lifted the bobcat up and began to beat its nose against the flat rock. Napi didn't pay any heed to the bobcat as it pleaded with him to let him go and not hurt him, as he didn't know that those gophers were Napi's food. On and on Napi hit the face of the bobcat on the flat rock until the bobcat's face was just short and wide and bloody.

Finally letting it go, Napi said after the bobcat as it ran into the willows, "*Ki-neye-i ni-staa-nuk.* Have this appearance hereafter." Today, if you look close at a bobcat, you will see that it still has a very short, wide face, the blood still can be seen too.

Napi was very mad at his butt. Back to the fire he went after he got done beating the bobcat up and putting a new look on him. Coming to the fire, which still had some very hot charcoal on some of the long wood that was used for fire, Napi grabbed a good hot one. Sliding his breechclout out of the way, he wiped his butt from one end to the other with the hot charcoal at the end of the fire stick. "This, for not waking me up in time to save my roasted gophers." The charcoal was very hot and it didn't take much to severely burn the butt.

He had burned himself and was feeling the pain as it came over him, and now he was thinking he had made a big mistake to burn his butt. It was his and no one else's, and he was feeling it, it was burning so much. He sat himself on the cool ground, but it didn't help any. He was in such pain, it made him temporarily out of his mind. He didn't think of water, but he was thinking of something cool or outright cold. There was a little breeze in the air, coming from the west. He stopped over and held his butt to that slight breeze, which kind of cooled it a bit. He wanted more cold air or wind to hit the burned area, so he stooped over more and began to say, "*Iik-so-boo-tah, iik-so-boo-tah, iik-so-boo-tah.* Blow harder, blow harder, blow harder." The wind began to come on a little stronger, and still saying the words, he began to hum them into a tune. "*Iik-sobe-see-say, iik-sobe-see-say, iik-sobe-see-say.* Blow harder wind, blow harder wind." Faster and faster he sang on as the wind picked up and got stronger and stronger. Napi all bent over holding his butt to the wind that was now getting mighty strong. As he sang on for it to blow harder, the wind got so strong that it must've been a hurricane. Napi couldn't stand up to it any more, he was beginning to blow away. At first he blew down and he held on to the grass. The wind got stronger and away he was tumbling along with the wind. He tried in vain to catch on to something, but everything gave way to that wind.

Napi was tumbling along, bouncing head over heels, rolling this way and that way, grabbing on to something only to break away, and along he would blow again.

Tumbling along with the wind, Napi seen a big clump of birch trees ahead. As the wind took him by these birch trees, Napi got ahold of a good-size branch and hung on for dear life. There he bounced around for the longest time, but this time he held on and didn't let go. After a long time the wind subsided and soon it was quiet. Napi laid there panting, all tired out.

It took a long while for him to catch his breath and to where he could let go of the birch tree. At last he let the tree go. Taking his flint knife out of its sheath, Napi began to nick the birch tree all over the trunk and limbs. Today those nicks Napi made on the birch trees can still be seen just as he done it. Napi was talking to the birch trees as he was hitting them with his flint knife, "*Ah, noom-tsi-tsi-bop-boke-op-oh-pub-oo-ky gits-ii-tsi-kyi-iss-seh-chi-bo-wah*. Yeah, I was blowing and bouncing along and you had to be there."

Napi was never satisfied, no matter how or who saved him from his predicaments. Napi left his mark on the red willow that he used for a dish to put the roasted gophers on. Today it looks like it's always greasy. And the wood he used to wipe his butt with—if you burn it in these days, it smells of human manure. We call it dogwood.

# Napi Cooks Babies

Napi didn't know the meaning of being in one place and staying out of trouble. He was constantly on the move from one place to another, and lately he was out of one trouble into another.

The incident about the bobcat was forgotten by Napi as again he walked along the old familiar trail of trouble. Where he was heading to was anyone's guess, but trouble was for sure at the other end of his trail. Into the open plains he walked, over hills, into valleys, ravines, coulees, across brooks, creeks, streams, and rivers. Through the brush, the forests and undergrowth, by lakes, big and small, endlessly Napi walked, on and on.

Just day to day was his life. As he walked along the brush, coming around a bend, ahead of him he seen a lone tipi. Being very cautious that he didn't scare the occupants of this tipi, Napi stole up towards the tipi. He was hungry and didn't want to scare them off before he could get something to eat. Many people didn't want to trust Napi anymore, so Napi had to be cautious all the time.

Stealing up to the doorway and eavesdropping, Napi heard women talking inside. He listened for a while, making sure there weren't others in this place. He didn't hear any male voice, he was sure there were no men present. Making very sure it was all right, Napi announced himself as he came to the doorway, "Oh-ho," and entered the tipi. Standing upright, he greeted the occupants of this place, "Oh-ki." The greeting was returned by the two women, "Oh-ki, oo-mi stu-beat. Hello, sit over there," and one of the women pointed to the opposite side of the room.

As he made his way in to sit down, one sweep with his eyes took almost everything in. Just a few rawhide bags or food bags and clothing were kept in the tipi. There were two babies swinging in rawhide swings at either side of this room, the rawhide rope was tied to the tipi poles. There were two beds, probably one for each woman. From what Napi seen, these two women didn't have much to them, they were a little short of most things.

The two women got very scared of Napi, but they didn't act it. Napi asked for something to eat, he was again very hungry. The women told Napi, "Right now, we just don't have anything to offer you. We haven't the men-folks to kill fresh meat for us, mostly we live on the roots and berries that we dig and pick. In fact, we were just getting ready to go and dig some roots and pick a few berries to eat. We were trying to put our babies to sleep.

"If you don't mind waiting and looking after our babies, we will go and get something to eat for you. You will have to watch the babies while we are gone." Napi readily said he would take care of their babies while they went to rustle for food. He was very hungry, didn't believe in exerting himself to find his own food. So now he became a babysitter.

The babies were old enough to know their mothers and to know a stranger. Not too long after the mothers left them alone with Napi, the two babies began to cry. Napi got up from where he was sitting, went to the swings, and swung the babies. The babies saw Napi and didn't know him, and things got worse for Napi. The two babies were hollering their heads off. Napi knew quite a bit about little ones, he done everything he knew to make them stop crying. Those babies cried that much harder.

Napi was always a little quick on the temper. When he couldn't make them babies stop crying, he was raging mad. Out came his flint knife and off came those babies' heads, both babies. Napi didn't stop to think. Realizing what he had just done, he was sorry. But it was too late now, the babies' heads were cut off, laying there silent. For a few moments, Napi didn't know what to do, he almost panicked. "I must do something before those two women come back." Taking the two babies out of the swings, Napi cut them up into very small chunks and into the pot they went. The heads he went out and buried deep in a badger hole.

Napi made two babies with the material he could get and wrapped them up. Into the swings these made babies went, covering them up very carefully. Napi went to work and boiled the babies. The babies were well done and tender when those two women got back with many roots and some berries to cook for Napi.

Right away, the two women noticed their babies were very quiet. They glanced at the swing, but the babies were still in them and fast asleep. Napi was a very good babysitter, the women thought, and they hurried to get something to eat for him. As they were getting prepared to cook the food, the two women noticed the fresh boiled meat. It looked so tender and fresh. Asking Napi where the meat came from, Napi said, "*Kook-ski-boo-kyi-yaw i-tsits-ko-pay-pi-yaw chi-chi-bi-ko-sin-ah-yaw*. Sharp-foreheaded baby animals jumped along close by, I kill them with a club. That's what I boiled for you two, as you do not have any meat."

Napi had to leave, he was in hurry now. He told the women that he ate his fill right after the fresh meat was done. As he left through the doorway, Napi told the women, "Your babies are fast asleep and won't be waking up for a while, just enjoy your meal while those two babies are asleep."

After Napi went on his way, the two women had the meal of their lives, they ate and ate of the fresh meat Napi got for them. Getting very full in their stomachs, the women sat around for awhile then to work they went, all of the camp chores that had to be done. And as they worked on, one would run into the tipi and find out about the babies in their swing. Without peeking into those swings, the woman would come back and tell the other, "The babies are fine and still asleep. Napi must sure know his stuff about babies, those babies have never slept this long." On with their work all day, it was getting quite late in the day when they went in the tipi for their evening meal, both were very hungry from working all day. The two had their fill of fresh meat again.

About this time, one of the women told the other, "The babies should be waking up by now. They have slept all day with not one whimper and they are usually crying their heads off all the time." Both women jumped up. To the baby swings they went, taking the bundles out of the swings, only to find the empty bundles.

They knew right away what had happened to the babies. The two women were grief-stricken. There wasn't anything they could do about Napi, he had gone too far, far away to catch up to him. All they had was their broken hearts over their little ones. And on top of that, they had eaten the babies, which made things so much worse.

This was another lesson to learn: Never trust the most trusted one.

# Rocks are Sweet

Napi, the disciple of Creator Sun, was told to go and invite all of the many kinds of life that existed here on Mother Earth. All were to come to Creator Sun's lodge.

Being the beginning of life, human life, it wasn't very long before all the many life of earth gathered in Creator Sun's lodge. Animals, birds, all water life, fishes and such, wind, thunder, lightning, rain, snow, hail, sleet, all the many kinds of plant life, trees, the rivers, creeks, brooks, streams, lakes, insects of all kinds, the many kinds of flies, rocks, mountains, and all life that existed on Mother Earth gathered in Creator Sun's lodge.

This was a day that all must get their specific instructions to follow throughout their eternal life here on Mother Earth. All this day, each one of these many kinds of life came before Creator Sun to get his specific instructions on what was to be done by him alone, as long as the sun shined. As each came before him, Creator Sun said, "From here on throughout time you will have to do this special thing always, nothing else but this." And the next life would come before Creator Sun to get its instructions.

It was getting late in the day, but the insects still had to come by Creator Sun. The many kinds of insects, big and small, came by Creator Sun and got their special instructions. All of the many kinds of flies went by Creator Sun first, then the insects, they were the last. Every one of them went by, and the very last one of the insects was the ant.

Creator Sun gave the ant his special instructions for the rest of time, as long as the sun was shining. Not mentioning the special food that the ant must eat during the time, the ant spoke up as if to finish Creator Sun's

*Creator Sun Tells The Ants,*
*"Rocks Are Sweet"*

words. "And we shall eat the nice tender, juicy, sweet flesh of all animals and all of the human flesh too."

Creator Sun was very quick to come back with his reply. "No, no, flesh isn't good for ants. Eat rocks, they are much sweeter." So to this day, one can see an ant chewing around on a rock.

# Napi and Two Ladies

In the days when this country was still an infant, the Natives of this land weren't too numerous yet. It was a sparsely populated place and them Natives were a bit afraid to venture out too far from their villages or camps, especially the woman. A lady was a virgin until a husband was selected for her by her parents.

Napi was doing things to make good at times, but would end up by making a fool of himself. He tried to help people, but he made mistakes. Most of the time, Napi had much trouble in getting food.

In those long time ago days, before the 1500s, this land was only inhabited by Natives, no foreigners had come to it. There was nothing like a place to go to eat and pay for it, no stores to buy at, no sleeping places to rent a room for the night. The Native people relied on one another to help each other without cost to the traveler or visitor. A free meal is given any visitor or traveler, and they are also given presents to let them know they are welcome. This has been our custom and is still the thing for us yet in these days of conflict between the whites and the Native. Life was good in those days before the whiteman. There was plenty to eat, plenty food all over. We didn't pay for food, it was free to us. All we had to do was to spend a little energy and hunt for food. It didn't make any difference which way one went to find food, he found it. Food was always plentiful until the coming of whiteman. Now the whiteman makes us, the original owners of this country and all that went with this country, food and the likes, pay for our very own food and all. All originally belongs to the Native.

Napi was going along this stream as usual, where it was very brushy and where usually food would be more abundant. Trees and willows just about covered either side of this stream. There were openings among the trees, known as parks to the people, and many of them went in through this brushy place.

It happened this same day that two women were coming along from the opposite direction. Not everyone knew Napi personally, but all people had heard of him many times in one way or another. Some said Napi was very good, and some said he was very bad, especially to women. So whatever, women didn't trust Napi too much, especially when they were alone.

It wasn't any different with these two women as they came along—their minds were on roots and barks, and not on Napi. Not once did they think of Napi as they strolled along, looking to either side of them, and once in awhile towards the direction they were going. It was one of these moments they happened to look ahead of them and seen, in a small opening among the trees, Napi, as he went along leisurely, in and out of the willows and quaking aspen trees. The women had heard of Napi, but neither one of them knew how he looked. The two women's fear came to them—it just didn't have to be Napi, any man was as bad.

How to avoid meeting with this man? How? They weren't that fast to run for it, they must do something right now so this man, if it's Napi, wouldn't harm them. A split-second plan came to one woman. "Let's play dead. No one likes dead people, they can't make any use of a dead person." There wasn't time to think a better way to fool this man.

The two women fell down on the ground and laid very still, playing dead as Napi came in and out of the trees and through the parks.

Napi was too busy to be looking far ahead of him as he walked along, he was looking to find food along the way. The grass was very high all over this place, and one had to look very close to the ground to see anything that might be eaten. Coming along and not suspecting anything unusual, Napi was taken aback when he almost stepped on a woman. In fact there were two of them laying there, and they were both dead. What a strange thing about these two women, both dead in this same place.

Napi got down on his hands and knees and felt the bodies of these two dead women, but Napi's foolishness was always there. He didn't even test the women's hearts, just their bodies, and those bodies were still warm. Napi was trying to solve this one out in his mind. "I must take them with me," he thought. "They might've just fainted or been knocked out by something. If they come to, I'll have me a couple of good young women for my wives."

The two women laid still, hardly breathing. Napi stood there, thinking how he was going to carry both women at once. Bending over, he picked up one of the women and slung her on his shoulders, and the other one he tried to carry under his arm. Just for a short way he carried the two women, they got too heavy for him. A plan came to him. He will carry one for a short distance and lay her down, then go back and get the other woman, alternate them.

Laying one woman down, Napi took the other over his shoulders and started out with her. One arm of this woman was swinging freely, back and forth, hitting Napi right across his nose. It was no time at all before Napi's nose started to bleed from those blows. But Napi was so set on taking the women, he didn't pay much attention to them blows to his nose. He wanted to get as far as possible before he laid this one down and went back after the other woman. He was all blood, nose bleeding from those blows. Napi didn't know it, but this womans arm was swinging more than it should and the arm was swinging intentionally as Napi went along. At last he came to where he thought was far enough ahead of the other woman. He laid this one down and went back to get the other woman, he was all bloody as he walked back to the place he left the other woman.

Getting back to the place where the two women laid, the grass was trampled down and the imprint of the women still there. But to his surprise, this woman was gone. Napi immediately started back to where he had left the other woman on a dead run, as fast as his feet could go. Reaching the place, again to his surprise, this woman too was gone. Napi was plumb left out on either woman. It finally dawned on him. He shouldn't have wanted more than he could handle, he should've been pleased with the one of them women. But now, he was completely left without even one woman.

There he was standing empty-handed, hollering out, crying out for those two women, "*Kip-ots-kun-its-teeg kahn-its-cheeb-o-wyi.* Lay as you were when you were laying here!" But Napi knew it was no use, he should've been pleased as it was.

# Napi Becomes His Own Son-in-law

Times were beginning to change. In the many, many years of Napi's existence here on Mother Earth, he had also started to change. The beginning was now in the past. Napi had taught the children of Creator Sun all that was taught to him.

It had been so long since Napi done a good deed that those deeds were forgotten by the people, and almost by himself too. He wanted to change his ways for some good now, as he was getting tired of the foolishness he had been doing. Napi wanted to settle down like all the rest of the people. To settle down, Napi must get a woman to soothe his nervous life of foolishness.

Napi went around calling on all of the many camps in the country, which weren't too numerous at the time. The world was just beginning, humans especially had only inhabited Mother Earth just a few thousand years, and so the places where these people were wasn't all that many. With the power that was loaned to him by Creator Sun, Napi could get to places by magic. So from one camp to another he was traveling to find the right woman that he could lead a good straight life with.

He had been to many camps and stayed a while to study the many single women that lived there, but none so far had attracted him.

He always set his tipi wherever he went among those many camps. Coming to another camp, it took no time to erect his tipi. From this tipi, Napi done his scouting for the right woman. Among the people he would mingle, asking about this woman and that one, mostly if the woman was single and talked about getting a man. As he was talking to someone, a fairly young woman with good looks and very appealing to Napi's eyes went by. His eyes followed the woman, he didn't hesitate to ask about her. Napi was told that the woman's husband had died, she had two daughters that were fairly old and she might be looking for a husband by now, her husband had died many moons ago. Napi had kept his eyes on the woman and seen where she went, which tipi she went into.

This was the first woman that really appealed to Napi. He had seen many, many women at all of the camps he had come to, no doubt this was the woman that was meant for him. Napi didn't waste any time to go see her. Right straight to her tipi he went. One good thing about Napi, he was always straightforward about his ways. He didn't fool around, he went right in the woman's tipi. Napi was greeted warmly by the woman, which was a very good sign that this woman was good-hearted and kind.

A few exchanges of words between them, then all of a sudden Napi asked the woman if she wouldn't want to get married to him. It wasn't such a surprise question to the woman, many men had come before her and asked that same question since she became an eligible single woman. Without any hesitation, which was quite a surprise to Napi, the woman said yes to Napi's proposal.

In those days of Napi, a woman and a man just got together and lived as a man and wife. There weren't any holy marriages then.

Napi didn't waste time to move in with the woman—in her tipi, his was kind of small for them. They set it up close to the woman's tipi and had it for the daughters of this woman, as a sleeping place for them.

Living together wasn't as bad as Napi had thought. The two were getting along just splendidly.

Things went along just as smooth as could be expected, every one of them were very happy. This went on for a long time after the two got together, Napi and this kind, good-hearted woman. Things were good until one day, Napi had a very good look at the girls, the daughters of his wife. These two girls were growing fast and looked very tempting to his eyes. In his heart, he got that jealous feeling about those girls. He knew it wouldn't be too long before some man will come along and ask them to get married. Somehow, Napi wanted them for himself. But how?

Napi didn't want to leave this woman who was so good to him, but the two girls were so tempting that he must have them for himself. Napi's mind was working overtime, trying to figure a way out of this and get with the girls. He couldn't find any kind of excuse to leave this woman. If he did leave her, there wasn't any way that this woman would take him as a son-in-law, it would be against the principles of the Natives. He must find a way to get these girls before it's too late.

One day as Napi was still trying to find a way to get the two girls, his stepdaughters, a death occurred in this camp.

At that very early time embalming was unheard of, and wakes weren't known either. When a death came to certain families, it wouldn't be too long until the body was wrapped up for burial. The same day the death occurred, the burial took place. No processions or a crowd, just the immediate family were present. The burial took place on a high hilltop where there were a lot of stones to cover the body, as there wasn't any digging of graves to put the body into. The stones were used to cover the body so no animals could get at the corpse. Or the body was taken to the forest among the trees, where a good big branch was found high enough so wild animals couldn't get at the corpse. There, the body is tied securely, wrapped all together with the branch with a tanned hide, most generally an elk hide or moose hide. The rawhide rope is wrapped closely together, around and around the body and the branch. With either burial, the body remains until it deteriorates and eventually goes back to dust, which is many years.

Napi was very quick to grasp an idea from this death. It wasn't too long after this death that Napi got sick. At first no one thought much of his illness, but as time went by, Napi was getting steadily worse. All kinds of medication from roots and weeds, even the best-known Native doctors came to help try to cure Napi. Finally everyone knew there was no hope for him. Laying on his sick bed, Napi called his wife over to him, the stepdaughters too. Napi told the three that a spirit had come to him. He knew he wasn't going to get well, he must leave for Happy Hunting Grounds. This same spirit also told Napi to be sure and leave this message for his wife and stepdaughers and have them make sure these messages are carried out as the spirit said.

Young people will notice some strange things right away, and it wasn't any different with these two girls. Not too long after their mother got together with Napi, the two girls seen a scar between his thigh and knee on the right leg.

In the early days of the American Native, right up to about the mid-1920s, Native men, the older ones, still wore leggings that were individually made. With a string of buckskin, each legging was tied onto the belt that also held the breechclout up. This made it so the naked thighs showed to others, and if anything is on the thigh, it would surely be seen.

Napi's leggings were no different from others, and the two girls had noticed the long scar on the right thigh of Napi's leg. They never mentioned this to anyone, especially to their mother, as they didn't want her to think they were nosy.

Napi went on with his last wishes and that of his spirit helper, too. He told his wife and stepdaughters, "My spirit helper wants you three to take care of my lifeless body after it departs for that great beyond, where Happy Hunting Grounds are. The three of you must make a bed of soft robes only, for my body on that high hill. You must not weigh it down like others with heavy stones that are usually piled on top of a body. My body is only to be covered thickly with robes and weighted around the edges with smaller stones.

"You, my two beautiful stepdaughters. I have a very important message for just you two, from my spirit helper. I want your mother to listen carefully too so she can enforce these last wishes for me.

"My spirit helper wants you two girls to get married real soon after I pass on. Four days after the new camp is set up, a stranger will come to your tipi. You will identify him the way he will be dressed. He will come painted all in yellow earth paint, clothes and all. This man shall be very easy to distinguish from all other men. Most of all, this man will come right to your tipi.

It's this man that you two girls must marry, which would help your poor mother out good by having a son-in-law that will take care of all of you.

"My helper of the great spirits wants everyone of this camp to move soon after my burial in that same day, and move to those lakes to the north of here. It will take about four days to get there. From the day all the camps are set up, for four days, everyone must sweat bathe to clean the bad illness that I am going to die over. After these four days of sweat baths the man appointed to become a husband to the two girls will come. Don't ask any questions, just hurry and get with the man. My spirit helper doesn't want anything bad to come to the people. If our wishes aren't carried out, very bad things will come unto the people of this camp, and I don't want anything to come over you three."

As Napi spoke, his voice was getting weaker and weaker, right after the last wishes was told to the three, the woman and her two lovely daughters, Napi died.

The three carried out Napi's last wishes as he had wanted it to be. Soon after the burial took place and the people got back to the camp, everyone got ready to move. It didn't take very long to get to moving, partly because no one knew what bad illness Napi died over and no one wanted to get it.

The woman was grieving very much as they moved along those first four days after Napi's death. The fourth day they reached the lakes Napi mentioned, and it was along the banks of these lakes the people set up their new camp. Soon after the camps were set, the sweat bathing got underway. The people of this camp wanted to sweat-bathe away the bad illness of Napi that might still be on them.

The woman and her two daughters were counting the days as they went by after camping. The two girls were very curious to find out what that man was going to look like. The woman was grieving through this.

Fourth day came after the camp was set, the girls didn't hardly do anything but sit while waiting for a man to come. The woman too was curious to see her son-in-law to be, so her grieving was temporarily forgotten.

Napi, as soon as everyone left the burial place on that hill, peeked out from under the heavy robes that were piled over him. He was very close to suffocating under those thick robes, he was all sweat. It was a good thing them women left right after the burial. It wasn't time to get up from this grave of his, Napi was just looking down on the people getting ready to move. He had fooled all of them and he didn't want to spoil it by having one of those people see him get up from his burial site. He must wait under these robes until everyone in the camp had gone and he better be sure of this. Waiting one or two nights under these robes should be it, Napi thought to himself.

After dark on the second day after his burial, Napi got up from those heavy thick robes and down the hill he went. Napi went on without stopping, walking as fast as he could go. He wanted to reach the new place where the camps were to be. Traveling alone and at a fast walk, Napi walked only two days before he came in sight of the new camp area. Waiting in patches of quaking aspens, Napi waited for that fourth day. He waited until it was a little later in the day before he went down to the camps.

Not once looking to the sides as he walked along, Napi went straight to the camp of his widow. He already seen where it was from his hiding place among the quaking aspen patch. Right on into the tipi he went. The three took one look and knew this was the man mentioned by the stepfather. He was dressed as he said, and was covered with yellow earth paint all over his clothing and skin, the face too. This was because Napi was in a disguise.

There wasn't anything said, this man went right to the bed and sat down. The sisters didn't have any questions either, they must take this man as their husband from now on. The mother moved into the girls' small tipi, as this new son-in-law took completely over.

The girls told their new husband that he had come to fulfill the prophesy and his last wishes of their loving stepfather, Napi. The three of them welcomed the new husband.

It was a happy marriage while it lasted, and while the mother was grieving for her poor dead Napi. The three of them, the man and his two wives, were very happy. Walks they took, and played around at all times after the chores were done. They even wrestled, all three of them, and this was Napi's undoing.

As the three of them were wrestling, the wives of his took him down as one of them sat on him. The man was struggling to get up from this, when the other girl happened to see a scar on his right thigh. It looked exactly like the one on their dead stepfather's thigh. The girl didn't wait. She told her sister, "Our mother is calling us for some reason, let's go find out what she wants." The two of them started off, telling this husband of theirs, "We'll be right back, you wait here." Their husband sat up and waited as the girls went on to their tipi, where the one girl that seen the scar told their mother and her sister. They had to make sure of this, so for the next few days they all kept a close watch of that scarred leg. All three of them made very sure this was the stepfather that had died—especially the mother, she knew every bit of him. Now it was Napi's turn to be surprised.

After making very sure about this, the three laid in wait for the man to come. Each had a club as they waited inside of their tipi. Napi came to the tipi and went right in, as he did all the time. To his astonishment, he seen stars as the clubs came down on him. Napi didn't wait to find out what had gone wrong, something told him that he must get away from here as fast as his legs could go. He knew instantly that these women had found out about what he had done.

The girls and their mother meant to kill Napi for what he did, but they were so mad with rage they couldn't hit Napi squarely where it would've hurt. They were missing wildly, and this was a lifesaver to Napi. He turned and fled from this camp while he was still in one piece, although he was badly bruised. The girls and their mother had their revenge on Napi, but only after he got what he had wanted, the two young girls.

# Napi and the Sun's Leggings

Napi was the exact image of Creator Sun. He was always so jolly and kind to everyone, all life alike, no matter what kind of life, humans, birds, animals, plant life, water life, and all life of Mother Earth, still life, and active life, he loved them as he was put on Mother Earth to do. He loved and adored life unless he was hungry. He was always hungry. So he uses the power of Creator Sun that was entrusted to him for his mischief, to gain food for himself.

This wasn't too many years ago, a few thousand years ago. Creator Sun came down to earth once in a great while, but it had to be a very, very important happening here on Mother Earth to make him come down to his children. He came down disguised so he could freely roam about among the life he planted here to find out what could be wrong without anyone knowing he was down here and about. He worked like a present-day detective. When he found out what the wrong was about, he didn't punish physically, but through his power and unseen force he meted out punishment to those that were to be punished.

It was one of these times that Creator Sun was down here with his wife, Mother Earth, to see what his disciple Napi was doing. He knew Napi was doing some funny things to the life he was supposed to be taking care of. This wasn't any different from any other time Creator Sun came down to find out the root of the wrong he was investigating. Camping alone or camping among his children of life, Creator Sun was there to get firsthand knowledge of the trouble.

Creator Sun was camping alone at this particular time, along a small creek where willows and quaking aspen were quite thick. People of those days had to camp always near a watering place, and where firewood was plentiful, with a lot of shelter from wind and weather. It was this way where Creator Sun put up his tipi.

Napi, always roaming about for adventure or mostly for food, always ended up doing something foolish. This day wasn't any different. It was getting quite late in the day as Napi walked briskly along by this creek. Again he was tired and hungry, he must find a bite to eat soon, his stomach was a-growling like always when he was hungry. He was going along at a fast pace, with nothing in sight to go to. As he came around the quaking aspens and the willow trees, up ahead he seen this lone tipi. There was smoke coming out from it, so Napi knew someone was home there. What luck, just when he was getting mighty hungry. He didn't waste any time to go there.

As he got to the doorway, before he could get ahold of the doorpiece, a voice within the tipi called out to him and told him to come right on in. This didn't surprise Napi, because he didn't even notice it. Probably he was too hungry to notice anything unusual about this place, or he was just plainly scheming for some mischief. It should've surprised Napi that the man inside of this tipi called him by name and told him to come right in without even seeing him first to recognize him.

Napi went on in and was greeted warmly by this man that was all adorned in red earth paint. "Come on and have smoke with me and we will have something to eat pretty quick." Napi thought to himself this man was extra friendly, for the way he was greeted and welcomed. Even before Napi sat down, his eyes were flitting here and there, taking in everything that was in view. Before Napi knew it, he was eating away, while the owner of this tipi sat talking to him. He offered Napi a place to sleep for the night, as it was late already.

After the meal the two smoked the pipe for awhile, talking as they visited over the pipe. All of this time, Napi's eyes were roving about, flitting here and there until they were attracted by a pair of buckskin leggings. These leggings were somewhat unusual in the way they were made. Instead of the regular buckskin fringes and the usual plain buckskin leggings, these leggings were doused with the red earth paint and the fringes were of red-winged woodpecker feathers, they were mostly outstanding in appearance. Very, very neat in the way they were made. It was these leggings that Napi's eyes were glued onto. He would look away from them, but those eyes rolled right back to those nice-looking leggings.

When it was finally time to go to bed, the man of this tipi pushed all the live ashes of the fireplace to the center and laid a few very large pieces of wood over the ashes. Then the man got into bed, while across the room, Napi was laying there wide awake. It wasn't very long after they went to bed that the man of the tipi went to sleep, breathing heavily and snoring once in awhile.

The night was young yet. Napi stole out of his bed when he heard the man snoring and breathing loudly, and went right to the place where the leggings were hanging. Going about as easy as he could, Napi took the leggings off of the pole they were hanging from and under his arms they went. Quiet as a mouse he went towards the door of the tipi and out he went. He had stolen the red-winged woodpecker feather fringed leggings.

Napi went along as fast as he could tiptoe until he was out of hearing distance from the tipi. From there he went into a run, on and on he ran as fast as his legs could go. He wanted to get as far as possible as he could before daylight came about. After he had gone over many hills and coulees, creeks too, then did he slow down. It was getting pretty well towards daylight when he laid down to sleep. He was very tired from all of that running and he knew he was far, far away from that tipi. He used the pair of leggings for his pillow as he laid down near a tree.

Napi slept a long time. It was late in the day when he sat up awake, but to his utmost surprise, he was still in the tipi that he stole those red-winged woodpecker feather fringed leggings from. It was quite astonishing.

Sitting up on the bed he slept in, Napi didn't have anything to say. He thought that it was just all a bad dream. And to make it worse, the pair of leggings were under his head as a pillow. Somehow he tried to lie out of this, telling the man, "I needed a pillow for my aching head, so I got up and got what was in easy reach for me in the dark, and they happened to be your leggings."

It was all right with the man as long as Napi would hang them back up on the pole where he got them from after he got out of bed. All that day it

*Napi Steals Creator Sun's Red-Winged Woodpecker Feather Fringed Leggings*

was a puzzle to Napi—how did he get back into the tipi after running away almost all night before he laid down to sleep? This didn't deter Napi's mind one bit, though, he was more determined to steal those red-winged wood-pecker feather fringed leggings.

Napi came up with several excuses to sleep there again, and got his permission from the owner of the tipi. Napi had made some foolproof plans for this night.

Night once more came to this tipi. Napi waited until the snoring got very loud this time. Napi did some very foolish things, but this was more foolish then ever. Before getting out of the bed he was in, Napi pinched himself as hard as he could to truly know that he wasn't dreaming again like the night before. He pinched himself so hard that he made tears come to his eyes. He even pulled on his hair as hard as he could to make very sure he wasn't asleep and dreaming.

After being very sure about being wide awake, Napi got up so easy and to those leggings again he went, taking them down, and under his arms he put them. Out of the door he went once again, running as he got out of hearing distance. On and on Napi ran, not stopping for a breather. Through the night Napi ran on. It was getting light enough to see, and Napi was just so very tired he couldn't go on, he must get rest and sleep. Down in the thick part of the willows he laid, and just almost as he laid down, Napi fell asleep.

Napi was so tired from all that running, he slept most of the day. It was very late in the day when he woke up. Without opening his eyes he sat up, and was stretching from the stiffness from that running he did the night before. As he stretched his arms this way and that way, he touched something with his fist or fingers, and it felt like a soft tanned hide. He knew he was sleeping in the thick patch of willows. His eyes still closed, he was wondering about the soft thing he had just touched. Slowly he opened his eyes and again, to his astonishment, he was back in that strange tipi where the those red-winged woodpecker feather fringed leggings belonged.

The man of the tipi acted like he didn't even know what was going on. Like nothing happened, he got a meal ready for Napi and told him to eat hearty, that he may be very hungry. Eating as he sat there in the strange man's tipi, Napi was almost going crazy trying to figure out what was happening to him, why he would wake up back in this strange tipi. He knew he wasn't dreaming like he thought he was. It was a very deep puzzle to him. But for some reason he was determined to steal those red-winged woodpecker feather fringed leggings.

In those early days, even to the time before electricity came into the coun-tryside, on the many Native reservations, those Native people went to bed with the sunset and got up with the sunrise, they were so devoted to Creator Sun. Their last act of the day was devotion to the setting sun, with sweet grass they made incense. As it smoldered on hot charcoal and the smoke went upwards, curling in the air, their prayers of faith could be faintly heard in their tipis, the smell of the sweet grass was all over in the room, that sweet aroma as the prayers were being said. About the time the sweet grass burnt out, the sun had set, and so on to bed they all went. Sometimes there was storytelling from the bed while all waited to go to sleep. As it quieted down, everyone went to sleep.

The older people would get up long before sunrise and the woman cooked by the light of the open fire inside the tipi. Just before sunrise, everyone would be awakened to get up and give their devotion as the sun rose up into view on the eastern horizon. All Natives grew up this way, all Natives know their rightful Creator. The sun that feeds them and gives them the breath of life. And Creator Sun gave to them Mother Earth's part of this devotion, the greatly honored sweet grass. Not only the sweet grass, but the cedar, the sweet pine, the juniper, the sage, and the pine tree moss—all of these for the people devoted to the sun as they burned them on hot charcoals as they prayed.

This camp wasn't any different from the other camps. This strange man, too, burns sweet grass as the sun begins to rise or as it begins to set and pays his respects and devotion too.

It was so late in the day that it was almost time to go to bed as Napi finished his meal. It wasn't too long after that meal he ate that it was time for bed again. Napi was more determined then ever to get away with those red-winged woodpecker feather fringed leggings. In his mind he knew he was going to try again to steal those leggings. To bed they went and again, as all things quieted down and it was fairly late in the night, Napi stole up again and got at those leggings. Taking them down once more and tucking them under his arms, he went out of this strange tipi once again and off into the night he ran. Away and ever farther away he ran through that night. This time it was morning when he finally stopped running, daylight. He had come to where large quaking aspens grew. Stopping by one very large one, Napi laid down to get some sleep. As he laid down, he tied himself securely to this large tree. Napi felt contented as he went to sleep, again he was just so very tired from all the running in those past few nights. No matter what powers there were to contend with, Napi felt absolutely safe now. Because with the way the rawhide rope tied him to a very large tree, there wasn't any way anyone could take him from this place. And so to sleep he went, this time no worries.

Upon waking up, Napi didn't wait to open his eyes. Yes, he was right back to where he got started, in that strange tipi again, and it was almost dark. Whatever it was that was urging Napi to steal the red-winged woodpecker feather fringed leggings, no one knew, just himself. For sure this time he was going to get away with stealing those leggings, this was the fourth time and the fourth night he tried to get those leggings from this strange tipi.

Once more they went to bed after the sun went down in the west and after evening devotion. Napi acted like he was fast asleep. But as soon as the strange man began to snore again, Napi got up and right back to those red-winged woodpecker feather fringed leggings he went. Down once more they came, right under his arms once again, and off into the night he took off. It was broad daylight when finally he stopped again, once more he found a very large tree to tie himself to, and as always he used the leggings as a pillow. The leggings were always a telltale sign, they were always still under his head when he woke up in that strange tipi. He just didn't have a guilty conscience about trying to steal those leggings from this good-hearted man that wouldn't even mention what was going on. Instead, Napi was treated with kindness.

Napi was sleeping heavily from the running again. When he finally woke up, he didn't open his eyes. He had felt the rawhide rope still tied securely to the big tree and around him too. That's what came into his mind as his eyes were still closed and laying there. This time he had won, he got away with those red-winged woodpecker feather fringed leggings and he was still tied securely to the tree, that's what he knew without opening his eyes yet. He could hardly move with the rawhide rope around him, but he was feeling so great that he finally got away from that strange tipi, and with those wonderful leggings too, that he didn't want to move or open his eyes, but just lay there and rest a while.

Maybe he slept a while again, it was such a relief to get away with something you liked so much. It was late in the day when Napi woke up again. He must go on now that he got free from that tipi. Finally, he slowly opened his eyes. I suppose he would've used all the profane words when he finally opened his eyes, when he seen where he was at. And to make it worse, he was still tied to something.

Fully opening his eyes, Napi seen that he was tied to the tipi poles. Turning his head slowly around towards the opposite side of the room, he was greatly embarrassed, he seen that strange man sitting there on his bed. Napi couldn't face the strange man, he felt so awful guilty of these past few nights, trying to steal those beautiful red-winged woodpecker feather fringed leggings. He just didn't know how to act as he slowly untied himself from those tipi poles he was tied to.

The strange man spoke up like nothing happened, "*Oo-ki Napi, nee-bo-wod, ka-ki-chooi.* All right Napi, get up and eat." Napi was very ill at ease over his behavior these past few nights, he just couldn't look into this strange man's eyes.

This strange man put him at ease with the kind words that came from him. He wasn't mad at Napi for trying to steal his leggings from him. Napi was still treated with respect and kindness.

As Napi ate slowly, this strange man was explaining to Napi about himself, letting Napi know that he too might've tried stealing the leggings from someone else if he got stuck on them. But as he spoke, he told Napi that the best thing one should do was to ask for something he wanted. Like now, Napi should've come right out and asked him for those leggings. "It would-n't've been a problem to give you them, as you are a visitor here. They were yours for the asking. You can have them red-winged woodpecker feather fringed leggings of mine, take them with you when you leave here." And Napi ate with haste as this man told him he could have those leggings.

Already through with that meal, Napi folded the leggings up neatly and was soon ready to leave. Before he went out of the tipi, this strange man motioned to Napi to wait and he spoke on. "I am the Sun, Creator of all things. Creator of this Earth you are on and the many forms of life here. Any place here on this Mother Earth is my tipi, which you were trying to run away from. You were only running inside of my tipi all the time you were running, that's why you always woke up in that bed you slept on.

"There is a restriction on those red-winged woodpecker feather fringed leggings of mine and if that restriction isn't complied with, you shall find out the consequences. Do not wear them just any time. They are made especially for certain times when one is very happy and devout for the coming day. Only wear them when you are to pray with all your feeling for your coming to this Mother Earth. Remember and take my advice to you, don't wear them just any time, unless your heart is all given to your Creator."

Napi was listening, but the words of this strange man were going right through Napi's ears. He didn't hardly hear a word of the words that were spoken by this strange man. All Napi had in his mind was to get a-going so he could try those red-winged woodpecker feather fringed leggings on, they looked so neat the way they were made.

As the strange man got through with the talk, Napi went on his way, hurrying as fast as he could walk. On and on he went, trying to get out of sight of the tipi. Far from this tipi and way out of sight, far out in the prairies quite a ways from the closest creek, Napi sat down and out came those red-winged woodpecker feather fringed leggings. Off came his own leggings, and on went the red-winged woodpecker feather fringed leggings. Slowly standing up and looking at himself, admiring the leggings on him, how good they looked on him. But then he took a step and as his foot touched the ground, the dry grass burst into flames. He immediately stepped the other way, only to see that foot touch the ground and the grass burst into flames. Away from these flames he walked, first in a fast walk, and then he broke into a fast run. But each time his feet got in contact with the grass, they burst into flame. Faster and faster he ran as the flames followed him right at his heels. His senses coming to him, Napi made a wild dash for the closest creek, where he didn't even stop, but jumped right in, leggings and all. Napi took off those red-winged woodpecker feather fringed leggings as fast as he could and left them in the creek. To this day, those leggings might still be floating down or hanging back in that strange man's tipi.

After all of this, Napi never learned his lesson: to be honest.

# Napi Doctors
# a Young Maiden

Napi was living in a large encampment. An older lady had taken pity on Napi because he was so all alone, she had asked him to live with her at her tipi.

Napi done his share of the chores, which was mostly getting wood and water for their use. He was doing very good at this time. He was right down to the right business. The old woman liked Napi so very much, she took him as her son and there wasn't anything that she wouldn't do for Napi.

In this camp a big get-together took place during the summer months. Many, many people came to join this particular camp each year. Games were played and there were many different things shown off during this time of the year, things that individual people or families done to show what they knew about life. This was the time people were beginning to be aware of Creator Sun, and they were honoring the Creator in their own ways. At this particular time, a regular routine religion wasn't in existence. There were very few holy pipe bundles that had already been attained by just a very few people that knew the existence of Creator Sun, and these were unwrapped at this time too. They were the only things that people knew about a sort of religion. Probably, at this time, people of Mother Earth had already forgotten where they really came from, and how and who created them. Also they knew hardly anything about praying to this creator. So! At this camp, there was always some sort of worship to this almost forgotten creator of Mother Earth and its beings.

Many of the men and women had been given power through visions and direct contacts with the spirits of the many different lives of this Mother Earth. To the Natives of these present-day Americas, everything that existed under the sun, whether it's on Mother Earth or away out in the great void or space, whatever it may be, it had life and a spirit within it. From these things of our great universe, the Natives of these Americas achieve their powers.

This power was used mostly for the good of the people as it was used to doctor with. Of course in those days, sickness was almost unheard of. It wasn't until the white people came to this country of the Americas that the Native first encountered the diseases of the whiteman. The whiteman's disease killed off huge populations of these Natives, because the Native was very vulnerable to the many diseases that came with the whiteman. One major disease was the smallpox that killed over half of the Native population. Many smaller tribes of Natives became extinct from this one particular disease.

One day the old lady of the tipi where Napi was living went across the encampment to the other side to visit a friend. She was there almost all day. Napi was alone at the tipi. All day he heard drumming going on across the other side of this large circle of tipis, and he thought it was one of the families doing their family dance.

It was quite late when the old lady came home for the night. When she came in and sat down, she told Napi that there was a very sick girl near the place she was at. The parents didn't have much hopes of seeing her get well and were calling all of the doctors of this camp to come to the girl's aid. Anyone that has power is needed there.

Napi is always fooling around, he told the old lady that he would go and find out what it was all about. Maybe he could help in some way. It was dark out already when Napi made his way to the sick girl's tipi. Instead of going right on inside, Napi wanted to see first who was inside of this tipi. He peeked in from the top of the door flap where the tipi was pinned together. There were many people inside, some of them were doctors and many were just concerned people, relatives and friends of the girl's family.

Napi seen that this young girl was old enough to be married off and she was a nice-looking girl. Right away Napi had a plan to carry out, a wicked plan about the girl.

Going back to the old lady's tipi, Napi didn't hesitate calling his adopted mother, "Go tell those parents of the sick girl that your son has the power to make her well. I would need seven gifts of their valuables." Napi had power from the Creator Sun to teach the children of Mother Earth and Creator Sun the ways to live accordingly to their ways. He was put here on Mother Earth a long time ago by Creator Sun. That power only worked mostly for the good of things for the people. To use it for something bad, it always went back on Napi.

The old lady thought that Napi had much power, he was always so all alone in many places where there would be powerful spirits, so Napi would have multiple powers by now. She didn't hesitate either, going right to the sick girl's tipi and telling the parents what Napi had to offer to help the sick girl.

The parents were more than glad, as they were frantically calling for help. They were desperate and didn't hesitate to agree to Napi's demand. The parents loved their daughter very much and didn't want to lose her to death.

The old lady went right back and told Napi the good news, that he was accepted to doctor the young maiden. It wasn't late when Napi got his medicine bag together and left for the girl's tipi, almost diagonally across the encampment. Napi must hurry to get his plan underway, as these summer months have very short nights. Napi was half running as he made his way to the sick girl's tipi.

It seemed like all were waiting for Napi's appearance. Everyone was sitting quietly as Napi came into the tipi. He glanced around him and seen many faces, all were concerned about the poor sick girl. Even the top doctors of this camp were waiting on Napi to come, probably from being tired from doctoring many nights or just plain curious to see Napi doctor—no one had ever seen him doctor before.

The parents of the girl were all ready for Napi. Immediately they told him to sit up and begin to doctor, as the girl was very sick. The parents informed Napi about her condition and where she was having the most trouble—it seemed like it was just below the waistline and all the way across her abdomen.

Napi went to the side of the sick girl and sat down in a kneeling position facing her. Instead of being worried or concerned about her trouble, Napi was giving her the once over. He glanced from her face to her toes and seen that this sick girl was a very well-developed girl, which made his mouth water. She laid there very tempting to Napi's eyes, she was a young maiden and ripe for womanhood—or was she already a woman?

Napi didn't hesitate anymore to start doctoring the young maiden. Talking partly to himself, and to be heard and at the same time, he reached under the robe that covered the sick girl. Napi was mumbling that he must feel around for the main trouble spot, which all good Native doctors do. Reaching under the robe, his hands went to the girl's breasts, which Napi felt around for a bit, then his hands went along the chest down towards her legs. Napi was pressing her body as he felt along. He sang a song that he doctored the sick girl by, which lasted a long time. It must've been probably two o'clock, as there was no such thing as time in those days. The way time was told was by looking at the stars and how they lay. The Natives could tell whether it's near morning or what part of the night it was.

There were several ways to tell the time of day or night. In the daytime, it was the sun that the Natives went by if it was visible to them. On cloudy days it was by the deep shadows of the sky and horizon, especially to the southern direction. At night, to know how late it is or how close to morning it is, the stars are the ones that tell. If it's cloudy and in the warmer days of summer, late spring, or early fall, it's the chirping of insects or chirping of certain birds that tell you what time of the night it is. To the Native of these Americas, time of day or night wasn't at all very important, unless there was a special reason to keep track of it.

Napi would sit very still at times as he doctored, as if praying or meditating. Everyone else would quiet down too. It was right after one of these quiet meditations that Napi spoke to the parents of the sick girl. "My spirit helper wants me to say this. In order for this sick girl to get well and to live, I must be all alone with her for a while. For my spirit helper to help directly, the fire must go out for the time being so there will not be any light. This is a must as my spirit helper only comes to me in complete darkness. So I'm asking the parents to cooperate with this spirit helper of mine. I want the parents to ask you all to leave until I give the word to come back in again."

The parents of the sick girl were ready to do anything to get their daughter back on the road to recovery. Immediately they asked the people to go out for a while until Napi and his spirit helper had done their doctoring in complete darkness. Even the drummers are to go out and sit in the back of this tipi and a little distance from it, so as not to scare the spirit helper away. When Napi has sung his medicine song through four times, then he wants the drummers to start drumming and singing his song and to drum as loud as they could, and also to sing to the top of their lungs.

Everything was now set for Napi. All of the people of this tipi went out into the dark of the night. The woman of this tipi, the sick girl's mother, poured water on the fire to put it out so no light would be showing inside. Napi was sitting close to the girl's side all this time. As soon as all of the people had gone out and away from the tipi, which Napi gave them plenty of time to do, he started his song. "*Ghi-ah-si-ki-wahts-ah, ghi-ah-si-ki-wahts-ah, ghi-ah-si-ki-wahts-ah, ghi-ah-si-ki-wahts-ah*. What is it going to do, what is it going to do, what is it going to do." Over and over he sang this doctoring song of his. Napi was daring the sickness to get worse, this was to make the parents of the girl know the power he had, that nothing whatsoever would happen to the girl.

Several songs over and the drummers start beating on their drums as loud as they could and singing to the top of their voices, the song that Napi was singing.

It was now time to put his plans into action. Napi was still singing as he climbed on the girl and began topping her, and as it got to the good part, Napi began to sing a little faster than his drummers. At the same time, the girl was calling for her mother, "*Nah-ah, nah-ah, dow-auk-ka-nook*. Mother, mother, he's hurting me."

Mothers are always so ready to jump to their children's side, the mother of the sick girl didn't hesitate to run and jump inside of their tipi, thinking that by some mistake Napi had burnt her or stuck her with one of his medicine tools. Jumping to her daughter's side in the darkness and feeling around for her, the mother felt Napi on her daughter, going after it as if he couldn't stop. It must've been at the very best part of the intercourse, Napi just couldn't jump off, the woman jerked him off and cussed him down in the Native language, "*Ki-ah-yo ah-nyi aa-soo-ki-nukiw aht-tum-too-kitay-chiw ni-doni imi-des-kiw* (*Ki-ah-yo*, an expression of resentment), him there, a-doctoring, laying on top of my daughter, the she dog."

(She dogs in those days were numerous and they were kept around at all camps because their litters were used in those days for moving. But if not properly taken care of, the she dog goes wild and has too many pups and besides, too many dogs hang around a certain tipi. It was awful to see a she dog and a he dog doing their thing among the people. All dogs remain tied most of the time at the encampment and over this, the she dog was a sinful dog. The Natives had lots of respect for one another, especially their relations and close friends.)

The woman got ahold of a stick and beat Napi on the back as Napi made a fast exit through the doorway, the woman right behind him. No sooner had he ran out, when the rest of the people went after him to help catch him. It was a good thing Napi was a fast runner, he outdistanced the bunch of people after him.

It is known that children are gotten out of bed when it's still dark out— the older children, teenagers, to learn of their Creator Sun, to help pray with their elders or parents. Reverence was of most importance to most people of that time. There still wasn't a routine religion yet, only their reverence to Creator Sun. So it was that the older children were out playing at daylight.

These older children were out playing already when Napi was running from the camp. The people seen the older children playing up ahead, all hollering at the same time to stop Napi as he ran by them. Napi was far enough ahead of them to talk his way out from these children that had got ahold of him. He told them that he was running and was beating those people back there in a race. They had heard of a pile of elk teeth, he would give these teenage girls elk teeth by the tens. Believing him, the teenage girls let him run on his way.

The people back of him began to holler ahead to the teenage boys that were playing a little further ahead to stop Napi. Napi talked his way out of this too. He promised them he would give them by the tens a pile of arrows that were down the way if he beat all of these people back of him. The teenage boys let him go, as they wanted to get in on those arrows.

On he ran, right into another group of boys and girls that heard all that hollering from the grown-ups. Napi talked his way out of them too. He promised these girls and boys arrows and shells by the tens if they would let him win this race to the piles of shells and arrows. They let him run on his way, thinking he would give each of them arrows and shells and elk teeth.

Napi was once more at large to do what he wanted. In a way, he was still leaving precedent things for the coming generations, even to this generation.

# Napi and the Elk

Napi would get out of one trouble and into another. Many times he had used the power that was entrusted to him by Creator Sun in a wrong way, mostly for the good of himself, not the people, which made the Creator very mad at this disciple, Napi. Mostly when Napi used the power for himself, Creator Sun would turn the power to make Napi look like a fool. This was his punishment for the wrongdoings. It was because Napi had done such a wonderful job to begin with that Creator Sun didn't want to harm Napi too much. He was hurting his ownself as it was.

After all, Napi been on this Mother Earth many thousands of years now and he had done a lot of good for everyone here—the people, the animals, the birds, the different kinds of live growths here, the spirits and nature itself. But now Napi was acting foolish to get attention, and he was getting it. He knew he was doing wrong, but it was a good way to have people and life itself like you and talk about you. Doing the right as a disciple of Creator Sun, teaching of survival and how to live a life here on Mother Earth—no one cared one way or the other about him then, no one patted him on his back for the good work he was doing. So now it was the other way around, everyone was talking of Napi.

Since he had roasted gophers for his meal that one day he played the roasting game with those gophers, Napi hadn't had much of anything to eat, so he was again on the hungry side of life. These were the punishments that befell Napi for his wrongdoings. Creator Sun didn't want to be too severe on him. But a little of this and a little of that punishment was what Napi was facing. Without his knowing it, that Creator Sun was causing him to suffer at times, just like at this moment of hunger. Because he had cheated the poor gophers out of their lives.

Going along on this fine day, his stomach aching for the want of food, growling as he went along and not a bite to eat in sight. All of a sudden, far ahead of him among those cliffs and rocky ledges, many, many head of elk were following one another in a single file, weaving in and out of the rough terrain. In fact, it was all of the elk got together in one big herd.

Back in the days of Napi, because it was only the beginning of time, there weren't too many of each life, so certain animals and birds would get together to play.

Napi stood for a while looking at them as they went along in a single file. Hungry and curious too, he had to get up close enough to see what was going on. He always sneaked up to whatever he wanted to see up close, and this wasn't any different. He went sneaking along until he had just about met the elk herd.

A closer look at them, he seen that all were following the one elk that was in the lead and the rest of the elk were doing everything that leader did. If he jumped, the rest of them would jump too. If he shook his head, the rest of the herd would do that. They were following the leader, only Napi didn't know it was a game and that the elk herd had just begun to play the game before Napi spotted them. Napi was highly intelligent, he caught on right away.

It didn't take Napi very long to think up a plan for nice elk meat, fresh and juicy.

The elk herd was playing towards him as he stood there watching them. As they came near the place where he was standing, Napi, always so humble and pitiful, came out to meet them. And as always he was crying, "*Aye, aye, aye, niss-gah-nuk ahni nah-goo-kah-wahn-ists-ah-hey.* Aye, aye, aye, this, let me do too."

The leader of the elk herd stopped as he met Napi and heard what Napi was crying about. Turning around, he told the rest of the herd, "Nothing to fear, it's only our big brother, Napi. We must let him play with us, he is lonely, we must brighten his spirits up." So the leader went on for a while. They had come to a very high, sheer wall of this cliff, and they were on the top of it. Napi, knowing just about when to spring his plans, stopped the leader of the elk herd and went up to him. He was trying to talk to the elk leader, but his laughing was getting the best of him. Every once in a while he would let out a loud holler. When he finally managed to talk, he told the leading elk, "I've been the tail end since I joined you in your game. It's so much fun to me that I'm having the time of my life with you all. It's been such fun for me, I would like to lead you all for a while and then another can take over after a bit or after I get tired. We will all take turns leading."

Napi was the leader now, he took the elk herd away from this sheer cut in these cliffs, and made a big circle back. In fact, he had them all turned around. Coming back to the sheer wall and before they all came in sight of it, Napi stopped the elk herd and told them that this was the funniest part of the whole game. He would run first and jump off a little place and when he hollered, he wanted the whole herd to run and jump off of the little bank he had found and in a single file, but close together so it would be over soon and they could again all climb and jump again.

As usual, the elk herd didn't suspect any wrongdoing by their big brother Napi. He told them to wait until he gave a holler and then all of them would have to come running to the jump. He took off laughing with glee to the jump off. But instead of jumping like he was suppose to, Napi made it down by a roundabout way where he didn't have to jump. As he got to the bottom of the cliff, he fell down and was laughing just so loud so the elk herd could hear him. Talking loud and clear so he could be heard by the elk herd, saying and laughing at the same time about how fun it was to jump from such a high place and not get hurt by the fall. Giggling, laughing, and hollering, rolling around at the bottom. He also hollered at the elk herd to come running fast and all jump at one time, that it was so much more fun when a whole bunch jumped all together.

The elk herd could hardly wait their turn, because of the noise Napi was making. It sounded like much fun. They all just kind of stampeded to the cliff and over they all jumped. Sorry to say, it was very high, too high for anyone to come out of it alive. The whole herd of elk got killed when they hit the bottom of this cliff. Napi didn't care, he was more happy and gleeful over his achievement. His mouth was a-watering as he began to dress out all of the elk herd. He stuffed himself with raw entrails of the elk to stave off his hunger. One lone female pregnant elk got away.

It took Napi a long time to dress out all of the elk. As he got through dressing them out, he made a shelter for himself with the hides of the elk. There he cut all of the meat into thin slices for drying. He made drying racks to hang the meat on and then made a smokey fire under them. Smoke-dried meat. Everything was dried so it wouldn't spoil. The tongue of the elk he put away up near the top of the rack, along with the guts and tripe. Now all he had to do was eat and sleep for a long time to come. Napi had enough food to last him a whole winter.

The next evening after the slaughter of the elk herd, Napi was sitting by his fire eating away as he always done, when along came a coyote to Napi's camp. Coyotes are known for their cunning too. This coyote had his right forefoot in a buckskin sling around the neck, he could hardly walk, his feet were all very sore. That's what he was telling Napi as he came there to bum for food. Napi was very stingy with his hard-earned food, he just couldn't afford to give even one little piece away. The coyote didn't give up, he acted more pitiful, groaning as he begged for just a taste of the delicious-smelling food. "Hi-you niss-ah, eyi-mug-its-si-nits-ahbi nu-gees-oog-it. Help me big brother, even a burnt piece, feed it to me." The coyote begged on.

Napi chased the poor crippled coyote away without giving him even a little

***Napi Leads the Elk Herd off of Cliffs
to Their Death***

piece of food, not even the burnt piece the coyote asked for. The poor coyote left Napi's camp almost falling from lameness and his sore feet.

He didn't give up that easy though, he came back to Napi's camp and told Napi, "I'm so hungry, I'll race you for a little something to eat." Napi didn't go for that either, the winter was coming on and he needed all of the food for that cold weather.

The coyote wasn't one to give up easily. He kept on nagging Napi to race with him, telling him, "I'm crippled, you will beat me even if you had to hop on one foot and leg. I just can't run with my sore feet, so you have no worry."

All that nagging by this coyote, Napi wishing the coyote would shut up for a while. But he kept on nagging for a race with Napi, just for a little something to eat. After a long argument between the two of them, Napi got so tired of the nagging that he gave in to the coyote.

The two of them set out to the starting line. They went quite far when Napi looked back and seen it was getting quite a distance to the camp. He told the coyote, "This should be right to start our race from." But the coyote argued again that it wasn't very far yet, he wouldn't have a chance to win the race. So on they went, every once in a while Napi would ask if this was all right, but it was always "no" to the coyote. Over hills and creeks they went, at last the coyote said this should be a good starting place for their race. It was almost a half-day's walk back to the camp of Napi.

The two got ready and stood at the starting point. All at once, Napi hollered, "*Oak-ki!* Go!" and off they went. The poor coyote seemed like he was standing still, Napi took off so fast. It was a level land for quite a ways, then down a hill it went. Napi went out of sight of the poor coyote. He didn't give a darn for him, he wanted to get back to his camp and food. He was still running along when something went by him so fast that it seemed to him a shadow went by. Getting a good view of the thing that went past him, Napi recognized the coyote as it went over a hill ahead of him. Napi hollered after the coyote, "Save me some of that food," but the wily coyote didn't even try to listen, he went on as fast as his legs could carry him back to Napi's camp and all of the fresh meat there.

This darn cunning coyote was acting pitiful so Napi would feed him, there really wasn't anything wrong with him, he pretended all that crippleness and lameness. It fooled Napi into a race and now the coyote was somewhere far ahead, no telling what he was going to do with all of the meat.

As the coyote reached Napi's camp, he got up on a knoll and gave several loud yelps in the animal language. This was an invitation to all of the animals around to come for a feast. It wasn't no time at all when all of the coyotes came running for the feast. The wolves came, the badgers came, the lynx came, the cougars came, magpies, crows, all of the many, many different birds of the area and all of the many different animals of that land. Even the mice were there to enjoy the feast.

Napi was all tired out when he finally got back to his camp. Everything was gone, ate up by the animals. Napi was very hungry when he got to his camp, but all the meat was gone except all those tongues he tied away up there at the top of the rack. There were still a few animals eating what was left of the meat and food, so Napi sat down watching them eat. Every once in a while he would say, "*Ohm-stees-chee mut-si-knee-tsi ohm-stees-chee mut-si-knee-tsi.* Those few tongue, those few tongue."

At last! The last few animals left the scene and nothing left of the meat, but Napi thought he had a hidden food where no one could get at. After everyone left the camp, Napi got up and went to the rack. He reached up and untied a tongue, but to his surprise, the meat part of the tongue was all gone, it was just a hollow tongue. Being so surprised, he said, "*Huh-ah-yuh awk-it-si-ni-wuas-iwah.* Oh my, this tongue is hollow." Over and over he said these words as he took each tongue down from the topmost part of the meat rack, right to the very last of the tongue. Those darn mice got up there and ate the meat out of the tongue, all of them. Not one was saved of the tongue. Napi was left out of his ill-gotten meat, punished by Creator Sun once again.

# Napi and the Mice

Napi had left the camp of people and was going back to the good old nature that he had lived with all the time. It may be a little hard to get by at times, but you sure didn't get left out. Napi came to what is now known as the Province of Alberta as he was going along, trying to get far from the people, at least for this time.

Napi never worried about where he was going to sleep or eat until the time comes. Napi laid down to sleep any place, as long as he had his old standby, the thick tanned buffalo robe. If it's to eat, that was something else, food wasn't always an easy thing for him to obtain.

Napi had traveled all that day. It was getting a little late as he made his way down into one of the rivers throughout the country. Along any waterway, it's always almost inaccessible because of the thickets, trees, and bushes. But there were always small openings where there wasn't any kind of foliage except thick, high grass. It was one of these fairly large open places among the trees and bushes that he happened upon. Darkness was coming on fast. Without going any farther, Napi throwed his robe down on the ground and there he was going to spend the night. As the darkness came, Napi covered himself good and closed his eyes to go to sleep. He was so leg worried that he just couldn't get to sleep right away like he wanted to. At last that drowsiness came to him. It must've been fairly late now. As he was falling asleep, something awoke him, a faint sound like singing. Napi thought he was just hearing things because of his tiredness. Not paying much attention to what he heard, Napi only moved about in his bed for a more comfortable position and tried to doze off again.

That was singing, and it got louder this time as it awoke Napi for the second time. Sitting up in his bed, Napi listened carefully for that singing.

There were many small voices singing and talking at the same time, whoever they were or whatever they were doing, there were many of them and they weren't very far away from here. Napi sat very still, trying to get the direction of the noise and what it was about.

Napi's curiosity was aroused. Slowly he got up from his bed and, listening for the sound. He went towards it, every once in a while stopping to listen for the direction of that small sound of singing. This was a small open park and wherever the sound was coming from, it shouldn't be too far. Napi crawled along towards that singing, he could hear them very plain now as he was going directly towards it and getting closer to it. He didn't want to walk right up to them or he would've scared them off, whatever they were.

Crawling along ever so slow, very careful not to make any kind of noise that might scare them off. It was very dark as he groped towards the sound of the singing. Crawling a little farther along, just ahead of him, along the edge of the bushes, Napi spotted something white. This something white was an old sun-bleached elk skull that had laid there for a long time. It was from within this elk skull the singing was coming from. Crawling ever so slowly and coming to the elk skull without even as much as cracking a dry grass, Napi peeked in through one of the eyes of this elk skull. This was really something, what he seen. It was a bunch of mice inside of the elk skull dancing and singing. The mice all stood around in a circle with their little paws held up about even with their little cheeks. They were jumping up and down on their little feet as they went around in a circle and sang as they went around. Those that were sitting down were against the wall of the elk skull, they too were singing to the rhythm of the dancers. Every one of the mice was having the time of their lives and like always, Napi wanted to join them.

"*Kyi-neh-ski-nah-yah ahwa-bi-new-si, kyi-neh-ski-nah-yah ahwa-bi-new-si, kyi-neh-ski-nah-yah ahwa-bi-new-si*. Mice fluttering your eyes as you are dancing." The mice sang on into the night. Over and over they sang this with a little interval to catch their wind, then back to singing and dancing they went.

Napi went sneaking back towards where he came from. Picking up his robe, he slung it over his shoulder and walked slowly towards the old bleached elk skull where the mice dance was taking place. As he neared the skull, his old, old familiar wail was heard by the mice. "*Aye, aye, aye niss-gah-nuk ohn-ni nah-goo-kah-wahn-ists ah-hey*. Aye, aye, aye, little brothers, what you are doing, let me do to." Over and over he cried this same cry as he slowly walked towards the old bleached elk skull where the mice dance was taking place.

His voice, being louder then those of the mice, was heard above their pattering little feet and their singing. All quit singing and dancing as they heard the crying coming towards their skull dancing area. One of the older mice peeked out from the skull and seen Napi coming, telling the rest of them, "It's only our big brother Napi, he's crying to join our dance." Without any further argument, all of the mice agreed to let Napi join them in their little dance. The leader of these mice telling Napi that it was too small of place for Napi's size, all he could do was to get his head in through the neck part of the skull and that had to be done by the mice's magic. He could sway his head back and forth to the time of their singing and dancing. This was all right with Napi. One of the elders of this mice family used his magic to get Napi's head through the small opening of the neck part of this old bleached elk skull.

"You are not one of us," said the leader of the mice, "we have a restriction for those that aren't one of us. We dance for four nights, this is only the first night. At daybreak, we disperse until night falls again. We continue this way until after four nights, then we go on our separate ways. Through all of these nights, you must not fall asleep or bad things shall happen to you. We will have to leave your head in here until after the last night, then we will let your head out of here. Don't fall asleep while we are dancing at night. Beware."

Napi was always ready to agree to all of this, he wanted to have a good time for once, he wanted to learn the mice dance. The mice once more began their dance, while Napi kept his head in motion back and forth and to the sides to the rhythm of the mice music. Napi was having the time of his life that night.

Just breaking day, the mice all left. Napi fell asleep with his head inside of the elk skull. All day he slept like a dead thing. If it weren't for the mice returning for their continued dancing that night, Napi would've slept on.. He woke up as the mice were coming in and all them with their happy voices, talking excitedly.

The mice dance went on as Napi done his part of swaying his head this way and that way to the time of the music. All night the dance went on with nothing happening except all were having a good time. At daybreak once again, the mice all disappeared out into the bushes for the day and Napi's

*Napi Watches Mice Dance in the Elk Skull*

head was alone once more for the day. This time he didn't get much sleep, he was getting very tired from laying one way, on his stomach mostly.

Nightfall brought the mice back again for their four-night dance. This was their third night of dancing. Through the night the mice danced as Napi's head bobbed about in time with the music, his way of taking part in this mice dance. Once more, daylight came and the mice dispersed for the coming day as Napi's head was left all alone again in this old bleached elk skull. He just couldn't sleep too much this day. He was awful tired laying on his stomach, he had been on it for three nights now, which was very long for anyone.

Trying to fall asleep, Napi's day just wasn't long enough. He just couldn't sleep and when he did start to go to sleep, it was night and the mice all returned for their last night of dancing. It started out all right with Napi, he was wide awake when the dance began again. His head was again bobbing about to the rhythm of the mice singing and dancing. Every once in a while Napi's head would fall forward as he would doze off, he was really fighting his sleepiness. It was well towards morning, Napi had almost made it to daylight, when he just couldn't get his head back up. He fell asleep as the mice danced on.

The noise didn't waken Napi back up, he was fast asleep. The restriction the mice mentioned to Napi had to be carried out, it was a mouse custom. While Napi was fast asleep, the mice chewed Napi's hair all off of his head, Napi was just plumb bald as he slept on into the day. The other part of their restriction was to leave Napi's head in the elk skull if he fell asleep, and he did. Waking up, he didn't notice his hair all chewed off, that he was just plumb bald, but he did notice that he couldn't get his head out of this old bleached elk skull. And to make things worse, he couldn't see where to go, the bone of the skull was in the way of his eyes. Napi couldn't break the skull off either, or he would hurt himself. He found out the restrictions of the mice for falling asleep while the mice were dancing.

Napi got up with the elk head over his head, feeling his way, this way and that way. The elk skull was top heavy, which made Napi stagger this way and that way. He went along as he felt the ground with the feet and hands. He fought his way through the undergrowth and trees, he really didn't know which way to turn. Stumbling and staggering along, trying to find his way out to the open land where he could get along better without his eyesight. Not knowing where he was going, Napi was still groping about through the brush, when all of a sudden the bottom seemed to drop away, and down into the river he fell. Not knowing which direction to swim, the weight of the elk skull would submerge him every once in a while as he tried to swim to where he thought the shore was. Instead, he was going out towards the middle of this river and it got deeper. There he was, floating down river bobbing out of sight with the elk skull still over his head.

Napi didn't know how long he had been in this river, floating down with the current. He had swallowed a lot of water, he was still going under the water at times, he was fighting for dear life to stay afloat. The darn old bleached elk skull made it that much worse, its weight took Napi under water as he floated along. Napi was hollering out every chance he got, but this elk skull muffled all of his hollerings, no one to hear him.

Far down this river was a large camp. The men of the camp had just returned from a hunt. The women were all down along the banks of this river, washing the fresh entrails off and readying them to eat. One of these women spotted the elk skull as it came floating towards them. She let out an excited scream, saying at the same time, "There comes an elk swimming down the river!" All of the women dropped what they were doing and turned to the middle of the river where the elk skull was floating. The elk skull got closer and closer. The women still thought it to be an elk swimming down river. As this elk skull was almost even with them, the women noticed it wasn't an elk swimming, it was a human being with an elk skull over its head.

The women lost no time to get a rawhide rope long enough to reach out to where this thing was floating, they could see the arms frantically grasping for something to hang on to. Now they could hear a muffled sound from within the elk skull, calling for help. One of the stronger women threw the rawhide rope out to the man that seemed to be in trouble. The first try was a lucky one. It had to be, otherwise someone would've had to swim out after the elk skull. He made a few wild grabs for whatever it was that he felt. One of his tries was good, his hands got ahold of this thing, some one yanked on the rope. Napi knew help was at hand. To the shore he was pulled, he was close to drowning again, his stomach was full of water.

Getting him pulled ashore, the women couldn't figure out how this man got his head in this elk skull. The women helped him further, after trying to pull the old bleached elk skull off of his head without success, the women got ahold of a stone hammer and broke the elk skull off as easy as they could from Napi's head. As the skull broke free from Napi's head and the women seen the naked head—it was just kind of shining—they all ran off screaming. All got scared of this hairless person, no one had ever seen a hairless person before this. Slowly reaching up to his head, as he stood there not knowing what the women were all running from, his hands touched his head and he almost broke into a run too. He felt nothing but naked skin on his head. This was a bit embarrassing to Napi, he didn't know how to act or what to do.

Being a good actor, Napi went into one of his acts. He acted like a man out of his head, crazy, running here and there and hollering as he went. The women all took off in many directions away from this dangerous character. All scattered, it was a good time for Napi to disappear from sight, into the trees he ran, screaming and hollering as he went, still acting like a wildman.

Running far away from the camp, Napi slowed down and became himself again. Reaching up and getting a better feeling of his head, Napi knew he was just plumb bald and he would have to stay out of sight for a long time to regrow his hair. And that's what he did, never forgiving those mice. And to this day he never did trust mice with anything.

# Napi and the Bobcat

Napi was camping along the Fox Creek at the foot of the Triple Divide Mountain in what is now Montana, just south of the St. Mary's Lakes.

Most probably, Fox Creek got its name from so many foxes in that area.

One day Napi was just so hungry, he had to have something to eat. He left his camp and went southward towards the Cut Bank Creek, as it's known in these days. There were many *pis-kuns* along its banks. Locating a good fresh used *pis-kun*, Napi waited around it for a few days hoping that someone might use it again soon. When nothing happened there he went on to the other *pis-kuns* to find out if they were in use. He had to have something to eat.

Napi was just all alone, he couldn't very well use those *pis-kuns* alone.

Several days went by, he had seen several camps in this vicinity along this Cut Bank Creek. Napi had his eyes on these camps that they might go out to bring in the buffalo to these *pis-kuns*, one of them at least. Napi was waiting around in the hills nearby one of the camps. One morning, just as it got gray in the east, an early morning activity took place at the west-most camp. Right away, Napi knew what was going on there, the men were all getting ready to go out into the plains to bring a herd of buffalos to their *pis-kun*. The camp was running short of fresh meat and entrails. Light was now showing more brightly in this early morning, the men were on their way out of the camps. Napi knew where a herd of buffalo were, and not too far from this camp. Running alongside the group of hunters but behind the rolling hills, Napi was trying to make his way to the leader of this hunting party to put him wise to the large herd of buffalo.

Napi was very desperate to get something to eat, all he had in the past few days was a few dried roots and berries, which wasn't too filling for him. He had to have meat to satisfy himself.

There were so many camps of these early Natives of these Americas, that people may have traveled together for many years, and they still all didn't know one another. In this camp, it wasn't any different.

Napi was always so very sneaky and very stealthy about his ways, any place he could be near by without being noticed. He snuck alongside of the hunting party until he finally got the chance to merge in with the hunting group without being noticed. He got in the hunting group up near the leader.

They made hardly any noise even as they all walked along, all had soft-sole mocassins that hardly make any noise. All had to be quiet on a hunting party to be able to sneak up to a herd of buffalo and to kill with a bow and arrow.

As he got as near to the leader as he could, Napi whispered to him, telling him of the big buffalo herd very near here. The leader didn't know Napi, so he wasn't in any way suspicious that a stranger was among this hunting party. The leader took the way Napi pointed to and sure enough, not too far away, a big herd of buffalo grazed about. Behind the hills, the leader gave orders to the men to make a semicircle around the herd, opposite from the *pis-kun*.

On their way, every so far, the leader would leave two men as guides to lay in wait for their return with a buffalo herd. These guides kept a sharp lookout for the hunters' return, and if they see a herd of buffalo coming towards them, these men must spook the buffalo on the right course towards the buffalo jump. All men were very important on a buffalo hunt in those early days. There weren't any horses to depend on, to get places faster, all people had to depend on were their legs and feet. Because of the way we ate our natural food in those early days, pure food with no mixture of anything, it was healthy to live on. It's true and known by many that those early Natives could run all day and all night if they have to without getting winded or getting weak.

These men were very skilled hunters. It didn't take much to get organized behind the herd, and it wasn't long before they got them a-moving towards the direction of the *pis-kun*. This day didn't see much trouble in herding the herd of buffalo in the right direction towards the *pis-kun*. All moved along so nice.

The day was still young when the herd of buffalo came in sight of the womenfolks near the *pis-kun*. They were ready too. The younger ones, the lame men, and the older men would hide behind those piled rocks that formed the V-shape pointing towards the *pis-kun*. Behind about every fourth pile of rocks, a man or woman hid to scare the herd on to a faster run, and eventually into a stampede over the steep bank, where they would fall on one another and all get killed.

The herd of buffalos came without any trouble and got into the V-piled rocks. From there on it was easier. The herd was scared on to a faster and faster run towards the jump-off, and by the time the herd got to the brink of the steep bank, they were in a stampede. Over they went and on to their death below.

The women came, all of them, and the children too, to help with what they could. It was the women's turn to work, the men done their share this morning, bringing in the herd to the *pis-kun* and to their death. Now the women got busy with the skinning of the animals, the butchering, dressing the meat, and preparing the entrails.

Napi was right among the women, doing his share of work, but for himself—he had no woman to do the work for him. He got all he could handle and carry on his back, and no one among those people was the wiser. No one as much as asked Napi who he was, they all thought he was one of them.

The men were sitting all around the corral of the *pis-kun* telling stories, while the women were in the corral skinning the carcasses. Every once in a while a woman or two would bring a tasty morsel for one of the men as they sat telling stories, raw tasty pieces of the entrails washed in blood. A piece of tripe, belly of the animal, manyfold, the food grinder of the animal, piece of liver or kidney, the brisket, or the cow might have an unborn calf in her.

This unborn calf is taken out and the womb cut open. Inside of this womb is some lumps that look like sweetbreads, and the Native calls them womb buttons. These are eaten raw too. The children are playing around with a lower leg bone broken in half, and with a small stick, these children dip into the hollow of this leg bone and dip out the marrow. A very tasty treat for the children and far better and healthier than all the treats they have these days.

It's about mid-afternoon now and the butchering of the animals was over. Everyone was hauling their load of fresh meat and entrails to the river close by to wash them, Napi was right among them as they all went down to the river.

Napi got away from there with his load of fresh meat and entrails without being noticed by any one of the people. To his arbor he went, and as he reached that arbor he throwed down his load of meat. This load should do for a few days, he thought. It didn't take him very long to make a hot fire, and soon he was cooking quite a bit of meat. It wasn't too long before the meat and entrails were ready for eating, and that he did. Napi ate and he ate, he ate so much that he fell asleep where he sat and naturally he didn't put any of the fresh meat or the cooked meat away before he fell asleep.

Napi woke up from his deep sleep. Gosh! It was morning already, he had slept all night. He was a bit hungry this morning, getting up he went to the pot to get something to eat from it, he found it empty of its contents. He jumped to the fresh meat he laid near the entrance to his little arbor, and those too were gone. Left without anything to eat again, he was boiling mad. He crawled around, looking where the things were, to find evidence of what became of them. Napi found a bone with the fat still on it, and there were teeth marks on this fat. By those teeth marks he knew what got away with the meat. It was a bobcat's teeth marks.

Napi went around his camp to find which way the bobcat went. In the loose dirt he tracked the bobcat going towards the hills. Tracking him here and there, the tracks led up into these rolling hills. As Napi came over one of the hills very slowly, there, down in the bottom of this hill, was the darn old bobcat that stole all of Napi's hard-gotten meat. The bobcat didn't notice Napi looking down at him, he was busy turning rocks and making quite a bit of noise with those rocks he was turning over.

Before this time, bobcats were very beautiful animals. They had perfect faces with a long beautiful nose and long beautiful ears.

Napi thought he would have some kind of fun with the bobcat before he done anything to him. Still a-hiding among those weeds and rocks and looking down at the bobcat, the bobcat thinking he was all alone here. Napi slowly peeked over the rocks and hollered out so the bobcat would hear, "Mey-stik-si-si! Oh slick butt!" The bobcat heard him and stopped to look all around him, and up the hills around him. Satisfying himself there wasn't anyone around, he went back to turning the rocks over again. Several more times Napi hollered at the bobcat, "Mey-stik-si-si," and each time the bobcat would stop and look all around him. Although the bobcat couldn't see anything, each time he looked all around him, he would be grinning. He knew someone was playing tricks on him.

Several more times of this, then Napi's anger got the best of him, he couldn't hold himself any longer. When the bobcat went back to turning rocks, Napi hurriedly went sneaking down to him, and with the noise of those rocks he was turning, he didn't hear Napi coming. Napi grabbed him by his hind legs and up and down he threw him, hitting the bobcat's nose on a flat large rock. Over and over again he threw the bobcat on its nose on that flat rock until the bobcat's nose was just so short. All this time the bobcat was hollering and begging for Napi to stop it, but Napi was making this thieving bobcat pay for all that meat he stole from him.

Napi finally decided the bobcat had enough, but before he let the bobcat go, Napi bit its ears off too. Then he let go of him. As the bobcat took off, Napi hollered after him, "From here on, you will look like this so people will know that you got your looks from stealing and they will watch you very close."

**Napi Shortens the Bobcat's Face**

# Napi and the Bull Berries

Hunger got Napi into much trouble, women got him into a lot of trouble too. In the days of Napi, about all the treasures one knew about was eating and women. No money to worry about, nothing of value to worry about.

No wonder Napi had converted to this sort of going on when he was only supposed to be a disciple of Creator Sun. He had carried out all the orders of Creator Sun, people of Mother Earth had learned much from this Napi. All the people were still learning from him, the works of foolishness.

One day Napi was going along as usual, and hungry as usual, there was nothing to satisfy this hunger until he found a camp or some kind of food along the way, but drinking water would stave off the hunger for awhile. Down to the river he went, fighting through the thickets to get to the water. This was a larger river and quite deep, especially where there were bends. As he reached the water's edge, Napi found himself a place where he could lay on his stomach and drink his fill. He drank a lot of water. Being a hot day and him getting kind of weak from hunger, Napi got up on the bank and sat near the water's edge. His stomach was growling something awful after downing the water, he must rest a while before going on.

As he sat there looking all about him, wishing he could see something edible, he looked under some bushes for shade. These bushes hung out over the water and right at a bend in this river where it was very deep. This particular place was one of the many green holes, it was so deep. He hadn't looked down into the water as of yet, his roaming eyes were all over through the trees and up into the trees. Nothing there he could see that was good to eat. Straightening up in a sitting position, Napi's eyes went down the river and slowly towards his place where he was sitting. As his eyes got to where he was at, right under him in the deep part of the river, Napi seen a big cluster of bull berries. They looked very large and juicy, sweet and delicious. His mouth was watering as he sat there gazing at those delicious bull berries.

Napi could swear they were under water, he would have to dive for them juicy red bull berries. Taking off what clothes he had on, Napi didn't hesitate any longer. He dove right down after those bull berries, his lungs almost bursting from want of air. He came up, his head popping out of the water and gasping for air. He didn't get any juicy red bull berries. Filling his lungs again with the nice fresh air, Napi dove again and was feeling around for those luscious red bull berries. No berries. Over and over he tried.

"I must stay under water longer to find those bull berries and I must use some weight to hold me down there. I keep on floating back to surface," thought Napi to himself.

Coming back up for air again, Napi found himself a few good, large stones. These he wrapped in his leggings and tied around his waist, and back into the river he dove again. Down at the bottom of this river in the deep hole,

Napi was looking all over for those red juicy bull berries. His lungs were very near bursting when he finally gave up to come up for more air. To his horror, he couldn't begin to float upwards from the bottom of the river, and he needed air so bad now. Trying to untie the ends of the rawhide rope from his body, Napi had already swallowed a lot of water. At last he freed himself and to the surface he went. He was almost drowned, gasping for air to breathe and all in from those dives he was doing to get at those juicy red bull berries.

This was about the closest to death Napi had ever come during all his doings. Laying there fighting for breath, on his stomach as the water drained out of him. For the longest time Napi laid there fighting to regain his breath from that near drowning.

After a long while Napi felt better and slowly turned on his back, still under those bushes, his eyes closed, breathing a little easier now. Napi slowly opened those eyes of his and the first thing he seen was those juicy red bull berries, a very large cluster of them as they hung out over the river. They weren't in the water as he had thought, but up in the air where he hadn't bothered to look. Angry again over his foolishness, Napi got up and got a good big club and start beating on them bull berry bushes, knocking off all of those luscious red juicy bull berries into the river and off they floated away.

*Reflection of the Bull Berries*

Napi didn't get to eat any of the bull berries, although he set another precedent for time to come. Napi told the bull berry bushes and the berries, "This shall be the way people will pick you from the bushes, they will hit the bushes and this will knock the berries off where they will be picked up by the people."

To this day, when the Natives pick bull berries, they lay a canvas under the bushes and beat on the bull berry bushes. The berries fall onto this canvas and, when they're all beaten off, the canvas is picked up at each corner and dumped into a box or some kind of container. This is done after the first frost hits, because the frost makes the bull berries very sweet.

# Napi and a Big-Breasted Lady

In the latter days of his presence here on Mother Earth, Napi's mind was constantly on women and food. Napi was a disciple of Creator Sun, to teach the people of Mother Earth the ways of Creator Sun and what the Creator wanted his children to be in the future. In most everything today we go by the precedents that Napi taught the people of those early days. We even live by those crazy things Napi done towards the last of his days as a teacher of Creator Sun's children.

In these last days of Napi's teachings he had gone astray, contrary to the good he was to teach all people of Mother Earth. Why had he gone astray from his errand for Creator Sun? Was it that he wanted to live here on Mother Earth like a common child of Creator Sun and not the disciple he was? Anyway! That foolishness that he done about food and women has influenced many of the people of today. Many of us do foolish things whence women and food are concerned.

Napi had the power that was entrusted to him by Creator Sun. Creator Sun couldn't take it back because of Napi's wrongdoings. Creator Sun knew it was his fault that Napi was here on Mother Earth and Napi had to have something to live by while he was here.

The children of Creator Sun were spreading out in greater distances now as time passed, and as they multiplied into greater multitudes. They needed the food in new areas they were to live.

It's the same as today, people are forever migrating from one country to another to find food and good living. Jobs of these days are part of living, and they concern food too. So! It's still the way Creator Sun and his disciple Napi had taught all people—to leave one place, find a new place of plenty, with room and food to live by. Now people even have a plan to seek a place to live in space. But there! The space is Creator Sun's domain and he will not permit anyone to live out there. He gave his bride Mother Earth to suckle all of his children, and those that are to live out in space aren't suckled by

Mother Earth. Nothing will come to them. They'll be forgotten and shall perish no matter what they might try to do to better it out there.

Napi had come to a camp, one of the ever-spreading groups of Mother Earth. Like always, Napi was very curious about this place he had just come to. The people and their ways were a little different from those he was used to seeing. It didn't make much difference to Napi, he could get by anywhere he went. There was something going on here at this camp. The people were all milling around, and Napi's neck was getting sore from turning his head this way and that way trying to see what was going on. Not only was he trying to see what was going on, he was also busy staring after this woman and that one. His head was something like a goose, it was almost twisting off from spinning one way then the other. Lust for women. He was scrutinizing every woman that came along, looking at the legs, the butt, the breasts, and the face. At times his mouth was drooling.

Staring at almost every woman that came along, Napi was walking around among this crowd. His eyes kept a sharp look out for women and their shape. Coming from the tipis, two women came towards the crowd, Napi right away noticed them, especially the one with extra-large breasts, exceptionally large.

Napi wanted to get at those extra-large breasts. He followed the two women wherever they went, his eyes steadfastly on those tender, juicy extra-large breasts. Asking around in the crowd about the woman and where she had her tipi and not getting any answers, Napi finally had to make some kind of lie to obtain an answer. Napi was told that this woman with big breasts was a single woman. She had children and her husband had died. She was a kind woman, especially to children, she got very upset and emotional whenever she sees a child crying. She went far out of her way to help others whenever and wherever help was needed.

Upon hearing this information, Napi soon had a plan to get at those luscious, juicy big breasts. Since he seen those big breasts, Napi hadn't gone much any other place, but always stayed close by those big breasts he so much wanted to handle and play with.

The tipi of the woman with the big breasts was pointed out to Napi. Napi kept his eyes on this woman with the extra-large breasts. He was always close behind them at all times, not letting her out of his sight. So when it was time for the woman to go to her tipi, Napi knew this. He followed behind her for a little ways, then he ran in a roundabout way to beat her to her tipi. Jumping inside of the woman's tipi, Napi put his plan to work.

He started to make himself small, like a baby or a small child. But as the woman was now coming closer, Napi's plan didn't come out just right. Because he was in such a hurry, the power didn't do exactly as he wanted it.

The woman was just getting too close, and he didn't have time to make it right. The woman came inside her tipi, and she was very surprised to see a different small child in her bed. Her children were getting big and were out there playing somewhere. This little one was crying very hard and she didn't have time to find out where this child came from, she had to take care of it now. This little one was still in its suckling age. Taking the child in her arms, she held the child to her breasts to feed him so it would stop its crying. Just what Napi wanted, him transforming into a very small child and now that wish for those luscious, tender, juicy extra-large breasts he hungered for. At last he was getting at them with his mouth, and sucking on them at that. But like it was, he didn't have time to righten the power he used, probably because he was using it for his own gain and a bad one, to get at those big breasts.

This child just couldn't get enough of those breasts he was sucking on. Every time the woman tried to push his head away from those breasts, this darn child would burst out screaming and she would have to let him suck more. Her friend living in the next tipi had been hearing those screams. Wondering what all the commotion was about, she came over to the tipi where the woman was suckling the strange child.

This other lady sat opposite from her friend as she sat there suckling the child. The lady that was giving suck to the child was telling her friend about how this child was already in her tipi when she came in and that it was crying, she had to take care of him so it would stop its crying. The other woman looked at her and the baby as they sat there busy feeding the baby. This other woman was staring at the child's feet and hands, they looked very strange to her. Her curiosity finally getting the best of her, she went over to her friend's side and had a closer look at those strange-looking feet and hands. The woman with the big breasts took a closer look too. Seeing them, she pushed the baby's head away. They knew right away what it was about, they had heard about Napi and his tricks before. Right away they knew it was Napi that was here. This child's feet and hands didn't change to baby feet and hands—they were still the hands of a grown-up, the feet too were that of a grown-up.

The two women dropped the child and ran out of the tipi. They dare not call for help as it was just too embarrassing to the woman with those extra-large breasts, letting Napi fool her into letting him suck on her big breasts. Out to the crowd they ran, while Napi transformed back into his own self, cursing his stupidity about the lack of transforming his feet and hands. Well anyway! He got to suck on those extra-luscious, tender, juicy large breasts of the woman, and that was what he was after.

Again on his way to the unknown places, Napi left the camp to seek elsewhere for more of his doings, especially for women and food.

# Buffalos Laughing to Death

Napi is always hungry and always out to find something to eat. He wasn't any different this day as he walked along the creek bottom along the brush, Napi looking here and there where he might find something to eat by luck, something he would be able to chew on. But no such luck. Nothing!

During the Napi days, things were a little hard to come by. It was bird eat bird, animal eat animal. Mostly everything in those days spoke language, no matter what kind of life it was. People were very hesitant to kill the birds or animals that were edible. It was so hard to kill them because many of them begged for their lives and the people, being very compassionate to all life, couldn't just see killing someone that's begging for its life.

This day wasn't any different for Napi as he walked along, if only he could see a camp to bum for some food or steal from he would do that, he was so hungry. But no such luck, there weren't many people about at that time. It was the first beginning of people. Groups were still sparsely settled.

As he was coming around a bend in the creek and around some bushes, just ahead of him a fox came and made its way towards the hills. Napi immediately followed the fox. He knew these foxes hid food for future use, and this fox just might have some food stashed away in those hills. Hiding around behind the fox, where the fox wouldn't see him, Napi followed.

Far up into the rolling hills went the fox, with Napi following as close as he could without the fox knowing about him. Up to the highest of the hills the fox went. Napi was just far enough behind so the fox wouldn't see him.

Coming to the highest hill, the fox went up, but not all the way to the top. From there he seemed like he was crawling on his belly and slowly peeking over the top of this hill. At the foot of this hill was a big herd of buffalos. Napi was trying to sneak up as close as he could without exposing himself to the fox. Napi was still crawling along when he heard loud laughter from the herd of buffalo. Just about then he seen the fox running with all speed down to the herd. Napi ran too, but still hiding from the fox. When he got to where he could peek down on the fox, the fox was already eating on a huge buffalo bull. Napi stopped short, surprised! How had the fox killed the huge buffalo bull?

Napi waited in hiding until the fox left after filling himself with the fresh kill. After the fox left and had gone, Napi went down to the carcass to eat on what was left of the buffalo bull. As Napi left after he had his fill, all the way home he thought of the fox. What did he do to kill a huge buffalo bull? "I will have to find out about this," he thought to himself as he got home.

Sleeping on it, the next morning Napi got up before daylight to keep his eyes on the fox. For several days nothing happened, no fox to see anywhere. Napi didn't give up so soon, he had to find out what the fox did to kill those buffalos and why all the laughter came from the herd.

One day as Napi waited around for the fox to come out of the bushes, and so very early in the morning, he wasn't surprised to see the fox come out and immediately head for those rolling hills again. Napi didn't wait either, he knew just about where the fox was a-going. He made a wild dash for that place to beat the fox to it, and he did. Napi hid himself well, where he could see what was going on.

Napi had just gotten hid when the fox came over a hill not far from him. The fox came trotting slowly towards the high hill again and slowly peeked over it. The fox waited a moment, then he made a noise that attracted the herd of buffalo to him. And as the herd of buffalo looked up at him, the fox went into the craziest dance anyone every seen. At the same time he was making all kinds of funny faces. When the herd of buffalos seen his act, there was a loud roar of laughter. Napi was looking down at the buffalo as they made the racket from laughter. He was still looking at the buffalo herd when he seen a buffalo staggering around and down it fell. The fox didn't wait, he went running down there in a hurry while Napi looked on. Stopping at the side of the fallen buffalo, the fox soon was eating the fallen one. It had died from laughing too hard.

The fox got its fill again and left, and Napi came out from his hiding and went to fill up on the remainder of the carcass. He too went home after his

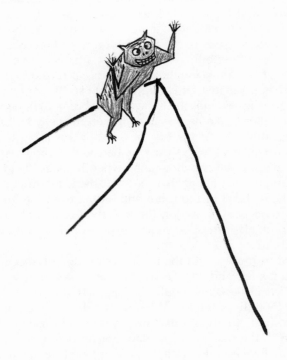

*Buffalos Laughing to Death*

fill. Napi wanted to learn how to do this, to kill the buffalo with laughter. It was several days before the old fox again took off for those hills. This time Napi didn't hurry, as he knew right where to go. Up, up the hills he went, waiting a little as he went along slowly. Napi came to the place just as the fox ran down to the buffalo that laughed himself to death. The fox ran down to it and began to eat off of it. As the fox ate, Napi slowly made his way down to him. And as he got close enough for the fox to hear, Napi acted very pitiful and humble. He came towards the fox crying and talking at the same time, "Aye, aye, my little brother fox, let me do this, what you have done, so I will not go hungry anymore."

The fox took pity on Napi. He quit eating for a spell to speak to Napi, "Yes! You can do this when you get hungry. Come here closer and I will teach you what you must do." Napi came closer to the fox, he was a willing student. The fox taught him to act foolish and comical and to make all kinds of funny faces at the same time. It was a short lesson for Napi, but he caught on, because it was a way to get food. Before the fox left the place he turned to Napi and told him, "Never be too greedy about this, do this only when you are very hungry and haven't any other place to get something to eat. If you do this one after another, bad will come of it. Remember, not for fun." The fox left for the creek again.

Although there was quite a bit left over from the fox's kill, it wasn't good

enough for Napi, not with the new power he got from the fox. He went to find himself the herd and, with the new act, he got himself a buffalo to eat. He took only a couple of bites from it and he let it go to waste. Again he went to the buffalo and killed another one by his act. The next day he went very early, and every little while he killed a buffalo. All went to waste, just one or two bites from each one. There were buffalo carcasses lying all over the hills now, Napi's dirty work. But always there is someone looking down at us, our Creator. And with the waste he did, Napi was sure to be punished for it.

It was getting well towards evening when Napi decided to kill one for his evening meal. Up the hill he went. Slowly looking over, he saw the buffalo herd again. Napi went into his act of the funny dance and the making of the funny faces. It was quite a surprise when the buffalo didn't even smile at his act. Instead the buffalo bulls pawed the earth and bellowed, and towards him they came a-running to attack him. They were after him and Napi didn't have a place to hide, all he could do was run like the dickens.

Over the hills, down the hills, and no woods to take cover in. Napi finally made it to the creek, among the larger trees. Grabbing a large limb, he swung himself to safety, and up in that tree Napi sat all evening. The buffalo herd didn't leave, they stayed around for several days watching Napi and laughing at him up in the tree. It was their turn to laugh at him for killing all of those buffalos for nothing.

# Napi and Women Selecting Husbands

Towards the last days of Napi, all of the single women left from camp where everyone else lived. The single women had their own head woman besides the Chief of the camp, and the single men had their own Chief too.

It was one of those things where the Chiefs couldn't get along too well, arguments and arguments between them, the head woman of the single women's group and the Chief of the single men's group and the head Chief of this camp. One day the arguments got so bad that the head woman of the ladies' group decided to move away from here where she could better take care of her followers. She moved far away from this main camp. It took the women several days to get to wherever they moved. The place was along a river, and the women camped on the north shore. The women went out to find their own food, and built their own *pis-kun* where they killed buffalo by the herds. They didn't have any problems. It could've been the very first women's lib.

The main camp got along very good for a while. The head Chief and the single men's Chief seemed to hit it off very good since the head woman and all of her single woman left this main camp.

Everything would've been all right if it weren't for the single men. They started to bellyache about no single women around this camp, they were only human beings too, they needed company of the opposite sex and there wasn't any single women in this camp. No one to flirt with or to take out and they dare not get mixed up with the married women, as that was a sure sign of death.

All of the single men began to let their Chief know what their feelings were. They hounded him and bothered him about this night and day until one day he got so tired of hearing about it that he got together with the head Chief of this camp and told him that him and all of his followers would have to leave and find the single women's camp. The head Chief of this camp, understanding the situation, didn't say much, except that it was a good idea for the single men. A few days after this all of the single men got together and got ready to move away from this main camp to find the single women. The Chief of this single men's group was none other than Napi himself.

One very early morning the single men sent out some scouts to go ahead of the main group of singles to try and locate the single women's camp. The rest of the men, the main force of the single men's group, gave the scouts time to get far ahead before they too got under way and followed the scouts in the direction they had taken. For many days the move was constantly a-going, their scouts would come back to report every once in a while and tell which direction they were to go.

Several days went by without any luck, but none wanted to give up. The scouts kept a-going ahead every day to look. One day, as the sun was getting low in the west and coming over a high butte close to the river, the scouts seen a good-size camp along the north shore of this river. They didn't hesitate very long, down the hill they ran until they got to the camp. They weren't surprised to find the group of single women. Meeting with the head women of this single women's group, she too was very glad to have the single men close by them. She gave the scouts the location of a place for a camp for the single men. The south shore of this river is where the single men's group will set up their camps. Everything was agreed to by the scouts. The scouts took their leave of the head woman and happily hurried back to the main group of the single men to report.

When the scouts had related their finding and the agreement with the head woman, Napi's group got ready and moved closer to the women's camp. Across the river, on the south shore, Napi's camps were set.

The river is the present-day High River, about forty miles south of Calgary, Alberta, Canada. This particular story of the two camps was located about eighteen miles west of the present site of the town of High River along the river. To this day it's still a landmark for those oldtimers, of course they are all gone on to Happy Hunting Grounds. Some of these people that held that particular place as a historic landmark of the Piegan Natives died only a few years ago, in the twenties, thirties, and forties, there might be a very few that might be alive yet as I'm writing this story in 1979. In the Northern

Plains Native area, where this story is written about, Napi left many landmarks that the older people point out to many of us younger people that are
being told those stories of the beginning of life and the legendary history of
our ancestors. Many of these legendary landmarks are still plainly visible,
but some have eroded away, and others are destroyed by the works of
progress.

The stories that I write about might sound fantastic, or like a lot of imagination, because of the supernatural powers that those people had, that were
given them by that life of nature, whenever they went out to seek for it. Of
course it isn't any different from the written stories of the days of King
Arthur and the great magician Merlin, or even the Bible stories of water all
turning to blood and canes turning into serpents. In those days, most people
had the power of Creator Sun if they went to seek for it, and they could do
almost anything with that power.

Both camps were doing their own thing every day. Most of all, each group
was minding their own business, not trying to bother the other, and all was
going well for a very long time.

One day the women's group went out to hunt buffalo, using a further *pis-
kun* than the one that was near by their camp. It was nothing to carry the
fresh meat to the tipis when the killing was done at their closer *pis-kun*, but
this *pis-kun* was very far from the campsite and all that heavy meat would
have to be carried all that way, and on their backs. It finally came to the
women that being segregated from men wasn't an easy task. With all the
work they had to do since they moved to a separate campsite, it was getting
mighty tiresome for many of the women. Oh how they wished their head
woman would change her mind about men so they could have help on these
heavy jobs. Many of the women were ready to give this up, but their leader
wanted to stay independent from the men.

From this distant *pis-kun* they began to take their heavy meat to their camp.
To make it all the worse, they had to make several trips to get all the meat
to their tipis. It was very late when the last load of meat was brought to their
camp. It was a workout for the head woman, a workout she wouldn't forget
in a few days. The next morning she was just so sore on her body all over
that it made her think she should get some sort of help for her and all of the
women with her.

That same morning, the leader of these women called a meeting. The
women didn't lose much time in getting to her tipi. Every one came to hear
what the head woman had to say. She never has a meeting unless it's
something very important.

First she talked of their good living since they separated from the main
camp, and then she spoke of the goodness of keeping away from the men.
They didn't have to worry about a bunch of little ones crying after them. But!
She told the women, "From our workout yesterday, I knew we had to get
help from the stronger people, the men. Now I have decided that we will
have a meeting with the men's Chief and plan out a way for all of us to get
together. We must get a man to marry to help us, and that goes for all of us

women here at this camp. We will have a meeting with the head Chief of the single men's camp, we'll set a certain time for this important thing for us."

After the women had met, their head woman went across to the men's camp with her closer aids to talk to the head Chief. After seeing some of the men, she asked for the head Chief of the camp. She asked for the Chief's name, and was told his name was Napi. By then, Napi was found and brought to the head woman of the camp across the river.

In the middle of Napi's camp the two head people of the camps met to talk about the good news with good understanding. An agreement between the women and the men was made. It was decided that the selecting of a husband would be after the morning of the next full moon.

The two head people of the two camps went to their camps to give the news to their subjects, the time of selecting of a husband. All of the women were glad to hear this, and the men were too. For all of them, it was like sitting on a porcupine's tail. All of them, both men and women, could hardly sit still to wait for the coming day.

The night of the full moon came at last. Most of the women and men just couldn't sleep any at all that night, it was a big day for them the next day. Next morning, for some reason, the head woman forgot about this special day. She was busy with her tipi work and was in her working dress when one of the ladies came to her and reminded her. All of the other ladies were ready, they were all dressed for the big occasion, a day that will change their lives for better living and more rest for each woman. The head woman had already delayed all the women. So she decided to go just as she was dressed, in her dirty working clothes, so the woman could have it over with as they were all very anxious to get a man. The head woman as a leader of this women's camp was to be the very first to select a husband, then after her all of the other women would have their turns.

It was all arranged at their previous meeting. When the women started across the river for the men's camp, all the men were to climb to the top of the bank along this river and stand in line along the edge while the women gathered at the foot, and from there they would take turns to climb up and select a husband.

All of the men had gone up the bank and made a line along the river's bank. Napi was placed right in the center of the men in the line, and he had dressed for this special thing. The women had already gathered at the foot of this bank and were all looking up at the men standing in line, waiting for the head woman to go up and select her future husband. The head woman was looking the men over. Because she knew her wit to become head of this women's camp, she could tell where the Chief of the men was standing in that line on the bank of this river. It was only fair to everyone that the head woman and the Chief of the men would take up with one another. The head woman went up the bank of the river and her dirty dress was still on her. She didn't straighten out her hair or even tidy up. She looked somewhat messy and dirty, but everyone knew she was a very good-looking woman and head of this women's camp. She was a very important person and shouldn't have any trouble at all. Any man would be willing to marry her.

Coming up the bank, the Chief of the women's camp made her way right straight towards Napi. Napi didn't recognize her as the head woman, all he seen was that this woman coming towards him looked awful fifthy and dirty. In his mind he visualized her as a dirty tipi-keeper, lazy good-for-nothing woman. As she got close to Napi, Napi stepped aside from her and each time she reached out for Napi, he would take a step out of her way. After her fourth try she gave up.

She gave up and she held up her hands to her followers, the other women. This head lady was very upset and embarrassed over what happened to her, the Chief of the men's camp refusing her hand, stepping out of the way from her. Being the head woman of her all-woman camp, naturally she was the first to choose her man. Napi had refused her, and she now held up the husband choosing for awhile until she had a word with her followers.

Getting back down to the group of women, the head lady called a huddle. There she told them not to choose the man that had refused her and to hold up a while, while she got changed into a better dress and adorned herself a little.

They all waited anxiously to get this choosing over with so they could see what kind of men each had chosen. The head lady went up the hill first again, all dressed up this time. She was about the nicest looking woman the

*Women Selecting Husbands—*
*Napi Turns into a Lone Pine Tree*

men ever seen. This time, Napi made his way to where she was headed to the row of men. Now it was her turn to side-step Napi. Each time she held her hand out to choose a man, Napi got in her way so that he might be the one chosen by her, as he was the Chief of the men's camp. The head woman finally reached around Napi and chose a nice-looking man. Napi was shocked over this, he didn't know how to act before all of the men and the women that had their eyes on the choosing.

Taking her man back down the hill with her, the head woman now gave the signal to her women followers to go ahead and each choose a man for herself. As each woman came up the hill to choose a husband, Napi always got in front of them so he might be chosen, but no such luck. All of the women chose a man and Napi was left all alone on the bank of this river. The women all began to go back across the river, their head woman was the last to leave. As she too left the choosing place, she seen Napi so all alone, still standing along the bank looking down on them as all left the scene. The head women hollered up to Napi and told him, "Stand there forever and turn into a lone pine tree."

Napi turned into a lone pine tree and stood there for years upon years. And as far as can be said, that lone pine tree still stands there on the bank of the Highwood River, Alberta, Canada.

This was the end of Napi, Oldman, a disciple of Creator Sun sent to teach the ways of our Creator Sun to those children and to us, children of both Creator Sun and Mother Earth. We all learned many things from Napi, both the good ways and the bad ways he influenced this world over.

But Creator Sun didn't stop there. He put another disciple here on earth to correct the mistakes that Napi taught us and to do away with evil powers. He was Kut-toe-yis, Bloodclot.

# KUT-TOE-YIS, BLOODCLOT TALES

## *The Birth of Kut-toe-yis, Bloodclot*

Creator Sun had done away with Napi, he was getting too foolish to teach the children of Creator Sun and Mother Earth. Creator Sun didn't go out to do away with Napi, but! Napi had done himself in from the foolishness he was doing with that wonderful power he was entrusted with by Creator Sun and Mother Earth. He was beginning to use too much of that great power for his own mischief towards the children of Creator Sun and Mother Earth.

Much wickedness had come to this land because of Napi. Creator Sun had to do something to stop it all. Napi was stopped by his own foolishness, and now Creator Sun must put someone else in that place to correct the bad.

It's always a mystery about Creator Sun and Mother Earth and the way they do things. The coming of Kut-toe-yis wasn't just an ordinary thing, it came about by Creator Sun's and Mother Earth's mysteries.

Among the people of this land, wickedness had been abundant, and somehow it must be stopped by Creator Sun. All of this wickedness had been spreading out to all the people that had scattered many, many hundreds of miles. Of course the people of that time didn't know anything about miles, distances were mostly by how many days it would take one to get there. It now was several thousands of years since the beginning of the humans, and the population of these people had gone in groups to many parts of this land. The language they once used to understand one another was different then that first language they all knew at one time. Almost all of these scattered groups had their own way of talking, a different language that the others couldn't understand.

Today that language barrier still is among the many various Native Tribes of the American continents, North and South America. If it weren't for the English language, we would've had to still talk with our hands in the old Native hand sign language.

All of these groups of people had everything their own, their own area of hunting and their own language, their own ways to live by. Very, very seldom would two groups meet. If by chance they met, it was all respect for one another. Fighting was unheard of in those days. What the whiteman wrote about, that all of the Natives of these Americas were savages and warlike people, is nothing but a lot of wind that come out of their mouths. Compassion for the life of people and for everything that was created by Creator Sun and Mother Earth was theirs and still is in these days. If it weren't for this compassion, I truly don't think there would be any other race to set foot on these continents, because sure as hell they would've been killed outright when they were landing. No one would have landed here without an invasion of this land if we were the savages, murderers, and barbarians that the white people often call the Natives.

It was one of these groups that had an area of hunting grounds somewhere near the present-day Sweet Grass Hills or the Great Plains of Montana and Alberta, Canada. It was a fairly large camp and hunting wasn't so good. A young man that had just married into a family of four girls didn't like the idea of how they were getting their food, and besides he was kind of a jealous sort of person, especially with his newly found young wives. He wanted to move away from here to find their own place to build a *pis-kun*. To his in-laws and to his wives he spoke that it was better for them to leave here and find a place where buffalo was bountiful. He didn't have to argue much to do what he wanted, the girls and his in-laws knew he was a good rustler for food. They all liked the idea, and one morning the little group left this main camp after telling the Chief of the camp their plans.

The small group of in-laws and son-in-law, the women and all, about seven people total, left the main camp one early morning to find themselves a good place to hunt and live. It was especially the young man's idea over his new wives, the four sisters. He was jealous over them and afraid that some other young man might cut in on him. He was an ideal young man, many parents would've liked to have him for a son-in-law. He was a go-getter, a good provider, even to his own parents. They sure were going to miss him now.

The in-laws had gained a son. They didn't have a son of their own that could help them around. They were very fortunate to get a son-in-law like this young man, and they liked him very much.

With their dogs and the travois that were used to carry their belongings, they were well on their way by the time the sun was up. They headed north and northwest from the main camp to find a nice place to live. For many, many days they traveled, over hills, across rivers and creeks, the young man always looking ahead to find where the buffalo and other game were abundant, even for fowls, the edible ones. This young man used his head, he was very intelligent.

After many days of weary travel, the young man at last found what he was looking for. Game was abundant here with buffalo, deer, elk, moose, even antelope, and many kinds of edible fowls that could be dried like the bigger game meat. It was here that the small group set up their tipis and made their home.

At the bank of the larger river, the young man built his own *pis-kun* with the help of his wives and in-laws. Right inside of this *pis-kun* in the bank was a very large cave. The young man had gone in there before the *pis-kun* was built, he knew how large of a cave it was and he had plans for it. So right over it he built the *pis-kun*.

It doesn't take long to set tipis up and get settled once it's decided to camp. It didn't take very long to make this place look like it was always lived in.

Upon completing the *pis-kun*, the young man and the whole family got out and brought in a herd of buffalo, which they ran over into the *pis-kun*. Many of the buffalo were killed, but there were many that weren't even maimed by the fall over the bank, as they were cushioned by those that fell first. The young man and his wives chased all of these unmaimed buffalos into the large cave for use as they were needed. Almost every other day the young man brought more and more into the *pis-kun*. As each herd of buffalo was separated, the maimed were killed and those that were all right were taken into the large cave, until it was full of buffalo. The mouth of this cave was right under a debris of logs and trees.

It wasn't always a lucky day for the young man. There were days that he came home empty-handed, no buffalo. All this time he was out alone most of the time, once in a while the father-in-law came along to help him. This was getting at him, he was beginning to get mean to his little family and his in-laws too, especially those times he came home empty-handed. The wives and the in-laws were getting kind of afraid of him when he got into those rages.

One day he came home empty-handed, he was in an exceptionally angry rage to his wives and he came short of beating them up. He told the father-in-law he was good for nothing, that he was a free-loader, that he must help a little more to earn his food and for his tipi too. It got so bad that all of them were very much afraid of him, they all had to jump around at his commands to please him.

This selfishness to his in-laws went on for a long time. Most of the time now, he made his father-in-law do a lot of work and he would send him home without anything after the clean-up in that *pis-kun*. The poor old man and his wife were very undernourished and close to starvation. If it wasn't for the youngest daughter, they would've been starved by now. The youngest of the wives of this once good-hearted young man would sneak some of the fresh meat out for her parents each day. The parents would cook mostly in the night when everyone was in bed, their fear of their young son-in-law was so great. They were barely existing on what food the youngest daughter stole for them to eat.

The son-in-law got meaner and meaner as he got older. He knew that the old man and his wife never really got much to eat, they were weak from lack of food, still he made both of them work more than the wives of his. He was getting very cruel to his family, especially the older couple. The two older ones, this cruel young man's in-laws, were always hungry. The old man was getting to the point where he picked up anything that looked like meat off of the ground within this *pis-kun*, he was getting mighty desperate for food. Whenever he picked anything up from the floor of the *pis-kun*, he made darn sure that he wasn't seen by his son-in-law. Everything he done for their good, he had to sneak doing it.

As the colder weather came and winter had set in, those buffalo that were put up in the cave now came in very handy. The son-in-law would let the old man go into the cave while he stood on top of the entrance to this cave. The old man then would scare one or two of the buffalo to the entrance of the cave, and as the buffalo got near this entrance, the young man stomped as hard as he could on the logs over this entrance, which would then scare the buffalo out into the open to be killed by the young man. The older man then went to work on the dirtier part of the butchering, only to be sent home without anything at the end. This went on through the winter. The days were getting longer and warmer again, and still it was the same routine each day for the old man and his wife, just barely hanging onto life itself by what meager food they were getting from their son-in-law and the three older daughters that went along with their husband. If it weren't for the youngest daughter sneaking food for them, they would've died of starvation long ago.

It was a nice spring morning when the two went to the *pis-kun* to get fresh meat (those people of that time got up with the birds, just when it's beginning to light up in the east), and as usual the poor old man had to jump around at every command his son-in-law ordered. He was sent into the cave like any other morning to herd a couple of buffalo to the entrance for slaughter, while the son-in-law stood on top of the entrance. As the two buffalo came under him, he stomped on the logs over this entrance to scare them out into the open and out into the *pis-kun*. The son-in-law then killed them with his bow and arrows.

But one of these two buffalo didn't die when it got hit with an arrow, the son-in-law missed the vital spot. The buffalo was wounded badly, but was still a-going around within this *pis-kun* a-running, which made the blood ooze out in thick squirts. Big puddles of blood were clotting up all over the place. The poor old man spotted an extra-big clot of blood, he had to get it to make a good old blood soup for them, him and his wife. He watched the son-in-law very closely that he might see a chance to get this big bloodclot as he ran behind this wounded buffalo.

It happened that the son-in-law was busy trying to pick up a fallen arrow, and the old man seen this chance to pick the bloodclot up. He had to be a good actor for what he done, he made out that he slipped and fell by this bloodclot, and at the same time his arrows fell out of his quiver, spilling over this extra-large bloodclot. He picked his arrows up after he crammed the bloodclot first into his quiver and the arrows on top of it. At last he finally had something to take home to make at least a blood soup.

The son-in-law, who always had his eyes on his poor old father-in-law, just to make sure that he didn't take anything that he shouldn't, seen the old man getting up from the ground, and asked the poor old man what he was picking up from the ground. The poor old man told his son-in-law that it was only his arrows that spilled out when he slipped and fell that he was putting back into his quiver. The son-in-law didn't see a thing wrong in that, he didn't say anything further. They finally killed the buffalo and the old man done the dressing out while the son-in-law looked on.

After everything was done, all of the entrails sorted out and the meat cut up by the old man, the son-in-law told his father-in-law, "You can go home and rest until we need meat again."

The old man hurried to his tipi, which was a little ways from the *pis-kun*. Soon as he came stepping into the tipi, in a very low tone, so he wouldn't be heard by all those older daughters, he told his wife, "Old lady, throw your rocks on the fire and get your rawhide pot ready." The old lady said, "*Ah-ya-ho, mah-coke-chewg ooh-see*. It can't be (*ah-ya-ho* is an old Native word only uttered by the older women) that your son-in-law gave meat to take home with you." The old man said that it was only a bloodclot that he picked up off of the ground in the *pis-kun*. At least now they can make a good blood soup to have for their meal.

The old lady got her rawhide pot ready and the old man put the rocks on to heat until they were red-hot. He spilled the quiver into the rawhide pot, out came the extra-large bloodclot. Water was put into the pot too and a hot fire built. It didn't take very long for the rocks to get red-hot. The old lady, with her two forked sticks, got ahold of a red-hot stone from the fire and into the rawhide pot it went. Instantly the water came to a boil, and as it boiled, a cry came from the rawhide pot. It was more like a scream by a baby, and the old man and woman both jumped to the rawhide pot almost at the same time.

To their utmost astonishment, instead of the bloodclot, a little boy was laying in the hot water. The old lady jerked the little baby boy out of the rawhide pot, wiped him off, and wrapped him up in one of the robes of fawn. Both of them were very tickled to have such a wonder, a baby born from an extra-large bloodclot. The two older people didn't care whether they had anything to eat, they were happier to get a baby boy, something they never had before.

Just about that time, right after it got dark outside, their youngest daughter came walking into their tipi with a fairly large piece of fresh meat for them to eat. This young daughter of theirs was always stealing for them to see that her parents didn't starve. Coming inside, right away she seen the little bundle on the old peoples' bed. She stopped short and looked again at the bundle. She finally managed to speak. "What is in that bundle? I know it can't be a new baby, you haven't even been big." The mother answered her daughter, "It is a baby and it came in a very strange way." The mother went on to tell her daughter about the bloodclot that her father brought home to make a good blood soup with, and the cry that came from the rawhide pot as the water got very hot. "The best part of it is, he's a boy. Now you have a brother. Don't give us away, don't tell your husband or your older sisters about this baby."

The youngest daughter promised up and down that she wouldn't say anything about this newborn baby. She went back to her tipi where the sisters and their husband were, she no longer sat down when a cry of a baby came from the old folks' tipi. The son-in-law jerked his big head up when he heard the cry from those old peoples' tipi. Right away he sent the oldest wife of his to the old peoples' tipi to find out if it was a boy or girl that was born to his mother-in-law. The oldest daughter came in and asked what the baby was, the mother lied and told her oldest daughter that the baby was a girl. Taking her mother's word for truth, she went back to her tipi and returned

**Bloodclot Near Birth**

with a little piece of bone with a little fat and very little meat on it. Throwing the piece of bone at her mother's feet, she told her, "My husband sent you this so you can make a rich soup to have more milk for the newborn baby girl." The oldest daughter returned to her tipi.

It wasn't very long when the second-oldest daughter came into the old peoples' tipi asking the same question, what the baby was. The mother sent her back to her tipi with the same answer, "It's a girl." She too returned to her mother's tipi with a soup bone, hardly any meat on it, and almost repeated what her sister said. "My husband sent you something to make soup with so you can have more milk in your breasts for the newborn baby girl."

Still the mean son-in-law wasn't satisfied with the answers. He sent the third-oldest to find out what sex the newborn was. Returning to her tipi, her answer was the same as her sisters. This time it was the youngest daughter's turn to find out about the newborn, only to come back with the same answer. And as each wife returned, the husband sent back a soup bone for the old lady so she would have more milk in her breasts to feed the newborn baby. The youngest of the girls was also sent back to her parents' tipi with a bone, but she also had a piece of good meat that she took without being seen by her sisters or their husband. This youngest of the girls had a strong compassion for her parents, the older ones went along with their husband, they too were starving their folks.

At last! The son-in-law was satisfied with the answers. The newborn was a girl! Another wife it meant for him, soon as she got older, or old enough. From there on the son-in-law was good to the old lady, each evening he sent the youngest wife to her folks with a soup bone, and the youngest daughter always managed to steal a good piece of meat for her parents. But the young man got much meaner to his father-in-law. Any time the old man done something wrong, the son-in-law was ready to strike him or kick him. This treatment was short-lived.

It was the night of the fourth day after the old couple were gifted with the baby boy, a newborn baby boy that came from an extra-large bloodclot. To their utmost surprise, the baby spoke to them. "*Nah-ah, nin-ah ace-ta-tote-chi-scibik-sig on-neek-si-ya ah-mon-stom-iks*. Mother, Dad, tie me briefly to each tipi pole."

The old Native tipis were made of tanned buffalo hides and were very heavy. The larger of them tipis took twenty-nine tipi poles to hold them up, with two poles on the outside to regulate the draft at the top of the tipi. From there down, as they got smaller, the tipi poles also came down in count—twenty-seven, twenty-five, twenty-three, twenty-one, and down to seventeen or even less then that. In all of them, there were two poles for the outside for regulating the draft, which added two more to each of the counts of each tipi.

Without hesitating very long, the two got busy and done what the baby boy wanted. They had already given him the name Kut-toe-yis, meaning bloodclot. To each of the twenty-nine tipi poles on the inside of their tipi, and going clockwise as the sun goes, the old couple tied Kut-toe-yis to each pole briefly. It took quite some time to tie this baby boy to each pole and let him hang there for a short time, then untie him and take him to the next pole. Finally they got to the last pole at the door. The two tied Kut-toe-yis to the tipi pole and for a moment let him be, then untying him. Just as the last wrap around was undone, down jumped a full-grown young man, medium tall and very brawny, muscular and well built, a young man instantly intelligent.

Kut-toe-yis made himself comfortable, next to his father and mother. This strange young man began to ask questions about the old peoples' livelihood, how everything was for them and how their son-in-law and their daughters were doing, if everything was going all right for all of them. How their four daughters and their son-in-law have treated them all this time. If there were any other people around close by. It was many, many things this Kut-toe-yis was asking about. This stranger was very, very intelligent for a newborn, he seemed to know many things about life and what to ask about.

The old couple told their new son about the treatment they were getting from their son-in-law and their three older daughters, how the youngest of the family was very kind to them, how she managed to sneak fresh meat in every day. If it weren't for her, they would've been starved by now, starved to death. How the son-in-law made the old man work so much and never even as much as sent him home with a good piece of meat. If the old man came in with anything of meat, mostly it would be gristle or bone with nothing on it, which the old lady could only make soup with. How the two would go down to the *pis-kun* before daylight, the son-in-law and the old man, that the old man was always sent into the cave to chase a buffalo or two out of the cave, and how the son-in-law would stand on top of the logs above the cave entrance where he would stomp on it to further scare the buffalo out and shoot them as they came running out of the cave. Then all of the hard work was done by the old man, dressing the slaughtered buffalo out and cleaning the entrails, and when all through, the son-in-law would send him home without any kind of meat.

This Kut-toe-yis never moved as he sat there listening to the old folks telling him about their troubles. After everything was told by his parents, this strange newcomer sat up straight and said, "I will find out about all of this that you told me in the morning. I have a plan to find out. Now let's all sleep a while and we will get up before daylight and I'll tell you of my plan."

Not even once dreaming of what had happened in his in-laws' tipi, the son-in-law knew only that a newborn baby girl was there. But! For a full-grown man to be there with his in-laws at this time, a full-grown son, in only four days since the birth of the baby girl he heard in his in-laws' tipi— who would ever believe such a happening?

In those very early days and even to the 1930s, a mother-in-law forbade herself to see her son-in-law. It was of the highest embarrassment to see her son-in-law. In many cases, in-laws moved or went into exile to a neighboring tribe of Natives, there to die or wait until either one passes on to Happy Hunting Grounds. They also moved away alone to the mountains or wher-ever. They would never see their son-in-law anymore until such a time that the son-in-law might die or vice versa, then the father-in-law could move back to his group.

Very early the next morning, Kut-toe-yis got up and got his father up too. "Let's get on down to the *pis-kun* before the son-in-law gets up and I will see what he does." The poor old man wasn't too sure of this. He was afriad, but his son reassured him that no harm would come to him by his son-in-law. Down to the *pis-kun* the two went. Kut-toe-yis didn't hesitate. Into the *pis-kun* he went, calling his father to come along too. Inside of the *pis-kun* he made his father wait like the son-in-law done, while he went into the cave and chased three fat buffalos. Before he went inside of the cave, his orders were to his father to shoot the buffalo as they came out into the open and kill them. The old man was very nervous as he stood on top of the entrance of this *pis-kun*, he managed to kill the first two head that came out from under him as he stood there on top of that huge log debris. He was so very nervous, any time his son-in-law would come along. Even with the new son, Kut-toe-yis, the poor old man was still very much afriad of the son-in-law and the temper he had. For what he was doing, the son-in-law would surely kill him, arriving ahead of him at the *pis-kun* and going ahead with the killing of the buffalo. The third of the buffalo was only superficially wounded and was running around within the *pis-kun*.

It was just light enough to see this morning. Both were chasing the wounded buffalo around the enclosure of this *pis-kun*, when they heard the son-in-law talking very loud in anger as he started out from the camp. He had come a-knocking at the old man's tipi this early morning to get the old man a-moving to the *pis-kun*, only to find out from the old lady that the old man had already gone down to the *pis-kun* this morning before daylight.

The son-in-law didn't know what to think when the old lady told him that. This made him very, very mad, the old man going ahead down to the *pis-kun* without the son-in-law's orders. He was mad enough to kill the old man. But! No one told him about the newborn son that grew up in the last four nights, none of his wives knew about it. Just the old lady and the old man knew it. So down he went to the *pis-kun*, almost running and stomping as he went along, talking very loud, angry words about his father-in-law. Every once in awhile, he mentioned killing the poor old man. This made the poor old man to shake with fear and he told his new son, Kut-toe-yis, that he was very afraid that the son-in-law would kill him.

Kut-toe-yis told his father, "Don't be afraid. He will have to kill me first before he touches you or harms you in any way, so depend on me and do what I tell you. I'll hide and you just keep on chasing the buffalo around. I want to see what that son-in-law of yours will try to do to you. He doesn't know that I'm here with you. He thinks you are still all alone yet."

As he came nearer to the *pis-kun*, the son-in-law was raging mad, he was so mad at his father-in-law. Native cuss words that were for the old man and all in an almost screaming tone, such was the anger of this son-in-law. As he seen the poor old man chasing the one buffalo and seeing the two that were already on the ground, lying dead, the son-in-law was that much more angered. He came running up to the corral of this *pis-kun*, calling ahead to the old man, "*Ah uh-noh-yi caw-caw-ni-sti-gaw-ma-do-do-nik-kiw a-newk-kis-ka-naw-do-nee-yig kuk-sty-yin-a-moo-goow.* Yeah! You there, just kind of went on ahead this early morning to butcher, no one here to hold me back from what I'm going to do to you."

Jumping right into the *pis-kun*, the son-in-law took out an arrow and to his bow he fitted it and aimed at the poor old man. He shot him, but missed as the old man jumped to one side. Again he shot another arrow. Four times he shot and missed the old man. The old man finally hollered out to his son, "*Ha-yo noo-coo-yih nah-coo-noo-wy-iss-see-doog maw-dut-sik-um-ops-bah.* Help me! My son, before an arrow hits me, I'm not as spry as I used to be." Hearing and seeing what the son-in-law was doing to the poor old man, Kut-toe-yis jumped up from behind one of the dead buffalo just to the right of the son-in-law. He jumped to the young son-in-law and grabbed him, telling him, "*Un-ahks ah-cah-nis-sta-baa-stew-do-yiw nin ki nee-kis-tsi, ki-stew-ah, kuk-sty-yin-amoo-goow.* So! This is the treatment my father and mother get from you. It is your turn, no one is around to hold me back to do to you what you have done to my folks." The son-in-law pleaded to Kut-toe-yis, but it was no use. Son-in-law too mean, it showed on the old folks. They were very thin from lack of food, the son-in-law had meant to do away with them in a kind of a natural way, to slowly deteriorate away from hunger until they died. These two old folks were getting to be a heavy burden on this young son-in-law of theirs.

Kut-toe-yis already had his flint knife in his hand. With one stroke, he got the young son-in-law right squarely in the heart, telling him as the young man fell, "You are one of those wicked people that I have come to do away with in this world." The young son-in-law was dead as he hit the ground.

Kut-toe-yis didn't stop there. He told his father, "Come on, we will go back to the tipis." Back at the tipis, Kut-toe-yis went on in to his mother, his father right in the back of him. He asked his mother, "How did my sisters treat you two before I came along?" The mother told Kut-toe-yis all about the way her three daughters treated them, while the youngest was the best one of them, she stole for them things to eat, she lied for them, and she loved them most of all. Kut-toe-yis told his folks, "Stay in here while I go to the girls' tipi." Out he went to the girls' tipi, going right in without stopping for an invitation, he stood in the doorway so none of the girls could get out. In his hand he had a shin bone, while with the other hand he tied a piece of fat, a belly fat down from one of the tipi poles, he was in the doorway all this time.

The girls hadn't found out about their young husband yet, they weren't told that he had already been slain by Kut-toe-yis. Kut-toe-yis told the oldest of the girls to come to him and stand under the belly fat that was tied down from a tipi pole. She came and stood under the belly fat, and Kut-toe-yis asked her this question. "Do you love your folks or your husband?" The girl said she loved her husband. Kut-toe-yis told her to get right under the belly fat and hold her head and lick the fat. The fat was almost too high for the girl, she had to stretch her neck upward to reach the fat and as she done so, Kut-toe-yis hit her across her throat with all his might, which killed the girl outright. As she fell, Kut-toe-yis told her, "It's better that you lay with the one you love."

He called the second-oldest girl and the same question was asked, the same answer was given, and the same fate was given her too. The third too was given the same treatment. All four of them were wicked and mean, Kut-toe-yis had to do away with them as he was sent here on Mother Earth to do away with wickedness.

After getting rid of the wicked daughters and their husband, Kut-toe-yis went on back to the two old folks and their youngest daughter. He told them, "Come on, we will go on back to the *pis-kun* and butcher those three head of buffalo we just killed this morning." Back to the *pis-kun* they went, four of them. No one was around to be afraid of now, the old people could do what they pleased now. Kut-toe-yis told them that the *pis-kun* was theirs from now on.

For a long time after this, Kut-toe-yis went out to replenish the *pis-kun* and the cave. He filled it up with a fresh herd of buffalo so the old people would never go hungry for a very long time. Again filled to capacity, the cave and the *pis-kun*. Kut-toe-yis and the old folks with the younger daughter, taking it easy, mostly busy on making new bows and arrows, spears too.

# Kut-toe-yis and the Bear Family

For a long time Kut-toe-yis mostly fooled around the camps, doing this and that for his parents and his sister. He was by no means contented with that, he wanted to go out into the countryside and find excitement. He didn't know right then, but that was the main reason Creator Sun had Kut-toe-yis come into this world of Mother Earth and Creator Sun. Mother Earth and Creator Sun wanted the wickedness to stop all over, this was the only way they could fight it, with someone to work with the human race. And so Kut-toe-yis was born from a large clot of blood.

Kut-toe-yis was very restless, he would take long walks into the country-side, many times overnight. He wanted to go and find out about the rest of the country and its people. Each night the old man told him about the wickedness that abounded in the country, and for some strange reason he wanted to go and find those wicked people or whatever it was that was wicked. He had a dream of doing away with all of that wickedness.

Kut-toe-yis had gotten himself a dog from his folks. Him and this dog were inseparable, day and night they traveled together.

One early morning as they got through eating their morning meal, Kut-toe-yis just couldn't stand it anymore, he had to leave here and go find real excitement some place. He told his parents his plan to go and find out about the people in this hunting area of this land of theirs. For a long time his mother had been secretly making extra moccasins for him, knowing that very soon, one of these days, he would be asking to leave to go out into the wicked world.

Whenever a man went out into the wilderness for several days and was to travel steady, traveling was done only by foot, as there were no horses at the time. Walking wore moccasins out fast, the traveler had to have several pairs of moccasins, enough to last him until he reached his destination.

Old people are very much aware of their younger peoples' thoughts, so it was no great surprise to hear Kut-toe-yis say he wanted to leave and go out to find excitement. The old folks also knew that this strange comer to them must have come for some reason—he didn't come as a regular-born child. And to make it more strange, he was able to speak the fourth day after his birth, and he turned into a full-grown man. He also helped the old folks with their wicked son-in-law and daughters, he done away with them. Now he wanted to go find out about the rest of the people and the land. The old people had him figured out very close.

Taking leave of them, Kut-toe-yis and his dog first traveled towards the mountains, the foothills of this great hunting area of theirs. For several days they traveled, over hills and rivers, through forests and the plains. No worries for the two, whenever they got hungry they found small game and fowl to kill and eat. Fish was plentiful in all of the streams. Whenever they got tired, they slept under trees or made a shelter with boughs of trees and branches, grass too was used, it was then a virgin land and everything was plentiful all over.

Kut-toe-yis had named his dog See-soum, Little Dog. It was many mornings after they left the parents, traveling always to the north and westwards. It was a little late when the two came over a hill towards a river that they seen ahead of them. There was a small camp close to the river and almost among the trees. As they came towards it they could see well into the camps. There seemed to be no movement of any kind, nothing lively. Only a few people, very few, walking around, and they walked like they were sick or something. The two quickened their pace to reach this camp, which was only a few steps away.

They came among the tipis on the outer circle of the camp. From a small tipi, two old ladies spoke to them. "Where are you going? And what are you going to do around here? If you are a stranger to this camp, you should head right back out and find another place to go, a different camp where it might be friendlier."

"Why is this?" asked Kut-toe-yis. Again the old ladies spoke.

"This is the Bear family's camp. The Chief is a great big bear and his wife, several little ones too."

Now when the old lady said they were a bear family, she didn't mean they were regular bears. It's a known fact that the real bear is very mean, it will attack anyone, they kill and are very strong. They will take food from anyone, by force or otherwise, just plainly take it away from whomever had the food. People who act like the real bear are known as bears. These are the human beings, but they are so mean that they bully their way to gain whatever they need. They are lazy and would rather just take things so they won't have to work for it.

"Who might you be?" asked one of the old ladies.

"*Ni-stu-wog-oak Kut-toe-yisa ki-moo ni-do-me-dom-ah ah-ni-sta Si-soum*, I am Kut-toe-yis, and this dog of mine, his name is Si-soum."

"You are crazy to come here, my son. It's no place for good people. That Bear family, they are very mean. There have been many people starved to death over the Bear family. Every time the people slaughter buffalo in our *pis-kun*, when all of the buffalo are skinned out and the fresh meat is all dressed out, the Bear family comes and takes all of the fresh meat for themselves, leaving only the gristle and the parts that can't be used. Them there is the only food we are getting, hardly edible. We can't fight them, as they are very strong and have killed many men that went up against them. None of us can leave here, the Bear family won't permit anyone to go. Even newcomers, the Bear family don't allow them to leave once they come into this camp. So! Before the Bear family notice you and your dog, sneak back out and leave here."

It was this kind of a family that was running this camp that Kut-toe-yis had come upon. He felt very sorry for all of the people of this camp, because! Looking around him as he sat there with the two old ladies, hardly anyone was moving about, and those that were seemed like they been in ill health for a long time. He told the two old ladies, "I guess I can't leave here, my dog and I, so we will wait and see what happens."

Those men that were still able enough to move around were out hunting. It was getting late in the day when the hunters' hollering was heard by the camp. That hollering meant the hunters were bringing in a herd of buffalo. The people were so afraid of the Bear family that no one moved to get to the *pis-kun*, no one even got excited over the herd of buffalo being brought in. Some of the livelier women slowly made their way towards the *pis-kun* to dress out the buffalo. In their hearts they all knew that it was no use, the Bear family would only come and get all the good meat and there wouldn't be any left for them, all a useless work for them. They just had to come and dress the buffalo out, they knew the Bear family would only jump on them and maybe kill them if they didn't do their job. Kut-toe-yis followed the women to the *pis-kun*. The two old ladies didn't want him to go there, they knew the Bear family wouldn't like that a bit.

The buffalo were all butchered, and the women were dressing them out, getting the fresh meat ready in a pile. Kut-toe-yis was right there helping them dress out the fresh meat. Right to the very last carcass he helped. The women had it piled where the Bear family could get at it without having to go around gathering it. This time, instead of waiting on the Bear family to come, Kut-toe-yis made the women sit down in a semicircle, all of them. Mostly all of the livelier women were down here helping to dress the slaughtered buffalo out. Several that were too weak couldn't make it down here. Kut-toe-yis piled the meat at each lady's feet and put enough there for those that couldn't come to help because of their weakness from lack of food. Kut-toe-yis hurried all of the women to take the fresh meat to their tipis and cook a meal for the families. For those that couldn't cook, he sent help for them, someone to cook for them and feed them and their families too.

Kut-toe-yis told all of them not to be afraid of the Bear family, that he would pay them a visit before they got around to come and get the fresh meat. It was hard for the women, most of them were very much afraid of what the Bear family would do if this brave young man couldn't back up his words. Kut-toe-yis even helped many of them take the meat to their tipis. After enough women took their meat to the tipis, the rest of them got braver and took theirs too. Kut-toe-yis, with his word of encouragement to the ladies, kind of took the fear out of them, and their confidence began to go along with this young man.

It didn't take very long to dress out all of the buffalo with all the help that came this time. Kut-toe-yis encouraged those women on, and even as much as sent them home with all of the fresh meat.

Everyone had gone on to their tipis with all of the fresh meat when the greedy Bear family came down to collect their fresh meat. But they found in the empty *pis-kun* just what they would leave—gristle and fat, a taste of their own medicine. Were they ever mad to return to their tipi empty-handed. This was the first time this ever happened to this Bear family. The Chief, this mean Bearman, right away knew who was behind this and he was going to make him pay for this embarrassment. He knew it could only be the newcomer, Kut-toe-yis. Raging mad, the family went inside their tipi to think of their next move.

Many of the women already had cut their fresh meat and it was hanging outside of their tipis on drying racks. Some even had the fire a-going under the drying racks. Kut-toe-yis took a load of fresh meat on his back to the old ladies that warned him of this Bear family, as they were a little too old to come and help out at the *pis-kun*. He heard the Bear Chief talking very loud about the embarrassment that just happened to him, talking angrily about what he was going to do to the people here. Kut-toe-yis got up and told the old ladies that he was going to pay the Bear Chief a visit right now, before he left his tipi. The Bear tipi was located right in the center of this camp, it was a painted tipi and the emblem was that of the Bears with the usual other emblems of the night, stars (the Big Dipper and Little Dipper), the butterfly, and the surrounding hills with the emblem of animal burrows or dens. It was a pretty tipi.

The two old ladies almost held Kut-toe-yis back. They pleaded with him not to go to the Bear family. The Bears would kill him, they were very mean, especially when anyone does things to them, like now, what Kut-toe-yis done, leaving the *pis-kun* empty and sending the meat home with the women. The Bear family wouldn't forget that very soon, and they will kill for that, the two old ladies pleaded with him. "He didn't have ears," said the old ladies as Kut-toe-yis left their little tipi and went on to the center of the camp to visit the Bear family.

Without the accustomed way of entering a friendly tipi, Kut-toe-yis went right in and made himself at home. He sat at the proper side for visitors, but not for long. Looking up at the inside drying rack, he seen much choicy dried meat and plenty of back fat (*oo-sah-key*), a very tasty fat that usually goes good with dried meat. This fat is taken from along the back of the buffalo, and when the buffalo are at their fattest, this fat is about an inch or so thick. Smoked and dried along with the meat, this combination is almost always the Chief's food or for Native dignitaries. Anyway! Seeing all these special parts of the buffalo cut and dried along with the back fat, Kut-toe-yis didn't have to be invited to get at the morsel. A couple of large pieces of dried meat and a large piece of back fat he took off of the rack. He sat back down and, without saying a word, ate them while the Bear family looked on.

The Bearman and his family just couldn't believe what they were witnessing. The Bear Chief didn't think anyone would do a thing like this to him, because he was the ruler here in this camp. Those that opposed him before this, it was a one-way affair— they lost their lives to this wicked Bear Chief. This one, Kut-toe-yis, he either hadn't heard about the Bear Chief or was just outright brave, probably a lot of power in him from unknown spirits.

Kut-toe-yis ate slowly. After downing the food, he spoke to the Bear Chief. "They tell me you are the Chief of this camp and you treat them awfully. They tell me many have died from your cruelty, starving them. You take all the best food, hardly leaving them with any or none at all. I'm now going to ask you that you and I have a game, the mystic game." This game is the original game among mostly all of the Natives many hundreds of years ago. Today it is known as stick game, bone game, hand game, or other names. "Between you and I, whoever wins this game shall be the new Chief of this camp."

This sounded all right with the Bear Chief. He had a lot of power in him, he wouldn't lose this game to this unheard-of young man. Who was he anyway to try something against this Great Bear Chief? "I'll show him," thought the Bear Chief as he got ready for the game. To the center of this Bear tipi he sat, telling Kut-toe-yis to sit down opposite him. There, in the center of the tipi, they faced one another. Kut-toe-yis had his spear alongside of him, and on the other side of him sat his faithful dog, Si-soum. The Bear Chief got his bundle from where it was hanging on the wall of his tipi. Out of it he took a small piece of bone, it looked like a half piece of bear claw. "We shall hide this bone. As I'm the Chief of this camp and you are the contender, I shall hide the bone first and you guess what hand it's in."

The Bear Chief didn't have a worry. He was mean and strong, a fighter and always a winner. He had very much power, spirit power to back him up to win this young man that spoke too big for his own good. "This young man is nothing," the Great Bear Chief was thinking, as he got the bone ready and went through the motion that his spirit helpers gave him. Facing him was Kut-toe-yis, watching him as he done his thing. For the longest time this Great Bear Chief went through the motions of his spiritual powers, singing as he went through the motions, "*Ah-hey ah-hey ah-hey-yay-yay-yay ah-hey-ah-hey-ah-hey-yay-yay-yay.*" This song, over and over again. At last he came out with both hands, with his fists tightly closed over the bone of bear claw. Which hand? That was Kut-toe-yis's problem, to find out what hand the bone was hidden in. But it didn't work out that way, Kut-toe-yis was all ready to do his guessing in another way.

The Great Bear Chief gave the grunt that he was ready to be guessed. Kut-toe-yis looked at him square in the eyes for a long time. Then, without a warning, he made a surprise move. He jumped up suddenly with his spear in his hands, and at the same time he made the guessing sound, "*Ah-ho.*" All in one movement and sound, Kut-toe-yis ran his spear right through this Great Bear Chief's heart.

Almost with a non-stop motion he kept on a-going with the spear. Before the rest of the Bear family could move, one after the other he stabbed them to death as they sat frozen, not believing what their eyes were witnessing right in front of them all. They had been the boss family from time unknown, they couldn't believe this was happening to them. Kut-toe-yis killed them all—all except a young Bear girl that ran out just before he got to her, finally realizing what was happening to the Bear family. She made for the timber, the wild. She was in family way, pregnant. As she made her way into the forest and out of sight Kut-toe-yis, looking at her from the doorway of this Bear painted tipi, said after her, "*Key ahwk-tsi-tsi-stub-op-oo-kuy-yi-scoo.* Let there be more Bear people from her." By then she had disappeared into the forest and Kut-toe-yis didn't have any intentions to follow her. He let her go free, the only one to escape his spear. The rest of the Bear family were slain and laying about in the Great Bear tipi.

Kut-toe-yis went back into the Bear tipi and cleaned it out. He drug all of the remains of this once brutal Bear family into the woods, where they would rot away. He went back again to the Bear tipi, straightening it out, and then Kut-toe-yis went to the old ladies that had befriended him when he first came into this camp, telling them that they could move into the pretty painted Bear tipi. It was loaded with all the special cuts of meat and all were dried. Kut-toe-yis helped the old ladies move to their new tipi that once belonged to the Great Bear family and the Chief of this camp. Kut-toe-yis made short work of that Bear Chief.

After the Great Bear family was done away with, Kut-toe-yis called a meeting for the whole camp. In this meeting a new Chief was selected by the group, their favorite man. They wanted Kut-toe-yis to become the new Chief, but he declined, making excuses that he had to go and find some other people living in a distance from here, and maybe when he returned he would accept that Chief position.

# Kut-toe-yis and the Huge Vacuum Monster

It had been so happy since the death of the Great Bear family. Everyone here in this camp picked up so much from worry-free minds and all of the good food they now had each day since Kut-toe-yis came around.

Kut-toe-yis had told the two friendly old ladies of his plans since he done away with the mean Bear family. He was only biding his time when to leave here as he got kind of used to the old ladies, they reminded him of his own parents. Somehow he almost hated to leave this small camp, but! Sooner or later, he must take leave. He had restless blood in him and must find excitement to slow down the restlessness in him.

One evening the evening meal was downed and the storytelling got underway by one of the old ladies. Kut-toe-yis sat there with something stronger in his mind. He sat there as if listening, but all this time he was wondering which way would be the best way to leave here in the early morning. He had made up his mind to leave here that very next morning, and as the story went on by this old lady, Kut-toe-yis didn't hear what it was all about.

Waking up from the deep wondering of his mind, he cut in on the old lady, asking her which was the best way to go, that he was leaving in the morning. The old lady stopped her storytelling to answer him. These two ladies were very old and they knew what they were talking about. It was good to listen to such wise old people like them. The old lady told Kut-toe-yis, "Don't go to the northwest of here, there is danger that way. People that go that way never return, there is a huge monster that lives over that way. It works like a magnet and when them people are close enough to this monster, this monster then uses a very strong suction that reaches far out from its location. It only vacuums those that go by on the west side of it, its mouth is located westward from its huge body. In case you do go that way, be sure that you go on the east side of it, where it hasn't any effect at all."

*Ma-too-too-ki-wah ma Kut-toe-yis.* No ears, that Kut-toe-yis. Early the next morning he headed out. But instead of going the way he was told to go, Kut-toe-yis went the forbidden way, he was all excited to find out what this monster was all about. To the northwest he went.

It took longer than he anticipated to get to that vacuum monster. He traveled all that day. When night came, him and his faithful dog, Si-soum, crept into the thickets. Always on his travels, his buffalo robe would either be on his back or in his arms. With the robe he was always warm in the nights wherever he might be, and the dog was there too, to keep him warm by curling up to him at nights.

Robes were very important to the people. They were made from the hide of the buffalo, or they could be made from the hides of deer, elk, antelope, or moose, as long as they were large enough to cover the body. They were

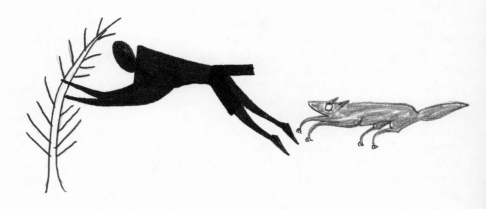

**Bloodclot and Dog Being Pulled in by the Vacuum Monster**

painted with the many different colors of earth paint. Emblems of the stars, the moon, the sun, birds or animals, or of the many things of nature are painted in emblems on a robe which is worn over one's shoulders and body. The larger robes were preferred on long journeys, because they could also serve as bedding as one sleeps out on the wilderness. Some robes were plain, worn just as they were tanned. The tanned buffalo hide was used for bedding in the tipis because it was heavy, like a modern-day comforter. All or most of these buffalo robes or tanned hides were tanned on one side, and the hair was left on, which made them all the warmer.

Food wasn't any problem, especially in the summertime, as long as one has his bow and arrows and flint knife. To start a fire, flint and a hard stone were struck together to cause a spark. The spark from this was held very near some hand-softened tree fibers. These are from the underside of the bark of a tree, a dry one. When it's tinder dry and softened by hand, it readily ignites from the sparks. That was the way Kut-toe-yis traveled, and many other men too, for they knew it was survival to be well equipped with the necessary things.

Kut-toe-yis bedded down for the night after finding some food for him and his dog. Having a very good rest through the night, early morning found Kut-toe-yis and his dog well on their way towards the forbidden area. Through the morning he traveled in that one direction. He was going along at a good pace when he noticed the wind was coming from the west. It felt like a wind, but it also felt like something was pulling him and his dog to the east. Right away, he knew he had come into the area of the Wind Sucker, or Vacuum Monster.

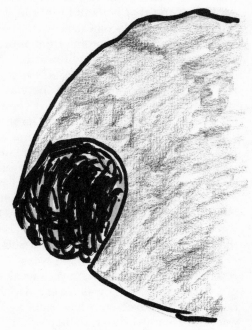

As he went along further in that direction, that suction got stronger and stronger until he couldn't walk much anymore without holding on to something. There was all kinds of growth along there—buck brush, saplings of the many kinds of trees—but they were scattered. Wild cherry bushes, birch, willow, dogwood, cottonwood trees, and quaking aspens, sage too. Kut-toe-yis and his dog grabbed onto things that came up in their way as this force pulled them along. But this force was so strong, that each time they got ahold of something, whatever they got ahold of came out by the roots and they kept being pulled along, him and his dog.

Hanging on to whatever possessions he held in his hands, Kut-toe-yis decided he would let nature take its course. He let go of what he was hanging on to, jumped up, and ran along with the strange force that was pulling them along.

For quite a run he went along with the pulling. All of a sudden the pulling stopped, and he must've had his eyes closed. Opening his eyes when this strange force quit all of a sudden, Kut-toe-yis couldn't see a thing. It was totally dark and very hot in this place, wherever it was, and most of all no more pulling from whatever it was that was pulling them along, him and his dog.

Standing there in total darkness, afraid to step on something or step into a hidden pit inside of this whatever it may be. His dog was quiet too, and leaned against him as they stood there very quiet. Getting his bearings, he stood there listening for something. He heard a lot of breathing and some moaning and groaning, very heavy breathing as if whoever it was or who they were needed air. It was very hot in here and very dark. There was another sound that bothered him too, it sounded like a thumping of something within this place of darkness. The sound was like a heartbeat, a huge heartbeat, and it was coming from above them.

Kut-toe-yis made his way towards what he thought would be the wall of this dark, dank place. It smelled like something raw in here and very wet. His dog bumped into his legs, he was so close. So very slowly they went along, his foot pushed up against something as he moved very slow. Kut-toe-yis bent down to touch whatever it was to find out what it might be.

Touching it very slowly and feeling it, he found it to be a leg and foot. Feeling further on he felt out a human form—not only one, but many of them all laying side by side of each other! He even felt complete human skeletons laying there too. As he got more used to the darkness, he got around better and investigated more with his hands, feeling around, touching this and that, feeling them out, only to find out they were mostly human forms and a few other things of animals and birds that may have gotten into the pulling force of this huge Wind Sucker, or Vacuum Monster.

Many of the people in there were still alive, some may just been gotten recently. Many of them were very weak from lack of air and food, no way to get water either. This was a very wicked monster, whatever it was, and it had to be destroyed somehow right away, before the lack of all these things got him. He must hurry or they will all perish in this place.

Since he got used to the total darkness, Kut-toe-yis could make out the forms of these people and what animals that were inhaled in this place. He had already found out they were all in a live place, this was a huge live monster that used a vacuum force to draw people to it if they got in the way of the force, on the west side of this location, and it was so strong that nothing could keep you from being drawn into this monster. This was what kept it alive, drawing any kind of flesh into its digestive chamber. The humans didn't know it, but they were being eaten alive by this huge Vacuum Monster.

As soon as he found out there were several people strong enough to get up yet, he called a meeting so everyone would pay attention to what he had to say. Kut-toe-yis told them that they were all being eaten alive by this wicked Wind Sucker, or huge Vacuum Monster. Right now they were slowly being digested and would all die soon. There wasn't any water to drink, hardly any air to breath, nor any food to eat, and there wasn't any way to get back out of here, that suction was just too strong at the entrance to this monster's mouth. They were here for this huge monster's life. Sucking in any kind of food, the flesh type, was what this thing thrived on. Kut-toe-yis told them they were only food for this thing and must find a way out of here, some way to kill it from its insides.

"Now listen close," he told them. "We are going to hold a dance, and those of you that are still able to get up, I want you to get up and join me in a dance. Those of you that are just able to move yet, get in rhythm with the music that I'll be singing, even if it's just your heads that can still bob around."

Kut-toe-yis hurried right along. There wasn't much time because of the very short supply of air in the monster's belly. He got his long flint knife out of its sheath, took his feathers off of his head, and replaced them with this long flint knife of his, the sharp point extending upward on his head. He had noticed a thing hanging down from the ceiling of this place, almost in the center. This thing hanging down was about the size of a huge buffalo head, an extra-large bull head, and it was throbbing. He knew it was this monster's heart. It sounded like a thump, thump, thump, like his own heart, only this huge one sounded much louder then his, it made noise all over in here as it beat to keep this Wind Sucker or Vacuum Monster alive.

Kut-toe-yis had it all planned out so he wouldn't arouse too much commotion in here as they got ready for the dance. Mostly all of the talk was done in a whisper. Slowly he got up, and out to the center he went, telling the rest of them that were still able to move to get behind him in a single file. To those that were unable to move, he told them to just bob their heads with the music of his.

They were ready now, and he told them to start jumping along with him when he started to dance and sing. All waited for the word. When all was ready with these people, he gave the word to start dancing behind him, to jump as high as they could and come along in the back of him, follow him around in a circle. Kut-toe-yis was singing and jumping up and down in time with his music, at the same time going around in a circle. Each time he came under the huge heart, he jumped all the higher and harder. As he did so, the knife was stabbing at this huge heart hanging down from this monster's insides. About the fourth dance around, Kut-toe-yis jumped extra-high and harder when he got under the heart. This time, the knife penetrated the huge heart.

Kut-toe-yis had become a victor again, he had overcome this huge Vacuum Monster to save the people inside of it. As all of the blood drained out of this huge heart, it stopped beating and everything became quiet. The Vacuum Monster was dead, never to bother people anymore.

Kut-toe-yis, with the help of the others that were able, pulled out all of those in the insides of this flesh-eating Vacuum Monster. Those that were dead were put away as they should be, tied onto large branches of the bigger trees. After all was over, Kut-toe-yis went on his way again to find other excitement.

# Kut-toe-yis and the Sliding Woman

If it hadn't been for Kut-toe-yis, people would still be sucked in by the huge Vacuum Monster, the Wind Sucker. Creator Sun had put Kut-toe-yis here for a purpose, and that purpose was being carried out. To go out and destroy all of the evil that was now very widely spread in this country.

After he got rid of the Vacuum Monster, the people wanted Kut-toe-yis to stay for a while and teach them and help them in their life. Kut-toe-yis wasn't ready to settle down in one place, he had roaming blood that was full of adventure. He told the people to stay around, as he would return some day to live with them. There were things that he had to do in other parts of this land.

When he was satisfied that the weak ones were going to be all right, as they were being taken care of by the livelier ones, and every one of them were able to get around better than when they were first saved from this huge Vacuum Monster, Kut-toe-yis took leave of them and made his way out to the northeast. In the northeast there was a wicked woman. This woman got very friendly with people and talked them into taking a sleigh ride. But once on that sleigh, they never lived to tell about it. She was a cannibal woman, she thrived on human flesh. Kut-toe-yis wanted to see this woman, so! Out in that direction he went.

On and on he traveled. Distances were great in those days, because all places were reached by foot. For several days he traveled along with his faithful dog, Si-soum, still by his side. Wherever night took over, Kut-toe-yis and his dog curled up under some brush, covered up with the robe that was always with him.

They woke to a very pretty morning one bright beautiful day. That night the two had slept near a river under a heavy growth of brush. Jumping up just as the sun came into view in the east, the two went along this brush following the river. At the same time, Kut-toe-yis was looking out for something to eat for their morning meal. Maybe a rabbit, grouse, or prairie chicken, something that wasn't too big. Natives never were a wasteful lot, they made use of everything on an animal or a fowl.

Coming around a big bend along this river, Kut-toe-yis looked very sharply in every direction. He had very keen eyes. Far ahead of them up on the bank of this river was a steep grassy slope that went down toward the river's edge, where no trees or any kind of brush grew. Just a cut bank to a deep green water hole. It was a whirlpool and very strong. When something once gets into this deep whirlpool in this river, it would just spin whatever gets in there until they disappear under. It takes a long time for them to reappear, and the reappearance right along the bank where the woman pulls them out of the water and does what she has to with them.

As the two came around this bend and were seen by the woman, she waved at them to come up to where she was at. She waved frantically to make sure that Kut-toe-yis seen her. Kut-toe-yis wanted to come up there to see her and find out if she may be in need of help, because of the way she was waving at him. He made his way up there slowly, his dog by him as they climbed the high sloped bank. Reaching her, Kut-toe-yis greeted her like anyone else, she was very friendly. But right away, with his keen eyes, he knew they had come upon the cannibal woman that gives sleigh rides to her visitors.

In the midsummer time, especially when the grass begins to dry a little, it gets very slippery. The Native children of those days done a lot of sliding on the grass on steep hills and slopes. The Native sleigh is made of rawhide dried in the sun and stretched with wooden stakes driven through the edges of the hide and into the ground. This dries the rawhide very smoothly and evenly and they slide on grassy hills. It worked as good as the modern-day toboggans. So this was what this cannibal woman used.

Kut-toe-yis's keen eyes seen the very deep whirlpool almost squarely at the bottom of this hill where the sleigh run was. The immediate bank of the river was perpendicular, several feet high, and there was no way to climb this bank. One couldn't very well swim across the river, because the current was very swift. You couldn't swim upstream to get out of this place, the current was against you too. If you went in there once, the strong whirl gets you first and eventually sucks you down in and under the water for a long time. This whirl was so strong that it held you down under water until you drowned. Every so often this strong whirl releases its circular current and things that are in it are released from it and wash upstream until they reach the bank, where the cannibal woman would be waiting to pull them out of the river and have something to eat—that is, the human beings.

He also saw how the sleigh was rigged. Two rawhide ropes, which were very slimly twisted, were the guides for the sleigh. They were on either side of the rawhide toboggan and strung through holes on each side of it. One of the rawhide ropes guided the sleigh to clear the whirlpool, over to the right of it. But the other rawhide line was rigged squarely to this whirlpool. Either line could be used just by the fast kick of a foot, and this would change the course of this toboggan. It was real neat the way she had it, and it was deadly to people. To her, it was fun as she rode it downhill. She used the safe line to assure her visitors that this toboggan ride was safe. She would ride it down just to show them it was fun. But when they got on, she kicked at the rope and the toboggan changed its course to the whirlpool, where they would fall in and drown. Then she had another meal.

All of this Kut-toe-yis seen with just one glance around. He was here in place of Napi, and he had to be very intelligent to notice all of the dangers of life. He didn't have as much power as his predecessor, Napi. His powers were very limited, his power was intelligence with some supernatural powers, but not like Napi's power.

The woman spoke smilingly. She seemed to be very nice person, and that was one of her ways to fool people. Kut-toe-yis knew right away that her way of speaking was just a blind. She had other things in her wicked mind. She told Kut-toe-yis, "O-ki, ah-ko-nip-sue-chi-cope. Come on, lets slide." Kut-toe-yis, pretending to be afraid of the steep hill and having seen how the cannibal woman worked the toboggan without her knowing it, told her to slide down first so he could see how it worked. The cannibal woman thought she had another foolish victim for the day, and probably her only meal in several days.

Without hesitation, she got on the toboggan. And as she got on the toboggan and started down hill, Kut-toe-yis kicked the ropes. This changed her course to the whirlpool. She couldn't stop the toboggan, as the ropes were on either side of her legs. And besides, it went down the steep hill like lightning, too fast for her to do anything. Before she knew it, she had fallen a victim of her own wickedness.

Following her down the hill, Kut-toe-yis recovered her body from the river, where she had drowned in her death whirlpool. As he was taking the body out of the river and laying it down, Si-Soum came running out of the brush barking excitedly. Kut-toe-yis, dropping her lifeless body down, went into the bushes where the dog came running from. In a little opening of the bushes, a huge pile of human bones laid there, the victims of this sliding woman cannibal. Now she had gone the same way in death, but not to a cannibal. All of these human bones that laid there was what she ate. Kut-toe-yis, always doing the right thing, laid away the bones as they should be, even that of the wicked cannibal woman.

He had forgotten the morning meal that they were looking for just before they had the encounter with the cannibal woman, the Sliding Woman. Kut-toe-yis didn't have to go far to find a pheasant that he soon killed with his bow and arrows. A fire soon got a-going, and him and his dog had a roasted pheasant for their meal. It was a very good meal, and now they were on their way again to find more excitement.

Kut-toe-yis didn't know which way to go. He held his flint knife at the very tip of the handle where it swung freely, dropping it and watching which way the pointed end fell. In that direction Kut-toe-yis went, almost due east, and a very little to the south. Him and his dog, Si-soum, struck out that way.

# Kut-toe-yis and Two Faceless Old Ladies

Population was widely scattered in the days of Napi and after him, in the days of the Savior, Kut-toe-yis the Bloodclot Man, born of blood, a strange comer that done away with wickedness at that time to save his people from the wicked beings that started to multiply in the land. Already he had done away with the Bear Chief and his family, and the Wind Sucker or Vacuum Monster. And now he had killed the Sliding Woman, and was heading out to the easterly direction and a little to the south.

Kut-toe-yis and his dog always fooled around along their way as they traveled. He never was in a too big of a hurry. As they went along, he made sure he seen everything that might mean danger to people. He was just full of adventure, his dog Si-soum never leaving him, always by his side. It was all fun for them. These wicked things that were present in the land, Kut-toe-yis didn't just go find them one after the other. He went along doing away with this danger to people, the wicked things that came into being on Mother Earth in many years, living for a while with certain groups as part of them and like an ordinary Native. No one knew he was born of a buffalo bloodclot.

Like always, Kut-toe-yis and his dog were going along, into valleys, across rivers, along some streams, and through the forests. Wherever night overtook them, the two bedded down for the night. Wintertime he traveled, but it was a long time in between his travels. They would hole up some good place where food was plentiful, and live there for a while until warmer weather came again.

Kut-toe-yis came to many, many camps, things in these camps were running smoothly, there was no danger of any kind in many camps that the two came upon. The two would visit the people of these camps for several days or for many days, it all depended on the hospitality by the people. There were places that Kut-toe-yis especially enjoyed, and those places he didn't want to leave right away. In certain places people were very friendly, while other places the people were very unfriendly and mean. These places Kut-toe-yis wanted to leave right now.

To the east and a little to the south he went after leaving the last camp they had come to. This land was sparsely settled by the Natives. In many instances, camps were several days apart or many days apart. It was a kind of forest that they were going through, Kut-toe-yis and Si-soum. They came to many small parks in the forest. Going through an especially heavy wooded area, and as they came out from among the trees into an opening of a small park, almost squarely in the middle of it was a lone tipi.

Stopping and very surprised to see a lone tipi here out in the middle of nowhere and especially far into the forest, Kut-toe-yis stood there looking to see if anyone would come out of the tipi, if it had occupants. Smoke was coming out from the top of the tipi. After several moments of waiting and no one showed, Kut-toe-yis walked slowly towards the tipi, he walked very stealthily, not making any kind of noise to forewarn the occupants. Very slowly he went, and slower yet as he came nearer to it. The door flap was set to the side and the door open, very slowly he snuck up to the doorway and peeked in. The dog always seem to know when to be quiet, he seemed to know danger and everything his master was doing. In one glance, Kut-toe-yis seen almost everything inside of this tipi. There wasn't much to see, the occupants didn't have much of anything in their small tipi.

Kut-toe-yis just couldn't believe what he seen. He seen two ladies sitting not too far apart on one side of the tipi. They had faces, but they were just flat and slick. There were no eyes where the eyes should be, and neither one had a nose—the two breathed through two small holes on their slick faces. There was a slit across the lower part of their face for their mouths, and they had teeth. There weren't any ears where ears should be, but there were only holes that the two hear from. They were strange women.

**Bloodclot and the Two Eyeless Women
with Spear Elbows**

Without making noise, Kut-toe-yis and his dog sneaked in there and made themselves comfortable on the opposite side of this tipi from where the two sat. Him and his dog were very quiet as they sat there listening to the old ladies talk. One lady said to the other, *"Sko-noots mahk-sahyeeze-tsah-qupe boo-me ah-kit-to-pot-ope*. I'm very hungry, why don't we melt tallow and dip?" Without waiting for an answer from the other woman, she felt around for their food container or parfleche case. There was a fire a-going and rocks in the fire that were already hot. All that had to be done was to set the rawhide pot upright and put a red-hot rock into it, maybe a couple to make the water boiling hot, and then put the tallow in it to melt. This she done without hesitation and then she broke some of the tallow, a large chunk, and put it into her pot of very hot water. As soon as she dropped the tallow into her pot, Kut-toe-yis jumped up to the pot very quietly and took the tallow out and threw it to his dog to eat, which Si-soum done gladly. The old lady waited for a while. Then, waiting long enough for the tallow to melt, she stuck her finger in it and tasted the broth. "Huh, it doesn't even taste like broth, I better put some more tallow in it." Breaking some more of the tallow, she put it into the pot again, only for Kut-toe-yis to take it out of the rawhide

pot again and feed it to his dog. Again the old lady tasted her broth, no taste.

"I wonder what's wrong," the old lady told her friend. "It still doesn't taste of the tallow and I've put in several chunks of tallow which should made it very greasy by now." The other old lady answered her and said, "*Ah-yo-o-o dokes-eeb-bee-stee-dug awk-stomi-gaab-sto-biw ah-yah-suh*. I'm very suspicious that he's present in here, the young man." Not waiting for a word from the other lady, she went on, "*Yahs, yahs, yahs ki-jip-stob-bi-pah*. Young man, young man, young man are you sitting in here?" Kut-toe-yis answered her, telling her he was sitting there.

The three of them visited for a time. After a long visit, and one of the old ladies, thinking that Kut-toe-yis was all ready to leave, told him, "Just before you're leaving, let us know, so we will know when you go out." Kut-toe-yis said yes, he would let them know when he was going. For a while after that, he told them he was ready to leave now. It took the old ladies no time at all to get to the doorway of this tipi. Feeling the doorway, each sat on either side of it. It was then that Kut-toe-yis noticed something else on these peculiar old ladies. On their elbows, each had a spear-like bone growing out of them, and they were very sharp.

Again! Right away, he knew what they were up to, they meant to stab him with those sharp elbows when he went by them through the doorway. He had to stoop way down to get through any tipi doorway, and that was their chance to use those spears on their elbows. These two old ladies were of the wicked people, they would get him right in his ribs if he went through the doorway. Kut-toe-yis was always aware of danger, he knew what should be done about this. He never wanted to kill any of the wicked people with his hands, he would rather see them die by their own fate that they destroyed their victims with.

Slowly he bundled up his robe, he was standing near the fireplace. The robe all bundled up, he held it ready, then making a sound as if he was leaving and telling them so at the same time, he threw his robe past the two old ladies. Thinking it was him going past fast, the two wicked old ladies used their elbows on the robe. They missed it and got each other right in their own ribs, both dying by their own method. Again, Kut-toe-yis done away with one more wickedness that his people wouldn't have to be afraid of anymore.

# Kut-toe-yis and the Woman Wrestler

Having no idea where to go this time, Kut-toe-yis struck out to the south and veering somewhat to the east. Kut-toe-yis was told by his father how large their hunting area extended on all four sides. He had described the invisible boundaries of it, and told him to respect those on the other sides of this boundary. Kut-toe-yis didn't want to go beyond those unseen boundaries. He hadn't spent much time with his folks, only a very few days, but his Dad taught him and told him many things that should be known to all. Kut-toe-yis, being a strange comer to this land, probably had already known the true facts as they should be. Anyway! He was full of respect for the other areas outside their own territory.

It was several days of travel for them. There were no houses anyplace you went. It wasn't anything like these days, now houses are only a few feet apart except in the mountainous terrains all over this world of ours. Then, what one saw anyplace, if any humans were around, were tipis made of tanned hides, particularly of buffalo hides. Most places where it was inhabited, one would see either many tipis or probably one lone tipi. There are times when the people has to set up a camp overnight, or for emergencies where the erecting of the tipi poles would take too long. Then, a fast shelter has to be set up. This was where lean-tos were originated. Three or four poles were leaned against a tree, or something that would hold up one end of them. Tanned hides were thrown over these poles, and under these a shelter was made. Today plywood boards and canvas are mostly used for this same purpose. The small arbors were made from small willows. The bigger ends are stuck into the ground and the protruding branch is then interwoven with the others into a dome-shaped structure. These arbors are small, probably about ten feet in diameter, but they are only used for overnight camping. They are also used for the sacred sweat huts. The skeletal structure of these are also used for drying racks for fresh-cut meat. A fire is made under them to smoke the meat too. On warm summer nights, a bed is made out in the open and under the stars to sleep. Other shelters are for shelter from rain or wind, and mostly for summer use. The people of these lands, the Natives, had their own wintering places where a winter camp was made, a place where there was lots of wood for fire and a good wind shelter, mostly along the larger rivers of the area.

This was the way people traveled overnight—sleep under the stars or, if it's storming, a lean-to or an arbor is erected to sleep under. This was the way Kut-toe-yis was traveling with his dog. Food was always gotten along the way. There were times when leftovers were taken along for lunch, but usually small edible game could be eaten up in one meal.

People always lived along a river or a small creek, because of the water and wood that grew along the rivers. Kut-toe-yis was going through the wooded area one day as him and his dog, Si-soum, walked along through the trees and bushes. Coming out into a small park, he saw a lone tipi. It was in use and been there for a long time, the way Kut-toe-yis seen it. In front of this tipi a lone woman was standing, looking at them as they emerged from the thickets. The woman was very broad and looked mighty husky. She looked strong, almost muscular, brawny. She didn't wait long before talking to them as they stood near the thicket's edge. "*Boo-sha-boo-ka ah-go-kit-doke-ish-waht-si-yoop.* Come here and let's visit." Kut-toe-yis and his dog didn't hesitate any, they went towards the woman and her tipi. Kut-toe-yis could've been hungry or wanted to find out what this woman was up to. The woman led them on into her tipi. She fed them, and as they ate the visiting went on. She was like any other of the many people around, she welcomed him and his dog, fed them like a good person.

As the meal was nearing the last bites and the woman was thinking that this man might just leave suddenly. When they were both quiet for a time, the woman told Kut-toe-yis, "*Sow-woe-moe-mah-doo-nee-key ah-kip-oo-doom-stsi-moo-tsi-yoop*. Before you leave, we will wrestle first." Kut-toe-yis knew instantly that she was one more of the wicked, she was hiding behind her friendly attitude all this time. This must been the way she worked it all the time. Behind this friendliness of hers she was a beast, a murderer, she was a wicked person. She thought she was going to add this Kut-toe-yis and his dog to her many victims of wrestling. Kut-toe-yis readily agreed to the wrestling as he followed her out to a specific area, not far from her tipi.

Reaching the place, Kut-toe-yis with his always sharp eyes, glancing around fast to see what the trick was, seen what appeared to be a long piece of large, sharp-edged flint dug into the ground. The razor-sharp edge protruded from the ground and the grass around this long large flint blade covered it, almost completely concealed from view. Kut-toe-yis's sharp eyes seen what would be in store for him if she overpowered him.

This large flint blade was her weapon. She throwed her unsuspecting opponents on their backs over the sharp edge of this blade, which would cut their backs in two and kill them. Kut-toe-yis was ready for her. She hadn't counted on this man's intelligence and cunning. "*O-ki*," the woman said to get this wrestling a-going. She wasn't aware that Kut-toe-yis had already seen the large sharp flint knife or blade sticking up out of the ground.

They squared off and were going in a circle around one another, waiting for the other to be the first to tackle. Kut-toe-yis was stalking her and trying to get her in a certain position without her noticing it. She thought this was another easy prey, that he didn't know about that hidden weapon of death, so she got a little careless of her position, and a sudden lunge by Kut-toe-yis took her by surprise. Over his knee he flipped her, her back falling squarely over the sharp edge of the hidden flint blade, another victim of her own wicked weapon.

After an ordeal like this one, Kut-toe-yis always looked around for previous victims. He and his dog looked around through the bushes. They didn't have to go far. In the thickets not far from the tipi laid a pile of human bones. This woman was just another cannibal that thrived on human flesh. It didn't take Kut-toe-yis very long to put away the remains of those that previously wrestled with this wicked woman in their rightful place of burial. Even the wicked woman's body was put away with the rest in the right way.

Kut-toe-yis wanted to leave here, it was just another wicked place that seen many deaths at the hands of this wicked woman wrestler. It didn't take them long to get under way, him and his dog, Si-soum. They wanted to be as far from here as they could by nightfall.

# *Kut-toe-yis and the Snake Family*

Amongst the people of those long-gone-by days, the earlier days of our human history, the people increased in population and certain kinds of peculiar, shady, mean, low-down, and unfriendly people started to abound the land. These people were called certain names, such as the Bear family, to put them apart from the others, from the natural people. They weren't real bears, but throughout their lives they acted like the bears of those days—mean, brutal, and ready to kill. This story is about people who acted like snakes.

Many of our people—the Piegans, or as we are called in these days, the Blackfeet Indians—have heard these legends. These legends were related to us by our grandparents, and in turn they were related to them by their grandparents, and so on from generation to generation, from time beginning right to the present time. In the past one hundred years or so, people began to go modern and forget the history of our past. Most old folks remember these legends as they were told by their grandparents. But! They tell them in the way they understand the stories. For instance, the Bear family and the Snake family, many of the storytellers speak of these families like they were the real snakes or the real bears. They weren't. These and others that were made out to be the real animals, they were the real people. But by their actions they are called after the way they may act. Just like the bear people, mean, ready to attack and roar every time they speak or like the snake family, they seem to crawl through the grass to do their wickedness. This I want to stress, so people will know what the true meaning of the old Native legends were really like and the truth of them.

As Kut-toe-yis and his dog traveled along, they came to this camp where several families lived. Coming into the outlying tipis, an old lady asked Kut-toe-yis where he was going. He said he was just coming into camp to visit and get something to eat. They were very hungry for home-cooked meal, they have been traveling for many days and the only meals were of rabbits or wild birds. They haven't tasted any dried meat and back fat for so long that they were beginning to forget the taste of it.

The old lady told him that he couldn't come into this camp, he could never leave if he did, so it was best for his sake and his dog that they move on to better places where they would be welcomed and given better hospitality by more friendlier people.

Getting curious by the way the old lady was talking—she was talking in fear of being heard—Kut-toe-yis wanted to find out what this was all about. Had they come again to another of those weird, mean families? He must find out. Asking the old lady what this was all about, the old lady answered him with a very cautious tone, "This is the Snake family's camp, they run this camp just any way they see fit. Their words are poison and they are very low in their way to the people of this camp. They stoop so low as to steal last food from the people, they are very sneaky in their ways. They don't hardly show themselves because of their way. All undercover they go around, so the people call them the Snake people. There are several in their family. They got even meaner when they drank that medicine of theirs that they made from the wild cherries." (They even had wine in those days of Kut-toe-yis. The Natives of these lands of the United States, long before the coming of the whites, knew how to ferment certain wild berries that they called medicine for the effects it produced. Those berries were mostly the wild chokecherries that grew very abundantly in this country.)

Kut-toe-yis must find out for himself, he must see about this Snake family and their medicine of wild cherries. He didn't argue with the old lady and he didn't tell her anything about his intentions. She was still talking on about the wicked ways the Snake family treated the people. "They don't hunt or leave this camp, any of them except the man, and all he does is go along with the men of this camp on their hunts to watch over them so none of them would try to escape from his camp. He watches very closely over all of the people. While he is out there with the hunters, his sons are here sneaking around and keeping a very close watch over the camp that no one tries to leave here to escape. Through the night, they are watching everyone's movement. They take turns watching. You will see, when they bring in the buffalo and all of them are killed, the Snake family will take over and take all of the meat for themselves, leaving very little for the whole camp.

"Most of the people have such little to eat that many of us are close to starvation. The Snake family has piles and piles of dried meat in their extra-large tipi. We dry our fresh meat out on our drying racks, what very little we get from them, even that meat they come and steal soon as we are not looking. They are a very low-down family that crawl on their bellies to steal what little food we have. It's no wonder they are called Snake family.

Kut-toe-yis got up after the old lady had told him of the wicked Snake family. It was about that time when the hunters had came back with many buffalo, they were now down at the *pis-kun*, butchering and dressing out the carcasses. Like always, the Snake family were all down there too, waiting for the meat so they could take it all. With many people butchering the many head of buffalo, it didn't take them very long to dress them all out. The wait wasn't too long for the Snake family before going into the *pis-kun* to get all of the meat for themselves and leaving very little for the rest of the camp. All this time, Kut-toe-yis was waiting for the Snake Chief to return to his tipi. The Snake tipi was a pretty painted tipi. It was just like any other tipi that's been painted with the original emblems up on the top and the bottom of it, but around the middle of it, the emblem of snakes was painted to show this was a snake tipi.

Kut-toe-yis kept his eyes on the snake tipi. It wasn't too long before the whole family of the Snake people returned to their tipi, and each had a load of meat on their backs and arms. He waited a while longer before making a move to go and pay a visit to the Snake family, waited for them to settle down and get organized or even to get through cooking some of the fresh meat they had just brung home to their tipi. He might even get a bite to eat there.

After waiting and giving them enough time to do all of that, Kut-toe-yis went to the center of this encampment where the Snake-painted tipi was erected. It was an exceptionally large tipi. There were many of them, the Snakeman and his whole family. Kut-toe-yis didn't hesitate as he reached the tipi, he went right on in without invitation. To the visitor's side of the tipi he went, he didn't sit down like an ordinary visitor, he walked right to where the Snakeman was sitting, on his bed. In front of him, about three bladders full of fermented wild cherry juice were laying. Without any hesitation, Kut-toe-yis took one of them and took a big drink from it. This action by Kut-toe-yis took all of the Snake family by surprise, and before they could recover from the surprise he jerked his flint knife out, and still without hesitation he jumped to each one of them and cut their necks off. They all were so stunned from the surprise that none of them had time to run or do anything. He jumped to all of them and just before he got the last of them, she took off through the doorway of the tipi, running for the thick part of the bushes. This last one of them was a Snake girl and she was in family way, pregnant, several months gone.

Kut-toe-yis didn't bother about her, he didn't chase her, he knew it wasn't any use to run after her, she would be hard to find in the thickets. He let her go, he only said after her, "Let there be other Snake people come from you to live on Mother Earth."

Doing what he had to do and the ordeal was over, Kut-toe-yis went back to the old lady that had tried in vain to talk him into leaving here because of the wicked Snake family. He brought her to this beautifully painted Snake tipi and told her she could have it, the owners were gone and would never return. She could have all that went with it, the food and the other things, belongings of the Snake people. Most of the fresh meat that was just gotten that day was given out to the people of this camp. All of the people were very glad to get rid of that awful family. Many of the men that now took over this camp were hollering for Kut-toe-yis to come and eat with them, invitations from all over the camp, and Kut-toe-yis was very busy trying to attend all of the invitations—because among the Natives, if you didn't attend an invitation, you were noted as a stuck-up, a conceited person, too good for others. Kut-toe-yis didn't want that to happen to him. All that day he ate and he ate, well into the night he attended those invitations until he had gone to the last of them.

He became a hero to these people. They didn't want to see him leave here, they wanted him for their head Chief, but always he declined. Never did he want to be stuck in one place if he could help it. For many days he abided with these kind people. He knew he would have to leave sooner or later.

# Kut-toe-yis and the Mean Cannibal Chief

After getting rid of those bad people of this Mother Earth, the wicked, the killers, and people eaters, Kut-toe-yis would hang around the camp that he had helped in getting rid of such. For quite some time he hung around the people. Because of the deed he done for them, they respected him a lot and soon got attached to him, even his dog was well liked, especially by the children. Kut-toe-yis was put here on Mother Earth by Creator Sun to take the place of Napi and to do a certain job for this earth, he just couldn't stay one place, he had to keep on hunting for the wicked. Not until it is cleaned of those wicked people could Kut-toe-yis sit around and enjoy himself.

Every place of this hunting area of his people was a new place for him, he didn't know what he would meet next. All he knew was that he had to do away with evil, all evil people and other kinds of killers of the Native race. He had gone to many places to find any evil that he might run across, and probably he had just about covered the whole area of what is known to us as North and South America. Kut-toe-yis cleaned much of the evil that was present in his time.

Today, this land of ours needs someone like Kut-toe-yis to clean the land out again of all the evil that has come in a mass among the people. If it was cleaned of the wicked people, this land of ours wouldn't have much over a couple of dozen of good people and for darn sure, I could bet, they would be all Natives of this country.

Kut-toe-yis was once again out there where he was a total stranger, in the unknown areas of his country. It was towards the west he was now traveling, and veering to the south. It had been a long, long time since he'd been out finding the evil things that didn't fit into this Mother Earth. The sun was just going down behind the hills, when far out in a distance he seen a very large encampment. A large camp meant many people that he would meet. It was just before dark when he finally reached the outlying tipis. Kut-toe-yis was always quick to spot certain things, and he soon spotted a small tipi, a likely place for an old lady. Kut-toe-yis always would seek out an old lady's tipi, they were easy to see. The tipis are small and the tipi poles are never too good, mostly what they could get for themselves that was easy to get at. Neatness wasn't their thing. As long as they had a shelter over their heads, they were satisfied. So the old ladies' tipis are easily spotted. Older women are easy to talk to, they are friendly and always give you the truth of what it is you are asking about. They also will feed you almost as soon as you sit down. Old ladies welcome you that much. This still is true among our Native people. To this small tipi Kut-toe-yis went. Clearing his throat as he got to the doorway to make his presence known to the occupants, he went in.

Without waiting for an explanation from Kut-toe-yis, the old lady of this tipi told Kut-toe-yis, "*Ki-yah ki-mom-maa-sah-da-bokes mah-gop-i-nahw ni-chi-naa-min-nona nee-die-yoat-seem-stuck-i-noan.* Well, it's a wonder you come, no good Chief, our Chief here, he is starving us all." While she was feeding Kut-toe-yis of what little she had and mostly the gristle part of the meat that was all she had to dry, she was telling him about the things this wicked Chief was doing to the people, especially the women.

"He takes women by force, married women, single women, and even the youngest girls that are still unknown by men. He forces them to his tipis and keeps them as wives. The husbands of these women, he kills them and eats them. You can see them tipis out in the middle of this encampment, they are all filled up with the wives he has taken by force.

"As you will see for yourself, there aren't any young men around in this camp. This cruel man has killed all of our young men and ate them. Those of us women that aren't out there among his many wives, we are the producers for him, we produce more young men for him to eat. We want to live, so we have to go along with his rules.

"I'd rather see you go back out of this camp tonight, hoping they didn't see you coming into camp. They have very sharp eyes. If you were seen coming into camp, they won't let you leave here, they will kill you and eat you for their meal. The menfolks are all old men, the wicked Chief only keeps them around to use them for the buffalo hunts, to supply fresh meat for him mostly, and a little for the rest of the camp. He is very greedy."

For quite a while Kut-toe-yis was very quiet, eating the food that the old lady had set before him, just listening to this old lady talk. After he downed the food, and seeing to it that Si-soum got some too, Kut-toe-yis spoke at last. "Does your Chief ever leave that tipi of his, or does he stay there all the time?"

The old lady answered him, "Mostly he is out there by the menfolks. He watches them very close so they wouldn't escape from here. He has some very faithful women in those tipis, them women watch over the women that he took by force. You must try to leave here tonight or you will be dead tomorrow."

Kut-toe-yis seemed like he hadn't even heard the old lady. He was asking her if it was all right to sleep in here until morning. The old lady couldn't refuse him, he seemed to be a nice young man. We will see what takes place in the morning. Kut-toe-yis lay down and went to sleep for the night, his dog curled up besides him.

The old lady always got up from her bed when it's just getting gray in the east. Getting out of her bed and looking to where Kut-toe-yis slept, the place was empty. That young man must've taken her word to leave here while he was still in one piece and alive. It was just getting light enough to see when the old lady heard someone coming, the rustling of the grass and the ground. Whoever it was, he was kind of panting as he was almost out of wind.

Whoever it was came to her doorway and not hesitating, he came on in. To her surprise, it was none other then that young man that slept here. He brought in a big load of fresh meat, in his arms and back. The old lady didn't know what to do, she was sorely afraid, it was death to her and this young man if the wicked Chief found out about this. Without waiting, he dropped the fresh meat right in front of where the old lady was sitting, telling her, "Hurry and cut the meat up, have it ready by daylight to hang on the outside drying racks."

The poor old lady was shaking with fear, she was thinking of the mean Chief. She hurried like the young man asked her to, but she was very nervous about it. It didn't take long to cut all the meat. Because of her fear, she really done a fast job. Kut-toe-yis was right beside her, doing what he could do to help her. The meat was all ready by daylight. Kut-toe-yis took the pieces out and hung them on the outside drying racks.

What Kut-toe-yis done the morning, he got up and went right down to the *pis-kun* and killed a buffalo so the poor old lady would have a good meal this morning. At the same time, this was to spite the mean Chief too. Hanging all of the fresh meat up on one rack, and a special high rack to hang a large shin bone from.

Kut-toe-yis and the old lady didn't have very long to wait after daylight. From the center tipis, the mean Chief's tipis, a very young boy came running to this old lady's small tipi. He was one of the only young men to be around, because this mean Chief and the family didn't kill their own sons, so their sons were the only young men around. The boy came dashing to this small tipi of this old lady. His father had sent him over to find out where the fresh meat came from and to be sure and bring back the largest and the best pieces of meat hanging from the drying rack.

Without hesitation, because they knew they were always the boss in this camp and no one could tell them what to do, this small boy went onto the drying rack and loaded up his arms with the fresh-cut meat. This small boy wasn't aware of another being in the tipi, namely Kut-toe-yis, otherwise he might've had second thoughts. About the time he had his arms loaded with the fresh-cut meat and the choicest of the back fat, Kut-toe-yis stepped out of the small tipi and asked him what he was doing with the fresh-cut meat. "My father told me to bring it back to his tipi." Kut-toe-yis was beside him by this time, he didn't even make a stop as he came along, his spear in his hands. The spear went right through this small boy's heart. As the boy began to fall, Kut-toe-yis told him, "Take that to your father and let him be happy like the rest of his subjects."

The mean Cannibal Chief got up and looked out towards the small tipi on the outskirts of this large camp, thinking, "The boy shouldn't be gone this long." Coming back in, at the same time calling on the second-oldest son of his to go find out about the smaller boy and to be sure to bring back the choicest back fat and meat.

In the meantime, Kut-toe-yis had already put the body of the small boy where it was out of the way, covered and not easily found. He knew there were others of the family to come after the small boy was missed by the father.

The next-oldest boy came a-running to the small tipi. Without going into it, he went right to the drying rack and loaded his arms up with the fresh-cut meat and back fat. He had eyes for choicy meat and back fat, because he took the same meat the old lady hung back up on the drying rack. That meat and fat was what the first boy had picked too. About that time again, Kut-toe-yis came out of the old lady's tipi. Right to this boy he came, and without stopping he ran his spear through the boy's heart. At the same time, Kut-toe-yis told him to go and join his brother.

It wasn't too long when another boy, the third-oldest, came a-running to this small tipi of the old lady, asking her if she had seen the first two boys that came this way. At the same time he was also taking almost the same meat and fat that his brothers had picked too. They were already put back on the rack again by the old lady and Kut-toe-yis. Kut-toe-yis was back in the tipi when this boy came a-running. About this time again that the boy had loaded up his arms with the meat and fat, Kut-toe-yis came out of the tipi and slew this boy.

It wasn't very long before a girl was sent to this small tipi of the old lady. The same fate she got, like her brothers. She too was loading her arms up with the fresh meat and back fat when Kut-toe-yis pounced on her and slew her with his spear. After this girl, two more older than her came, one at a time. The same fate befell all of them as they came one at a time to find out about one another and also where the fresh-cut meat came from. No more children to do his errand, he then sent one of his faithful wives. It was his uneasy wife as Natives call them—*eese-oo-key-mon*—that went next, and she too ran into the same fate.

From time untold, men of these Native Americans had multiple wives. There always is a favorite wife that is known as *ee-dote-oo-bee*, sits by him. This sit-by wife doesn't have much to do, except to make her husband as comfortable as she can, and she does his hair too. The uneasy wives—it could be one or more of them, most times it all depends on the number of daughters in one family where the girls or women came from. These uneasy wives are the ones that does all of the work of cooking, tidying the tipi up, the tanning of hides, getting water, getting firewood, cutting fresh meat for drying, and making the clothes for the husband, and so on. The sit-by wife doesn't do much except to be by the man at all times, even away from the tipi, and do his hair.

The mean Cannibal Chief had only two wives that he could trust closely. The others that he forced to him, wives of other men and the younger girls, he didn't want to send them as they might get the notion to run away and never come back. It was this one uneasy wife and the sit-by wife that he trusted to do an errand for him. The uneasy wife already met her fate the same way as the daughters and sons. It was all up to the sit-by wife now to go and find out what was going on at that old lady's tipi. Why haven't the others returned yet?

The sit-by wife was sent there too and she too done just like the others did. This one Kut-toe-yis treated a little differently, because she mentioned she was the sit-by wife of the mean Cannibal Chief. Kut-toe-yis didn't use his spear on her. He led her to the high drying rack where the fresh shin bone was hanging. Her arms were loaded with the fresh-cut meat and the back fat, and not wanting to drop them, she held onto the meat. As they got up to the high rack, Kut-toe-yis told her to reach up to the shin bone with her tongue and lick it. She really had to stretch her neck, and stood on her tiptoes to reach the shin bone. Just as she licked it, Kut-toe-yis hit her across the throat with another shin bone with all his might. It killed the woman.

No one was left to do his bossing but the Cannibal Chief. Up he got to go do it for himself, he'll show them how it was done. He was very mad at his family, thinking they were just fooling around. Right to the old lady's tipi he came. As soon as he came within hearing distance, he was asking the old lady what had become of his family. Without waiting for an answer, he came up to the drying rack and began to load his arms just like the rest of them. He asked the old lady where his family went to. Before the old lady spoke, Kut-toe-yis was at his side, grabbed him by his arm, and led him to the high drying rack. He stood the Chief under the hanging shin bone and told him, "If you want all of your family, you are going to have to lick this shin bone first and then I'll tell you where your family are." The Cannibal Chief done this readily, he wanted his whole family back. Just as he stretched himself to lick at the shin bone, Kut-toe-yis landed the other shin bone right across the mean Cannibal Chief's throat with all of his might. This Kut-toe-yis done it again, done away with pitiless, selfishness, murdering, and all wickedness as this mean Cannibal Chief laid still in death.

Kut-toe-yis was already thinking about where he would go next to find the wicked.

People say Kut-toe-yis is still out looking for the wicked. But if he is, he's done a very bad job of it because today wickedness is so abundant all over the world. So Kut-toe-yis must've passed on after he done away with the mean Cannibal Chief. Creator Sun and Mother Earth must've took him back to the place of good spirits.

# HONORING CREATOR SUN

# Beginning of Native Religion

The people of Americas, North and South America—namely, the children of Creator Sun and Mother Earth, the Natives—had spread to many parts of these two continents. When the first Europeans seen the Natives of these two continents, they thought they had come to India. Over this mistake, they called us Indians. Rightfully, we should be called Children of Mother Earth and Creator Sun.

All of the Natives of these two continents are the very creations of Mother Earth and Creator Sun. Before the coming of the Europeans, things these Natives done was for their Mother Earth and their father, Creator Sun. Many, many things the comers from other lands see of our past points to that true fact. For example, our religion of the Medicine Lodge, it really isn't supposed to be Medicine Lodge. It is to honor our Mother Earth and Creator Sun. Most of our legends point to this. The circles from the past that are found in many places in these two continents are influenced by our father, Creator Sun. Many things are made in their pattern, in circles. The circle of the Sun, the circle of Mother Earth. Many other things point to Native faith, the surrounding facts of natural things of the whole universe. For instance, many people of these recent years have seen the movie *Close Encounters of the Third Kind*. All of these things seen on the film are the works of our Native people, and not of the outer space beings scientists say made them. The Natives of these two continents are just as intelligent as the next person, even those who lived way back in the past, thousands of years ago.

The ancient pyramids that are found from the northern area of this North America to the southern tip of South America are the works of our ancient people, the Natives. These pyramids are worshiping places. A Native climbs the high place to get nearer to our Creator Sun and still be standing on Mother Earth, so the prayers could be heard more distinctly by the two Creators. It took them both to create men—the mud or clay from Mother Earth and the breath from Creator Sun.

In the last 150 years, our Natives were shamed into forgetting our faith of Creator Sun and take in place of it a very foreign religion that we didn't know anything about. Those Natives that now believe in the European religion are all brainwashed into believing such by the missionaries that invaded our Native areas. What they done to our religion was very contrary to their reason for coming—freedom of religion.

Other things that point to our faith of Nature and the whole Universe itself and also shown in the movie *Close Encounters*—the straight lines and designs on the mountaintops, on high places, that point to a certain star or the sun or a special place in the universe—were all made by our ancestors, the Natives. These were special places of worship to the sun and stars, the moon too. Many of these places were sacrificial areas, a place of self-torture, a place to strain one's body for the sake of a certain religious and sacred object, a star, the moon, the sun, or a particular place here on earth. Nature as a whole was all sacred to our Natives. Our way was all reverence for the universe.

The Native knows that there aren't such beings from outer space. Otherwise, our ancestors would've told about such things as outer space beings in our legends of the past. Also, the Native's legendary history knows that there is but one Creator for all people of this world, and that human life was created here on this continent of North America. Instead of our Natives trekking from Asia, on the Bering land bridge, like the whiteman's history points, our ancestors know that this was vice versa. Humans went from North America across the Bering Straits to Asia and Europe. The culture of these Natives, compared to the Asian and European culture and traditions, is easily distinguished. If the Native of North and South America had come from Asia and Europe, our languages would be about the same with all of the tribes and those of the Asian and European people. As it is, in these days, there isn't any kind of correspondence in one another's language, particularly of the Caucasian and the Aryan languages that were and still are spoken widely by the people of the Asian and European countries. The Natives of the North and South American continents should have been influenced by such a language. On the other hand, many of those people of the Asian and European countries still carry some of our traditions from some of the words that are used by many of our own tribes from these Americas. So! Instead of us being influenced by the ways of the Asian and European people, they are in some way influenced by our ways and languages too.

The people had been saved by Kut-toe-yis. He had killed all of the wicked people and beings of this land he had encountered. The people were now living free from their fears of wickedness, and all were very happy for many years after this. Kut-toe-yis went somewhere to find more adventures and was never heard of again.

Living was very good to the people for many years, then a few bad things began to appear in the different parts of the land again. People were going against the rulings of our Creator Sun and Mother Earth. They couldn't let well enough alone, they had to follow their own beliefs or someone else's. For many years, all of this was not enough to be alarmed about. The people's reverence to Creator Sun and Mother Earth was still very strong among most of their children. They were obedient to his words and promises, mostly prayed a lot to the two for deliverance from this evil that was now coming back to this land, and it seemed that it was getting worse each time it came to the evildoers.

Even in these days, many of us are so strong in our Christianity and whatever faith we may follow, we just come short of pulling that God down from the heavens or pulling the great Native Spirit down to us. But then comes a time when we forget that great faith of ours, especially if we are bribed with a large amount of money or something that we really need in our lives. Whenever these things arise, to get them in some easy way, we forget our great belief of our faith. We do evil then, just to get our needs the evil easy way. Even to these days, things still work that evil easy way, and it was the same way right from the human beginning. We give up our Creator for the easy way of evil.

Creator Sun had always tried to find a special way to have his children go and live with good always. He had Napi to be with the people and taught them many things of goodness. Napi faltered at his job of teaching good, and he passed on from this world from his own foolishness. Then came Kut-toe-yis, a being from a clot of buffalo blood, to do away with the evil that he could find in the land, and which he did for Creator Sun.

Leaving disciples here on Mother Earth wasn't working out. The people only stayed good for so many years, then back to the bad they go. Not many of them at first, but as they go along they seem to drag others into this wicked way of life. Creator Sun must find a way to straighten his children out, it has to be a definite way to hold their thinking of him always. The imprint of both Napi and Kut-toe-yis shows in many forms and the traditional ways they both taught the people, the culture that stands out, even in these days of our modern Natives. This is the basis for the way children grow up into adults. A very young child in the first few months of life and within the first year to the ninth year of life—what they learned in those few short years is what they live by throughout their adult years. This holds the same for those first humans that were created here on Mother Earth, their beginning in those first few thousand years are the ones we are all living by.

The smoking of tobacco was given to the Mudman and the Ribwoman in the beginning of human life. It was a part of the honors for Creator Sun and Mother Earth, a sacred purpose used in speaking with these two that put us humans into Mother Earth's body. Those first people were given the tobacco to smoke. As the smoke from the tobacco curled its way upward, the smoker prays and the smoke carries the prayers to our Creator Sun. When the tobacco burns out, the ashes are then dumped into a small hole in the ground made with one finger of the last to smoke the pipe, and is again prayed with. In this way, it is also given and prayed to Mother Earth. Everything that is done for sacredness is done in two ways, always for Creator Sun and the other for Mother Earth.

Many mixtures for the tobacco were also given to the human race by our Creator Sun and produced by our Mother Earth. Several different kinds of roots were dried and mashed into a powder-like form. Many kinds of leaves were also dried and pounded into a powder form. I remember the kinnikinnick leaves, and the red willow bark. Wild cherry bark was used too. The layer under the top bark was used for smoking with the tobacco. All of these are of nature and are the productions of Mother Earth and Creator Sun for the purpose of sacredness.

I have to contradict many of the writers of American history in many things I say in this book. First, I must say that we Natives have very much compassion for one another. An old couple of many years of age would never give their children any harsh words, never be mean with them. All the time, these adult children are given stern advice by their parents. Among the Native Americans, before there was much contact with the white people, the children lived with their parents until the old couple died or the children moved away. Never was your children kicked out into the world to make a living for themselves, no matter how old they may be.

For another thing, I have read books that mention the pipes, the first smoking pipes of the Native. These writers tell about the old ways tobacco is smoked. The first pipe of hollow bones, mostly of the shin bones of animals, hollowed-out wood that was used as the first pipes of the Natives. These were supposed to have been the primitive invention of a smoking pipe. But I must argue with this way. I'm a Native full blood of the former Piegan Tribe, now called the Blackfeet Indian, and I have a full knowledge of my own Native history as it was related to me by many of my elders that have long ago gone on to Happy Hunting Grounds.

My informants told me that the lazy people, of which there are many, are the ones that would smoke in shin bones or improvisations of a smoking pipe. They are just too lazy to make a regular smoking pipe for themselves, especially in the past couple of hundred years.

The smoking pipe was given to the Native by our Creator Sun and Mother Earth to use in its way of praying. It is so, whenever something is given to anyone, it is to be given completely and not only a part of it. Creator Sun and Mother Earth gave the tobacco to smoke in a pipe, to be used in prayer. The two divine beings of our birth as humans gave it completed: both pipe and tobacco and also how to use it. They also gave those first beings how to get their next tobacco and how to ready it for smoking. The very first pipe given the first people of Mother Earth was a complete package deal—pipe, tobacco, and the full instructions for the use of it. It was from the body of Mother Earth and made in a red color from Creator Sun's element, its rays. Creator Sun even taught those first humans how to make a pipe out of the soft stone that was left here for that purpose and especially made for the people from the two divine beings' elements, Mother Earth's and Creator Sun's.

I will name a few of my informants who have now gone on to that eternal place of our people, Happy Hunting Grounds. They told me of our legendary past, right from the beginning, as I have told this story: my Grandma, Catches Last Bullchild; Weaseltail; Owen Heavybreast; Percy Creighton; Homegun; Manyhides; Dustybull; Pete After Buffalo; Yellowkidney; Chief Twoguns Whitecalf; James Whitecalf; Bearhead; Bearmedicine; Rides at the Door of Cardston, Alberta; Old Lady Littleleaf; Jim Littleleaf; Yellowhorn; and many others that I have since forgotten. My best informants were my own dad, George Bullchild, and Grandma Catches Last Bullchild.

All this time, Creator Sun's mind was on the subject of how to make his children more aware of him and their lies, what was the best method for them to keep in their minds the reverence of each one's life and how to make them always thankful to him for that life he created for the purpose of compassion here on Mother. In other words, they had to know to thank him and Mother Earth always, because it is the two that is keeping them alive. The breath of Creator Sun and the suck we get from Mother Earth. Breath and food that comes from both of their elements, Creator Sun and Mother Earth.

One day as Creator Sun sat thinking of that matter that was so very important to him and Mother Earth, thinking back to the beginning of time when he first gave life to the very first people, the smoking pipe and the tobacco he gave them to smoke and pray with as the smoke from the pipe slowly rose into the air and upwards, an idea struck him. "Why not use this method to keep their minds on the reverence I want them to keep in their minds."

Creator Sun knew these people loved the smoking pipe very much, and he taught the men how to keep that tobacco and pipe within reach at all times by putting it in a small bag and letting it hang from one's belt. The bag that contains the tobacco and pipe is known as a pouch. With this in mind, Creator Sun had formed an idea that would work for him among his children always. He would give power to a few certain ones of his many children, the most obedient of all the people that had spread to many parts of these lands.

The power was only to a certain extent and it would come to them in a mysterious way that Creator Sun thought of.

Around this time, as these Americas progressed, the population increased manyfold. Many, many camps of all the Natives were all over the lands, and the language had changed so much that all separated camps spoke a different language of their own, that one language they begun with was forgotten. In many instances the same words were used, but they meant something else to each group.

Creator Sun was always looking down on his children. Day and night he was watching them, their daily activities, those that were doing good for themselves and them that weren't doing so good with their lives, not paying much attention to the holy ways of most of the people. Creator Sun had to start someplace with the idea that was utmost in his mind, salvation for his children. Creator Sun knew that in some way women were very obedient to his ways if they wanted be, but they could be just so hard to manage once they got out of hand. This was going to be a test in what he thought best for his children's ways, a way that would always remind them of his presence among them each day and night. He had a plan that would bring this holy way into the people without having to appear before them himself. At this time he picked out a very obedient girl, a teenager who still was a virgin. Creator Sun had to hurry before this girl knew of adulthood. She was already thinking adult bad ways of life, but she actually hadn't done anything wrong. She had to be brought out of the wicked dangers of life.

It was a summer night, and the day had been very hot. Many of the women were out gathering wood for their fireplaces in their tipis. It was late afternoon when they all left camp to go to the woods. Each one piled wood that they could carry on their backs tied together with rawhide ropes, that was the only way of getting wood to the tipis. None was in great big hurry, they were visiting as they gathered what was needed. It was almost dark when all of the women started out for the tipis with the wood on their backs. All of them went along the trail without any trouble. This very nice girl that Creator Sun had in mind and her friend didn't go very far from where they gathered the wood, when the girl's load of wood came loose of the rawhide rope. She tied the load back together while her friend waited for her. On her back once more she threw it, and on their way they went.

They didn't get very far when the wood came apart again and fell to the ground the second time. The friend that was by her all this time was getting tired, the load on her back was getting heavy and wanted to get it home to their tipi. This girl that was selected by Creator Sun didn't want to be alone, she talked her friend into waiting for her a little more. It was the second time the load on her back came apart and fell to the ground. Her friend was getting impatient to hurry and get her load of wood to their tipi.

Trying to make her friend wait a little more after tying her load back together once more, she made her take her load off of her back and sit down beside her to rest for a while. The darkness had come and the night was moonlight, there were many beautiful stars shining bright from above. The two sat there among the trees, laying back against their loads of wood and gazing up into the sky with its many, many stars. Girls will always be girls. As the two laid there gazing upwards, looking at the stars, the selected had her eyes on one particular bright star, a large one. It was shining so pretty, glittering in all sorts of colors.

Tapping her friend to get her attention, she told her, "Look at that extra-bright pretty star shining in all kinds of pretty colors." Her friend agreed, she too was looking at this same star. Without waiting for her friend to say anything, the selected girl spoke out loud as she talked to no one in particular, "If that bright star was human, I would marry him, he is so handsome." Both of them giggled after she had said this out loud.

"Come on, let's get to our tipis, everyone else must've got their wood home and here we are still breaking down with our loads." They didn't get very far when the selected girl's load fell to the ground for the third time. "If your load falls again, I'm going to leave you. This load on my back is getting me very tired, I want to get it off of my back." Slowly tying her load together again, the selected girl got it on her back once more and off they went. They didn't go very many steps when her load came apart again. Her friend went on, telling the selected girl that the tipis weren't far, she could make it with her load after she tied it back together again.

There she was, the selected girl, only she didn't know she had been selected by Creator Sun to bring her people back into reverence of him. She was getting tired from the load breaking apart and retying it so many times already, and she was slower this time to tie the load together once more. Kneeling beside her pile of wood, tying it together, her head bent over as she worked on the rawhide rope, when to her surprise a young man tapped her shoulder. As she she turned to see who it was, the young man spoke with authority, "Come on, I came after you to come to my place. Come and let's put distance between here and get to where I want to take you." The selected girl was taken aback. She had never been near men, she was a virgin yet. Why would a man come to get her? She didn't know any man.

She said, "I don't know you and don't know of any man or boy, so why should I go with you anyplace?"

The young man argued, "You said with your own mouth that you wanted to marry me."

The girl argued back, "No, no, I didn't tell anyone I'll marry him!"

The young man told the girl where she said it. "It was when you and the other girl, that went on to the tipis, when you and her were resting the second time your rope broke from your load of wood. You and her were laying back on your pile of wood resting, when you said 'If that bright pretty star were a man, I'd marry him.' Well, I come after you, I'm that pretty bright star that shines with all of the pretty colors. Come on, we must get started before someone comes after you. You can't back down, it was your own wish." Taking her by her hand and arm, he pulled her up and led her away into the night. She couldn't back out from her wish, she had to go along with him.

It was still in the days of many mysteries. Her folks would miss her, but being left all alone in the forest, anything could happen to her. Wild animals could get her and eat her up, she could've lost her way, it was dark when the other girl left her. Many things could happen to her. Her folks and friends would look for her, but there would be no trace of her and they would all come to the conclusion that she must've been eaten by wild animals, probably a bear. No one would ever know it was a Star Being that took her away, and by her own wishes.

Through the trees the two went, the Star Being holding her hand as they went along. She knew it was no use to argue with this man. He was right, she did say that if the very pretty bright star were a human being, she would marry him. The girl didn't get scared as they went along for quite a ways. She was secretly tickled to know she was heard by a Star Being.

They had gone quite a ways from where this man had first appeared to her, when he stopped. He told the girl to close her eyes until he told her to open them again. Without hesitation, she closed her eyes and waited for him to tell her to open them. She didn't have to wait very long when he told her she could open eyes. Upon opening her eyes she saw a very pretty valley with such nice fields and trees, but it was a strange feeling for her. She felt she didn't belong here. She didn't say anything to her new man, for she had a secret feeling of love for this Star Being. The Star Being told the girl, "This is your new place to live, here in this land we live. There isn't too many of us here yet, but we are increasing slowly."

After several days her parents became very, very bereaved, they knew something dreadful had happened to her. Many of their friends went out into the woods to look for her, but she wasn't there. In a very large radius from where her friend saw her last, they looked. They just couldn't find anything of her or her clothes, but they did find the pile of wood she left where the rawhide rope last broke from her back. After many days of looking, the parents gave her up for dead, killed by some wild animal and eaten. For a very long time afterwards, the parents mourned for their daughter, they loved her very much.

The girl got very used to the new place, she came to love it because her man was from this land. She did whatever the other women were doing, her tipi chores first. She got to know all of their habits, their ways, the culture and traditional ways they lived. This selected girl got to love her Star Being husband very much. She had forgotten all about her own people and her parents. She lived with content among these people of her husband's. Always something new that she learned each day. She had been here for many years, she had grown up into an honest young woman, true to her husband in every way. She was an ideal lady.

This day was another day in her husband's land, but it had come to that time again when it was time to dig for certain roots that were used for food. Roots were gathered at certain times of the year, mostly in the summer months or early spring of the year, when they are just fresh in growth. This time it was the wild turnip roots that were to be dug and as always, this selected girl was very happy to go out into the fields to find the wild turnip root. She had done this many times since she came here with her husband. The women made a regular party out of digging for roots. Lunches were made to take out and eaten after they were through digging for the day, or sometimes about midday. It took several days for each kind of root to be dug out of the ground. Each one of the women would dig for so much or a bag full, then they were through for the day until the next morning, when they went out again to dig some more.

The women had to gather enough of these roots to last through the coming winter, and this was the only time of the year that this root could be gathered. All other roots too had to be gathered at a certain time of the year, and each kind of root had to last through the coming year. It wouldn't be until the next year before the roots would grow again, so enough had be gotten.

The husband kind of hesitated to let his wife go. For a long time, when the other women were getting ready to go on their first morning's diggings, the Starman argued with his wife about going out into the wild turnip fields. He had gone through the field with the other men, and all of these men had seen a special turnip out in the middle of a certain one of the many fields. A very large turnip, it must be four or five times bigger than the regular turnips, the leaves grew high and large. It could be seen as soon as one got into this field.

This Starman, having such powers to know what things were about, knew this was a year that wasn't going to be very good for him. He had dreamt about this long before now. His wife, the selected girl, argued back with her husband. She's been out there digging with the other women ever since he brought her here. She told her husband that it would be very lonely for her to be all alone here at the camps. There wouldn't be one lady or girl to visit with for the next few days, all of the womenfolk with their children would be out there digging for as many roots as they could get for the coming year.

After a long argument between the two, the husband finally gave in to her when she went out into the fields of wild turnips. "You must work along by one of the old ladies that I'm going to tell to watch over you, so that you do not forget that restriction. There is a very large turnip in one of the fields. Do not touch that one large one, don't even go near it. Use your ears and hear me right. It is a forbidden one of those turnips in that field. It is especially you that must not go near it, let alone touch it or try to pull it out from the ground. Hear me, hear me, my wife, and stay away from that one large turnip."

"I will, I will stay away from the turnip you are telling me about. You can tell the old lady to watch me out there in the turnip field. I have never gone against your words at any time since we've been together. I'll take your word that it will bring bad luck for us if I pull it out of the ground. I promise to not even go near it when we come to that particular field where that extra-large turnip grew."

All of the women went out for the roots, bringing their children along to help them with the digging and the gathering. The selected girl went along with them. It was their first morning out in the turnip fields, all of them happy to be out away from their tipis. It was just a lovely day to do this job. Everything went smoothly this first day. The women were just so busy to dig as much as they could for the day. The selected girl was no exception, she too worked fast to dig for as many roots as she can by the time they went home to the tipis for the day. It was time to get everything together and go home to prepare their meal for their husbands and families. After their evening meal, all of the women went right to bed, they were all so very tired from the digging.

Of course everyone rises very early in those days, everyone gets up at the first light in the east, with the birds. Before sunup, right after the morning meal, the women were well on their way to the turnip fields again. It started out like yesterday, smoothly. They had dug most of this field and were ready to move to another field of wild turnips. They were just waiting on a few stragglers to finish up. All of them were now ready to move into the next field, as this field was all dug out of turnips for this year.

All of the women went on into the next field of turnips and immediately went back to work at digging for the root. They hadn't worked too long before one of the older women said she was getting mighty hungry. She didn't have to say it again when all of them threw down their digging tools and in the same spot they all sat down to enjoy their lunch. Soon after she got through with her meal or lunch, the selected girl asked her overseer, the old lady, if she could come to the bushes to let her digested food out in nature's way. The old lady, sitting so comfortable, told her she could go alone, but hurry back, as it was nearly time to get back to work, they had to dig for so much of those roots each day. She didn't argue with the old lady— she had to go, and soon, she could hardly hold her water any longer. She ran to the bushes and in among them to hide from the other ladies' view, so she could let her water run out.

It didn't take her long to get through, and on her way back to the other women. Not far out of the bushes, going along with her eyes ahead to where she was stepping, right along the way she took was this very, very large, extra-large turnip. It had the biggest leaves on it and it was quite a bit higher than the rest of the field of turnips. Seeing it made her stop in her tracks. It was a surprise for her to come to the forbidden turnip her husband told her to stay away from. This extra-large turnip didn't in any way look any different than the rest of the regular turnips in this field, it was only very much larger than the rest of them. In some mysterious way, this extra-large turnip had aroused her curiosity. She hesitated by it several moments, but in her heart she remembered her promise to her husband, not to try to bother the extra-large turnip if by chance she came upon it. And this she did, she came upon it by chance.

It was very hard for her to walk away from this turnip. There was something about it that kind of pulled her to it. This turnip had a strange force, and she couldn't get it out of her mind. She tried to work hard to get it out of her mind, but it was just no use. It was a long day for her and she just barely dug enough to fill her bag up this day. The extra-large turnip was too strongly on her mind.

Getting home that evening, all of the women got their home chores done, the family meal, and then to bed they all went. All were tired again and they must have enough rest for tomorrow. The selected girl tossed and turned that night, she couldn't sleep for some reason. That something was thinking of that extra-large turnip out in that field. There was a strange reason why she alone must not dig it. Of course, the restriction was for all of the women, not to bother it, let alone digging it. But for some reason, she felt this restriction was directed at her mostly. The more she thought about it, the more curious she was.

Early the next morning the women and their children all went out into the turnip fields. This morning the girl was a little slower than other mornings. She was just straggling along in the back of all the women—even her overseer, the old lady, was among those ahead of her. This was the third day of digging for the turnip roots. The girl just barely made it through this day, her thoughts were heavy.

The digging had gone on around a patch of trees in this field. The forbidden turnip was around behind the other side of the trees where one couldn't see. All were digging as hard as they could—all except the girl, she was too busy thinking about the extra-large turnip. It was almost their lunch break when the girl got an idea. She must wait for the lunch break. It wasn't very long until one of the old ladies said it was time to eat their lunch.

The girl could hardly wait, she sat right down and ate as fast as she could. This would give her more time to do what she wanted to do during her rest period with the other women. She didn't lose much time after she ate her lunch. She asked the old lady, her overseer, if she wanted to go and relieve herself of water before the other women started to work again. The old lady didn't want to at this time, maybe later on, she said. She told the girl she could go alone if she had to, but to hurry and get back to start the digging again. The girl didn't even wait for her to get through saying what she had to, she jumped up and away she ran for the thick growth of trees.

It wasn't anything unusual for a woman to go alone into the woods to relieve herself and come back and work again, so no one even noticed her. She didn't stop in the trees, but went right on through them, still a-running, and right to the extra-large turnip that was left all alone in this last field the women picked over.

This extra-large turnip had really made her nervous in the past few days, she was thinking all sorts of things about it. She just had to go back there and see this extra-large turnip once more. It had a magnetic force, it seemed to be pulling her back to it, her mind and herself. She came to the extra-large turnip. Its extra-large leaves, sticking up even with her knees, were very large, wide, flat, and long. She walked around it a couple of times, looking at it. This time, her mind was on her work and her overseer, the old lady. She had to get back soon, before the old lady missed her. She got ahold of those extra-large leaves and pulled on them a little bit. They seemed to give somewhat, and this gave her more courage to pull faster and with all her might. The extra-large turnip came up slowly as she pulled. She didn't easy any at all, and she almost landed on her seat when the turnip suddenly came out of the ground very fast from her last, hard pull.

The extra-large turnip left a deep hole in the ground where it grew, but the girl was busy looking at the turnip as it laid on the ground beside her. Her mind was on hurrying back now that she had pulled the turnip out of the ground and nothing happened this far. Jumping up fast to get to running back to the rest of the women, her glance fell to the deep hole in the ground, the deep imprint of the extra-large turnip. Not thinking of anything certain, she jumped on over to this deep hole in the ground and looked in it. She almost fell over with the biggest surprise of her life. The extra-large turnip left a deep hole in the ground, it was so deep that a light came from the bottom of it. The girl got on her stomach and looked down into this deep hole where the turnip came from. Tears came to her eyes as she laid there looking down into the hole. Almost directly below her was her people's camp. She recognized many of the tipis, she seen people as small as tiny insects walking around down there. One thing certain, it was her people's camp. She got very lonesome now that she seen her people far below the place she was at.

Getting slowly up again, she started back towards the women. Her heart was very heavy and those tears kept coming out of her eyes. She must get her self-composure before she got back to them. She mustn't let them know where she's been. Drying her eyes and wiping them the best she could and fixing up a little, she hurried back to the digging area. Most of the women were up and some had already started digging. She didn't wait, but went on to digging too, keeping her head down as much as she could until there wasn't any sign of tears anymore. She must get up some sweat to hid the tearstains on her cheeks.

This was her fourth day of digging the turnip roots, and already she had found out about the extra-large turnip that grew in that one field. It brought very sad thoughts in her mind. Those days she was at home with her parents and all of her friends. Thinking back on all of these precious times before she was taken away from her camp by this Star Being brought tears back again and again. It even made the day go so fast that it was time to quit before she knew it. Trying not to think of this anymore, she tried to bring herself together before they reached home, so her husband wouldn't suspect anything of her.

She had come out of the feeling before she got to her tipi, and looked like herself again. Her husband wasn't at their tipi when she came in, he was out somewhere, which made it all the better for her. She went ahead to make the evening meal, keeping as busy as she could to forget the day, but it just wasn't that easy to forget about seeing her parents' camp far below them that day. This kept on stirring her mind as she tried to forget the whole thing. It was just no use. After preparing the evening meal, she sat quietly alone, waiting for her husband to come home and eat.

The Starman husband of hers came in just before dark, there was still light enough to see and eat their evening meal. Both were very quiet as they sat there eating, which was very unusual for the two—other times they were always busy talking. After their meal was gone, the Starman husband cleared his throat and asked his wife why she was quiet. He didn't wait for an answer, he went on talking to her, telling her that he knew already why she was so quiet this evening, that she found out about the extra-large turnip out in that one field. She had seen her parents' camp and had recognized them and now she was very quiet because she was lonesome for her real home, her parents' and her friends' camps. He told her that she shouldn't have broken her promise about not bothering the extra-large turnip root. He told her that they would have to go on despite of what happened. Furthermore, he made her promise with her heart that she wouldn't go against her husband's words the next time. The Starman also punished his wife for being disobedient to him. He kept her home in their tipi for the next several days.

The Starman husband went out each day and didn't return until towards the day's end. He was busy helping get prepared for the coming year. Things were only gotten once a year, and it was work until those things were all safely stored in the rawhide cases and preserved for use. The Starman husband kept a very close watch over his wife those next several days. Each time the husband came home in the evening he would look his wife over very carefully, without letting her know of this. And each evening her eyes were red from weeping the day through. Her eyes got redder and redder. He knew she was very lonely now that she seen her parents' camp and the friends that she grew up with until he came and got her away from that happy life she had. But it was Creator Sun's plan to let it come this way, and it was falling right along into the plans for his children of Mother Earth. Something that would always keep those children's minds on his presence on Mother Earth each day.

The Starman husband was very compassionate to life itself, for it was the life of nature that all beings were alive wherever they may be. He loved this woman with all his heart and would be very sad if she had to leave here. He knew she was getting so very lonely for her folks and friends, and it was all because of the broken restriction of the extra-large turnip that she pulled out. That turnip was the sole power that kept her mind off of her parents and her friends after she was taken to this place of her Starman husband's land. Now that it was out of the ground and she seen her parents and friends, it would be very hard to take her mind off her folks. This meant the Starman had to comply with her wishes, whatever she wanted to do. He must let her rejoin her parents and friends if she wished so. The Starman husband knew that loneliness was very serious to most people, one could get sick and eventually die over loneliness. It wouldn't be any use to try and keep her here any longer, now that she had seen with her own eyes the camps of where she came from.

He was hoping against hope that it may not be so, that the girl would overcome her loneliness and have more thoughts about their love for one another. Secretly he knew it wouldn't be that way, because there wasn't love involved to begin with. He just came along and took her away from her camp, her parents and friends, suddenly, without knowing one another previously. This getting together was sparked instantly, it was her childish, girlish, and foolish wish to get married to a brilliant star that sparkled in all sorts of colors. He was foolish too, to come and take her away just on that childish whim. He knew he was very wrong to do what he did, and now he must pay for that crazy deed. This would hurt both of them in many ways.

The Starman husband couldn't stand his wife's loneliness any longer, he hadn't let on that he knew what was taking place with his wife, pretending that all was normal. Early on the morning of the fourth day of her loneliness, the Starman went to a very wise old man to consult him about his troubles. The old man listened very carefully to the young man as he told his story about going to take this wife of his away from her folks and friends. The old man, after he heard all, told the young man that all of this was very wrong, he should have waited before doing this wrong to a girl that hadn't known anything about adulthood yet. In a way, it was good that the two had found out soon enough, before there was a little one involved. This young man must bring his wife back to where she was originally from. Before he brought her back, he must give her something that was very valuable to all of these people of this land, the Ancient Pipe Bundle, to ease their parting for the both of them. This pipe would also make up for all of his wrongdoings.

The Starman husband went home to his tipi with a heavy heart, but he must let the girl know that he knew all along what happened to her, that she was a very lonely girl and he must take her back to her parents and her friends. He went in slowly, not a word from him as he made his way to his place of sitting, on his bed. His wife immediately realized what it was all about, being so very quiet. Somehow she knew that this was a lecture to her and also something else more important.

Sitting down and being quiet for quite some time, the Starman husband finally found the right words to begin with. This wasn't easy for him, this was the beginning of the end for him, the end of his marriage to this once virgin girl he took from her people by force. He told her that he knew all the time that after she seen and pulled the extra-large turnip root in that certain field, and had looked through the hole it left after pulling it from where it grew in the ground, and had seen directly below, her own camps that she left long ago, that she became very lonely for her people. He seen the tears each day as he came in that stained her cheeks, that he was wishing that this would be overcome by their love for one another. He also said that he knew that this couldn't be so, because he made the mistake of taking her forcefully away from her people. There wasn't any previous love between them, and this made a lot of difference.

Their living would be very different now since she found out about the forbidden turnip, and her loneliness would get worse. He told her that he had consulted one of the wisest old men around to find out what should be done about this. This wise man had given him advice that he must follow, and that was to take her back to her people. She would never overcome this loneliness, as she had pulled the only power that kept her here, the extra-large turnip.

He further told her that they must get her ready before she left here, she must go through the mystical powers of Creator Sun that he had given these people. Also, this same power of the great spirits must be given to her to take as a sacred gift to her and her people. He said, "This readying takes about four days, well into the night of the fourth day, so you will be leaving me for good on the very early morning of the fifth day. You will travel with the rising sun. But now we must get ready for the coming event, a transfer of this very holy bundle to you, the Ancient Pipe Bundle. There's many things we have to do, prepare food for all of those that are taking part in the transfer of the holy pipe. Anyone that asks for this pipe, to own it as a keeper, must pay for it with their most valuable possessions. But that's almost only once in a lifetime to own a sacred thing like it. To you, my wife, it will not cost you anything. I'm giving it as gift to you especially, and this will eventually go about among your people. This Ancient Pipe Bundle comes from a long ways back, it is a gift directly from Creator Sun to sanction our thoughts of him always so we would not do bad things. I done wrong in what I done to you, but this Ancient Pipe Bundle will make things right for us both in the eyes of Creator Sun."

The two hurried along as the day went slowly, getting ready for the next morning. Everything had to be so in the Starman's tipi, and all of the elders must be invited to attend this great transfer of this Ancient Pipe Bundle. Both were so very tired when everything was ready that evening. There was no time for thinking, there wasn't anything to think of for the girl, because she already knew she was getting ready to go home to her people. The only thing on her mind was that the days were so very slow from one day to another, these last four days with her Starman husband. In a way she hated to leave this man, yet in a way she was very glad that she would be seeing her parents, her friends, and her native land again.

Her Starman husband was the one that was getting mighty lonely already, even though she hadn't left yet. But it consoled him when he thought of the way he took her away from her home, suddenly! The two fell on their bed and fell asleep as they hit the bed, they were so very tired getting ready this day.

Very, very early the next morning, things got underway at the Starman's tipi. All of the invited people came early to get this transfer of the pipe a-going, it would take four days to transfer it to the selected girl. Just before the ceremony began, the wise old man came in and went right to where the young man and his wife sat. The Ancient Pipe Bundle was placed at the center of the head of this tipi. The Starman sat on the right side of it, and the wife, the selected girl, sat on the other side of this holy pipe, so both were at the either end of the pipe. The wise old man sat himself directly behind the pipe and the two, Starman and his wife.

After making himself as comfortable as can be, this wise old man hung his head and began praying. After prayer, he sang a song that fitted into place of the ceremony. Then again he prayed more. This went on for four times, a prayer then a song. After the fourth song, he took a little bag from the bundle and opened it. The bag contained a bright yellow earth paint. This paint was then annointed on their face and hands by the wise old man. After this was done, the main sacred ceremony began. The Ancient Pipe Bundle had several pieces to it, and each piece to this Holy Bundle had a song of its own. Before each piece was shown, right after it was taken from the bundle, it was prayed for and held over the sacred smoke of the sweet grass. This was done four times. All this time a prayer was being said by the wise old man conducting this sacred ceremony of the Ancient Pipe Bundle.

This is for the truth of Native religion for all the sacred pipe bundles. Whenever they are taken out of the bundle, each piece must be held over the smoke of the sweet grass, back and forth between the smoke of the sweet grass and the bundle where it is all kept. Four times back and forth to the bundle and the smoke of the sweet grass, accompanied with prayers. After this back-and-forth procedure, then the song that goes with the particular piece is sung by the headman or curator of the holy pipe. (The previous curator of the holy pipe had gone through it several times and knows it all— this would be the wise old man, a previous keeper of the pipe bundle. These holy bundles are given to a keeper with several restrictions. If a restriction is broken, some kind of ill luck would befall the keeper.)

This first holy pipe bundle was given the name Ancient Pipe Bundle by the people several thousand years ago. It was also named because it was given to the Star people many thousands of years ago by Creator Sun. Some time ago, within the last five thousand years, the Ancient Pipe Bundle was transferred to the people of Mother Earth. It was given as I've told it in this story, to the selected girl of Creator Sun. It was given according to his own plans for the sake of his children of Mother Earth, to be saved from the evil that has been plaguing his children of Mother Earth, even from the beginning of creating the human being.

After this first piece of the sacred pipe bundle had been through the routine, the song to it was sung. This particular song to that certain piece is also sung four times through. The song and its chorus are sung four times, then it is laid back down alongside of those pieces that haven't been touched by the conductor of the ceremony, an original keeper of the holy bundle. Each piece that goes with the holy pipe has its own ceremonial way of handling it, the prayer that accompanies it and the singing of four songs after the prayers.

This pipe bundle ceremony takes all day and sometimes into the night. All of the special pieces of the pipe must go through the routine way of sacredness, no shortcuts. About halfway through a ceremony of handling the sacred pipe, a meal must also be fed to the participants of the holy ceremony, and this meal takes a while too. The tongue of the buffalo is always the sacred host of all religious doings. It must be cut a certain way and in front of all those attendants of the sacred ceremony. Everything is four, because four is a charm for the Native. Handling the boiled tongue from the pot it was cooked in, the selected girl is the holder of this pipe, because it is being transferred to her from her husband. So this made her a host to this particular sacred ceremony. She is also the co-keeper, because her Starman husband is the present keeper of the pipe bundle.

Because of the transfer to her and a co-keeper, the selected girl had to handle the food. She must be the first to touch the many kinds of food being fed to the participants of this sacred ceremony. Starting with the sacred buffalo tongue, a prayer is said as she stands near the pot that contains the host, the sacred food, buffalo tongue. Then a song, a prayer again, followed by a song again. Four times this praying and singing is repeated.

This is followed by taking the tongue out of the pot with a forked stick that is sharpened to penetrate the top tissue of the sacred tongue. This forked stick too has to go through the special ways according with the ceremony of transfer. This forked stick that is to be used to get the tongue out of the pot had to be held over the smoking sweet grass and to the pot, back and forth four times before it is actually stuck into the first tongue. There must be four tongues of the buffalo for these religious ceremonies at all sacred doings.

The tongue is now taken from the pot and laid on a platter of closely netted willow branches. Again that four comes again for cutting the tongue into small pieces, because it is a host. In those days, a flint knife was used for all cutting. The knife is held over the smoke of the sweet grass and then on the tongue, back and forth over the tongue and back to the smoke of the sweet grass, four times. The fourth time, the tongue is cut in just one tiny piece by this girl. A piece of this very small piece is torn off for a prayer. It is held between the thumb and finger as the prayer goes on and is held towards the sun and down to Mother Earth. After the prayer, this tiny piece is stuck into the dirt, a taste for Mother Earth and Creator Sun. (The Native has always been reverent from time beginning, and even now this tearing off a small piece of the meat or tongue is done at every meal by the early Natives. It is still done by a few that still revere the Sun and Mother Earth among the tribes of Natives in these two continents.)

After this is done by the girl, she then eats the other small piece of tongue. All of the many different kinds of food are done in this same procedure, a small piece is taken first and held over the sweet grass smoke and then to the girl's mouth, and the fourth time she puts it in her mouth and eats it. Everything is now prayed for in this way. Then her helpers come to do the rest of cutting and then serving the people.

After the meal is over, a brief rest, then back to the sacred ceremony of transfer of the holy pipe bundle. It may be late at night when the last of the pieces of this bundle are prayed for and held over the smoke of the sweet grass. More praying and singing is done by the old man conducting this ceremony as he slowly puts each article back in the same order as he had taken them out of the bundle. When everything is back in order in the bundle, it is covered up for the night. Most of the participants of this ceremony go to sleep right where they are sitting in this tipi of the girl and the Starman husband.

It's not even getting gray in the east when the morning meal is served, the only meal without a hitch. It is served just like at home. The meal is well over with when the first sun rays hit the tipi. Back to the sacred ceremony of the pipe transfer.

Through this second day, all things done the day before are repeated again until again, late in the night when things are back in order in the bundle, then a little sleep for the night. All of this is repeated over and over again for four days, this is for the benefit of the receiver of the sacred bundle. To learn all that goes with the transfer, the many different ways that goes with each piece, the songs. To learn it fully so he or she could conduct the ceremony if they were called on or in time of a transfer. The selected girl of Creator Sun, as a receiver of the Ancient Pipe Bundle, had to pay very close attention to the routine way of the bundle. This same thing had to be repeated each year when the Sacred Thunder was heard, all of the pieces taken out, then replaced in the same order as they had come out of the bundle. But they are just taken out when the thunder is heard in the spring of the year, and only for the one day.

The final night of the transfer of the sacred bundle, the Ancient Pipe Bundle, it is over with. The wise old man, a previous keeper of this bundle, sings and prays as he puts everything back in order as they came out of the bundle. When this is done, and everything is put away in order, the holy bundle is then wrapped very carefully with the tanned hide of an elk and bound tightly with a stripped tanned elk hide, known as a buckskin. These wrappings are so very old, they are soft as cotton from being handled each summer twice or more if a vow is made to the particular pipe bundle. By this time all of the participants in this holy ceremony have gone home to sleep and rest, a rest that is well earned from these last four hectic days and four nights of the transfer of the holy bundle. The wise old man's job is done after he hangs the bundle up on a special hanger just for this particular bundle. He just moves across the room of this tipi and lays down to sleep and rest. He has done most of the main work of teaching the girl all about this bundle these last four days and he feels it now, he is very tired.

The selected girl by Creator Sun and Mother Earth and her Starman husband go to bed too, together for the last night of their marriage. Early the next morning, before the sun came up, they must be at that hole in the ground where the mysterious extra-large turnip had grown. It was a night to remember always for both of them—their last night together, never again shall they see each other. This was a punishment to both of them for the sin they had commited the way they got together in the first place. No one shall get by the sharp eyes of Creator Sun and Mother Earth, it was wrong for them to get together the way it worked out.

It was still very dark when the wise old man woke up the two from their wonderful sleep and told them it was time for them to go to the turnip field to do the rest of what has to be done. The wise old man carried the Ancient

Pipe Bundle on his back. Before he took it off of its special hanger, those prayers and the handling song are never forgotten, because the holy pipe was very, very sacred, the tobacco it holds too. The tobacco is very important to the bundle, the pipe and the tobacco is smoked all the way through the religious ceremony, almost at the end of every song that was sung during the ceremony. It is for this reason that the main part of the bundle is that pipe that goes with the bundle. Without that pipe, it wouldn't be sacred. This went for all of the pipe bundles that came into existence after this Ancient Pipe Bundle, the very first of all the Native Holy Pipe Bundles to be transferred to the people of Mother Earth.

On their way finally, it was still dark, the wise old man walked ahead of the two, leading the way with the holy bundle on his back and carrying one of the longest rawhide ropes anyone had ever seen. This rawhide rope was freshly stripped, it was green, very raw. Some of it was carried by the Starman husband. This fresh stripped rawhide was very heavy, but it didn't feel heavy to the two carrying it, the wise old man and the Starman husband. This is the ways of our Creator Sun, a very heavy burden is light when he takes a hand in his own makings.

The east was just turning very light when they reached the hole in the ground where the extra-large turnip had grown. Again the wise old man got ready, sang four songs, then he took the paint of yellow, a natural paint from the dirt, and annointed the girl's face and hands again. He was praying and singing all the time as he done this. After all of this the wise old man made a small fire to burn the sweet grass on. As the smoke rose upwards from the sweet grass, the girl crossed over it back and forth four times as the wise old man still mumbled the prayers and was singing from away down deep in his throat. The first rays of the sun were now showing in the eastern horizon. The old man tied the rawhide rope around the girl's middle and made a harness for her shoulders. The rawhide rope was secured on her, then the Ancient Pipe Bundle was securely tied to her back.

Everything was now ready. More prayers and singing for a safe trip down by both the wise old man and the Starman husband. A safe trip down to Mother Earth from the land of the Star people, riding a rawhide strip down there. The wise old man and the Starman husband easing the rope as it began its journey downwards just at the first light, the top edge of our Creator Sun's appearance in the eastern skies. Down, down down she went as she descended to her own land and her parents, her friends too.

Just outside of the camp of her people, the southeast side of this huge camp, other clans had moved in with this clan for the coming religious celebration that took place annually here. Up to this time, smoking of a common pipe was used for praying, and the tobacco was picked from the prairies. It wasn't a routine way of reverence. This smoking the pipe and tobacco was done any time and any place, whenever the people felt up to it.

Her people had seen something coming down from out of the sky as she descended slowly. Most of the people of this camp had gathered, watching her as she came downwards. They hadn't known what she really was from way down here. As she came closer and closer, the people made it out to be a human form tied to the end of a rawhide rope. But what was that? Something on her back, it was quite large, probably a child, maybe she was deformed on her back. All kinds of guesses.

The people followed her as she slowly descended to the southeast side of this huge camp. The people guessed just about the very spot she would

***Bringing Home the Ancient Pipe Bundle
from the Star People***

land. Sure enough, it was there that she came down. But the fresh stripped rawhide rope wasn't long enough to reach all the way to the ground, it was short by a few feet. If the people of those days knew the foot measurement, they would say, "Short by about twenty-five feet." It was short enough for her to fall fairly hard the rest of the way to the ground as the wise old man and her Starman husband dropped her the rest of the way. Again, it was meant to be that way as a remembrance of this particular descent by the girl, just as Creator Sun wanted it to happen. She wasn't even hurt in the fall.

All of the people ran to her as she tumbled on the ground, but before they could come near her, she stopped them all by warding them off with the sign language of the hands. The people understood right away, they all stopped a little ways from her and all around her as she slowly got up to her feet. She asked for her parents by their name. No one in this crowd seemed to know who this girl might be. She had changed so much since she was taken away from here. It happened that the parents were in this crowd too watching her descend from up there. She, too, didn't recognize her parents, they had grown much older now, and her disappearance was an awful shock to the mother and father. Everyone thought the worst of it, no one in this crowd ever thought she would be seen again. So no one knew her at this time.

Her parents, hearing their names called by this girl came towards her slowly, as if afraid of her. She asked the two, her mother and her father, if it were really them she was talking to. The parents hadn't recognized her either. They said it was their names that she called. Being confirmed by them personally and her knowing this was really her folks, she told them who she was. But there was a restriction before they could touch her that must be taken care of at this time. They must make four sweat huts in a row near the creek where the water was gotten by the camps, and she must sweat alone in the first two huts. Then, the last two huts, she must be joined by her mother and father and as many of the wise elders that could get in this sweat hut with them.

This was no sooner said by her than it was done by mostly all of the available help that was at hand. It didn't take those people very long to complete those four sweat huts. They were completed with their covers, and the fire that went with each of them, and also the rocks that were put on the fire to heat until all of them were red-hot.

She didn't waste any time to get in the first sweat hut, the Ancient Pipe Bundle went on top of the first sweat. She went through the routine way of sweating in every way, except for her singing and her prayers, which her people had never before heard. Four times the entrance to this sweat hut was thrown open to get air in it. On the fourth time, the girl emerged and went right on into the second of the sweat huts, only this time she again told her father to take the Ancient Pipe Bundle and put it on top of this second sweat hut. These four sweat huts were built like small arbors, a dome-shaped structure about ten feet in diameter, according to the present day measurements, with around twenty long branches of the willow. The ends of these were stuck into the ground and the remaining ends of them were woven together in that dome shape of our skies. The finished structures were then covered with tanned robes of buffalo, almost airtight. Water is taken in with the people that are sweating. This water serves two purposes—for drinking, if it gets too hot in the sweat hut, and to throw on the red-hot rocks to make the hot steam that makes one sweat more. This also makes the inside hotter and hotter. The more water thrown on the red-hot rocks, the hotter it gets on the inside.

Again the routine way of sweating, except for the prayers and her singing. Four times again the entrance to the sweat hut is thrown open to let cool air in briefly, and it is closed again. On the fourth time it is opened, those inside emerge from this sweat hut. She emerged and went right into the third one, only she called those that would have room in there to come in and sweat with her this time. All of the people of this camp were very curious to find out what kind of a girl this one was that descended from above. Everyone stuck around the sweat area, there was no shortage of help around this sweat area. Enough attendants to maintain the necessary ways of sweating. This was the third sweat hut that was now in progress.

Several of the women and their husbands, with a few powered elders, came in this third one with her to help her pray and sing the songs that were given for this particular sweat. These people must learn these songs too, it was really meant for them. She was only selected by Creator Sun and Mother Earth to go to the land of the Star people and bring back this Ancient Pipe Bundle to her people for their salvation from wickedness. This had worked out just as Creator Sun wanted it done. The selection of this particular girl was done by cleanliness of her body and soul, but before she got intimate with men.

They went through the routine way of sweat again, with the making of power for the elders that were in there with her. Four times again, and on the fourth time they all emerged from this sweat hut she went into with the elders of her camp, and the day was getting very close to the end. It was the third opening of the sweat hut, and all of them inside of there were very quiet from the heat that all were feeling. She called her mother and father, who were sitting right beside her all this time in the darkness of the sweat hut. She told them who she really was, their long-lost daughter. She had many ways to prove this, but had to wait until they all emerged from the sweat hut. About now, it was time to throw the entrance open the final time, then all will come out from this last sweat hut. Once all of them were out, they gathered around the girl, amazed at her story of how she was taken to the land of the Star people and what she brought back with her to renew her people with more reverence for their makers, Creator Sun and Mother Earth.

The parents of the selected girl didn't know whether to believe her or not until she showed them things on her body that only her parents knew of. It was time for rejoicing. After all of these years the parents thought they would never know what became of their daughter, and now they were feasting their eyes on her and she was still alive, only grown older with wisdom. Many feasts in the honor of her were given all over this large encampment. People were calling from all over the camps, hollering out invitations for the girl and her parents and the elders of this camp, singing and praying by many of the people for the return of this girl and the way she returned. It was an astounding mystery for the whole camp to see her come from the skies with only a fresh stripped rawhide rope tied around her middle and shoulders. Also, the holy bundle that everyone seen tied on her back—who would argue with that? She was telling the truth.

It was four days now since she had returned to her own people, and each day was just like the day before—all of these people so glad to see her back, the invitations she was asked to go to, feasts of thanks to Creator Sun and our Mother Earth. They weren't forgotten in these feasts, each prayer was with a piece of the food to offer them to share in those feasts of thanks.

The morning of the fifth day, the girl told her folks that she must go on through with what she was told to do by the wise old man and her Starman husband. She must show her people how to conduct a religious ceremony with the Ancient Pipe Bundle. Her folks must enlarge their tipi so it could hold many of the elders. They must set up a double lodge, two tipis together to make one big room. It was done as she wished it, with plenty of help and the preparing of food to go with it. This was only to be a one-day honoring of this Ancient Pipe Bundle, and also to show the people of hers how it's done.

In a very little while, everything was ready to go for this great event of showing the Ancient Pipe Bundle. The girl conducted the religious ceremony just as the wise old man had shown her to do. She repeated all of the doings of that wise old man. The songs she sang in order. It was so fresh in her mind that she thought she heard the wise old man singing along with her in many of the songs that went with the bundle, even in the praying she thought she heard the wise old man of the Star people praying along with her. It seemed to her that he was leading her in the singing and the praying, he was so near her with his spirit.

Everything was done in the same way they showed her in the land of the Star people, right to the very end of the holy ceremony. The putting away of all of the pieces to the Ancient Pipe Bundle and the way it had to be wrapped, and the last of all, to hang it right, on a special hanger for the holy bundle. So, from that time on to the 1930s, this Ancient Pipe Bundle had existed, and the particular religious ceremony that went with it was always conducted in the same way. But then came the whiteman with its foreign religion that the native didn't understand, even to this day. It is so corrupting to humanity.

# *Preserving Pelts Pipe Bundle*

Before I go on with the story, let me explain a few things.

We had translators of our Native words. Many, if not all of them, are mistranslated from the Native to the English. This is because of our language barrier, especially in the last half of the 1800s. Our interpreters or translators were either half-breeds who understood very little of the full-blood Native language, or a hobbyist of the white race, who may have lived among the Natives for a few years. In either case, those interpreters grabbed a chance to make a fast buck for themselves, whether they got the wording right or not. It didn't make any difference to them, they were just doing it for a few bucks. It wouldn't hurt them one bit if they made mistakes, as long as they got paid for it.

So, in today's files of all BIA offices in the United States, and Canada too— and I guess I can say the same for the South American Natives—many of the valuable documents, especially those of our treaties, are off from their true meaning. This is according to the old Natives that took an actual part in those treaties. Their explanation of how the treaties were agreed upon by both the Native and the government, or what those non-English-speaking, non-English-understanding Natives thought they really made with the government at those treaties, just aren't as they thought. Many of the written treaties are worded mostly in favor of the U.S. government and for their white laws.

How would those Natives, the Chiefs of the many different tribes of the Natives, understand the written part? I can truly say that there wasn't much chance for a person unfamiliar with the two languages to fully understand them, especially the Native language. No one had that much savvy of any Native language in any of the places—U.S., Canada, or South America, not at that time. It was an important barrier between the Natives and the whites. It was most important for the Native's future living. Today, we are living with those wrong translations, I can say that those wrong translations, especially of our treaties, have the government and the white people stepping all over the Native in these past several years, trodden in the mud. That's us Natives.

On with my story of the Native past. The Ancient Pipe Bundle had started a somewhat routine way of Native religion. The bundle had to be exposed to the people, honored, at least twice a year—when the first thunder is heard in the spring of the year, and again when the last thunder of the year is heard. This was a way for the Native to welcome the thunder for the coming year, and it was also a wakening for the pipe bundle and the contents of the holy bundle.

The bundle keeper honors it by giving a feast immediately after the first thunder. Everyone who comes to this particular feast must get their faces painted with the sacred red earth paint to protect them all from the coming thunder and lightning storms during the summer.

After the last thunder is heard in the fall, this holy ceremony of the holy pipe bundle is repeated almost like it was done the spring before. Only this time, the bundle is carefully wrapped and tied securely for the coming winter—it works out like a hibernation for the pipe bundle. A face painting is done to all the people that come for the last doing of the year. This time, the red earth painting of the faces and hands of the people that come for this ceremony is for good luck through the winter months.

There are times when the bundle keeper must take the contents out in a special religious ceremony to fulfill a vow someone had made towards this particular pipe bundle during the time when the holy bundle was wrapped up for the coming winter and the time it is exposed to nature after the first thunder in the spring of the year. A vow was also made towards the bundle between the time of the spring and fall handling of the pipe bundle. A vow is made for a very sick member of the immediate family who is very close to death, or anything that concerns life and death—someone might got lost out in the woods, been in an accident, and so on. A vow is made for a very serious reason. If a vow was made in the winter months, the ones that made the vow must honor it during the spring unwrapping of the holy pipe bundle. If a vow is made right after the spring unwrapping, these vows have to be honored during the midsummer religious encampment that took place annually when the meat animals are at their fattest and when all berries were ripe. If any vows are made after this midsummer ceremony, the vows had to be honored when the holy pipe bundle is wrapped and put away for the winter months.

Our Natives had much faith in this truest form of religion, because everything was of the very nature they lived in. And most of all, our holy beings can be seen with our naked eyes. Our Creator Sun created the earth and all living things, from the beginning to this life we are living, and still he is creating new things. It has the power to destroy life through the many different ways of its own—storms, tidal waves, earthquakes, and even the wars that are fought by the human beings. Not only humans are affected through his powers, but the many kinds of life, too—birds, animals, insects, reptiles, and the living things of nature, be it a spiritual life of the surrounding growth of trees, rocks, mountains, any kind of water, stream, lake, and the oceans. Just think of what you may see in the newspapers: avalanches, landslides, floods, forest fires, breaking of dams, and volcanoes. People just don't have to believe it, but these are caused by our Creator Sun to punish the lives of the people for a wrongdoing they have committed towards his children or his creations of nature.

We see all sorts of life wherever we look, everything in this world of ours is alive with its own spirit of life. Even Mother Earth is alive. She feeds all of us, we all are her suckling children. Things come out of her body, the ground, growing up towards our father Creator Sun with their arms held out to him as the growth slowly grows upward from the ground. Everything is purified by nature as it grows along. Water too is purified as it sifts through the rocks, gravel, and sand. So our faith in the things we see with our naked eyes as they do their work for humanity is the Native's way of life.

The Piegan Native has a pipe bundle. Some call it medicine bundle, which isn't the right translation. It isn't for medicine at all, it is a sacred holy bundle, it is a faith for the Native Piegan, it was given by the holy spirit of nature of Mother Earth. A pipe bundle is really called holy pipe bundle. This holy pipe bundle was given to a young man and his wife by the animals of Mother Earth and of her body.

Among us Piegans, this particular pipe bundle is known to as *ni-nam-sky-yah-koo-yi-nee-mahn*, Selecting a Chief Pipe. This is wrong according to the right translation of Native words, and the story of where the holy pipe bundle came from. In our beginning we all spoke the same language. As we slowly drifted apart and had no contact with one another, our languages began to differ from one another until our languages differed so much that in time we didn't understand other groups of people. So it goes today, we have many dialects among our Native people of these continents, which the other groups of tribes cannot understand.

The right translation of what it meant in the first place was, "Preserving Pelts Pipe Bundle," and is pronounced in our Native tongue as Preserving Pelts Pipe. It is known to be a bundle of our holy faith. The original word for this was *ee-ins-kaa-yauk-oo-yin-ee-mahn*, which explained the origination of this particular pipe bundle. It meant "peeling the hide or pelt off of an animal and preserving it by tanning it." This Preserving Pelts Pipe Bundle consisted of mostly the many small fur-bearing animals of the Piegan area at the time this pipe was given to this certain young couple. Bigger animals and bigger birds were represented in the pipe too, but just certain small pieces of these large animals and birds were in the pipe bundle. Others, like lizards, were also represented by a charcoal drawing of them on a stiff dried rawhide that was used to drum on. Thunder and lightning was represented in the bundle by using the yellow and blue earth paint.

Within the once great hunting area of our people, the Piegans, which took in half of the Rocky Mountains northward and back up to the original head of the North Saskatchewan River, the story of the Preserving Pelts Pipe Bundle all began.

The Piegan Tribe had increased to manyfold, and they had divided into clans. Each clan had its own hunting area within this great hunting area of ours. Throughout the year the separate groups camped about within their own areas until a certain time of the year when they all gathered in one place down near the Sweet Grass Hills. (Sweet Grass Hills is another of mistranslations of those interpreting for the U.S. government. The Native word really means Sweet Pine Mountains.) This gathering was to get one group acquainted with another, and also for a religious gathering to unwrap the holy bundles, and also to do some dancing of the many clans. The dancing wasn't anything like our present-day *pow-wows*. In those days they had clan dances such as the horse dance, the fox dance, the fly dance, victory dance, brave dance, dove dance, and bear dance, and so on. There are many forgotten dances that those clans done at the gathering.

It was in these gatherings, once a year, that boys and girls met and got married. A few were married by the trade marriage between their parents and relations, and many of them went the blanket way, which is even worse in these days. In these days it is known as shacking up. This was the beginning of a very routine way to realize the wrongs that were committed with those blanket marriages and the everyday ways of forgetting our Creator Sun.

A young man came moving into the annual encampment of the year with the others of the clan—an annual encampment was also an encouragement to many young people to go seek the supernatural powers that was very important in those days for sickness and other emergencies. This was because most of the annual doings were religious. At the time, there wasn't any intertribal dancing like we know of in these days. All doings were individual family dancings, or what we would call semireligious doings, and were done in each clan that took turns through the days of the encampment.

After a few days of watching, this young man saw many of the people put on their shows of certain powers. There were many young people in these doings of the clans, which got up his ego to go seek his own supernatural powers.

He called on his parents for advice, and they told him to go and talk with one of the elders that had the most power, and whom they called by name. The parents gave their son the right instructions on how to do this. This was done a certain way among the Natives. The parents told their son to use the family pipe and have it ready for smoking when he approached the right old man. The son must go up to the old man, holding the pipe in the offering way of asking for religious help. The young man must tell the old man, "This is your smoke, I would like to have you tell me how to find the most powerful area of all spirits, as I want to seek power for myself." If the old man accepts the pipe smoke, the young man must then light the pipe for the old man. The old man, after he is through smoking the pipe, will give the young man instructions of how to go about the supernatural seeking.

The old man will point out a very special place the young man must try first. It is a place where there are no other people, it's away from all human life. It could be on a mountaintop, near a lake, a river, the forest, a high hill, a big rock, or any of Mother Earth's natural places. The young man must go alone to find a supernatural spirit, taking along with him only his robe, the tobacco and pipe, and his flint for lighting the pipe and for the the fire that he must make the smoke of sweet grass incense. The burning sweet grass is an invitation to all spirits that may be in the area and on friendly terms.

If there wasn't already a place for sleeping, then the young man must build one. They are made with rocks piled on top of one another in a small oval shape, for a windbreak. The rocks are piled to only about three feet high, and long enough for a man to stretch out in. It is within this enclosure of rocks that the young man must spend the next four days and nights, coming out of it only to urinate and going right back into it. No food of any kind for him and no water for him these next four days. He must live on prayers and wish a spirit comes before he gets too hungry. If he is a smoker, he can smoke and pray with the pipe as he is smoking it.

His parents told him of a particular old man whose power could be about the most powerful of all the power people. It was to this particular old man the young man went to offer his pipe of hope. He was very lucky, the old man was in a better mood today. He was very pleased with this young man, and he willingly accepted the pipe smoke that was offered to him. As the young man lit the pipe for the old man, he told him what this offer of pipe smoke was for: The old man knew where he had slept to acquire his powerful vision that was very useful to him and the people. Not only one vision he had, but several! He was a multi-supernatural-powered old man.

The old man didn't say a word until he finished his smoking, cleaning out the pipe with the stick that is always handy to smokers and always tied to the pouch. As he began to hit the pipe bowl on the ground to shake the ashes out from it, he began to talk to the young man about his seek for power. He told him everything from the beginning to the first time he finally achieved his first power. Old men are naturally that way, they are very thorough. At last! The old man came to the description of the first place he had spent four nights to achieve a supernatural power. He talked for quite some time about the first place before he went on to talk of the second place he got his second power, and then on to the last one. It took almost half of the day to listen to him talk about the powers he acquired, ending with where to go for the power the young man was seeking.

After the old man finally got through with his directions on where to find the places of power, the young man gave him the basic pay for his advice and directions. The pay consisted of furs, shells, robes, and a large amount of smoking tobacco, which was the most for the older people. A sweat hut had to be made for him and the old man, and that came that same evening. Older people knew all about these things, so it was no surprise to the old man when he was told to go have a sweat bath with the young man and his father that same afternoon. It didn't take long to get a-going with the sweat. This was just prayer sweat and only one sweat hut was used, but there are always the required four openings of the sweat hut. On the fourth time it's opened for air, the sweat bathers had to emerge from the hut. While inside and sweating, songs of power are sung, and all the time a prayer is being said.

It was almost sundown when they finally came out of the sweat hut. The readiness for the seek of power was done. All went home to the young man's tipi and had an exceptional meal that was especially prepared for the old man. The bossribs of the buffalo were soft boiled, a liver of the buffalo was charcoal cooked, the tongue of the buffalo was boiled along with the bossribs, and a long crowgut was the very special part of the meal. To go along with this delicious food was the back fat of the buffalo, from an original kill, that was smoke-dried and preserved with dried wild peppermint. This was a meal for a Native Chief. The meal was eaten and, being a long day, everyone was very tired. To bed they all went after the special meal. Before the young man went to bed, he got all that he needed for his vision quest and got them together, ready for the next morning.

The young man didn't sleep much, he had the quest in his mind and was very anxious to get to the places the old man had pointed out to him. He wanted a supernatural power. He was a very popular young man and a power would certainly make him that much more popular among the older people. He must've dozed off somehow, but he was awakened by a dog's bark. Looking out, the morning star hadn't come up yet. Back inside he went, and ate what he could of the leftovers of the evening meal. After the last bite he got up and got his things together, bundled them and slung them on his back. Bidding his parents goodbye, the young man left for the unknown places of the supernatural spirits that were pointed out to him by the old man. He headed in the direction that was to be the first test of gaining his own powers.

Those places of power were far from the camps. The young man walked and walked, but he didn't reach the location that day. He laid down and slept for awhile. The Big Dipper was just half turned when the young man got up and on his way again he went. Since he got started the day before, he had walked at a very steady gait, a fast walk. He thought he could make the place the same day, even though it was far, far off from camps. Again he had walked almost all day when he seen far ahead of him the high butte the old man told him about—that was his first destination. It took him quite a bit longer to reach the place. He got right down to business when he found the exact location of the seeking area. One thing that was strongly in his favor was the weather, it was very nice all the time. Days were hot out and even the nights were very warm.

This place was all ready, the old man had set a place of shelter with rocks. Into this he went. The sun had already gone down and it wouldn't be too long before it got dark. He had his pouch with him and the sweet grass, and he picked up a few sticks to make a small fire within the rock enclosure for the burning of the sweet grass and the pipe. This he done. When the ashes got good enough, the young man took some out from the burning fire, and on these he burned some of the sweet grass. He sang a song the old man told him to use. After singing, he prayed a long time. Then, taking the pipe and tobacco, he filled the pipe up and lit it from the ashes that were handy. Again he prayed a long time with the pipe as it slowly smoked upwards. After smoking the first bowlfull of tobacco, the young man again filled the pipe bowl.

All of the things that he took along with him on this vision quest he laid out alongside the dirt where he made the burning of the sweet grass: the pipe and tobacco, alongside of it was the pouch and the braided sweet grass, a small pouch of red earth paint, and the flint and striker. Making very sure he left nothing out, he laid down. All the time as he done these things, he is praying under his breath, at times he is humming a sacred song. This was to encourage the power spirits to come to him, coaxing them along. It was dark when he laid down for the night, but as long as he stayed awake, he never let up on his praying and his humming a sacred song.

The young man didn't know when he fell asleep that night, he was so busy with the prayer songs and praying for the spirits to come. Nothing happened that night. There wasn't anything else to do for the day. He couldn't eat or drink water for the next three days or until he had achieved his wish, if it came sooner then the required four days. He knew by the sayings of the older people that nothing happens until the last two nights of the quest. He left the sleeping area and went down near a small creek. There he made himself a small sweat hut and again asked for spiritual help to find the powerful spirits of this place. Always at hand is the necessary pieces of a quest—the robe, the sweet grass, the pipe and tobacco, the flint and striker, and the pouch that holds them to his belt. Prayers were the main things for a quest.

Spending the good part of the day down near the creek, sweating himself, and laying in the shade of the trees. It was well into the afternoon when he went back up the steep climb to the same spot he spent the night before. Getting back inside of the rock shelter, he took out all of the things for the rest of the day. Just before dark, he again got things under way. Smoking and praying, singing to coax the power spirits to hurry and come to him. Night fell and all was ready if anything came for the vision. Singing and praying as he laid there until he fell asleep. Nothing came that night either.

Waking up very early again, just as the east was turning gray, the young man made his way down the mountain and again to work making another sweat hut to help him along in his quest for a vision. Spending most of the day by this creek again, he couldn't eat anything, as he had to fast all of the four days that he is seeking a vision. He couldn't even have water, he must live on prayers and smoking the pipe these four days he is here. Two more nights to go of this. The best he could do was to sleep as long in the day after his sweats as he could to make the time shorter for him, and that's what he did. But as long as he was awake, he did nothing but pray and hum the songs the old man taught him.

Not too long before dark again, he went back up the mountain or the high butte to have things ready for the coming night. Reaching the sleeping area, he laid his things out again and smoked, praying and singing for the spirits to take pity on him and come and give him power. (Many of these vision seekers don't only plead for the spirits to come to them, they also cry, they weep, begging the spirits to come and take pity on them, give them the power they are seeking.) It was dark when he laid down for the night to try to sleep again. He must've fallen asleep. Although he slept all day down by the creek, it must've been the hot climb back up this steep place that tired him out. Anyway, he fell asleep not long after he laid down.

He didn't have any idea how long he slept. He was awakened by something that hollered as loud as it could, by his ear or very nearby. He woke up instantly, sitting up and listening for another holler or any noise. It was a shrill whistle that he heard next, right in back of him. By the lay of the stars, it was only about midnight. The young man was frightened somewhat, but he kept on praying to whatever it was that hollered and whistled. He almost forgot what he was to do. Getting his self-assurance again, he remembered the pipe that he filled with tobacco before he laid down. Grabbing it, he began to strike the flint to make a light and spark the moss to flame. Small sticks are fed to the flame, which turns into a fire, and from the ashes of the sticks the pipe is lit, or the burning of sweet grass can be made. It took him a little time to light the pipe and offer it to the spirit that came there. Nothing happened. No one accepted the pipe, and nothing more happened that night.

The next morning he again went down the hill to the creek and immediately made a sweat for himself. Again he prayed and he prayed for the spirit to come back to him. Almost all day he stayed in the sweat hut praying and singing. He finally came out of the sweat hut and ran to the creek and jumped in to wash himself off. It was getting late, he must get back up the sleeping area to ready himself for this last night. It was the fourth night, and tomorrow he could go back home after he had something to eat. The young man was already very gaunt from the four days of fasting and no water. Getting up to the rock shelter required a little more time, he was getting weak from lack of food and water. He made it up there just in time to get his things ready, and even then, it was dark already. He was very, very tired. He laid down and almost immediately fell asleep. He didn't forget the prayers and the humming of the song, he was doing that as he fell asleep.

About the same time as the night before, the spirit didn't just holler or whistle. Whatever it was grabbed the young man by his feet and grabbing for his pipe as this spirit was dragging him out of this place. He was praying and begging it to give him power instead of treating him rough like this. Before this spirit drug him out from the enclosure of the rocks, he managed to grab his pipe. Whatever kind of spirit this was, it drug him to the steep side of the hill and was trying to roll him down the hill. The young man's heart had almost stopped from fear, scared half to death. But deep in his heart he would remember the old man's words, he would distinctly hear him talking to him. "Whatever the kind of spirit, and no matter what he is doing to you particularly, don't let it scare you or you will never achieve your want of supernatural power. Pray and beg him to pity you, and keep offering him the pipe."

With these words in his ears, the young man was fighting off the fear that had almost overcome him. He was praying to this spirit and handing it the pipe. It was a long fight with the spirit. The young man, almost overcome with fear, was ready to let the want of a vision go and let others seek it. All at once the spirit quit and left the young man lying there for a moment. The young man couldn't even jump up, he was left windless. Before he could get up, something came over him. He passed out and didn't remember anything more. He didn't know for sure if it were a dream, or if it actually happened as he seen it.

The young man didn't know how he got back into the rock shelter, but he was in there and he seen a very old man standing beside it. As if looking at him, this old man came stepping over the rocks into the compound and kneeled down close to this young man. It was there and then he received his first supernatural power from the spirit of this high butte. The spirit gave him all it knew about strange powers for good and bad, and a few restrictions to go along with the powers.

Just before daylight, the spirit of this high butte disappeared from the young man's vision, and immediately he woke up from a deep sleep. To his surprise, he was back in the rock shelter laying on his robe, and all of the things that he used were almost as he had laid them out before. Now he didn't know for sure if what he went through that night was for real, or if it was a bad case of nightmares. He sat up, and as he did so, he spotted the bag that the spirit had on his side, tied to the belt. The young man took it slowly, as if half afraid or in disbelief. Sure enough, it was the real thing. The young man got up very happy, he knew he had overcome the fear of receiving a vision. Before he got up from his place of sleep in this rock shelter, he made the usual fire to burn sweet grass and smoke his pipe. He even sang the songs the spirit left him with before it disappeared. This was all in giving thanks to the this particular spirit of this high butte and also to any other spirit that could hear him. These were in the prayers he was saying. It was time to go down the hill.

Reaching the bottom of this butte, it was getting warm, the sun was way up. The young man didn't hesitate, he immediately made a large fire and heated the rocks that he had used before. This was one of the things that he was told to do before he got in contact with any other human being. To have a good sweat and give more thanks to the great spirits of Mother Earth, and particularly to the spirit that just gave him power. The sweat wasn't anything fancy, it was the same as those he had made before this, but there were a few things that he must do to remember all of what had happened up there on the butte top, and what to do and what not to do.

It finally came to the fourth opening of the sweat hut. All of this he had to do himself, from the beginning to the last of this sweat bath. He was all alone, way out nowheres. After coming out from the sweat hut and getting his clothing on, he remembered that he was mighty hungry. After all, it had been several days without food for him. He got busy to find a grouse or anything that was available to get and eat. He didn't have his bow and his arrows. Because this was a quest for a vision and supernatural powers, he wasn't allowed to take weapons along. Whatever he could get by his bare hands or a trap was what he had to eat. But this was the land of plenty, it didn't take long to rig up a trap to get one of the plentiful grouse. There weren't any guns to scare away any kind of edible game, whether it had wings or four legs, and everything was plentiful at the time. It didn't take long to cook the grouse and down it, washed down with water from the creek. He was full now. He laid down to digest his food, and as he laid there, the young man got an idea to go another place to get more powers from the spirits.

It was still very early as he laid there, and once he had the idea it didn't take long to put it into action. The young man went on to another place the wise old man had pointed out to him if he didn't get any results in this area. He traveled for a whole day before he reached this other place, which was by a large lake in the foothills. The old man had pointed out a place very near the water's edge, a shelf-like place along the cliffs along the lake. It was evening already when he finally reached the area. Along the way he had killed small game to eat by throwing rocks at them, so it wasn't any problem to have a little bite before it got too dark.

Up with the first sign of gray in the east, enough spark to start his fire and get a bite for his morning meal. After his meal, a cottontail rabbit, it was light enough to get things ready for another vision seek. He made sweat huts near the river, four of them in a row. He made them ready for the next morning, today he wanted to eat all he could as he wouldn't be eating again for the next four days and mornings. All that day he ate and drank from the river. Once the sun went down behind the mountains, that was it. He couldn't touch food again for the next four days or until he achieved a vision on this quest, even within the four days.

The sun was just coming into view when the young man entered the first of the sweat huts. Everything he had to do for himself—make the sweat huts, get the rocks, and ready the fireplace to heat the rocks. He had to bring the red-hot rocks into the sweat hut, and once he got to sweating, he had to open the sweat hut for air when it was time. His smoking pipe and his tobacco pouch and sweet grass were always at his side, in and out of the sweat. All this time he was praying and singing as he went about his chores and into each one of the sweat huts. It almost took him the whole day to go through the four sweat huts. Once out of the last one, the young man annointed himself with his own read earth paint that was spiritually given to him at his first quest for spiritual powers. Just before dark, the young man made himself comfortable in the sleeping area the old man had advised him of, on a ledge near the lake's edge.

He went through the ways that were shown to him—getting the pipe ready, the sweet grass, his flint and striker, all the necessary things he had to have. As he sat there waiting to get sleepy, he sang his new power songs and prayed. This went on far into the night. The young man finally fell asleep, but nothing happened that first night, nor the next night. The third night he thought something came around, but it could've only been an animal or an owl, a night being.

The fourth night, as the young man sat there praying and singing, something happened—he didn't know exactly what it was, if he got hit or struck by lightning. Anyway, whatever it was, it knocked him out without warning. As he laid there, unconscious, this supernatural spirit came onto him and bestowed those powers onto this young man, it was the power of lightning and thunder from this lake. This was an easy quest for the young man—he didn't get thrown off of the hill, like the last time. This was a kind spirit until it gets mad at things that do not agree with it.

The young man didn't give up there, he went two other places that were pointed out to him. In all, the young man had gotten or achieved four supernatural powers. All of the quests were much like the first one, except for the location and the different kind of spirit that gave a gift of power. After the fourth quest he thought of home, he had been gone over one moon. He relaxed for a few days after his last quest. He was weak because of his fasts, and he had to get his strength back before he started for home, which was a long ways off. Probably might take him several days to get to his camps, and he must have food to hold him until then.

For the next few days the young man ate what he could get. At first he used his hands and a trap, then he rigged up a bow and arrows to use, which were much handier. Drying meat was his next project, he had to have dried meat to take along on his long trek back to his camps. He wasn't in any hurry. He had achieved what he went to seek, and now had a few of the supernatural powers to take home with him and to use for the good of his people.

The day finally came when he was ready to start for that long way home. He carried on his back the food for lunch to eat on his way and the things that were given him through the mystic quest of power by the spirits that pitied him. He had quite a heavy load. He didn't mind it one bit, in fact he was very glad to achieve what not too many young men could ever wish for. On and on he walked, over hills, across rivers, through the forests. And whenever night fell, he camped to sleep and eat. He was having the time of his life as he trekked homewards. It was several days when he finally came over a slight rise. As he slowly came over it, far ahead of him he saw some camps. He knew he was coming in the right direction, straight for his own camps. It took him almost all afternoon to reach those camps, still he didn't mind all the walk he had made so far.

The young man didn't go right into the camps, he stopped short of entering them. He waited among the many growths of quaking aspens surrounding the camps, he had to catch someone coming out to use this cluster of quaking aspen as a toilet. The first to come out to use this place a middle-aged man. One would think everyone knew one another in these camps, but that never is the case. Most camps of those times were divided into groups or clans. Each clan kind of keeps to themselves within their own group until such a time as a get-together for the whole camp. At these doings the many different clans get their chance to meet one another and get acquainted, make new friends. Probably the one that might know almost all of the people in a camp is the Chief, the men he might know but not the women or children. So! Most of the folks of each camp are strangers to one another, until they meet and make friends with each other.

The young man sent word to his father and mother that he was back at last from his quest of seeking powers of the great spirits, and he needed them to lead him into the camps early the next morning. This was an honor for someone that had achieved greatness all alone. He sent the word to have his best clothing brought out to him when they came out the next morning to lead him into the camps. The clothing was his best regalia of buckskin.

The parents rejoiced over the good news the man had given them, because in many cases a green young man often disappears when out all alone for a period of time in the wilds, especially on a vision seek, and he is never heard from again. But this young man had returned after he'd been gone for over a moon. Their son had returned to them and they were very happy, the relations too. By the look of things, he had come back with a great achievement or he wouldn't have asked for this honorary entrance the next morning.

The father of this young man would be on his right side, holding his hand, and the mother would be on his left side, holding that hand and leading him into the circle of the camps and out into the middle of the camps. All of his relations coming along in a long procession, all of them singing their power songs, their chanting songs. All of them hollering and chanting his name as they came along in a slow march. They start from where he had them come, over the hill and out of sight, from where only that one man that took his message into his parents had seen him, the only one to see him before this honorary entrance into camps.

The next morning the young man was up long before daylight and got himself ready for the grand entrance. He had a sweat and adorned himself with what he had and with the new things he had achieved on his vision quest. He was all ready when his parents finally came, right at daylight. They brought his best regalia, his buckskin suit. These he got into and was completely ready for the entrance. Mostly all of his relations had came about the same time, because the grand entry was to be done just as the sun began to come up over the horizon. Before the procession began, the young man and his parents, all of the relations and those that came for this, gathered in a group, singing and chanting for the brave young man that had achieved something very great all by himself. They were hollering his name, while others were just hollering. All of them were making one big noise before the procession got under way. This was to attract the attention of the whole camp, for this was a great entrance for a young man.

The grand parade went forward towards the camps, a noisy procession as it came over the hill and onward towards the camps. Hollering and singing and chanting, calling the name of this brave young man as the parade came along. Slowly it came on and on, it took a long time to come to the edge of the camps. All of the people of this camp were standing on the outside of their tipis, watching the great parade as it began to come on into the camp circle. Even these people, these spectators, were hollering now and chanting and grouped there in a big circle. Those that were waiting in the camps now came out, all of them in this large camp came out to see this young man and to hear what this was all about. When everyone got out there in the middle of these camps, it got noisier. Everyone was singing or chanting, hollering at the top of their voices. This lasted all morning. The noise finally subsided and then this honorary entrance got into its final stage of talking by the young man's folks, parents, grandparents, and all of the relations. All encouragement for the young man and for other young people, this was an example for all of them young people that were serious about their lives.

After the talking and singing, a special meal was served for the whole camp out there in the middle of the camps. The usual prayers that always goes with the serving of food before the food was eaten, and sharing with Creator Sun and Mother Earth and the holy spirits of this universe.

After the meal and the smoking of many pipes, the ceremony got back into action. This time it was a name-giving ceremony. Back in the early days of our ancestors, whenever someone does something great, especially of bravery, their name is changed. They could be given a name from an ancestor of great bravery or a close relation of great powers, someone that had done a great deed. This was a very young man that had done something very outstanding among his own age group, and he had done it all by himself. This was outright bravery and for his folks to emphasize it, his name was going to be changed to that of one of his very elders who had made a great name for himself. And so it was, that late afternoon. Again, very late that evening, a meal was served to all of the people out there by his relations and then, after the meal was over, all went to their tipis and into bed.

Long before daylight, the young man and his father were out near the river. They had got a sweat hut set up and readied for a big sweat for the morning. Just as it was getting gray, the young man went to several of the very old men that had powers, strong powers, and invited them to a sweat for the morning. Just before the sun came up over the horizon, all of the old men and the young man and his father were ready for the sweat. Just a moment before the sun came into view on the horizon, all of them were waiting in the sweat hut. And as the sun peeked over the horizon, the doorway of the sweat hut was closed and the sweat began. This was a one-sweat-hut deal, but it could last a long time. It was well in the afternoon when the last of the four openings of the doorway was thrown open and all of the men came out. Right into the river they all went to wash and cool themselves. It was an exceptionally long sweat, but it was all for prayers and singing. This was an encouragement for the young man, and at the same time, he was getting anointed for what he had done. The great sweat was to sweat off any evil powers that might have come onto the young man at the time he was alone. This sweat was done before he mingled with the crowd too much.

From all of this, the young man's bravery was heard of so much that he became known among his people in those few days he had come home. It didn't take very long till the Chief of this camp came to the young man's tipi and asked him to become his son-in-law. All of the young men of this camp had eyes on the Chief's daughter. She was something special among the young girls her age—she was very intelligent and a hard worker for her folks. She was an ideal girl for a wife. Knowing this, the young man readily said yes to the Chief. The Chief went home to his tipi with the good news.

A great wedding was in the making and the parents of the girl and young man got busy and began to get things ready for the great wedding.

Among the Natives, whenever the young people were asked to become married, the wedding would get underway in a little while, probably the very next morning. Those Natives didn't wait for several years until they knew the girl real well. A native wedding was something of an instant wedding, and most of the marriages went smoothly to the end of their lives. Some men even get more wives as time went along, and the women all got along splendidly, no jealousy among them, they worked hard together.

The very next morning the wedding took place, and it was a great wedding. In all of the old Native weddings up the first half of the 1800s, a wedding was sort of a trade. It really wasn't a trade, but a giving of gifts. Each family traded with the opposite family their most precious and valuable belongings. They tried to outdo each other in this trade, no valuables were held back.

It really wasn't a trade, but giving of gifts. Immediately after the trade of gifts, the young couple were blessed by the most powerful old man. Their faces and hands were painted with the red earth paint.

Right from the beginning of human beings, the red earth paint and the tobacco, the pipe, the sweet grass, sweet pine, juniper, cedar, and sage had a lot to do with life of those people. They were the forerunners of faith. The red earth paint was the body of Mother Earth, colored by Creator Sun. As the smoke would slowly rise upward from pipe smoke, smoke from the sweet grass, smoke from the sweet pine, smoke from the juniper, smoke from the cedar, or smoke from the sage, a prayer was being said. That smoke carries the prayer up to Creator Sun and spreads onto Mother Earth.

After this was done, the wedding dinner was brought on by both the girl's relations and young man's relations. The whole camp was given food to eat. By this time, it's getting late, almost dark out, and everyone goes home to bed.

The newlyweds came home to the girl's tipi, which was given to them by the girl's parents with everything in it, well furnished, including a good supply of food, which was a lot of dried meat, dried roots and berries, lots of mashed dried cherries, and a whole parfleche case of pemmican. They were well fixed for a while. They had many robes that were given them as presents, buckskin clothes, and many dogs to use. Dogs were essential in those days, the dogs were the load carriers, families with many dogs were known as well-to-do, like the people of today with many livestock.

The young couple lived very happy after the wedding. Both of them had many friends their same age. For a while they were alone to themselves. When their friends hadn't seen them for awhile since their wedding, and those friends wanted to know how the two were getting along now as a married couple. Young people are very nosy people. The young couple began to get visitors, friends that they used to play with before their marriage. From the first it seemed fun to all of them, especially the young couple. But every day the couple got many visitors, their friends, both boys and girls.

The young man had some very close friends that he had as partners, his same age. Because he was so close to them, they in turn got very close with the bride, they would tease with her. To the young man it seemed like the close friends were getting a little too chummy with his wife. It just seemed that way, it really wasn't. The young man was getting a jealous streak in him, which got worse as time went by and more of his friends came in to visit them. He didn't let anyone know of this, not even his wife. The jealousness raged in him every time his friends came in to visit them, those young men friends of his teased the girl very much. To him it seemed like the boys and girls were favoring the girl, getting closer to her, and this boiled inside of him. The jealousy got so strong that the young man started to bring his wife everywhere he went. He didn't trust her to be alone anymore because of that jealousy. The girl was sensing this jealousy now and she didn't like it very much.

For several moons the couple lived together and were not very happy among the crowd of their people. The jealousy of the young man got worse each day, but he didn't want anyone to know it. He hid it really well, just his wife knew about the jealousy of his.

One afternoon he told his wife of a plan he had. A good wife always lets the husband do what he thought best, and she was a very good wife. He told his wife to get things ready, get them all packed, they were going to move away from their friends, especially all of those single young men that he thought were getting too friendly with his wife. They were going to move some place where just the two of them would be alone. The young man loved his wife so very much, he didn't want anyone to be cutting in on him, now or ever. He wanted to live all by themselves somewhere, where no one would bother her or him. She didn't argue with him, like a good wife. She knew he must love her a lot to think about moving away all by themselves and living far from other people. Not too late that night, she was all packed. They weren't going to take their tipi down, they had some other tipis that were given to them for their wedding. Also, if they left their tipi standing, the people of this camp wouldn't know right away that they had moved away.

It was very late that night, when all things were just so quiet, except for some owls hooting and coyotes howling just a way from the camps. Tying a buckskin string around the dogs' noses and all loaded, the couple went sneaking out of their people's camp. They were very lucky, no dogs of the other camps barked at them as they left very, very quietly. By daybreak they had gone a long, long ways from the camps. Right at daybreak the two made camp for the day far in the thickets, where their dogs wouldn't be seen if someone happened by. All day they slept, it was getting late in the day when the two finally got up and got busy getting something to eat and for their dogs too. After their meal, with everything packed away once more, the two set out again. They were headed northwest towards the Rocky Mountains. This time the two didn't travel all night long, they went along until they got sleepy, probably it was past midnight then. They camped down for the night again. By now they had covered a lot of ground and were very far away from their folks' camps, they didn't have any fear of someone finding them now.

For several days they were on the go, they were getting closer to the mountains each day as they went along. After a long wearisome travel, they got into the foothills of the Rockies. For a while they went along the foothills until the young man seen a lake that went into the mountains. They set up camp along the shores of this lake where mountains were on three sides. It was a natural place for them. This lake is now known as the Waterton Lake in Glacier Park in Montana and Alberta, Canada.

Everything was made as comfortable as could be for the both of them. The tipi was made very warm on the inside. The days were still very warm and berries were plentiful and very ripe now. Things for the coming winter had to be preserved and other things gotten ready for that time. After the camp was made in order, the young man told his wife that he had to get meat to dry for the winter. He must leave her every day, probably all day long, until there was enough meat to last through the winter, smoked and dried. While the girl gathered berries and roots to dry for their winter use, the young man was out hunting for deer or elk. He had to go a little farther for buffalo, and that would take a little more time. Most often it took about two days to get back with a good supply of fresh buffalo meat, but he done it, he was a hard-working young man. In her spare time, the girl tanned hides for their clothing and their bedding. These tanned hides would also make new tipis for them, if needed.

There just wasn't any time to get lonely now, because they worked late into the night to get these things ready for winter use. Busy, busy, each day, there wasn't time to even think except what you were to do for the day and tomorrow. In more ways than one, the girl loved this life of living all by themselves away out here in the midst of the mountains, she just didn't have time to get lonely or think about her folks, nor the life she had left behind her. The two were so very busy right to the time snow began to fly. Their times together, when both at their tipi, wood was gathered for the coming winter, they seen to it that everything was plentiful so there wouldn't be any hardship for them. They wouldn't have anyone to call or borrow from, there wasn't another soul in sight for several days walking in any direction from here, so they had to be sure they had plenty of everything.

Occasionally, through the cold days and the winter, whenever they got hungry for fresh meat, the young man went out to hunt. It didn't take long, as he didn't go very far. Game was always plentiful everywhere, there weren't any guns to make noise and scare them away. It was during these leisure times, during that winter, when the girl got lonely for her folks and friends, but there wasn't anything that could be done about it. It was cold and it was far, far away from here. She just had to stay lonely or forget about her folks and friends. Her husband did the best he could do to console her whenever those lonely days came around on her. It was a long cold winter but they survived it, no problems. They had plenty of everything to carry them through this cold winter.

The days got warmer each day and the two got a restart on everything again, getting prepared early this year for the next coming winter. It took the young man a little longer to go hunt, probably about two days every time he went. Game was going a little farther away, it was being scared off by their noise. Those nights her husband stayed away hunting were hard for the girl. She got just so lonely, especially when she had awful thoughts about her husband encountering a mean bear or something that might kill him. She just couldn't shut those wicked thoughts out of her mind, and this took place whenever he went out or was gone for a few days. She even as much as cried about those silly thoughts of hers. But her husband returned each time he went out. The girl had often secretly wished her husband hadn't been so jealous-hearted, so they could have been still with the main camp of her folks and friends.

Summer came and went, but as usual, there was plenty of everything for that winter. Lots of dried meat and roots, lots of wood for the fireplace stacked up outside, and many thick robes that were freshly tanned this past summer to cover themselves with on cold nights. The tipi was like a warm nest, because of the way they had it lined with warm buffalo robes, and their rugs covered the floor. What else could anyone wish for? It was just the girl's loneliness that was the problem, but it wasn't so very hard, as long as she could stand it.

Spring once again came around, the days were getting warmer and longer. The young man soon began his hunting. This was the second year here, so game had really gone farther away. Sometimes the young man was gone three or four days at a time before he came back with the fresh meat, so he had to go almost immediately back out to hunt for more each time he returned. This made it very hard for the girl. Her loneliness got worse each day she was alone, and she was alone almost from the beginning of the warm days of spring. She knew it was necessary for her husband to go right back out each time he came home, because they were thinking of the coming winter again and must get prepared for it. They must have plenty of food and wood, too, for the fireplace. She must face the lonely life she was leading far out from nowhere, and she loved her husband. She couldn't bear to leave him, and besides, she wouldn't know where to go from here.

It was during this time, as spring was still in the air, that the girl could feel something piercing her through. It felt like eyes were always on her, wherever she was during her work around the camp area. It was something she felt on her in the past few days, and it was strong on her. If it were piercing eyes, they had a magnetic force. But she couldn't see them, although she would look and look all around her. Whenever her husband came home for a short time or overnight, the girl would tell her husband about, but it seemed like the young man didn't have the time to find out what it was that was bothering around, he was always so busy with his hunting, trying to get the food in for the next winter. He talked to her a lot to make her feel better, telling her there wasn't anything to be afraid of around here. "We are all alone here, there isn't any other people around us for many days of walk from here." The young man told his wife that it may be the eyes of some wild animals looking at her move around near her tipi each day, and just to be careful not to go too far from the tipi. This always consoled her, she wasn't afraid of animals.

After a night of sleeping with her husband, he would be off again to hunt. At a certain time of the day, that feeling of eyes watching her would come onto her. She knew it wasn't her dogs, but it may be some animal that was always looking out of the bushes nearby. In the next few days this feeling increased, and again she told her husband about it, but he still didn't have time to look into it or he didn't believe it to be true. Feeling this thing, whatever it was, and knowing she was alone most of the time, she got a little scared and very lonely. She would cry at times. Who would know she cried when she was alone?

It was one of these very lonely days for her, her husband had been gone for these past two days. She was sitting inside of her tipi on her bed, lonely for her folks who she hadn't seen in the past two years, and all of her friends. And to make it worse, her husband had only been with her for just a few nights in this past Moon of Frogs, since it got warm. She was crying, thinking about all of this, when she heard the dogs barking. The dogs never bark at their master, the young man, the girl's husband. She knew something was coming from the lake, because the dogs were barking towards it, and she knew it wasn't anything the dogs knew, because they were barking as if they were afraid. The dogs would come a-yelping, and then turn around and charge whatever it was that was coming towards the tipi.

She seemed frozen to her seat. She wanted to look out, but couldn't move for some strange reason. The dogs' barking came nearer and nearer, soon she heard the rustling of feet coming towards her doorway. It was the feet of a person that was coming. Soon, the feet came to the doorway. The girl was very still, holding her breath, when the door flap was lifted and opened. She seen a foot and a leg come in, then another, then came the whole body of a person and he stood just inside of the doorway. She could see him plain now. For some reason she wasn't a bit afraid of this man, though he was strange-looking in a way. He had a short chubby face, he wasn't fat, but he was husky and not too tall. His eyes were pitch black and round. He had noticeable teeth, they were slim-like and very white. In other words, he was very handsome. The man was very friendly. As the girl told him to go sit down, she pointed to the visitor's side of the tipi.

The girl asked him what was he doing around here. The strange man told the girl that he lived close by, that he had been watching the two since they moved in here and he had noticed the woman was left alone most of time, especially this spring. He knew that her husband had only been home overnight just a few times, and he knew the girl was getting mighty lonely with a life by herself. For some strange reason, she became attracted to him in just that short time since he had come into the tipi only a few moments ago. She didn't want anything to get in between her and her husband. She loved the young man, he was doing his best to do right with her. But this strange man had that strong attraction she couldn't get it out of her mind.

The strange man told her that there were many dangerous animals around that lurked in the woods close by, that her husband hadn't even thought about that danger for her. As he was talking to her, she just sat there staring at him, as if in a daze. The strange man got through talking and was ready to leave. He got up, went towards the girl, and he held his hands out for her. She readily held her own hands up to him. She was charmed by this man's powers, there wasn't any resistance in her to refuse him.

"Come on, come with me, I'll take care of you better than your husband. You are too nice a woman to be left all alone by yourself every day. There is a lot of danger around here for a woman. Come on." There wasn't any resistance in her, she seemed glad to go along with him.

The strange man had her by one hand as he led her out of the tipi. Right towards the lake they went, and as they got by the shore of the lake, the strange man took something out of his pouch and held it to the girl's nose and mouth. Then he went on into the water, still leading the girl by her hand. The water got deeper as they went towards the middle of the lake, deeper and deeper, until the water went over their heads and on under the water.

Far out in the middle of the lake, under the water, they walked slowly toward a beautiful tipi. It was very large, there was paint on it all around. The mid-part of the tipi had beavers painted around it, and the bottom had the usual painting of mountains and burrows of animals. The top too was the usual paintings of the darkness with the Big Dipper and the Little Dipper, while in the top back was the usual symbol of night, the miller or butterfly design. Coming to it, the two went in. It was almost the same as other tipis with everything in them, the only difference was a huge bundle at the opposite end of the doorway or head of the tipi.

The girl was stunned. She didn't seem herself at all, it was like she was doped with something. Once inside of this tipi, the strange man told the girl this was going to be her home for the rest of her life, because she had now become his wife. She seemed glad in a way, but she was in a trance by his strange powers. It was a wonder that she was able to breath underwater, she didn't mind it one bit.

The young man was gone about four days before returning to their tipi, like always, with a big load of fresh meat on his back. There was a hill to come over before he could get a glimpse of their tipi. Although he was gone almost all the time, he loved his wife and was always glad to get home from these hunts. Anyway, it was for her own good, they had to have food for winter, and winters in these mountains were something else, they were very severe and wicked. Food and wood to burn was always their main job to get ahead on.

He was coming towards the hill, thinking he would see their tipi and his lovable wife, who was so true to him and always was there to greet him on his returns from a hunt. She done this each time he came home, she was always so very glad to see him back, and his dogs too that were so faithful to stay by his young wife. Slowly coming over this last hill, he got a glimpse of their tipi before the dogs noticed him a-coming. All of the dogs were sitting in the front of the tipi, as if looking towards the lake into the water, and he could see by the way the dogs were sitting that all wasn't well. The dogs seemed lonely as they sat there. Coming fully over the hill, the dogs sensed him a-coming and came running happily towards him, barking with glee and happiness. They were all over him, licking his hands and jumping up to him. He walked towards the tipi, he was expecting his wife to come out and meet him, but at the same time he knew something was drastically wrong here. His dogs were jumping up to him and running alongside of him, whimpering, trying to tell him something. To the tipi he was going, almost running now. The young man was all out of wind with the load of meat he had and walking very fast, half running towards his tipi. He dropped his load of meat on the ground just before he reached the doorway.

Jumping to the doorway of the tipi, he opened the doorflap and looked inside. His heart almost dropped out—no wife was inside. He went on in to look around, maybe there might be something that would tell him where his wife had disappeared to. Looking around very carefully, first on the inside of the tipi, then coming out, he began to scout around to find tracks leading away from the tipi. Walking all around the tipi, the young man struck it lucky—he found a man's track and his wife's, a woman's tracks, and they both went towards the lake. The tracks led down to the lake's edge and they seemed to go on into the water. Maybe someone had came there with a boat, a hide boat, or a bull boat as they were known at that time. The young man must find out for sure, but it was already too late now to start around the lake, he must wait until morning.

Walking back up to the tipi, his heart very sad, he didn't even feel like eating. He went inside and sat down on their bed, thinking about his wife. He was crying, thinking he never should have left her so much all these times he was out hunting, he should've taken her along with him. All that night he sat there, crying and thinking of his wife.

The woman had settled down far out in the middle of the lake and far under in a beaver tipi and a Beaverman had came and got her from her own tipi. This was a life of two different things of nature, an animal and a human being. The Beaverman was used to eating his own food, and the woman was very used to her food. So, from the very first day they came to this Beaverman's tipi under the water of this huge lake, the two didn't quite hit it off on their eating. The food was strange to the woman, she couldn't eat very much of it or none at all, she didn't like it. But she was still in a trance from the powers of the Beaverman, and she had to nibble some of that strange food, she was hungry.

The Beaverman had told her about himself. He was a beaver that lived in this lake with many other beavers, and all of them had seen the two when they first moved in. They were under observation day and night since then, especially by this Beaverman that transformed into a man. He seen their every movement each day and night, and that was the reason he took this girl away from her husband. The girl was being left all alone so much and she was lonesome mostly all the time since they came here, but she loved her husband.

Probably a lot of you have visited the Waterton Lakes Hotel along the international boundary between the U.S. and Canada, and probably you have walked around the lake. It's a big lake and it would take about two or three days to walk all the way around it. Well, that's what this young man done to make sure that his wife didn't come to the other side of the lake and walk off to somewhere else. It took him almost three days to walk all the way around the lake, but he was sure his wife was still in this lake somewhere, most likely drowned by now. This made him all the more lonely for his wife. He didn't actually know if she were alive or if she had drowned. But those other tracks, what did they mean? He couldn't understand them, since now he couldn't find any tracks leading out from the lake or away from it, no tracks could he find when he went around the lake. So his wife and whoever the other tracks belonged to were still in this lake.

By this time the young man's eyes were very swollen from crying for his wife. He was lost without her, but life had to be lived, with or without. The best he could do was go on and not give up hope of finding her until such a day that he might find her body somewhere around this lake. The young man knew his wife or her body was near here, because the tracks of her and whoever it was with her didn't lead away from this lake. He made up his mind that he must stay right here until he knew of his wife's whereabouts. It made it all the more lonely when their dogs begin to holler and whine around, they too were thinking of their mistress. As for him, he cried every day. He couldn't sleep or hardly eat anything, he was so broken-hearted. Winter in these mountains never took very long in coming, so he couldn't just sit around and be lonely, he had to get out and get things for the coming winter—food, wood, and even down to the tanning of hides. His work had doubled since his wife disappeared, even this work tanning, the wife's job, brought memories of her, and each day ended with his loneliness getting worse.

One day he came back to his home with a big load of fresh meat. It was early yet when he came home. He was taking care of them, cutting them up into dry meat, and he had a very slim meal. It was getting into about mid-fall. His wife had been gone several moons and the thoughts of her were worse. Getting through with whatever he had to do that evening, the young man sat back on his bed and filled his pipe. As he was filling it, a thought came to him that made him sit up and take notice. In all these days since his wife's disappearance, the young man forgot his prayers, because he was too bereaved. This young man had a lot of powers, and his prayers were very strong with Creator Sun and Mother Earth. But being too upset about his wife, he had never once thought of calling on his father, Creator Sun, and his mother, Mother Earth, for help. He got up and put live ashes into the incense burner, a round stone hollowed out in the middle. In this he put the live ashes and the sweet grass. And as it began to smoke, the young man used his prayers for the first time since his wife disappeared. He prayed a long time, asking the sacred folks for help in finding his wife alive or finding her body someplace so he would know what became of her.

For the very first time since the disappearance of his wife, the young man fell asleep without trouble or thoughts to stay awake. In his sleep, the young man had a dream of his wife, he dreamt of this strange man coming out of the lake to visit him and told him about his wife being down in the lake, living with this strange man. He found out this man was a Beaverman and lived out in the center of this large lake. Not only him, but many of them living here in this lake. These Beaver people were claiming this lake as theirs and their home, but they were not stingy with it, they could always share it with others. That wasn't why she disappeared, though.

This Beaverman told the young man of his compassion for other beings. The Beaverman knew the girl was lonesome for something, for each time the young man was gone, this girl would walk around crying for someone and the Beaverman couldn't stand the loneliness of such a beautiful girl. So he took her from him and now was living underwater with the Beaverman.

Now it's the other way, the Beaverman can't stand the loneliness of this young man who was trying so hard to make a good living for his own wife. The Beaverman admitted he had done wrong in taking the girl without first finding out the truth of these two people, the young man and his wife. It was getting cold and very late in this fall, the Beaverman told the young man that he would have to go without his wife through these cold days alone, but he promised he would come very early this coming spring and do right about his wrongdoing. It was a promise.

The Beaverman just about had to do this without thinking of the young man. The girl was very used to living out in the fresh air of the open. Living underwater was getting to her, and the food wasn't right with her either. He used most of the powers he had to keep her in the trance so she would be able to breathe underwater and eat his food. But she wasn't eating too much of the Beaverman's food, she wasn't made for that kind of food, she was losing weight and getting very thin from undernourishment. She was eating the barks of trees and the many kinds of bushes that beavers ate, but she needed more meat and roots. This was a great concern for the Beaverman, he didn't know just what could be done about this. The Beaverman knew she had to have her own kind of food, and that he couldn't get at, no matter how much supernatural power he had. His supernatural powers were mostly about water and natural life.

Just before the Beaverman left the young man's tipi, he told the young man, "This isn't just a dream, but this is the only way I could come to you and tell you what wrong I have done to you. On your doorway, just inside of the tipi, I'll leave my mark. This will let you know that I did come to you for real." And the Beaverman left the young man's tipi.

Just as the Beaverman disappeared out of the doorway, the young man woke up with quite a start. He thought his dream was true. He thought he saw the doorpiece fall back in place as he opened his eyes, but he wasn't sure, his eyes were still half asleep. As he got used to the light after waking up, and still looking at the doorway, his eyes fell upon a piece of wood. It was a beaver chopping about arm's length and big as his wrists, the bark of this wood was all chewed off and had the markings of beaver teeth. The young man didn't hesitate a bit longer, he jumped up and went to the piece of beaver chopping.

He picked it up and held it in his hands for a bit. Then he took it back to the bedside with him and laid it down just beyond his pillow. The young man had the beaver chopping wrapped up in a tanned deer hide before laying it down. He made a fire, and as the fire got hotter and had more ashes, more live charcoals, the young man made a sweet smoke from his sweet grass, giving thanks for what he had dreamt about. He thanked Creator Sun and Mother Earth for hearing his prayers this past night, and he thanked the Beaverman coming to tell him what really happened and that his wife was safe down under the water where the Beaverman lived in his own tipi. The Beaverman mentioned early spring, when he would bring back the young man's wife. The young man thought he heard the Beaverman say something about the first thunder of the spring, when he would come and do something before giving the girl up and back to the young man. The young man wasn't too sure of what he had heard.

The young man had the beaver chopping that he picked up just inside of his tipi, and this made him feel very good. He knew that this wasn't just a dream, but a real promise from a Beaverman. It made him feel so happy to know about his wife and that she was coming back to him this spring. From there on through the winter moons, the young man couldn't do enough to keep himself busy so the moons would go faster. He hunted a lot and tried to spend as much time away from his tipi as he could to make time go faster. He trapped a lot too that winter, he done many things to keep busy. Doing so many things, he did forget about time a little. The winter came and left, it was getting warmer as spring started coming around, but the young man was still a busy man, doing his odd jobs to kill time.

One night as he crept into bed, just so very tired from all the things he was doing and just as he began falling asleep, he woke up from the noise of the first thunder. Immediately, the young man was wide awake and the thunder made him think about the Beaverman's promise. This made him sit up and take notice of how fast time went since he dreamt about the Beaverman and all what this stranger wanted when the first thunder was heard. The young man could hardly sleep anymore waiting for daylight. He had many things to do. He had to get everything ready for the return of his wife.

Soon as it was light enough, the young man left the tipi and got busy doing what he had to do. The sweat huts were the first things that he had to set up before sunrise, and there were four of them. Along the lake these sweat huts were to be erected, side by side, from east to west. As the young man was very anxious to see his wife—it was close to a year since he had laid eyes on her—it wasn't too very long to set the sweat huts up. Soon as the first one was set up, the fire was lit to get the rocks red-hot in time for the sunrise. And as that fire was burning, he got busy with the other three sweat huts. The rocks were all ready by the time he got through with the three sweat huts, they were red-hot and ready for the first sweat hut.

The young man was all alone through this morning, and as he was doing what had to be done, he was wondering if it were all true, or if it was just in his mind and he was fooling himself about all of this. Just before the sun came up over the horizon, the young man let out a sigh of relief. For just out from the four sweat huts, a strange man appeared in the water and began to come towards the shore and the sweat huts that were in a neat row, east to west. After he had a close look at him, the young man knew that this strange man came from the Beaver family. In every way this man resembled the beaver—the eyes, the face, the mouth, the teeth especially, and the body of him. His wife didn't appear, which was very disappointing to him, he wanted so much to see his wife. The Beaverman came right out to the first, the east-most one, and without saying anything this Beaverman got ready to go into the sweat hut. About that time, the sun was just beginning to come into view. The young man immediately got the red-hot rocks inside of the sweat hut, into the hollowed-out place for them. After this was done, the Beaverman told the young man to come in and the sweat was under way.

It took the better part of the day, sweating with the Beaverman. He prayed a lot and sang songs of the ways of faith among the beavers. During the last sweat of the four the Beaverman told the young man what else he had to do for the next morning. The young man must have two tipis set up together to make one large room, food must be cooked and ready to serve for many people that were going to be here. Lots of firewood was needed for this, but of course the young man did have a lot of firewood gathered and it was piled up very high and ready to be used. The Beaverman gave the young man further orders of what to do and what not to do. The tipi was to be ready with all that the Beaverman needed—small willows for the seats all around the inside of the tipi, mixed with straw; most was to be used for the floor and mud for the sweet grass burner.

The Beaverman told him that when everything was ready, which had to be the next morning, the young man was to lay down inside of the tipi, at the head where he was to sit, the righthand side, and cover his head. No matter what he heard, the young man wasn't to pay any attention to the noise. He must keep his head covered, he mustn't see what was taking place or who was doing the talking. The main thing was to keep under the cover and to close his ears.

The fourth one of the sweat huts was over, but it was still early enough to do some of the things that had to be done for the next morning. As soon as the Beaverman had left and gone back into the water, the young man got busy. He knew no tiredness, he must get his wife back. The young man worked until far into the night, and everything was ready for the next morning before he laid down to sleep. Waking up before daylight again, the young man took the thickest robes he could find to cover up with. As the light of day began to show, the young man was ready for the first of the many restrictions that he had to put up with, for now and for the future as it came, and it was all for the sake of his beloved wife.

By daylight, the young man was already covered up with the thickest of the buffalo robes. He didn't want to make a mistake and look up, he didn't want to hear anything that might tempt him to look up, so he covered up very thick. He laid there for the longest time without hearing anything, it seemed like forever to him. He didn't know the time of the day it was, as he was still covered up thick, when he heard the first of some people talking. First it was just about two or three people that he heard, but it wasn't too long before he began to hear more and more people talking and they sounded very happy. Everyone he heard was laughing and talking excitedly, but the young man held to the covers. At times he almost became tempted took up and see who it was that was doing all of the talking. The thought of his wife would keep him from doing it, he must be patient and not get overexcited, he must remain covered and not look up. The voices became many, it got very noisy here with all of the people talking and almost all at once. But the young man stuck with the robes, kept his head under there, fighting the urge to look up and see all of the people talking. It's been a few years since he last seen many people and all of this he was hearing was very tempting to him, to get to talking to other people after three years alone, just him and his wife.

He was using all of his willpower and supernatural powers to stay put under the covers. He was doing all right until, among all of that noise, a sound made him perk up his ears a little more. Among all of that noisy talking, and it seemed like it was above all of the talking, he had heard his wife's voice. He wanted so much to see her once more after all of these winter moons that went by, it was all he could bear. Her voice was right next to him, he even felt her moving around very close to him, and this he couldn't stand. He uncovered and took a look. As soon as the covers of the robes came off of his head, all of that noisy talking subsided, it became just as quiet as this morning when he was alone. He knew right away he had done wrong, and he didn't know what to do. It was only a little while before he heard the voice of the Beaverman from the outside of this enlarged tipi. The Beaverman told the young man to lay down again and cover up and this time not pay any attention to any noise, no matter if people bump into his legs or any of his body.

Again the young man covered up his head. He thought to himself, "This time, nothing will tempt me to uncover my head or try to see who is around." He covered up thicker this time to keep out the noise of those happy-sounding people, he even held his fingertips in his ears to help keep all of that talking out of his ears. Again he done very good, the voices increased as the time went by, more and more peoples' voices could be heard. It wasn't very long till he thought he heard the Beaverman talking, and again he heard his wife, he kept his head under cover, while every once in a while the sound of his wife he would hear. He was doing it right, staying under covers until he heard her so near him, saying "This one must be asleep, and everybody is so happy today because of what's going to happen." It sounded so real and besides, at the same time, with her foot, she bumped him on his side. Like a fool, the young man, by mistake, jumped up again to see and tell her that she could easily step over him. But as soon as he uncovered his, it got very quiet. Just him again, no one else was around. His heart almost fell out of him, it got very heavy from doing what he did.

It wasn't too long before the Beaverman's voice again came from the outside of the tipi, the voice came from somewhere in the back of the tipi. The Beaverman was telling the young man once again to do his best and not look up from under that robe he had over his head, that they couldn't be doing this all day.

Once again the young man hid his head under the covers of the robes and again he heard those talking people as he laid there. Only a little while before, the talking increased with many peoples' voices. Again he heard the sound of his wife above all the other people. The sound of her was coming towards him as he laid there, her spirit must've come right by him where he laid. He felt her footsteps alongside of him, stepping on the robes he was covered with. This was so tempting to see her that the young man couldn't stand it any longer, he jerked the covers off again. But again to his disappointment, there was no one else around except him.

This time the young man started to cry, he knew he had done wrong again. He sat up and made a smudge of sweet grass and as the smoke began to rise into the air, the young man asked Creator Sun and Mother Earth for help. He knew he was running out of time, all of this foolishness he was doing, and sure enough, after a long prayer, the Beaverman spoke from the rear of the tipi again. "This time use your ears and do what I tell you. If you don't, it will be the last time a chance will be given you and your last chance to get your wife back. If you look up again this time, that will be the end for you and your wife. You will never see her again. So do your best and stay there until I tell you to look up. Use those ears of yours to keep your wife for the rest of your life, be sure you do it this time."

He was praying for help after he covered up his head, and at the same time he was trying to shut out a noise of the people, who had started to come in again and were making a lot of noise talking. The young man must've really gotten help from Creator Sun's and Mother Earth's spirits, even his own spiritual helpers must've combined into one big help. Those spirits put him to sleep through all the noise that came into the tipi. He didn't know what went on.

The young man was just plumb dead asleep. He was being shook up by the Beaverman, to get up and take part in the doings now, but the young man was hanging on to the covers, his head still under there. He was half asleep yet, he was arguing with the Beaverman that he didn't want to spoil it this time, he wanted to get his wife back. He didn't want to look up. The Beaverman was shaking him to get him fully awake, and talking to him at the same time. The Beaverman was telling him it was all right now, to go ahead and look at all of the people. The young man didn't believe what they were talking about, so he kept his head covered up. It wasn't until his wife spoke to him, shaking him at the same time, that he realized it must be so. From under the covers he asked his wife if this was true. He was very afraid to look up, because this was the last chance that was given him to really see his wife. His wife gave him assurance that everything was all right now. He felt her hands shaking him on his shoulders and telling him to look up, that he could see her now, but not to touch her, because this was still a restriction. He must keep his hands off of her until the Beaverman told him to touch her.

The young man was finally convinced. He uncovered his head and looking all around him, he seen many people with many different features. Right next to him sat the Beaverman, and on the other side of the Beaverman sat his wife. She was all adorned for this doings. The Beaverman told the young man to sit right beside him to his right, that this religious ceremony was for him and his wife.

The Beaverman was talking on, explaining about what had happened this last summer and since the coming of this young man and his wife to this area of the many beaver families. This was a big mistake on the Beaverman's part to have stuck his nose into another's life. He was very, very sorry to be trying to come between these two, the young couple. The Beaverman wants to make up for his wrongdoings, he wanted to give the young woman his worldly and his most precious belongings, his pipe and the tipi he owned, and which was lived in by this very young woman and far under water.

The young man was so very glad to see his wife in person, he tried to grab her over the Beaverman. The Beaverman pushed him back to his seat and told him, "I haven't told you yet, but we still have four days before you can't touch her, this religious ceremony will end and we will have to do something else before you can touch your wife. She's had a different kind of life through this last winter, she must be transferred and adjusted back to her normal life before you can touch her." All the young man could do now was to look at his wife, his heart ached for a touch of her. But that was out for the time being until the Beaverman had done the things he wanted to do.

The praying went on and on, the Beaverman's prayers were so emotional to the young man, at times he had tears in his eyes. The Beaverman was asking forgiveness about this wrong he had committed. It was all a mistake, he wasn't aware of their closeness and their love for one another. His heart was so heavy from all of this, he doesn't know if he will ever forget this or forgive himself for the rest of his life. The Beaverman prayed very loud, and all of the people in this tipi heard him pray as he did. Making smudge with the sweet grass and singing prayer songs, the ceremony went on. Now it was time for the young man and his wife to pay close attention to the Beaverman and what he was doing, the main ceremony had begun.

The Beaverman told the two, "Watch my every movement and what my hands do. My body is your body whenever this ceremony is being done. After you have received this bundle, watch very close what you see in this bundle. Those you will have to acquire by trapping or hunting." There were several drummers, four of them. These four weren't using the round-made drums, they were drumming on a hard-dried rawhide. The ceremony was just now beginning to get very lively and everyone present was a-buzzing with excitement as this thing got started good. This was the Beaver Pipe Bundle then, and it was being unwrapped for the benefit of the young couple to learn the way to handle and preserve it. This bundle consisted of several beaver pelts, earth paints, some bones that were parts of the beaver, the cuttings, and it was anointed with beaver glands to make it sweet while bundled for a long time.

Once this ceremony was well underway, the lady to the left of the young woman motioned to her husband who was to the right side of the young man. The people were seated double all around. The women were seated all on the north side of this tipi, while the men were all seated on the south side. Everyone in here had a mate or a wife. The first couple, as the man came to his wife, she whispered into his ear. The man nodded his head as a consent to his wife's saying, and he sat back down. This man raised his hand to the conductor of this ceremony to hesitate a bit and hear what this man had to say. Immediately things got quiet, as curiosity got the best of everybody. All wanted to hear what was going on, what the couple wanted.

The man spoke loud so everyone could hear. He said to the conductor, the Beaverman, "Because of our presence in here and for the sake of this young couple that you have made a big mistake to, we too feel responsible in some way, because we are of the water too, we live there. We want them to have us as representatives in this pipe bundle you are giving as a forgiveness gift. We are of the Mink family, our representation in this Beaver Pipe Bundle shall be the clothes we wear." This was the mink's fur that they gave for the pipe bundle.

About that time, the dogs started to bark very hard as all of the people were sitting there listening to the Mink family give towards this Beaver Pipe Bundle. It was about midday now and this religious ceremony was just getting under way. The dogs quit barking by the doorway, and as they quit the barking, into the tipi came a-waddling two lizards, mates. As the two lizards stopped by the doorway, waiting for an invitation to a seat for them, the Beaverman, as a conductor of this religious ceremony and transferrer of the pipe bundle, didn't hesitate a bit as he seen the lizards waddling in. He let go what he was doing and hollered at the lizards to get back out and go back to the place they came from. The lizard didn't want to hear him, they didn't pay any attention to his words. They asked if they could come in and join this religious ceremony, this pipe bundle transfer. The Beaverman didn't want to hear either. Each time the lizards asked to come in to join this ceremony, the Beaverman asked them to leave. Four times they were told to leave by the Beaverman, and four times they asked if they could come in to join the doings.

After the fourth time they were refused by the Beaverman, the two lizards finally left. They were sorely hurt, their heads were hanging down as they went out of the doorway. Before they disappeared outside, the male lizard turned at the doorway and spoke. "We will leave now, but watch out for what is going to happen to your doings." To the lakeside and into the water they went. The male lizard was singing as he left the doorway and the female was talking as if praying to someone. Not too long after the lizards had gone into the lake, it began clouding up and very fast too, they were thick black clouds. Thunder and lightning started, then all of a sudden rain poured down. It rained so hard and the thunder and lightning was so severe, the religious ceremony stopped for the rain to quit. But the rain went on and on, it seemed like it was raining harder each moment.

Before long, the creeks and riverbanks began overflowing. The water was steadily rising as the rain poured down. There were several of these people present that knew about weather through their powers. Either the rain water began to form a lake, or the lake was getting higher and higher, it was slowly filling this valley. The Beaverman was getting very nervous about it all. He asked those that knew the weather through their mysterious powers to stop this rain and thunderstorm. All of those that had the power of weather took turns to stop this downpour of rain, but there wasn't anyone of them that had enough power to stop this rain, and it poured down steadily. The valley was filling up and the religious ceremony was temporarily out, because of the rain. The Beaverman tried with everything within his own power and those of the others to stop this rain.

It finally dawned on him, this rain and thunderstorm was caused by the lizard pair. He had hurt their feelings and they got mad, they started the rain. The Beaverman began to pray to the lizards to come back and join the religious ceremony, they were welcome to sit in this tipi. The Beaverman offered them a pipe smoke and he prayed some more to them. For the longest time, and as the rain steadily poured down, the lightning striking close by the loudest of those thunderclaps all around them, the lizards didn't answer those prayers by all of those in the tipi. The Beaverman prayed again as hard as he could to the lizards. He was talking very loud and clear towards the lake, after the prayer, the Beaverman offered the lizards a place among the holy Beaver Pipe Bundle. A place among the pipe bundle was a rare honor, it was something those lizards couldn't reject. They wanted to be represented in the holy pipe bundle.

Not too long after this offer, the lizards came waddling out of the lake, they had been listening all the time for this. Them lizards knew they were the only ones that would be able to stop this downpour with the lightning and thunder. It was still pouring rain and the valley was filling up fast with the water. This lake of these beavers had enlarged since it started to rain this day, it wasn't only dropping raindrops, it was like pouring one big bucket out. The water was inching towards the tipi of the young man, and still all of those in there sat tight, holding their breath. The two lizards slowly came along, taking their good old time to get to the tipi. Those in the tipi took turns looking out from the tipi, and everywhere they looked there was water. It was mostly the hills as high as this one the tipi sat on that were still seen, the rest of the place was now a huge lake. The two lizards finally made it to the tipi. They stopped just outside of the doorway, waiting for the invitation to come on in.

By now the Beaverman knew what the lizards wanted, and that was the representation among the Beaver Pipe Bundle. He asked them to come right in, and room for them to sit was cleared as the people moved to make a space for them. Now as the two sat down, the Beaverman jumped right up himself and offered the male lizard the pipe and tobacco, a smoke for him. He spoke in a prayer-like way to the male lizard, asking him to make this rain stop and make the sun shine.

"The water is overflowing all around us now, use your pity, your compassion for others that know not of water life. All of us here in this tipi aren't the same, many of us live on dry land. Them are the ones that will suffer for what you are doing. Accept this smoke of this pipe and stop the rain, let us all be happy from this day. Give us a big promise that you will never use the rainwater to take advantage of others after this. We are all scared of the powers you have, because you can destroy all life and Mother Earth too."

The lizards didn't put up any kind of argument, the male lizard accepted the pipe smoke readily. He puffed the usual first four sacred ones of this pipe smoke, then he hesitated to say a prayer to stop the downpour of rain. A very few moments after he had taken the four sacred puffs of the pipe and said a little prayer with it, the rain stopped as suddenly as it began. A little while longer, the sun came out and beat down on Mother Earth. It got very hot out. This was all a mystery. In a little while that water that was all over the valleys was now quickly receding back to normal.

The waters were now quickly getting back into their usual flows when the Beaverman gave thanks to the lizard couple. He also promised to always recognize the lizards and have respect for them as long they are here on Mother Earth. As those heavy black clouds were swirling around up there, the male lizard pointed up into the clouds and told the crowd to look for themselves and see the mark of his promise. Everybody in the tipi was curious what was up there. All looking up into the clouds, they seen the prettiest sight up there, it was the first rainbow.

"This mysterious thing you all see is my promise to all of you folks. Never again, as long as Mother Earth and Creator Sun are alive we lizards will never use this power of water, the rain, lightning, and thunder as an advantage for our good. Things shall come natural, as nature wants things to come. Now that our promise is made, let us get back underway with the transfer of this holy Beaver Pipe Bundle."

The storm was held by a lizard's rope of mystery, the Rainbow. The ceremony could go on, but again before it really got started, the rest of these people in this tipi took turns rising and telling the Beaverman that they would like to donate towards this pipe bundle too. Everyone in this tipi donated the clothes they had on them, which really was their fur, towards the holy pipe bundle. So this was representing all of those that were in this tipi, everyone that came for this transfer of a pipe bundle ceremony, a highly religious doings for the animals. For the young man and his wife, the only representation of theirs was that the pipe bundle would now belong to them as a gift from this Beaverman that was conducting this religious ceremony.

This pipe bundle now became a very large bundle with all of those fur-bearing animals and the many different kinds of birds, both large and small, the animals too, that had donated their fur or feathers. These fur-bearing animals and the many different birds are those that habitate the Northwestern region of the now United States.

When all of those present had donated to the holy pipe bundle, the conductor of this ceremony, the Beaverman, told the young couple to keep in their minds the order in which animal or bird donated to the bundle. It was very important that these birds' and animals' clothing are kept in the very same order as they were donated by the owners. As each animal or bird donated its clothing, each of them also gave a song that was to be sung as their clothing was being either taken out or being put back in the bundle. So it was very important that all was kept in the order as they came to the bundle. The song for each of them was to be sung four times through as they were being handled by the bundle keeper. As each one of the animals and birds gave to the bundle, that particular pair would tell the young man where to go and find that particular clothing of this particular animal or bird.

Of all the stories that were told to me, as close as I can tell, the many fur-bearing animals and the many birds that were truly represented in the Preserving Pelts Pipe Bundle are the mole, mouse, rat, ferret, weasel, rabbit, mink, otter, badger, porcupine, fisher, squirrel, marten, gopher, rednose gopher or mountain gopher, wolverine, coyote, wolf, lynx, bobcat, cougar, mountain lion, deer, elk, antelope, moose, mountain sheep, mountain goat,

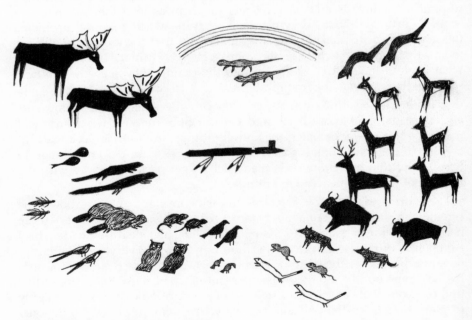

*The Beaver Pipe of Waterton Lake,*
*Preserving Pelts Pipe Bundle*

black bear, brown bear, muskrat. The first of these fur-bearing animals of the bundle is the beaver. There is more of the fur-bearing animals, the names of them I don't know. But that particular pipe bundle consisted of all the Northwestern fur-bearing animals of what is now the United States. The same of the many kinds of birds, too. Of those I know that are with the bundle are the hummingbird, robin, meadowlark, sparrow, wren, magpie, crow, both the raven and the regular crow, red-winged woodpecker, owl, several kinds of hawks, skylark, eagle, blue jay, camp robber, kildeer, curlew, duck, geese, mudhen, sagehen, pelican, rainbird, stingy berries, blackbird, grouse, prairie chicken, pheasant, and a tiny owl we call the mitten. If there are more birds of the Northwestern United States that I didn't mention, then they too were included in the Preserving Pelts Pipe Bundle.

We know that there are some birds and probably some animals that have been extinct since the organization of the Preserving Pelts Pipe Bundle. The lizard was represented as a symbol on the rawhide that was used as a drumming piece. The bullfish was also represented in the pipe bundle as a rattle. Four of these rattles, made from rawhide and molded into a rattle, with little pebbles inside of them to make the rattling sound, are used for drumming on the rawhide, dried somewhat like a board and with the symbol of the lizard. The water strider is also represented in the pipe bundle of the Beaverman as a symbol too, so are the water beetle.

This pipe bundle was known as the Beaver Pipe Bundle only for a very little while, just during the ceremony. After all of the animals had donated to the pipe bundle, the name of it was changed to Preserving Pelts Pipe Bundle.

After every one of the attending beings had donated to the pipe bundle, the ceremony finally went on. For four days it went. Four of a kind was a charm for all Natives of these Americas, so everything was done by fours. In these four days, the young woman and her husband got to know all about the pipe bundle with its many songs. Think about it for a while. Each song was to be sung four times through as each of the donors took their turns with the rattles and sang that special song for their own donation. This went on for four days, from early morning until late at night.

I personally experienced this kind of doings when my uncle had this pipe bundle transferred to him. I was only about five years of age, but I still remember many things about it. It took four days and nights, songs were sung before the people retired for the night, and songs for the rising of the people the next morning before the sun rose. Everything had a song to it.

In these four days the young couple learned the secrets that went with the Preserving Pelts Pipe Bundle. It was learned again, by this mysterious force of power that existed with the giver of the pipe bundle and all of those that were present there. It was such a desolate place where it took place, several thousand years ago, the closest humans were several days away from there. In these days it's known as Waterton Lakes National Park. There was no way to invite the real people, the real humans, so the Beaverman had to make up for that in some way. He called on all of the animals and the birds to come to join him for this one occasion of transferring the pipe bundle that was given in place of what he had caused the young couple. It was a sort of a gift of forgiveness to him, for what he did. He wanted to save face for taking someone else's woman away from him when it wasn't any of his business. Through the Beaverman's power, combined with the powers of each of those that attended the ceremony, all of the attendants transformed to human beings. This is a wonderful feeling to be human, you are held high among all kinds of life. All of these animals and birds transferred into your kind, a human being. They didn't transform you into a bird or an animal, but your kind. This is something to think of, you are higher than any kind of life.

It was very late after all was done at the transfer of the pipe ceremony, it was the last night and everyone was very tired from the four-day affair. All went to sleep on the spot they were sitting, the young couple too. Before they fell asleep the Beaverman told them not to touch one another just yet, there were a few more things that had to be done before they could touch each other. He was still sitting between them when this was over, so there wasn't any way the two could touch one another. Anyway, they were very true to their faith with Nature, to Mother Earth and Creator Sun, it was all from the young man's seek of powers, his vision quest. There was no need to worry about them. The young man was told to get up before daylight and set up four more sweat huts. These would be for his wife to go into and sweat out that power that was used on her by the Beaverman, enabling her to live underwater. That must come out of her before her husband could touch her.

The anxious husband woke up before daylight and looked to see if everyone was still asleep. To his amazement, there wasn't anyone else in here, just the three of them. All of those that attended this doings were gone, they came mysteriously and left mysteriously. In both cases, the coming of them and the leaving of them, the young man didn't see where they came from or where they went.

He jumped up from where he was sleeping. It didn't take very long for him to set the four sweats up. The fires lit as it gets light enough and everything that was needed was ready just before the sun came up into view. The young wife was ready to go in the first of the four sweat huts. When the young man seen his wife several days ago, all he could do was to look at her yearningly. He could not touch her until the Beaverman that done them wrong said so, and this would be sometime this day.

Into the first of the four sweat huts the young woman went. It took a very long time in between the openings of the sweat hut for air, and there were four openings to each sweat hut. Coming out of the first one of the sweat huts, the young woman left a huge pile of sand where she sat. She ran to the lake and jumped in to wash off. She wasn't wasting any time, she went right back and into the second of the sweats. These first two sweats took half of the day. When it was time for her to come out of the second one of the four sweats, she left a pile of sand again, only not as much as the first time. She went into the lake again to wash herself off and went right back into the third of the sweats. Four openings for each sweat, this third one took just as long. When the young woman came out of this sweat hut, there wasn't much sand left where she sat. Going into the lake again to wash off, she immediately went right back into the fourth and last of the sweat huts. The sun was just going out of sight when the Beaverman said it was enough. Right away, the fourth of the openings of the sweat was done. There wasn't a trace of sand where she sat this time. Running to the lake, she jumped in to wash herself off once more.

She got her clothes on and while she was doing that, the Beaverman was talking to her. "I'm sorry for what happened, but I really cannot see anyone so lonely as you were. I only tried to help you, but I done it wrong. I shouldn't have taken you under water with me like I did. I should've only talked to you and kept you company each time your husband went on those hunts. It is over now, you and your husband can go back to living like a man and wife. Your husband can touch now.

"I sure hope that I have repaid you and your man in full for what wrong I did to you people. I gave you folks my most precious belonging, the Beaver Pipe Bundle. It made it all the more powerful when all of those that attended the transfer ceremony gave to the pipe bundle you now have. It must be preserved as long as life goes on. It must go from hand to hand by doing this transfer ceremony. Anyone asking for it in the right way, and if you accept the smoking of the pipe offered to you, what was done in these past few days must be done again. That goes for each time the pipe bundle is transferred, when it's aired out at the first sound of thunder in the spring of each year, and when it's rewrapped for the winter months when the thunder is last heard in the fall of each year. These two times for airing it out and rewrapping it in the spring and fall, you will have to feed the people. If it's a transfer or if someone made a vow towards the bundle, they do the feeding of the food and provide the tobacco too, the people take care of that.

"So, both of you, remember all of the details, no matter how small or how big they may seem to both of you, do it for the sake of the bundle. Now I must leave you and I shall not bother you again. Live as you may and you shall have all good luck from this Preserving Pelts Pipe Bundle."

The Beaverman now had his turn of heavy heart. He got used to the girl in these past few winter months that he had her with him underwater, but he must face it, he was the one that done wrong. To the lake's edge he went, and without a bit of hesitation he went right into the water and went out of sight. After this, the Beaverman was seen occasionally by the two as they continued to live by the Waterton Lakes. It was several years later, and with a fairly large family, that the young man and his wife left the lake. They didn't forget the Beaverman as all was ready to leave, they went to the lake's edge to throw into it some gifts for all of those beavers that lived in the lake. The Beaverman had immediately transformed himself back into a beaver soon after the holy pipe transfer and ceremony to live a life that was meant for him.

After the gifts of value were thrown in the lake, the young man and his wife prayed to the beavers and asked for their prayers that went with the holy pipe bundle and as long as life existed. This was because the beaver lives a life of mystery, half under water and half on land, power had to be with them to live such a life. There isn't any remains to be found of them when they died of natural causes.

In these days we are living, the older folks that still remember all of these mysteries of life and nature of this universe still throw whatever they can to the water people or water life, because we remember the powers they gave to human life as gifts whenever a vision quest took place near their habitat. These water life powers were very important to the existence of our own human life and they still are, whether we know it or not.

The young man and his family left the mountain country and the lake to go back and join their families once more and to introduce the Preserving Pelts Pipe Bundle to their people. They had been gone many years. Their folks didn't know their whereabouts, they had moved out in the middle of the night and no trace of them was ever discovered. They were well received by everyone at their original camp, everyone was so glad to see them back unharmed. Many feasts for them were called for the next few days at their camp. They had come back just in time for the summer ceremonies of religion. They hadn't told anyone about their Preserving Pelts Pipe Bundle, because they haven't had the chance to, they were so busy with the feasts they were invited to.

After all had cooled down somewhat and they got more time for themselves, they had a camp crier announce their doings to show off their Preserving Pelts Pipe Bundle. At the ceremony, the two told the story of how things went for them during these past several years they were gone and how mostly all of nature throwed in for a holy pipe bundle to be given to this young couple for one beaver's wrongdoings. The name of Preserving Pelts Pipe Bundle stuck with this holy pipe bundle. It had many names, but the more outstanding names were Nature Bundle, Beaver Pipe Bundle, and Mountain Pipe Bundle. Preserving Pelts Pipe Bundle sounded more to the liking of most of the bundle keepers for this particular pipe bundle, and so that name stuck until a few years ago, when this particular pipe bundle went out of existence, probably sold to a German museum, and those that came along with the power of it all died off.

Among us few older ones left, we shall never forget these holy pipe bundles, all of them. They had brought to us such a wonderful life of existence, all clean life, almost sinless existence among our people of the Natives during the many, many years of the holy pipe bundles' existence. The whiteman came in the last few hundred years, but with him came a turbulent life that still exists in these days. What kind of faith or what kind religion did they bring to this Native land of calm and love to make it become as it is today? Full of hate to one another, among the people and among all nations. Each one trying to outdo the other at this, their greed for money and their inventions of death.

# *Honoring Creator Sun*

Most all the people of this great earth of ours, the many nations, right down to the last of them, know there is a very high one above us all. This extreme high one, our Maker of life, is known by many names—God, Buddha, Allah, and many other names. The truest of these names of our Creator is the name he is called by the many Natives of North America and South America. Our people of the Piegans call this Creator Nah-doo-si, Holy One, or as others call him, Sun.

I think praying to the sun itself is the truest form of religion or faith. The sun doesn't have any certain nationality or color, it is just the sun, and high above us all with its life-giving elements, the power of its rays to make our food grow. The sun has been in existence from time beginning, when no other beings were on this earth, no one to call it something else, God didn't come into existence until the Europeans brought him into this world, when they invented God to make their misdoings good. The Egyptians knew their true God was the sun, and many other natives of several different countries also prayed to the sun. They too knew the true maker of this universe and all the many kinds of life that exist on this Mother Earth.

The sun can heal or it can kill with its strange powers. It purifies what we eat and drink. We, the Natives, understand life as it is truly supposed to be. We have lived many, many thousands of years on these continents before the coming of any whiteman. We never heard of any other great spirit besides the sun. The sun and its heavenly bodies, along with Mother Earth, was our guidance, the sole support for our living and lives. The sun brings us warmth when it brings summer back into our side of this Mother Earth. It replenishes our food, our root medicines, and fattens the meat food of the land. It has the power to bring any kind of weather for us. But the truest sign of the sun as a Maker is that it definitely doesn't have one certain color or nationality. It can be seen as almost pure white at its brightest in the midday. It is yellow at certain times of the day. It is red or orange at other times, and it even turns black when a total eclipse occurs during the daytime. This shows us that the sun is with all of the many colors of nationalities of the world.

Many times after people changed or invented a God for their benefit, many thousands of years ago, Creator Sun has tried to let the people of this Mother Earth know the true Creator. Many have read the Bible, and of Moses when he went to the mountain and received the Ten Commandments as it was written. He spoke with the true Creator of life. This was one of the times Creator Sun tried to set this Moses straight on who was the true Creator. Moses couldn't look into the brightness of this speaker there, he had to hide behind a growth of thick bushes. The heat, as he stood there, was too intense, he had to get behind those bushes to get away from the heat of the Creator. Another of Creator Sun's tries at revealing his true identity was at the Miracle of Fatima. At this gathering on a hillside, God was to appear to all those people to show his true self. The only thing that happened that day was the people seen the sun falling down towards them as they all stood standing there to see the true God. All of those people seen the true Creator as it really was supposed to be. All seen the sun falling down towards this multitude of people, it was the sun showing the people who their creator really was—no one else but Creator Sun. There are so many things that we use of the Sun's elements, that people just can't do without the power of the sun.

I may be all alone, but for me, the Great Spirit of the sun is my faith, my life depends on it. There will be no other spirit to take its place in my heart. I know the sun is my true Maker. It provides for me and my family and all people of this earth. It gives me the breath of life from its many kinds of elements, the powers of it. The sun has existed from where no one can say but only guess. To me, it has been in existence always, and always will it be up there to show all people that he is the only one to give life and no other.

The Natives of these countries of the Americas have built many kinds of structures to use as our points of faith. Many of these are still seen as ruins of many thousands of years ago. All of these structures are built by the Native with their bare hands, and are built so that certain sides of these structures point a certain way. The corners, maybe the top part, the doorway, the steps, or just the lay of a structure points to their strongest point of faith, usually a star, the sun, the moon. Many times it's to an extra-high place, like a sharp-peaked mountain, a large, high hill, a lake, or a river. It might be an extra-large tree. It has to be something of nature and visible to the eye. All things of nature are alive and have spirits in them, and our structures of faith are pointed to the particular one we have high belief in.

Most of these structures are built very high. Pyramid shapes or temples are seen throughout Central America and into South America. These are places of worship. The Native can get closer to the sun when he is up on top of this structure of faith, this place of praying. This was a sure way of contacting the sun, because no shade from anything could get in between the man and the sun. A place for the burning of incense is usually up there at the place of prayer. The Northern Natives had a somewhat different way to reach the sun with their prayers. Many kinds of holy pipe bundles were used among the Northern Natives to carry their prayer to the sun for them. All of the Natives used either a pit or a small structure with a very airtight enclosure to take a sweat bath, heated with red-hot rocks—this is also the element of the sun, heat. These were used for prayers too, to the Mother Earth spirits and to Creator Sun. Creator Sun is married to Mother Earth, and all life is their children.

Some of our ancestors lived on leveled mountaintops just to be always near our Creator Sun. We, the Natives of these Americas, had that faith where we couldn't look into its face, because of the brightness, and also we are ashamed of it, always ashamed to face him. We look at it squarely in the middle when we are at prayer. Creator Sun looks down at us to listen to our prayers. It isn't a one to be ashamed of us, where it can't see us or we cannot see it. Our Creator Sun isn't bashful like the God brought to this Native country by the white people. We see our Creator Sun. The white God you just can't see, it keeps one a-guessing what it really is doing for its subjects and how that God looks.

There are many things the white people cannot accept of us Natives, like intelligence. The whites claim that the Aztec ruins, Mesa Verde ruins, the petrified ruins of Arizona, and many more were done by the outer space beings. The white people are funny people. They don't want anyone to surpass them in their intelligence, and yet they find these marks of the Natives but claim them to be done by outer space beings. How dumb can one get?

The whites also try very hard to disprove our original ownership of these Americas. They claim the Native came to this country by crossing the Bering Strait on ice at one time or another, that the Natives settled down wherever they got tired along the coast. Well, I'm just as sure of our prehistoric presence in this country. We have been here from time unknown. In fact, life began here in this country, and spread elsewhere in the world. It's just vice versa from the white peoples' thinking. Our Natives don't have all those many different gadgets that can tell of the past to prove our point—but then, those gadgets don't always give the truth of things. It's our long line of oral history passed down from one generation to the next that we have, and the landmarks that went with those legends of the past. Unbelievable, but very true to us.

But like I said, the white people don't want to believe our story of our beginning and our presence here. It's simple to guess why they don't want our true side of our own history and their coming. Our country is rich in many valuable resources. It's over this they didn't want to listen to us. Now those resources are just about all milked out, sucked out—our timber, our oil, our gold, and the many different kinds of minerals, all of our valuables of our country, and now the white people are trying for our lands in many different ways. Because our Creator Sun gave us this land to live in, Creator Sun in many ways helps us so the whites don't take full control of our land.

I write these things because they do pertain to my story and our original beliefs or faith.

I was told a story by Cutnose After Buffalo back in the 1920s. She told it as if she were there when it happened. I must emphasize the next few words. Cutnose After Buffalo was just like another seventy-year-old lady when she related the story. This too was before I knew there were great oceans or waters all around us, I didn't know there were other lands beyond these lands I knew about, the Blackfeet Indian Reservation. I didn't know anything about English language until I was six years of age. This old lady didn't know one English word, let alone understand one word of English language. She didn't know how to read, so she couldn't have read this story out of a book.

In this particular story, she mentioned our prehistoric life. She mentioned some people who left from here many, many years ago and went across a great body of water that froze over, and those people never did return. They stayed wherever they went to, and they increased manyfold and lived there. She told of our beginning, as I have written it. She told of life that got its start from this continent. She mentioned people that had just about the same culture and dress we do. I find that the many nationalities of Europe and Asia have about the same culture that we have. The Scandinavians, the Basques, Norwegians, the Swiss people, the Laplanders, and the Finlanders all have similar customs and culture such as ours, even their way of dressing is much like ours. The Egyptians were very similar to our ways, too. I'm writing about this because in this chapter of my story you might notice many things that seem similar to stories in your own religion. The reader can either take it or leave it, but study the history of the world before you leave it. Furthermore, research our Native legends, because we too know what we talk about, and probably more than anyone thinks.

Our greatest gift from Creator Sun is our routine religion which he sent down with a young man. Before this, there were prayers to him through the smoking of the pipe and by burning the sweet grass, the cedar, the sweet pine, the sage, and the juniper. The smoke carried our prayers and askings upward to Creator Sun. But Creator Sun wanted his children to always remember him throughout the year. He had to think of some way to keep their minds on him every day.

It was nearing midsummer, just as he was beginning to start back to the southern hemisphere, all of the many different berries, the roots, and the meat animals were at their ripest and fattest, when Creator Sun thought of an idea. It was also the time of the year the Piegans held their annual observance of the many holy pipe bundles and other sacred things. It was a time when the people got together for their annual meetings and social gatherings. This would be about the second week of July. Moon of a Big Circle Encampment was the Native name for July at the time, and it was named after what took place each year from time untold at a place between Cypress Hills and the Sweet Grass Hills. This was an annual gathering place for all of the members of the once-great Piegan group of Natives. This annual gathering lasted about eight weeks. This was also a place where the many Chiefs met and got their orders from the one great head Chief of all clans of this Piegan group. So this big encampment and the time of the year gave Creator Sun a plan that would enable all of the people to remember their Creator Sun.

Creator Sun's plan began to take shape the very next year, quite a while before the annual encampment was to begin. At this particular time, the head Chief of the Piegans was a very kind-hearted man. His compassion was for all life—human life, animal life, bird life, spiritual life, and all existing life of nature. When you are some certain way, it rubs off onto your immediate family, so this Chief's family also were very compassionate to the Chief's subjects. Anyone in need of some sort of help, the Chief and his family were there, ready to assist in any way. In turn, they too were loved by their people. It wasn't much of a family this head Chief had, there were only three of them—him, his wife, and a daughter that was now just old enough to get a husband. Generally, parents of all the girls selected their son-in-laws from the available slickerfoots, the single men and boys. They could select anyone for their daughters, a very young man or a very old man, and the daughter must always take what is selected for her by her parents. There wasn't any talking back to parents in those days. Parents always knew best.

The head Chief and his wife were so thoughtful to their only daughter, that they got together and between the two of them decided to let her find her own man that she wanted. She only answered them that she wasn't ready to find a man yet. This went on each time they asked her who she wanted for a husband. At this same time, the young and old slickerfoots came to her, asking her if she would marry them. Each one she told the same thing, that she wasn't ready for a selection of a husband yet. The girl was always in their tipi with her mother, helping her around, instead of being out there playing with the other girls. It seemed she didn't ever want to leave the tipi to be seen by the other people. There wasn't anything wrong with her, she was very pretty and neat. She dressed just so good with the dress they wore in those days. She wasn't sick or deformed in anyway, but for some strange reason she didn't want to mix with either her age group or even the older people. The people was already talking about this behind their backs, and it was getting stronger as it went along. The Chief and his wife had already got wind of this talking, but they weren't saying much about it. They loved their daughter, and deep in their hearts they knew there had to be very good reason why she didn't want to get married. Nevertheless, the talking went on.

Practically all of the slickerfoots had already approached the Chief's daughter asking her for marriage, and all of them she refused, saying she wasn't ready to pick her man just yet. Now those single men began to talk of the Chief's daughter, saying she is deformed, she is both a man and woman. Many talks of her went on. If she heard any of them, she didn't mind, she was set on her ideas and her belief. As time went on, it got worse, people were now talking of her openly. This was getting to her parents and it was making things look bad for them, because he was the head Chief of all the great Tribe of Piegans.

One night her parents couldn't take the talking anymore. They had to know once and for all why their only daughter hadn't taken any of these many men, young and old, for her husband. They sat down by her after she had gotten in bed. The Chief bluntly put the question to her. Why did she refuse all of those wonderful men, both young and old? Some were very well to do, and all of them seemed to be worth marrying. "Why, why have you continually refused a marriage? Are you what they all say about you? Give us a straight answer."

The girl sat up in her bed, tears were coming out of her eyes, she looked straight into her father's and mother's eyes. She wanted to make a lie about all of this, because they might think of it as very foolish why she hadn't got married. But it would hurt the folks if she lied to them about all this, she must speak the truth that she may be upheld by her parents after this. And she must make them believe her story, because it was very unbelievable.

The girl began, "I love you two very much. There isn't anything that I wouldn't do for you, even if you two asked me to jump off a high cliff or a high mountain, you wouldn't get through talking to me before I jumped. I love both of you that much. Now, whatever I have to say is very unbelievable, and maybe the two of you will not believe me, but it's the truth.

"It is true I have been asked by all of the single men of this camp in marriage and I have steadily refused them all. It's not that I don't want to get married, and there is nothing wrong with me. I'm healthy and I'm whole, I'm not deformed like the people now are thinking and talking, and most of all, I'm very pretty and young. I haven't ever been with any man or boy since I became of age. All of this is very important for you two to understand.

"I have a very powerful restriction by someone above us all, not to marry anyone. I am his and he is mine. I must stay as I was at my birth, no man must bother me, because he has taken me as his wife. I belong only to our Creator Sun, and if he lets me free of him in some way, then I can get married to anyone else. But as long as he has forbidden me and owns my body and soul, I must obey him.

"People are talking about me, but let them talk. I must not please them, I must please him, our Creator Sun. Believe me, my beloved mother and father, it's a high honor to be selected as a bride by a very high spiritual being, and it's more, he is our Creator Sun of all life. Just let people talk. I know and you know why I don't get married, why I have refused all the men and boys that approached me for my hand in marriage. We know the truth and we talk with the truth."

It was a surprise and quite a shock to the parents of this young girl to hear their daughter's story of a marriage to Creator Sun. They believed her story as she told it, and they would go along with her. They must not listen to other people talk about them all. Their daughter had told them that in time they would find out the real truth of her story, but right now they must just go along with her. If this was real true, then there must be a very great goodness within this small family for Creator Sun to pick their only daughter. Deep in their hearts, the mother and father of this girl felt very proud to have a daughter that was good, kind, and obedient, which had paid off now in something very, very great. She told them further of how it all began.

As she laid sleeping one night, the girl dreamt of Creator Sun coming down to her. And without any warning, Creator Sun came right into their tipi and sat down by her. In her dream, the Creator Sun was very hot as he sat near by her. The girl didn't mind it a bit, and right then she didn't know who this being was. As he sat by her, he came right to the point of why he had come to see this girl. Creator Sun told her that at long last he had come to the right place to find her. He's been all over, he said, everywhere he had looked, it was the same with most young girls—they had either been around men and boys or they were too mean to be around. But now Creator Sun had come to this place and it was about the last place he could have looked. He found her, just what he was looking for, a young girl that was old enough to get married, very pretty, and she had everything Creator Sun wanted to find in one girl—mainly, honesty and virginity.

As the girl was telling this story, she pulled a small buckskin bag from her own carrying pouch. This small bag was adorned with red-winged wood-pecker feathers, all of its fringes were of these feathers. Handing it to her father, she told him, "This is what he gave me in the dream I had of him. This bag was left by him in my own carrying bag." The father and mother were astounded over this bag their daughter showed them. They knew she was telling the truth, she hadn't ever had a previous experience of Creator Sun. These fringes on this pouch proved to them that it was true. Creator Sun really did come to her. As far as feathers went, the red-winged wood-pecker's feathers were the most sacred of all feathers. All Natives respect them, they belong to Creator Sun. Creator Sun was the only being that could use the red-winged woodpecker feathers on any of his belongings. All of his clothing was fringed with these red-winged woodpecker feathers, no one else was entitled to use them. How could she have known about it, about the red-winged woodpecker feathers that belong to Creator Sun? No one has ever told her the story of the great being, Creator Sun, and the way he dressed the few times he came down to Mother Earth and walked on it.

It was nothing but happiness they all felt, a blessing from Creator Sun. The three of them didn't spread this news around, for the simple reason that the people wouldn't believe this crazy-sounding excuse. It would seem just that way to the people, a crazy excuse for their daughter. Who would ever believe what they would say about their daughter's marriage to Creator Sun? It was just too unbelievable to anyone. Even at that time, people thought of the sun as just a sun of the day to light things up and warm things. And besides, it's far from the ground, away, way up there where no one could ever get at it. So the three of them kept their mouths quiet, they knew what it really was all about.

In this same camp, all of the teenage boys and young men were making fun of another young teenager, harassing and teasing him about the Chief's daughter, telling him that she and him were alike. "She has something wrong with her, she can't get married because she is both a girl and a boy at the same time, she is a cross woman." (A cross woman was really a hermaphro-dite, both a man and a woman.) "You can't get married because you have that big ugly scar on your cheek. You two would make very good mates, so why don't you ask her to have you for a husband?" They teased this young man on and on, harassed him about his big ugly scar on the right cheek. A big ugly welt that went from his ear to the corner of his mouth.

This young lad with this big ugly welt of a scar was called Scarface by all of these people that knew him. Scarface was raised by an old lady. His parents had died when he was still an infant, and this old lady was one of his grandparents. He wasn't very well to do, the old lady and him were very poor. He was too young to do very much in the line of living, so mostly, the two of them had to live on whatever food was available to them. It was mostly leftovers at the *pis-kun* that the two had to pick over and eat. It was seldom that one of the hunters would throw a good piece of meat at the old lady. She would eagerly grasp it and make small pieces of dried meat with it. But, even for this meager food they got almost daily, the two always gave thanks to their Creator Sun before they took one bite of the hard-gotten food. As poor as they were, they were very devout to Creator Sun.

Day after day, this poor lad was teased and harassed over the girl, the Chief's daughter, that the two of them should get married, they were two of a kind. It got so tiresome for the young lad with the ugly scar to hear every day all through the day, until he went to bed. One morning, bright and early, Scarface got up and ate his morning meal his grandma had prepared. After he had ate the meal, he told his grandma, "I'm going to the Chief's daughter and ask her to marry me, I'm so tired of hearing it every day from these boys my age, I have decided to really go and ask her, it might keep these boys quiet about teasing me over it. I know I'm very poor and I don't have a chance with her. I don't think she would give a second look at me. But I'll only try just for the simple reason that the boys might leave me alone after this." He got up, and just as he was going out of the doorway, his grandma said after him, "Ah-yah-ho, ah-goo, gah-kit-skay-chiwoo-keem. It's a useless try, go on and get an excellent wife."

Scarface didn't listen to anyone now, he went right to the Chief's tipi. Without hesitation, Scarface went right on in. It just happened, the mother and father of this girl were out somewhere. It didn't surprise the girl to see Scarface come in. In a way, she was expecting him for quite some time. Scarface was about the last of the single men that would come to propose to her. She told Scarface why he came. Scarface was dumbfounded, he could hardly answer her. She went on to say Scarface had come to propose to her like all the rest of the slickerfoots that she had turned down. She also told Scarface she would give him a different answer. She was willing to marry him, but it was going to be one of the hardest things to do for both of them, and it was even harder for him, Scarface. But, if he really wanted her, he would go all the way for her.

Scarface couldn't believe his ears. He asked her what had to be done to get married to her. She told Scarface that he must go look for Creator Sun and ask him if he could have this girl that he claimed as his bride of this earth. "Creator Sun must un-do that big scar on your face to prove that you really seen him and talked with him. Creator Sun will tell you what has to be done so we can get married."

This was almost too much for Scarface, his heart sank almost down to his feet. How! How in this world could anyone talk with Creator Sun when he's far, far away up there, the heat is so intense it could be felt all the way down here? How am I to get near him? All of these questions flashed through Scarface's mind. To him, this was impossible.

It seemed as if the girl was reading his mind. She told him, "When anyone wants something so much, there is nothing impossible to do for them. If you really want me in marriage, then there is nothing to stop you from getting me. But first, Creator Sun must let me go from the bonds he has me in, he must release me from that sacred tie he has around me. I'm his and he is mine and it shall be that way until he gives me up from the sacred tie. So go, Scarface. I have a lot of pity for you, the way you are teased and the way they talk about me, too. I know for sure, Creator Sun has a lot of pity for the both of us. But you must seek him and find him, tell him what we have to do to stop all of the talking against the two of us."

Scarface was still thinking he should just as well be dead than to try and do all of what the girl had told him. Thinking and thinking how it could be done, it was impossible. He was thinking this all the time he was standing before the girl, in her tipi. Her words would flash through his mind. "If you really want me, there is nothing impossible." Then again, he could see all of those boys and young men harassing him. Further, Scarface could see if he done all of this, this pretty girl that none of these boys and men could get as a wife would be his. She had said so herself. At long last, Scarface broke his silence and told the girl he would try to find Creator Sun. He would start immediately to seek him.

Scarface bid goodbye to the girl, and she in turn bid the best of luck to him, to find Creator Sun and soon. Going to the small tipi he lived in with the old lady he had known as his parent, Scarface told her what he had encountered, the obstacles he had to go through to have the girl. No one of this camp knew of the girl's marriage to the Creator Sun. Everyone thought she was off of her rocker or a queer or a cross woman. Now it was Scarface, the girl, and her parents that knew the secret of her steadfast refusal to marry. Scarface got some advice from his grandma, the old lady, how to get started on this great love venture. First, Scarface must go find an old wise man that had the know-how of quest seeks. The old lady, too, was quite skeptical about this venture. "How could my grandson possibly talk with Creator Sun? He is so far beyond our reach, far away from our Mother Earth. I truly don't think anyone could do it," the old lady thought. "But! It's him and not me that is going out to seek Creator Sun. In a way, my grandson is crazy to do this."

Scarface went out and began to ask around for a wise old man that had a lot of power, while his grandma got to work on several pairs of moccasins he should take along on this venture. Everyday moccasins were plainly made, no fancy stuff on them. They were made very sturdy for long wear and as thick as could be made on the soles, so they wouldn't wear through so fast.

Scarface made some good contacts with several powered old men. He sorted them out and compared them with one another. He found about three that would be good to talk with, and it didn't take Scarface very long to find the right one, the most knowledgable one and with great powers.

He was anxious now to begin this journey of finding the Sun. Somehow! The girl had given him much courage, and his courage to find Creator Sun got even greater after he talked with the wisest of the older men that had powers. Before he could start to seek Creator Sun, Scarface must meet all requirements and restrictions set by this wise old man. First, it was a long sweat bath with this old man to cleanse off his body in order to go to the first stop of this journey. The sweat lasted all day and with all of the things that went with it—sweet grass, tobacco and smoking, prayer after prayer, and a big meal after all of this had taken place. Then it was pay for the old man. With whatever Scarface could gather, and with help from some of the old lady's relations, the wise old man got quite a few valuable things for his part. Last of all, last-minute information and advice on how to go about this—where to go, what to do, the next place to go to until the seek is completed.

All was ready for the next morning. That night, the old lady and Scarface sat up almost all night, the old lady giving Scarface her last advice for him, and to take along enough tobacco to last for a long time, sweet grass, his robe and other smaller things, such as flint, dry moss for starting fires, and his flint knife. Scarface had quite a load after he got packed for the next morning. It was getting near dawn when they finally got to have a little rest for the night and for his trip ahead. He was to leave with sunrise. Scarface didn't sleep much. Before sunrise, he was up and ate lots of dried meat and back fat. His lunch was ready for him—a large piece of whole liver that was cooked in the hot coals of the fire, and back fat to go with it, seasoned and sprinkled with dried wild peppermint. Patties of dried berries too to go with the meat. Lots of dried meat, smoked with quaking aspen wood, yum yum. Most of all, he didn't forget the many moccasins his grandma made for him to take along on this venture.

Moccasins were a very necessary part of travel in those early days. The moccasin can be made from tanned buckskin of either elk or moose. But the buffalo hide, after it's tanned, was the toughest for use in making moccasins that would wear for a while, in any weather or terrain, especially when it is smoke-tanned. For some reason, a smoke-tanned hide seemed extra tough. When a traveler is to travel for several days, he makes sure he takes enough pairs of moccasins to last him until he gets back from his trip. Before travel, if the folks aren't able to help you with the several pairs of moccasins, the traveler hires someone to make him several extra pairs to take along. A good smoked-tanned robe, large enough to cover one's body and yet soft and light, was a necessity for a traveler.

If the trip is a hunting trip or just a common trip for plain business, weapons—such as the flint knife, the light hammer of stone (known by white people as a tomahawk), the bow and arrows, and even a spear—were taken along. All of these came into use at one time or another.

If a travel was for a divine purpose, such as a quest of vision, seek of supernatural powers, or just plain devotion, weapons are left at home. Just the flint knife, pipe and tobacco, sweet grass or whatever kind of incense one uses, a pouch, and his robe are the only things that are supposed to be taken along. No food or water for the seeker until he either sees a vision or he stays the full four days of a quest. No more then the required four days and nights to contact a spirit. If it isn't done in those four days and nights, the one must begin all over again. Seek a different old man with powers and begin anew from there.

The sun was just starting to peek over the east horizon when Scarface got on his way. His first seek was at the east peak of the Sweet Grass Hills. (Sweet Grass Hills is one the mistranslated words of the Piegans. The right translation was Sweet Pine Mountains. Sweet pine is another of our nature incense, and the Sweet Grass Hills are full of sweet pine. The hills or mountains of that particular range is a landmark for the Native, because sweet pine is so abundant there, in the Sweet Grass Hills. There are three peaks of the small mountain range, running west to east in the north central part of Montana.)

Scarface had a long ways to go as he left his camp. He didn't know how this seek was going to turn out, good or bad, and he wasn't too sure himself if he was going to return safely or otherwise. Maybe this was a no-return trip. Good and bad things went through his mind as he started leaving the camps behind. He could feel a lump in his throat as he got further and further away from the camps. Looking back every now and then, he soon realized he was out of sight of those camps he loved so much. A tear or two came running out of his eyes as the day wore on and as he got further from the camps that were a long time out of sight. But on the other hand, if it was Creator Sun's and Mother Earth's wish to achieve this impossible seek of Creator Sun, it would be his turn to belittle all of those men and boys that made so much fun of him and of the Chief's daughter, too.

It was several days' journey to the Sweet Pine Mountains. The old man told him that it was all right to eat and drink water as he went along. But once the sweat hut was erected near the location of his quest, eating and drinking water was prohibited until he achieved his quest or the required four days and nights were up, whichever came first. Then again he could eat all he wanted to and as much as he wanted to. Restrictions about eating or drinking on a vision quest were only the four required days and nights of the actual quest, no more or no less. Prayers, smoking of the pipe, and singing of holy songs—songs your advisor told you to sing or holy songs that may belong to your parents or grandparents—are the order for the duration of the four-day quest.

Once he got to the base of the easternmost of the three mountain peaks, Scarface made a camp. He erected a sweat hut to cleanse off his body and to purify himself for the next four days and nights of his vision quest with the right incense he was told to use by the old man that had anointed and conditioned him for this special vision quest. It was well towards evening when all was ready for Scarface. He was all alone, no one to depend on or to call on for aid. Everything must be done by him from now on until he completes this quest in one way or another. For the last time in the next four days and nights, Scarface ate all he could and drank all the water he could before he began the sweat.

Scarface was already at the exact location on top of the easternmost peak of the Sweet Pine Mountains where there was a shelter, a round mound of rocks piled up for this particular purpose. He had his tobacco, pipe, and pouch, with the incense of sweet grass braided for easier carrying (the tobacco is mixed with mashed or fine-cut kinnikinnick leaves that are sun dried and are nature's natural tobacco mix for milder smokes), and his flint knife. The knife isn't used for a weapon, it's carried for cutting many things, especially for meat, tobacco, digging for roots, and many times for cutting small branches that are used in the making of a sweat hut or arbor.

This was the first evening of his quest for a vision that would take him to a meeting with Creator Sun. It was an impossible mission, that's what he had in his mind most of the time.

Scarface's thoughts went through his mind as he sat there on the mountain top. In the years he has been on this Mother Earth, never has he heard of anyone that met Creator Sun personally. He had heard of the legends of Creator Sun at the beginning of time many, many years ago, hundreds of years ago. Creator Sun would often come down to his children to comfort them or to help them with their problems, because it was only the beginning of human beings and it was a very young world then. In the past several hundreds of years, Scarface hadn't ever heard of anyone to meet personally with Creator Sun, only in dreams was such things. Now Scarface was sitting on this easternmost peak of the Sweet Pine Mountains to find out how to meet personally with Creator Sun and ask him for the Chief's daughter that he claimed as an earthly bride. Somehow, this seemed kind of foolish to Scarface, but he is already here, he might just as well go through with it to the finish.

Nothing happened in the next two nights, the first two nights of this vision quest. It was the third night that a spirit came to him. The spirit did not come too close and he didn't bother. The spirit just stood in a distance from the stone enclosure of the sleeping area. Without making a sound, the spirit left after he got through with his observance of Scarface and the surrounding area. After a good night's sleep, Scarface woke up bright and early in the morning of the fourth day. This would be his last night up on this peak, and if he didn't do any good here, he must give it a try on one of the other two peaks of these Sweet Pine Mountains. There was nothing to do this last day, he still couldn't eat or drink anything yet because of the one more night he had to spend up here yet. All Scarface could do was to lay around, sit up, and sing holy songs and pray for something to come of this vision quest. All this last day he done this. It kind of made the day short for him, he was very gaunt and dehydrated from the lack of food and water in the past three days and nights. The sun went down finally after a seemingly long day. As twilight shadows fell, Scarface was as ready as could be for the last night's quest for a vision. He prayed and sang the holy songs the old wise man told him to sing. His pipe was filled with the mixed tobacco and he was burning a little bit more of the sweet grass. In other words, he was trying very hard to coax the spirits to come this last night.

Darkness came. Scarface laid down for the night, but he was wide awake laying there. He was still a-singing the holy songs of the old man and praying very hard for the spirits. He must've tired himself out. Before he knew it,

Scarface fell asleep. There was no telling how long he slept, when he had a rude awakening. Someone had grabbed him by his ankles and was throwing him out of the stone mound he was sleeping in. He grabbed onto the bigger stones and hung on for dear life. He was squirming around and trying to free himself from whatever it was that had ahold of him and was throwing him all over. The thing let go and Scarface went tumbling a little ways downhill. He didn't give up or even get frightened, he was warned of such things by the wise old man that anointed him for this vision quest. As soon as he got his breath, Scarface went back into the stone structure. Grabbing his pipe that was all ready to light, Scarface had just enough time to light it. The spirit of this peak hadn't given Scarface much time since the spirit grabbed him by his ankles as he laid there asleep. With the few moments of time that he had, and before the spirit had time to get at him again, Scarface was able to light the pipe with the ever-present live charcoal in buffalo horn he had just for that purpose. As soon as the pipe and tobacco came alive with the live charcoal and it started to smoke, Scarface a-puffing away, offered the smoke to the spirit before it came at him again. The spirit wasn't so mean after all, it readily accepted the pipe smoke, which calmed down the rough stuff.

A vision quest is very mysterious, because one is dealing with supernatural spirits. A spirit is one of the many lives of nature. All things that are visible to the eye are alive—mountains, rivers, lakes, trees, rocks, the birds, animals, stars, moon, wind, thunder, lightning, clouds, and the sun. Creator Sun is the most powerful spirit of them all, it is above them all. The sun has more supernatural power than anything else within this void, as far as your mind can wonder in space and earth. No others can surpass or even come close to his powers. Scientists can search forever in space among the many stars and planets, they will never find anything more powerful than Creator Sun. A spirit can be so rough or so timid, whichever way it wants to treat you before it bestows his power on you. A spirit can put you to sleep in a split second, and that's what mostly happens on these vision quests of the people. If the spirit accepts the pipe smoke, he'll only take seconds to put you to sleep or in a trance. It's then that the spirit will give you its powers of mystery.

That was happening to Scarface. As the spirit of this easternmost peak of the Sweet Pine Mountains took those first few puffs of the pipe, Scarface fell slowly to sleep, maybe a trance. The spirit bestowed his powers on Scarface. Before the spirit left him, Scarface asked him what the old man said to be sure and ask any spirit—where to go to find the way to Creator Sun. The spirit told him he wasn't the one to know, but he knew there was a way to get to Creator Sun. Scarface must go far to the west to some very large mountains and to the highest of them all. Scarface must sleep there to seek out the spirit of that mountain, who should know the answer to Scarface's question.

To be near accurate, Scarface started on this particular mission, the North

Flight of Geese Moon, which is about the mid-part of what we know as the month of March. It took him four months to complete his journey to Creator Sun and get back to his camps.

Looking west the next morning after he woke up from that vision or dream on top of the easternmost peak of the Sweet Pine Mountains, Scarface almost cried. The distance seemed so far, far away. He was terribly hungry too, and getting sort of weak from lack of food. He made his way down the peak to the small creek he made a sweat hut by, before his adventure on the peak. Scarface had tied some of his lunch high on a limb of a tree. Getting it down, he sat down and ate his fill, drinking from the running creek. After the meal, he felt better. He got busy again and made a new sweat hut to cleanse himself off and purify himself for his next journey to the high mountains west of him.

After a good night's sleep, Scarface left the Sweet Pine Mountains before daylight the next morning, headed westward to the high mountains far away. It took him several days to reach the present-day Rocky Mountains, going westward. Scarface had seen the highest peak and he made his way towards it. It was late in the evening. Before climbing to the top of the high peak Scarface made his sweat hut again to purify himself and to cleanse himself off from any contacts he might've made with bad things of nature. Scarface once again ate very hearty, the next four days and nights he wouldn't get a taste of food or water again. He was all ready for this next day, he had his fill of food and water the last evening. Today he just sat and was reverent. He sang many holy songs and almost continually he burned the incense of the sweet grass. Along with it, he never hardly stopped praying. The day was now getting late, the sun wasn't too far from sinking in the west. It was time Scarface must go up on to the top of this high mountain and seek for what he was out looking for, a way to Creator Sun.

Some places are calm all the way through the quest, while in other places the spirit gets kind of rough with the seeker of spiritual visions before it gives out any of its powers to the seeker of vision. This high mountain was one of those that was calm all the way through. The mountain spirit came to Scarface the third night and on the fourth night too, Scarface got more powers from this mountain spirit and information about the way to Creator Sun. He was told by this mountain spirit that he must continue on westward to the land of higher mountains and where water is all over, no end to the water. Scarface must sleep on top of the highest peak, where summer moons are never seen. After reaching this place, Scarface must prepare for the cold on top of that mountain or he would surely freeze up there on top.

Once more Scarface set out again on a journey where no one ever ventured before, his quest to find the way to Creator Sun. For days Scarface traveled on and on, ever westward, his eyes glued to the places ahead of him, far and near, always looking for the bigger and higher mountains the spirit talked about and the big water of no end. Scarface was walking against time, he must make it to the place before the berries start coming off of the bushes. The berries were now only blooming, the weather was getting warmer, and as he traveled onward and forever westward, the days were getting hotter and hotter. Scarface's heart really raced over this, he thought he was getting closer to the land of Creator Sun. On and on he walked.

One day as he came over a high ridge, far out among the sand and sagebrush-covered land, where one couldn't get under anything from the hot sun, Scarface seen, far, far away, in the blue horizon, the outline of some great big high mountains. It took his breath away. He was almost there, he could see those big high mountains now. Scarface hadn't been eating too much of anything, there wasn't anything to eat along the way, it was mostly roots that kept him a-going. Once in a while he ran into the lakes where the ducks already had laid eggs, these he would take and boil for his lunch. Lack of food was showing on him as he went along. He had lost much weight, but onward he went.

Those mountains he seen weren't all that close. For many more days he had to walk before he ever reached the lowlands of those mountains, and they were still further on. Scarface couldn't turn back now, he thought to himself. He would find what he was after or die looking for a way to Creator Sun. Scarface always had this in his mind, no one ever talked about anyone reaching the land of Creator Sun, but he was ready to die trying to find it.

One day, as it was getting a little late, coming up a steep hill through the timber, Scarface came out into an opening, and it seemed to be the top of this long steep hill. From this opening among these trees, Scarface seemed to almost kiss the side of a huge mountain. It was the mountain he was looking at many days ago from far to the east of here. Closer to it, Scarface soon seen that it was almost covered over with the cold snow, it looked like one big pile of snow in one place. It looked very cold to Scarface as he stood there gazing at the great big mountain. He knew he must climb this high cold mountain to find out if that big mountain spirit knew how to find the way to Creator Sun. Scarface wasn't all that close to the big high mountain just yet. Because the mountain was enormous, it looked just so close to Scarface from where he was standing in that opening. It took him a few more days to reach that mountain. Once again, at the base of this big huge mountain, Scarface made the usual sweat bath to purify himself and to cleanse his body of unpurified things. The day was still early yet after his sweat. He didn't wait for anything, he must get up there before dark so he could at least get this first night over with up there. The mountain looked awful cold. Scarface battled his way to the top through snow drifts, the slick ice. He had to go this way and that way. It took him a very long time to make it to the top, but that was the main thing, to reach the spot up there to sleep in quest of a vision.

Scarface, with his ever praying to the great spirits of this mountain and his continual singing of the holy songs, made time seem a little short, kept his mind off of what he was facing. He was well prepared for this, because he was warned of the cold by the last spirit from those other mountains, far, far to the land of sunrise. On the second night, the spirit of this huge mountain came around to the place of quest. The spirit didn't get rough with Scarface. In fact, it didn't even say a word, Scarface only seen it once that second night, and it disappeared. The third night the spirit bothered Scarface for a while. Scarface would see the spirit on one side of him and it would disappear and reappear somewhere else all around him. The spirit seemed to be playing tricks on Scarface. This went on for quite some time, then the spirit left for the night.

The fourth night came. Scarface was now feeling the cold very much, it was penetrating the warm buffalo robe he wrapped himself in, and all this time he was singing and praying for the spirit to come to him so he could get off of this cold huge mountain. The spirit didn't come like any of the spirits before. With no warning at all, something very cold seized Scarface. It was just so cold and it happened so suddenly, he didn't have time to think. Scarface passed out like lightning as that sudden cold touched all of his body. He was in this condition when that huge mountain spirit came onto him. All of his powers were bestowed onto Scarface, but the question of the way to Creator Sun, this great big mountain spirit couldn't answer.

The spirit told Scarface, "I have great powers to help all or to kill life, but I must say, I don't own the power to find Creator Sun. You will have to go on to the water of no end, there you might find someone to show you the way to Creator Sun." When Scarface woke up from that encounter with the huge mountain spirit, he was laying near the place where he made the sweat hut before he went to up to the mountain top. Scarface was very thankful for this, at least he didn't have to fight his way back down the mountain side, but he was very disappointed in his vision. He didn't find out what he wanted most, to find the way to Creator Sun.

Scarface cried. He was getting weak from lack of food and he didn't bring anything along to use as a weapon to kill deer or elk. He couldn't even get a duck or pheasant for meat food. His moccasins had all worn out long before this and he had no hide to make more moccasins with. His feet were already bleeding from the rawness of them, walking through rocky terrain and the sharp dry branches in the forests he had to go through. He was ill and tired, but he must go on. Scarface again made a sweat after he woke up from the last quest on the cold mountain. He cried, pitying himself to be going through all of this torture just for the girl that was claimed as bride by Creator Sun. Scarface had been suffering since that Chief's daughter came of age to marry and wouldn't accept any proposals from any man or boy. Now it had to be him, Scarface, that the Chief's daughter had accepted a proposal from, but with many, many restrictions and hardships along with it to be faced as each day came and gone.

Scarface was all worn out, very, very tired, close to giving up the whole idea and never returning home as he sat there thinking. That hope of doing the impossible no one had ever done from time beginning to this present time he was living in. Scarface didn't want to show anyone up, he didn't want to get even with anyone or hurt anyone. But he felt so close to it now. He couldn't make it back now even if he tried. He must go on to the big water of no end, there he would either accomplish his mission or die. Scarface picked moss and large leaves to pad his raw feet and tore some of his shirt to wrap around over these leaves and moss onto his feet. He again went on his way towards the big water of no end.

It wasn't that far, but it took Scarface several days before he reached the big water of no end. Ragged clothing of buckskin, shaggy hair, dirty face, and very, very haggard, very thin from lack of food, and he felt it. Scarface was getting weaker each day. Coming to the high banks of this big water of no end and looking out over the big water, the water seemed to run on over a hill— deep, far out there, away as far as the eyes could see. He stood there amazed over such a big water. Scarface made his way down to the big water's edge. His body ached all over from many, many days of travel. His feet burning and aching from going barefooted for many days through jagged rocks and the thorny timbers across those rugged mountains. Scarface came to the water's edge. Without hesitation, he waded right on into the water to bathe his poor aching body and feet. After a long cool bath, Scarface came to shore and held his feet in the water to continue cooling them off, they were burning and hurting so much.

As always, he sat there singing his holy songs and continually praying, only this time he prayed for death to come to him if he can't find the way to Creator Sun. It seemed to him this was the end of the trail to Creator Sun, because of the big water of no end. How could he possibly cross it? How far does this big water go? Surely, he couldn't begin to swim it, this has to be the end of the impossible trail to Creator Sun, and it meant the end for him too. He couldn't return to his camps and face all of those men and boys, they would tease him to death, so he might as well die here now. All of this was going through his mind as he sat there bathing his raw, aching feet. Hungry, his feet too sore to look for roots or something that would give him a bite to chew on. He couldn't even drink any of the big water, it tasted awful.

Scarface cried and sang songs, the holy songs of the old man that had anointed him for this mission of seek for the trail to Creator Sun. He prayed almost continually as he sat there with his feet in the big water of no end. The water must've soothed his feet and aching body, he must've fallen asleep with his feet still in the water. Sleeping there with his feet in the cool water, he had a dream or a vision. Just a ways out, several large white birds were swimming around, they weren't afraid of him. Those birds swam very close to him. There was among them a very large white bird, he must be their leader, Scarface thought. Scarface knew these large birds as the Piegans call them, white large quill feathered. They were swans. As he sat there still a-singing and praying and crying for help in his dream or vision (it might have been a trance by that extra-large white bird) this extra-large white bird swam towards him. This bird asked him why he was crying, praying, and singing with his feet in the water.

Scarface didn't hesitate to tell of his troubles. He told his story from the time this all started, how he traveled to find a spirit that knew the trail to Creator Sun, the promise from the Chief's daughter if he found Creator Sun, and right up to this place. He was too weak to travel back to those far-away camps he left many, many days ago. Long ago, Scarface had lost track of the days since he left those camps.

He told the Swan Chief, "I'm all in now, I have given up all hope of ever reaching the land of Creator Sun. I can't go on from here, I'll never be able to cross this big water of no end. I can't even swim out to where it disappears over the hill out there, almost as far as the eye can see from here on land. I have gone through a long suffering trying to reach our Creator Sun to ask him for the Chief's daughter that he has claimed as his bride and now I can't go back to where old men and the younger men alike would tease me to death, I'll be the laughingstock of that camp. I could never live it down. I'm so weak, I can't even rustle for food. Look at my feet, they are so raw from all of this seeking they are bleeding, I just can't take another step barefooted. Even with moccasins, I couldn't begin to walk for several days at least, I would starve to death within that time. My clothes are nothing but shreds on me. I wouldn't want that Chief's daughter to see me in this more pitiful shape than I was before I left that camp. Everyone sees my big ugly scar on my face, with that on my face and the way I would look to them, it would even be more rugged. No! I must die here and forget the trail and the land of Creator Sun."

The Swan Chief had much pity for Scarface after he had heard Scarface's story and had seen those very raw, bleeding feet of his still in the water. The swan Chief told Scarface, "My son, I will help you. It's my tribe that knows the trail to Creator Sun and the land he lives in. It is very, very far from here, but only we know where to go. Just be ready before sunrise in the morning to leave here. Never mind how, we will worry about that.

"There is a very hard restriction to this. From the time I tell you to close your eyes, you must keep them eyes closed. If you open them eyes of yours, that will be it. You will not have another chance to ever find that invisible trail and land of our Creator Sun. Use those ears of yours and do what you are told to do. I pity you very, very much my son, and I'm the only one that's going to help you achieve what you are seeking. To find Creator Sun and have him remove that big ugly scar on your cheek and for him to hand over the Chief's daughter that he claims as his bride of earth. Beware, my son Scarface, and keep those eyes of yours closed until I give you the word to open them.

"This isn't a dream, but I'm actually talking to you while you really are in a trance from fatigue, but you will be all right when you wake up at dawn. Under your pillow of moss, you will find a rattle, a head of a swan made into a rattle when you wake up. This will prove to you that I didn't come to you in a dream and this is for real, that you will reach Creator Sun after all, if you keep those eyes of yours closed until I tell you to open them." The Swan Chief swam out to the rest of the swans, who had all bunched up in one place while he was talking to Scarface.

Scarface found out something in his lifetime. He found out that to achieve something was a very hard thing to do, it had many catches. It had many pains with the good of it too. It had much suffering where one's life is gambled in many ways. One must go through torture for something he wants so very much.

It must've been a long sleep. As the Swan Chief swam away, Scarface woke up, or so it seemed to him. Scarface remembered the dream so well, he cried as he seen a flock of swans swimming around not too far out from where he was sitting after waking up. He was wishing that what he dreamt about would be true. Praying, singing as he sat there looking out at the swans and at the big water of no end. This was surely the end of the trail for him, and he had such a good dream. Without looking around on his bed moss and his robe, Scarface was reaching around for his pouch, he wanted to smoke and at the same time offer a smoke to the Swan Chief. Scarface touched something strange to his hand at his pillow of moss, he turned fast to see what it was. His heart almost stopped as he seen a swan-head rattle. Scarface was very surprised to see this. He knew right then that it wasn't a dream he had, but it actually happened while he was asleep. Without wondering about it, or hesitating, he immediately got busy and lit a little fire. There he burned sweet grass to pray and thank the Swan Chief.

The east was beginning to light up more as the sun would soon be coming over the horizon. The swans, all of them, swam towards Scarface as he still sat there on the bank of the big water of no end. Closing in on him, the Swan Chief spoke to Scarface. "I told you what has to be done to achieve this mission of yours. Spread your robe and lay on it, close your eyes very tight and don't try to see what is happening or where we are going. Just lay still and don't move. I'll tell you when to move and look."

Scarface felt himself as he began to move. He didn't know if he were up in the air or if he was being pulled over the water. All he knew was he was going along at a very rapid speed. At times he was almost tempted to open his eyes to see where he was heading. But he must keep those eyes of his closed if he wanted to accomplish what he was after. He laid still, so still that he dozed off. Scarface had his eyes tightly shut when the Swan Chief woke him up and told him to open his eyes. He was afraid to, he thought he might be dreaming all of this. The Swan Chief had to pick at his ribs to fully awaken him out of that sleep. "Open your eyes, open your eyes now, it's all right, you have made it to the land of Creator Sun. We can't wait around here, we must go back away from here and now. You will make it from here." It was the Swan Chief talking to Scarface as he laid there, and as it was by this large body of water, it looked like the big water of no end. The swans flew away, Scarface looking after them as they slowly flew out of sight far out over the water.

Scarface didn't know what to do after the swans had disappeared. He knew he couldn't walk because of his feet being so very raw and bleeding. He sat at the same spot for a very long time thinking. A scream broke that long silence. It was to his right, along this beach. He seen a figure running like mad, he looked like a small boy, and not far in the back of him was a huge bird. The bird looked like a crane, only this one was a huge one and he was after this boy.

Scarface didn't have time to think about his aching feet. Jumping up, he ran to intercept the enormous bird. Without stopping, jerking his flint knife out of its sheath, Scarface met the huge bird head on. In one smooth movement as he ran along, he sank his flint knife into the huge bird's throat near the chest. The huge bird knocked Scarface partly off his balance, but he managed to right himself. The little boy was still running and looking back as he ran on, he seen the whole thing, what Scarface done to the huge bird. The huge bird was so heavy and this happened so fast, that Scarface's knife was still in the throat of the huge bird. The huge bird didn't go far, only a body length when it fell to the ground, dead. Watching Scarface, the little boy ran back to him. As Scarface bent over the huge bird, he knew the bird was dead.

Scarface was very much surprised. When he first landed here, and not too long ago, he wasn't able to walk because of his feet being very raw from the long journey to the big water of no end to find the trail to Creator Sun's abode. But he just now noticed himself that he ran without pain to this feet. He didn't even feel anything as he ran to aid the little boy. Another surprise was, he had on a pair of moccasins, which the swans might've put on him as they brought him to this place.

Coming back to Scarface, the little boy was very happy about what happened. He was friendly, greeting Scarface in the most friendly Native way. A big smile and a hard handshake with a very loud, "O-ki." He told Scarface he was a brave man for facing the huge bird with only a knife to use to kill it. All of the people that live here are afraid of those birds. The boy was inquisitive too, he asked Scarface what his name was, what he was doing here, and where he was from.

Scarface told him his name was Boh-yi-yi, Welt on Face, because of the big welt on his right cheek, a big ugly scar that he was born with. In turn, he asked the little boy what his name might be. He said it was Ibi-so-waus-sin. Ibi-so-waus-sin means hanging as a jerky from a tripod. Jerky and dry meat are two different things. A beef jerky or buffalo jerky is a chunk of meat. It isn't cut thin, but is pulled from the lower legs of the buffalo with the muscles and tendons still in the meat and dried that way. It is dried as fast as one can, before it sours or spoils, over a fire and smoke. Dried meat is the softer flesh of the buffalo with hardly any muscles or tendons mixed with the meat. It is cut very thin in pieces as wide and long as could be cut. This cut meat is dried in the same manner as the jerky. When dry, it is very crispy and tender. This dried meat can be cooked in any way—cooked over the fire, boiled, or it could be eaten that way. The chunk dried meat or jerky is cooked only one way, it is soft boiled because of the muscles and it dries hard because it is a chunk of meat. So! Ibi-so-waus-sin really means Green or Wet Hanging Jerky.

Scarface also asked him where his folks lived. Ibi-so-waus-sin told Scarface where he lived with his parents, Ksah-koom-aukie, Earth Woman, and Nah-too-si, Superpowered or Holiness. Many people of these days translate Nah-too-si as the Sun. Again, this was a great surprise to Scarface, meeting someone of Creator Sun, his own son, Ibi-so-waus-sin. Scarface tried not to show his surprise at the boy's answers and his questions. Scarface had a hard time to conceal his uttermost surprise, that he was in direct contact with Creator Sun's own son, Ibi-so-waus-sin—Hanging Jerky, or, as it became known, Morning Star.

It was about this time when another small boy about the same age came around to the two. Ibi-so-waus-sin introduced the two, this other boy was his close cousin, Bah-tsi-dub-bi, Doer of Mistakes. He related to Bah-tsi-dub-bi what he just did to one of the huge birds. This other boy didn't stay too long, he left the two near the water of no end, going his own way. After leaving, Ibi-so-waus-sin told Scarface the boy wasn't very good about his ways, he made trouble for other people by the way he talked.

Scarface was still taken aback from the surprise of running on his feet. He sat on the bank with Ibi-so-waus-sin by him. Ibi-so-waus-sin was talking on, but Scarface wasn't listening to him, not at this time. He was praying aloud to the spirits that helped him along to here and giving thanks for what had happened this far. Looking at his feet, they were healed with no sign of the rawness on them and no pain whatsoever. He heard Ibi-so-waus-sin talking and asking the questions, but Scarface had to take time out to give thanks for all of this.

After his thanks, Scarface paid more attention to the little boy and what he had to say and ask. Ibi-so-waus-sin told Scarface that his cousin, Bah-tsi-dub-bi, was also very jealous of him, because his father Creator Sun thought of him so much. Always and always, Creator Sun took him out and taught him many things that were very necessary to life. Devotion and crafts of necessities for every day.

Ibi-so-waus-sin just couldn't stop thanking Scarface for coming to his rescue from that awful wicked bird that was after him. From there on throughout Scarface's stay with the Creator's family, Ibi-so-waus-sin idolized him for his great bravery. Scarface had staked his own life for this boy, he didn't know anything about the huge birds, but met the huge bird head on without thinking of his own life. "My father will never forget this. When I tell him of your bravery, he will do anything for you as long as you are going to be here with us." Scarface was very pleased to hear this, but he didn't show his excitement. He knew he needed something like this to get the favor he wanted so very much, but he was hoping that it would be the same with the boy's father, Creator Sun, that he be just as thankful for the boy's life as the boy himself thought of it.

The little boy, Ibi-so-waus-sin, was anxious to please Scarface to show him his appreciation for saving his life. He told Scarface, "*Oo-ki*. Come on. Let's go to my tipi and find us something to eat, you look hungry." The two jumped up. Scarface was very hungry. After all, he hadn't eaten any good food for several moons now. Up and away the two went, the little boy leading

the way and Scarface right alongside of him. It wasn't too far of a walk to
Ibi-so-waus-sin's tipi, and it was surrounded by trees and brush, green grass,
even the rolling hills and some mountains were in sight. It was a very
beautiful place. The place made Scarface stop in his tracks, to take it all in,
the beautiful surrounding countryside and Creator Sun's tipi. This was a tipi
so very pretty painted, there was none other like it. Everything in this area
Scarface noticed and took a good, long look at, to remember this for his
lifetime. He knew he would never be able to come to this place anymore, nor
could anyone else. He was just plain lucky to find the right spirits that
directed him to this place.

The tipi was a huge one, around the top of it was painted with a light blue
from the earflap to the middle of the back of it and on the right side of the
top. The emblem of the seven stars or Big Dipper was painted yellow on this
right earflap or draft regulator of the tipi. In the middle of the light blue
paint, horizontally, yellow stars were painted all the way to the back top or
back middle of the tipi. The left side was painted black around the top, the
same width as the light blue paint. On its earflap was the emblem of the
Little Dipper, a cluster of five stars in a small circle towards the top point of
the earflap and a string of stars in the middle, horizontally to the back of the
tipi. These stars were painted in red. The black field and the blue field, with
their stars of red and yellow, met squarely in the middle of the back top.

Right at the place the two paints joined with the stars and even with the
painted stars was painted the emblem of good sleep, a miller or butterfly.
The left half of this butterfly is red, the right half is yellow. Squarely in the
middle of the butterfly is a tail hanging down, the long hair of the tail of a

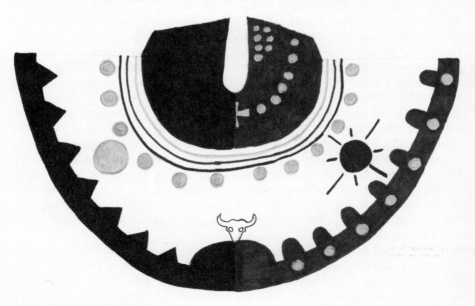

*Creator Sun's Tipi Design*

buffalo. This tail is a protection against bad spirits. Bad spirits were known to be afraid of hair in those days. Around the midsection of the tipi and on the right side, the huge emblem of the Sun was painted in red, the left midsection of the tipi was the emblem of the moon, twelve yellow moons horizontally to point out specifically the number of moons it takes for one year. Around the bottom of the right side of the tipi was the emblem of the hills all in light blue with yellow emblems of animal burrows. On the left side of the tipi, around the bottom, is the emblem of mountains with red-painted animal burrow. In the back bottom where the two paints met, in between them was painted the emblem of the sweat hut. The right half was in light blue, the other half was in black. On top of this sweat hut emblem, a buffalo skull emblem was painted. This emblem of the buffalo skull is for food and for this tipi to always have plenty of meat, because meat was the main staple of food for the Plains Natives.

Scarface stood like a statue as he took this all in, this beautiful sight, so speechless. Ibi-so-waus-sin's "*Ogie hun-nu-mok*. All right, this is it, we are here at our tipi," woke him out of his stupor. Scarface still didn't move, he was singing and praying in a low tune. He managed to utter a barely audible, "*Ki-kah*. Wait." The boy waited, he knew what this was all about. Scarface was again thanking his spirit helpers for this. The two went on into the tipi after the thanks to the spirits. As soon as Scarface stepped inside of this tipi, he felt the power of Creator Sun and Mother Earth. It felt very warm and very cozy. His mind had a very easy feeling, as if he had never been around trouble or any kind of bad thing. Breathing was much easier, Scarface felt like he could live forever in here.

He noticed everything in here. There were the Native bedsteads or pillows, the usual tipi wall liners of tanned hides. These were painted with the life of nature—mountains, hills, trees, rocks, streams, birds, animals, the emblem of lightning, thunderbird, and even the emblem of insects were painted all over the tipi wall liner. A rawhide cooking pot alongside of the fireplace and a tripod over the fireplace for cooking. A pile of granite stones, a little larger then the fists, probably about ten of them for cooking, boiling in the rawhide pot. Two beds at the far walls of the tipi, one to the right of the room and one on the left. In between the beds was a pipe bundle, and right next to it, towards the fireplace, a hollowed-out stone for burning incense of sweet grass, cedar, sage, juniper, sweet pine, and the tree moss. Between the stone and fireplace was a forked stick for getting hot coals from the fireplace and all of the different kinds of incense alongside of this forked stick. As one goes inside, to the left is the cook's area, and many partly tanned hide cases are along the wall. In these rawhide cases were food, dried roots, dried berries of many kinds, both whole or mashed, even pattied. A large rawhide case of pemmican. (Pemmican is dried meat that is pounded soft. It is mixed with either the dried sarvis berry or the mashed wild chokecherry and a little of the animal fat, most generally the backfat, which doesn't harden very much, it stays soft.)

Several of the rawhide cases contain mostly all smoke-dried meat. Dried back fat is in between the dried meat, and preserved with wild peppermint. This is also dried, pounded into bits of pieces, and sprinkled over each layer of dried meat and fat, which preserves the meat and the fat for long storage in the rawhide cases.

Scarface again was told by the boy, Ibi-so-waus-sin, to sit down and he would find some food for them to eat. Scarface was spellbound by these sights of the tipi, everything was so different from his way of life and living as he knew it at their own camps. Ibi-so-waus-sin dished out a lot of food for Scarface in a plate of closely knitted willow branches, and gave him some meat broth in a cup of a buffalo horn to wash the food down with.

As they were eating, the two were busy talking to one another. The boy was talking mostly, Scarface listening closely, this was information to him. The boy told about the huge birds, there were many of them here, and one had to be careful not to meet up with them. He told Scarface about his mother and father, Mother Earth and Creator Sun, their love for all life as it existed. Ibi-so-waus-sin told Scarface that he was left alone mostly all day, his Mother

*Creator Sun's Tipi as Set Facing East*

Earth and his father, Creator Sun, were out doing their work all day and every day. He said he was told by his mother and father to stay in or close by their tipi all the time. This was one of the days he was very careless and almost paid for it with his life. He told Scarface, "If it weren't for you to be around at that moment, I'd be in one of them huge bird's bellies right now. I'm very glad and happy that you came when you did, my pardner."

Ibi-so-waus-sin also spoke of Bah-tsi-dub-bi, Doer of Mistakes. He was a spoiled child, always doing things wrong and getting into a lot of mischief. This Bah-tsi-dub-bi was jealous of Ibi-so-waus-sin, he tried many times to get Ibi-so-waus-sin into trouble with his own parents. Ibi-so-waus-sin was too good and raised right to do anything wrong, so the parents would never believe this boy, Bah-tsi-dub-bi.

After the two got through with their meal, they went out along the beach of the big water of no end, walking and talking as they went along. They were still walking along when all of a sudden Ibi-so-waus-sin became aware of the day. He told Scarface, "We must be getting back to the tipi. It's getting a little late this day, it won't be too long before my parents will be coming home for the day." Ibi-so-waus-sin warned Scarface not to be seen by Creator Sun right away. Scarface must hide from the folks when they came into the tipi. He told Scarface, he must hide behind the tipi wall liners until he is told to come out, this was a must. Coming to the tipi of Ibi-so-waus-sin, the two went on in and waited for the folks to come home. Ibi-so-waus-sin said, "They usually come home right after the Sun goes down over the mountains. We never hardly have visitors, we will see how my father takes to visitors when he finds out you are here."

Sure enough! Right after the sun went down, the parents came home and without hesitation, came right on into the tipi, Creator Sun first, with Mother Earth close behind him. Creator Sun stopped short as they came fully into the tipi. He looked at Ibi-so-waus-sin as he sat on his bed to the north side of the room and he sniffed the air. Without talking to anyone particularly, he said, "I smell something strange in here, another human being, a stranger to this place." He didn't say anything further, he went on to his bed and sat down, Mother Earth went to her side of the room in this tipi to prepare the evening meal for them. Preparing the meal didn't take long, Ibi-so-waus-sin already had a hot fire a-going. It was then Ibi-so-waus-sin spoke up, telling his father all about the day he had. He wanted to play by the big water of no end. As he went there, about halfway, one of the big huge birds stole up on him from behind. He couldn't turn back to the tipi, he ran on to try to find something to hide in from this huge bird. The bird almost got him, but this man came about the right time to come to his rescue. This man went head on into the bird and killed it with only his bare hands and the flint knife, so Ibi-so-waus-sin took to him for his bravery and brought him home to their tipi because the man looked very hungry, he needed something to eat. "His name is Scarface, because of the big welt on his cheek. He came a long ways to find us."

As Mother Earth and Creator Sun came inside of the tipi, Scarface was hiding back of one of the tipi wall liners. But as the man came inside, immediately Scarface felt the heat, as if the fire was turned up higher or more wood was throwed on it, and the room of the tipi got so very bright that it was hard on the eyes. Scarface could hardly look over the brightness, he closed his eyes and laid very still. He listened to the conversation that took place and was waiting to hear what Creator Sun had to say about his visit there.

Creator Sun stood for a long moment before saying a word. He told Ibi-so-waus-sin, "My son, I'm very happy to hear about your new-found friend, and it gladdens my heart so very much that he saved your life from those awful huge birds. He put his own life last to save you. This Boh-yi-yi must be a brave man, he not only saved your life with his bare hands, but he came to find this place that none of my children from Mother Earth has ever tried to find and he made it here. We must treat him with kindness. We owe him a life for yours, whatever he wants for the asking, it shall be his. Bring this Boh-yi-yi to me and let your mother and me meet him. But first I must condition him for this land of ours, it may not suit him very well if I don't. Right after the conditioning of him, we shall eat. He will be staying with us for the duration of his visit, because you and him have become very good pardners."

All Ibi-so-waus-sin had to do was call Boh-yi-yi out from behind the tipi wall liner. It was just so much hotter and so much brighter out here in the room of this tipi now, it was hard to stand. Scarface had to close his eyes as he came out from behind the tipi wall liner, his body was almost burning from the intense heat. Ibi-so-waus-sin had to guide his pardner to where his father sat on bed after Creator Sun beckoned Scarface to come to him for the conditioning so he wouldn't mind this brightness and heat. Creator Sun sang a song and in his hand, he held a deep red earth paint and he also had a piece of back fat of a buffalo, which he used for mixing the paint into a soft, creamy paste. As he sang the song, Creator Sun began to smear the deep red paint all over Scarface's face first, his hair too, then all over the body. No part of Scarface's body was missed by this deep red earth paint, every bit of him was painted. Scarface was now ready to live like them, not feeling the heat, nor was it so bright for him anymore. "Now go sit by your pardner, Ibi-so-waus-sin, and we will eat," Creator Sun told Scarface.

It was this same time when Scarface also noticed Creator Sun wearing the eagle feathers and eagle plume on his hair to adorn his head and also wearing a white buffalo robe around his shoulders, and that was smeared with the red earth paint all over it, which made it look like it was a red robe. His face and hands, even his hair and all over his body, this red earth paint was smeared or painted. He looked very red to Scarface.

It is for this reason—because Creator Sun had the eagle feathers and eagle plume on his head for adornment and the red-earth-painted white buffalo robe around his shoulders—that the eagle feathers and eagle plume and the white buffalo robe are held in such a high esteem among the Indian race.

(Of course there are many versions of this particular fact, but this the most true fact.)

Scarface felt more at home after the conditioning Creator Sun done to him with his power. As the family ate their meal, Creator Sun and Scarface were exchanging stories of their own environment, the condition of their people, and many things of good information for one another. After the meal, the pipe of Creator Sun was lit up for the visitor, Scarface. This was the usual custom, the host provided the meal and the pipe smoking, a hospitality that still is done by the Native of this continent.

Natives never stay up very long. Like the old saying among them, "getting in bed with the birds." Practically all the Natives of this country go to bed after the birds of the land quiet down for the night. Once in a while a big storytelling will go on where all of the older men and their wives would gather in one tipi. The storytelling sometimes goes on for several nights, eating and telling more stories. This is seldom done and mostly done in the winter time, when nothing else is taking place.

Actually! Scarface thought he would never find the place of Creator Sun and be sitting with him and his family. Right at this particular moment, he

*The Sacred White Buffalo Robe*

felt just so very good and happy, sitting where he now was facing this family of Creator Sun. Just a day or two ago, Scarface felt he would never wake up to another day as he sat by the big water of no end, his feet dangling in the water to ease the rawness of them and to soothe the soreness from the long walk. Now! By a miracle, he was sitting before Creator Sun. He had to do something to himself to know this wasn't only a dream, but actually happening. Scarface hadn't ever heard of anyone of Mother Earth to find the land of Creator Sun. A few people talked with Creator Sun personally, but that was on the body of Mother Earth and in the legends of the people.

Scarface had a very long visit with Creator Sun and the family. His stay with them lasted for one moon, part of Leaf Moon and part of Sarvis Berry Moon. Most every day he was with Ibi-so-waus-sin, walking or just sitting and talking. The two got very attached to one another as the days went along, and as each day ended, Ibi-so-waus-sin related their day to his parents as they returned to their tipi. It was mostly about his pardner, Boh-yi-yi, the good things he done during the day while they were alone. This news from their son, Ibi-so-waus-sin, put that much more compassion for Scarface in their hearts, which was very good for Scarface when he was ready to ask for what he really came for.

Ever since the Moon of Geese Migration North, Scarface left his camps to find the way to the land of Creator Sun. It's been four moons ago and going into the fifth moon, the summer moon. Scarface was beginning to think of home a lot. He missed the camps, although some of the boys his age and even the older men had treated him a little bad over his scar and the Chief's daughter, thinking she wasn't all there because she refused them in marriage, all of them. Each day was a day longer away from that camp and it was getting heavy on the heart.

Creator Sun knows everything, you can't hide anything from him. All this time, he knew what this visit by Scarface was all about. Creator Sun was waiting on Scarface to tell him about it. Thinking about his own camps and what the people might be doing at this time brought Scarface to hurry with what he came for, and even that Creator Sun knew about it. During that day, Scarface became very quiet. Mostly he just listened to Ibi-so-waus-sin talk, sometimes he didn't answer him because of his own thoughts about his own camps. He could just visualize the goings-on in his home camp, particularly his grandma that raised him to this age. About this time of the year, all of the people gather at the sacred camping grounds northeast of the Sweet Pine Mountains to honor all of the sacred spirits, helpers of the people. This encampment consisted of nothing but religion and sacredness, holiness, it was all about prayers to the holy spirits and the Creator of all life. It was fun to be there, just to meet your relations from another clan and camp and your friends too. After the religious doings were completed, all of the many sub-Chiefs would be invited by the head Chief to talk over their problems and where each Chief might spend its fall hunt of buffalo and where each might winter their band of followers. A head Chief is the wisest one of them all, he must advise them of all the do's and don'ts after this meeting and after they go their own way again. This particular encampment lasts for six weeks or more, probably eight weeks. Of course, there weren't any specific days or week at that time. The Natives only went by the moon and its visibility, according to the quarters or half moon to the day it disappears from view. That was their days of each moon.

The summer moon was already in its eighth day of visibility, Scarface was thinking he really should be getting back to his own camps to help his grandma with the fall hunt of buffalo. The old lady wasn't getting any younger for her to be carrying heavy loads of meat on her back. "Who's going to help put up the drying rack? Someone must cut down small trees and carry them out, and that runs into heavy work. Besides all of that, I want to see my people, I've been away so long," these were Scarface's thoughts.

Creator Sun knows what each of his children is thinking about, and Scarface was no exception. That evening, when all of them were getting ready for the evening meal, Creator Sun put Scarface at ease with what he said to him. "My son, I love you very much, you have been so good to Ibi-so-waus-sin and he likes you so very much, he's taken to you so strongly, taken you as his hero for saving his life from those big ugly birds that we have here. Your feet were bleeding the evening before, but you didn't notice them at that particular time when my son needed help, you hadn't seen your feet since the evening before. You were aware of them, because you were not able to walk on them then, and you slept right there until the swans took you the next morning. You woke up where you were sitting when you heard the holler for help, and without thinking about your feet first, you jumped up and ran to aid the boy. What you did, my boy, was a great honor for my son, Ibi-so-waus-sin. You put your life before his, you thought of his safety before you thought about your bleeding feet and aching body. For this brave thing you done, anything you might ask for will not be hard to meet. I'll do anything for you, that's what you did for my son Ibi-so-waus-sin.

"You have come from far away, you went through the torture of life as you slowly came along the trail to where you are at now. What you went through, my boy, it's to show you that to be honest isn't a smooth trail, it's a hard, torturous trail to follow. You have followed it, you didn't give up when you could have along the way. That was the easy way out, but this trail took you to the place no one else of my children from Mother Earth's body has ever come before. It's your honesty and sincerity to find me, your honesty to the girl you want so much and who is mine. Remember, from now on, anything you might want in your life by honesty is never easy, it's torturous and narrow and easy to fall off course. Stolen things never do any good. You pay for them, one way or another. In the end, you will lose more value than the stolen goods. To steal is a wide-open trail to follow, it's the easiest trail, but it never pays.

"You have been with my family now for almost one moon, and I know you are thinking of your own people very hard the last few days. You have been so quiet and very deep in thought. I think it is time for you to get back to your camps to give my children a message from me, they have been forgetting about me lately and I'd like for them to come back to me in their prayers. Now, my boy, ask me for what you really came to look for me for, do not get ashamed, don't hesitate to ask me for anything you want, big or small, highly valued or not. It shall be yours. We really owe a life. I know that you didn't come on that long torturous trail just to visit me. It must be something very important to you, to seek me out. I leave at daybreak every day and I'm gone until the Sun goes down over the hills and mountains. So while the evening is still young, tell your true visit to this place."

Scarface was still a little hesitant about asking for the Chief's daughter, because she was Creator Sun's bride and he was sitting before Creator Sun now. And to face anyone squarely and to ask of them something—that is altogether different then asking for something immaterial. Silent prayers in his heart put him at ease and gave him the courage to ask for the girl.

Scarface began. "I came a long ways to find you. I didn't come by mistake, and it was a very torturous trail to find you. My life, I almost lost it looking for that trail, several times. I'm here now and very glad to find this place where you live. I do have an important thing to ask of you, it's hard to find the right words to say. First, it's my ugly scar on my face—I'm told to ask you to make it disappear from my face. A girl told me to find you and asked that of you, the Chief's daughter of my camp. She said you're her husband, her man. She's been talked about by all of the slickerfoots in that camp. They make fun of her and say bad things about her, because she has refused them all in marriage. All of them, young and old alike, have come to propose to her, but always she refused without giving some kind of excuse. It got so they call her a cross woman, a person that is neither a real woman or a real man, but in between. They say she can't have a natural husband because of this.

"They made fun of me, because of my scar. It doesn't look good to them, but I didn't care. Then they started to make fun of me over the Chief's daughter, that I should go and propose to her, that her and I were alike. That the two of us would make a fine couple, we had certain things in common—she was a cross woman and I had this ugly scar on my face, none of the girls or single women would have me, because of my big ugly scar, except the Chief's daughter. That made me mad, not for my sake, but for the girl. I know it's not a bit true what they said about her, so I decided to do just that, to approach the Chief's daughter and ask her for a marriage. I did and this is what became of it.

"I'm here before you because she told me to ask you for her, that she belongs to you and she must get your consent for her to marry me. She also told me to ask you to do away with this scar on my face, which would be the sign that I really met you personally and the sign that would give us the permission to really get married. She said that would be her only acceptance, if I came back to her without my scar. So now! I'm asking you to give us your permission and blessings, for us to get married and make this scar disappear from my face so she will know I was with you personally and you had gladly agreed to all of her askings.''

Scarface sat there very still, waiting for Creator Sun's answer. In a way, he was kind of nervous waiting for the Creator's words, and uneasy. He was thinking of a bad answer from him.

Creator Sun sat still for a long time, studying Scarface's words. Maybe he was weighing the words and all of the things Scarface went through to come to see him and ask him, and probably Creator Sun was also thinking of the girl's side too. She couldn't protect herself from all of the talking of her, because it was one of her restrictions that he put on her. It sure must be embarrassing to her, to hear all that bad talk of her going on. She was whole and without a sin yet, still a virgin, a very kind, healthy girl.

It was a long wait for Scarface, waiting for an answer. For no reason, he got very sweaty sitting there. After a very long time—maybe it was just another of the many tortures that Scarface went through—Creator Sun finally spoke. ''My son! You are a brave man to come to look for me. Never before has anyone from Mother Earth come to my place when they are alive and living there. You've gone through many tortures to find me, what you are seeking must be very important to you, and I know it is for the girl too. I must warn you that what you have asked for is still full of tortures for you and for the girl too. There are many do's and don'ts before you two get together. You can't expect to get anything for nothing, you must pay and she must pay too. I have given you my blessings to marry one another. She must pay for her release from me, as she is bonded to me for the rest of her life and to sever that bond to me, she must sacrifice her body in a way that it must suffer along for so long. I too will suffer for the feelings I have for her when she is no longer mine. We will all go through a bodily torture for one another.

''From this time on, the same things we are going through about this girl this day, people in the future shall also go through a similar way, a torture of the body and torture of the mind. The binding of a man and a woman is from love for each other, a very strong feeling for one another. For when we are binded with the opposite sex, we are as one people with one mind, and to part is a heart-felt sacrifice for both. It is a very sacred thing to get together with each other as a man and wife. It should never be broken through their lives, unless! It's for this particular reason we are now faced with. To be broken apart, then both man and woman must suffer the pain of divorce from one another.

''It is made so it would happen as it is now, particularly for the message I have for my children on Mother Earth, that they will know I think of them so very much each day. That is the reason I come up in the east and travel all day to the west until I retire at night. To keep my eyes on them and for them to see me each day too, so my children will remember to praise me as they see me as I pass over them. I must provide for them too and keep them alive with my power that is always there for them. Through my own powers of mystery, all food and the like shall grow for them to thrive on always. I have shown them all what food is good for them to eat. I have shown them what foods are bad and shouldn't be eaten, in both the vegetation and the animals and birds too.

"It is my promise to keep them alive with what I have to offer them to keep them alive. It is up to them if they go by my words and do the right things they must do that I have taught them all to keep that life I give each of you. My breathing is yours, it is my own breath that all of you breathe in to stay alive. If I didn't exist, there would be no kind of life anyplace. Life is my power, love is my power. No other being other than myself, Creator Sun, can provide anything like this, anyplace, all over.

"All life that exists must in some way honor me and thank me for that life I have provided for each thing that exists as a life. I think of all the life I have put there on Mother Earth, that's why I equal the days so all of my children can have its equal share of my powers. It gets cold in one place for so long, because that's when I go to the other children of mine so I can provide for them for their food and life. The other children have already put away enough food to last them through those cold days, and I must leave them and be gone to help my other children of life. My children are so far apart from each other and scattered on Mother Earth, that it takes me so long to help one group in getting food for them and enough to store for the days I'm not around to help those children far away. I must go back and forth to help all of the life that exists.

"I'm letting you go back to your camps with this message and for their own good, all of my children. You will have to set this message for them to follow personally with the help of your future wife, the girl I must give to you. At this same time, you and her must suffer for the sin of taking from a bind, she would have a bind to me for the rest of her life if you didn't come along and ask for her. You will be home very soon, it is now the mid-part of the summer moon, when all of the berries and roots are fully ripe and all of the meat food is at their fattest. It will be night when you get home. I want you to send a word to the girl as soon as it's daylight, with one of the people that go out away from the camps to relieve themselves at daybreak. She must come out to you to help you with what you have to do for that day. As soon as she hears it's you, she won't lose any time. She will find the place you are at. The girl awaits your return, she loves you very much.

"From here on out, I must let the girl be with you. I mustn't ever bother around her again, if I did, I would be breaking my own rules of life.

"For a very long time, I have been looking around for a woman to do the things for me on Earth, the people's mother. It was in her, the Chief's daughter, that I found the kind of love and behavior I was seeking. It was her I was seeking for so long to hold a secret and never let it out for any reason, except in this case of great importance.

"The kind of love she will have for you is one of a kind, she will do all of your bidding without a thought of herself. Both of you have made a very wise choice, she for you and you for her. It was made to be that way, so that my plans for my children of Mother Earth may survive the wicked things that will come in time. All of my plans are coming into place as I have planned them.

"Scarface! My Son! I want you to remember this very thoroughly. Remember the length of time it took you to find my place here, and how long you have been here with your pardner, Morning Star, with me and the family and our lodge. Keep in your mind, too, the surroundings—the hills, the forest, the trees, and whatever you see all around us where we live. It's the utmost importance to you now, and for others that will have to go through the thing you are about to go through, to observe and remember well all that takes place with all the surroundings as they are.

"Just in case you don't exactly remember the days it took you to find your way to this place, it's four moons from the day you began your quest to the day those birds set you down along the shores of the water of no end. (According to our count in these days, there would be approximately 140 it took Scarface from start to the day he arrived on that strange shore.)

Again, Creator Sun spoke to Scarface. "From the day you came to these shores, you have been here with Morning Star and the family for one whole moon, and this moon is half gone." (Our count would be approximately forty-five days from the time Scarface landed, or was landed there by those swans, and the time he spent with Creator Sun's family.)

"All of this is very important, especially to you, because you are the one that is taking this message for me to your own people of Mother Earth. Mine and Mother Earth's children.

"From this time on—it is midsummer on Mother Earth's body—at this particular time of each year, someone must erect a lodge for me, in honor of me, and it must be made from Mother Earth's growth.

"You will have to be the first to put up an honor lodge for me. The material you must use must be of the wild growth of the body of Mother Earth, mainly the trees. Cottonwood tree and quaking aspen, with a little birch."

For four nights before Scarface was to go back home, he stayed up with Creator Sun as he told Scarface what to do. Not only did Creator Sun put a blueprint in Scarface's mind of how to erect the Honor Lodge, but he also had to remember and to learn the many different songs that went with the several things Scarface had to do in erecting the Honor Lodge, and all of this in four nights.

"Now, my son, listen very closely so every word and information will be within your head where you will not forget it.

"You will be near home, by the camp where your grandma and the girl are, some time towards morning. People of the camp will be coming out to drain themselves, one or two of them at a time. This usually happens just as the east is turning from gray to blue. You will be in one of the many quaking aspen patches. Several must come your way as they go find a secluded spot.

"In that early morning light, no one will recognize you. Stop one of them. By that one person or two, send a message to the girl to come out to you. She will come out immediately. You! Yourself must not go to the camps at any time until the right time is at hand. Keep in your mind what I have taught you and what all I'm going to teach you in these four nights before you return to your people.

"Once the girl is by you, tell her of your travel and show her that scar which is no more now. This is what she asked for, to know that you have truly found me, Creator Sun! The most high being she belongs to. She must know all of what you two must face soon. The passion you both must endure. It will be torturous. This must be, because it will be the sacrifice you both must go through. This is the payment for what the two of you are doing to me. I am your Creator Sun, above all life wherever it exists in this universe or elsewhere. My words are the most high, my doings are the most high. But! Look at what I have to give in to, Scarface and my bride of Mother Earth."

(In the earlier days of this continent or continents, because Creator Sun had more then one wife, Mother Earth and the Chief's daughter, the virgin wife of Creator Sun, the Native men followed his footsteps and had more then one wife. Some men had two or more girls of one family as their wives. This was so until the last of the 1800s, when it was outlawed by the federal government.)

"Remember also, that all females are mine until they find a man who will revere them and their virginity is taken from them. After losing her virginity, a woman shall pay for her sins by losing some of her blood each moon throughout their lives until they are too old to bear other lives.

"The girl's sincere honesty found her a place in my heart. It is this honesty I want of those that will set up an Honor Lodge for me. The maker of this Honor Lodge should be an honest person, and all of the others who take an active part must also be of the highest in honesty.

"You will tell her what to do to get things ready for the coming sacrifice of you two. First of all, she must go back into the camps to find and select six of the most honest women. They either have to be virgins, or have been known by only one man, their own husband. Four of the women shall be as her maids or attendants. The four women will see to it the lodge she is in is well taken care of, kept neat at all times during this period of the sacrifice. Two women, her closest friends, must be by her side every moment during this time of the sacrifice as her personal servants. She must bring these women out here where you can personally advise them and coach them to learn what they must do during this period of the sacrifice.

"The girl must also find six men, the most honest of the camp, men that only know their wives or men that haven't been in contact with any women. These men will be for you. Four of them will take care of the camp chores. They must see to it that there is always enough wood and water for the lodge and to help inside of the tipi whenever possible, if the women attendants need that help. The four men will be your servants for the duration of this holy ceremony, to help in every way.

"The two women and two men that are to be by you and the girl, they must constantly be there by your sides at all times, night and day. While one rests, the other must be at your side. Same with the girl, too. Neither of you must ever be left alone at any time throughout this holy ceremony, which will last for about half a moon."

Scarface got his instructions from Creator Sun, from the time he arrived very near his camp. For the last four nights he was with the Creator, he was taught many things which no ordinary man would've learned in several moons. Scarface knew what had to be done to a T in those last four nights, and this was done by Creator Sun's supernatural powers and his own supernatural powers he got from many spirits while he was on his quest to find Creator Sun.

It was well past the mid-part of the night on this last night with the family of Creator Sun, and Creator Sun was pressuring those instructions of what had to be done for the memorial Honor Lodge for him. Scarface had to remember all of the instructions he was told.

Creator Sun told Scarface, "You must be very careful of others that will try to steer you wrong. Remember well that other little boy that comes around here, he's the same age as Morning Star, Ibi-so-waus-sin, your pardner. That boy tries his best to impersonate Morning Star in every way. We changed what we use to call him from Bah-tsi-dub-bi to Bah-tsi-bi-so-waus-sin, because he closely resembles Ibi-so-waus-sin. Pay close attention to what I have told you. We call that little boy, Bah-tsi-bi-so-waus-sin, Mistaken Morning Star. He is very jealous of Morning Star's doings, especially now that you are here with us. You will have to be extra careful of him that he doesn't foul things up for you or Morning Star.

"I'm warning you now so hard because Morning Star, your pardner, will become as your guiding light. The morning you are to take a sweat bath with the others, Morning Star will appear as it's getting light in the east where I rise from, and as soon as Morning Star appears above the horizon, the first fire of the first sweat hut must be lighted up. The rocks of that first fire for your first sweat will be ready the time I come peeking over the eastern horizon. At your first glimpse of me, those red-hot rocks must be put inside of the sweat hut in the pit that should be already dug for them. Twelve of them and of the red stones and a bit bigger than your fists."

With all of the instructions from Creator Sun, just how this Honor Lodge was to be erected for him all in Scarface's mind, Creator Sun told Scarface that it was time to leave for that camp on Mother Earth where all of the people he knew were at. According to the stars that night, it was well past midnight.

Creator Sun gave Scarface a tanned buffalo robe. The left side was all black with star emblems from top to bottom near the center. And in the center of this black was the emblem of the moon. Yellow stars, yellow moon. The right side was all red with red earth paint with an emblem of stars in black to the right of the yellow stars. And in the center was the emblem of the sun.

Creator Sun got ready. He told Scarface, "My son! Your long happy visit with my family is at end now and we are all going to miss you so very much. Never again shall we ever have any visitors from Mother Earth in their natural human form. People will be able to be with us here in this land that is on the other side of the big water with no end, but! They will only be here when the time comes for them, and that's when their bodies are still and their spirits will leave those bodies. Their spirits will be with all of us that are living in this strange land I live with my own family, and only until that time shall the people of Mother Earth come to live by us.

"Scarface! My son! Come now, I shall take you home to your own camps." Just outside of Creator Sun's doorway they stopped. "Now close your eyes, and don't open them until I tell you to."

It really didn't seem very long before Creator Sun told Scarface to go ahead and open his eyes. When he had his eyes closed, he knew he was moving, although he knew he was sitting very still too. He felt the move as if he was a-sailing through the air or floating at rapid speed, but! For some strange reason that speed wasn't taking his breath away. There he was, sitting among a patch of quaking aspen trees. As he slowly opened his eyes, Creator Sun's voice came to him with these last words for him. "You are now home, do all what I told you to do and do them right." Opening his eyes fully, Scarface looked all around him, but he didn't see Creator Sun then or ever again. But! Creator Sun's words rang in his ears for the rest of his life.

As Scarface sat there, he distinctly remembered all of Creator Sun's words, word for word. He had to wait until the east began to get light. Soon after the light began to show in the east, Scarface began to see dark objects appear from the camps, only to disappear into the quaking aspen patches all around. He knew that people had begun to rise from their beds to take their morning

*First Appearance of Morning Star*

strolls. It really didn't seem too long for him before a couple of people came along near the patch of quaking aspens he was sitting among. The couple went into the patch of quaking aspens, and after they had gotten through with relieving themselves they each gathered an armful of wood for their morning fire. It had taken them a while longer to come back through, each with an armful of wood.

As the two came very near where he was sitting, Scarface hollered at them, *"Hey ki-kah!* Hey, wait, I have an important message I would like to have you two deliver for me." The two came to him to find out what this was all about. As the two stopped before him, he told them the message he wanted to have delivered to the Chief's daughter. "When you come back into the camps, tell the daughter of the head Chief to come out here where I'm at. Tell her that Scarface, *Boh-yi-yi,* would like to have a talk with her. It's very important for all of us, and she must come right away, as it's very urgent what I have to tell her. Now go, and go directly to her camp lest you might forget what I told you two."

The two hurried back into camp. Without even stopping to dump their wood, they went directly to the head Chief's camp. Making their presence known just out of the doorway, he told the Chief he just had a message for his daughter from Scarface. Hearing Scarface's name mentioned, the girl stopped short. She was all ears. "What is it?" the Chief asked the man. "We all know that Scarface disappeared many moons ago. Is he really back?"

Without hearing more, the girl asked the man where Scarface might be at this moment. The man took the girl outside to show her about the exact place where she would find Scarface.

The girl hurriedly went back into the tipi to get her shawl of deerhide. It was now getting quite light in the east when the girl hurried to the location she was shown by the man. It took her a little while to come to the exact place. Sure enough! There was Scarface sitting there among the quaking aspens waiting for her to come.

When the girl saw Scarface sitting there she rushed toward him, but Scarface held his hand up for her to stop before she got any closer. He immediately explained why he done this. "I am very sorry, but we must wait for several days before we can even touch one another. We must stay apart, but we must work together throughout this religious observance to our Creator Sun. He told me this to tell you, he said you would understand. This is the reason he had me to send for you at the first light of the morning, so we can get together on this message of his."

Hurriedly, Scarface related the message of Creator Sun, from the beginning right to where he was sitting, where Creator Sun had brought him to. "And now we must carry it out for our Creator Sun. He is very powerful, he removed that big ugly welt on my face, that big scar. Creator Sun also by his mighty power brought me right to our own camps, don't ask me how, he had me close my eyes before he done anything and I didn't open them until he told me to, right here where I'm sitting, and I didn't see him after we got here, I only heard his voice. He also told me to do this right, both of us."

The morning was getting brighter. Scarface told the girl all that must be done. "We must begin now, as we have only four days to get ready for the big observance to our Creator Sun. The others that must help us must learn their part within these next four days before the Honor Lodge is set up."

Scarface told the girl, "First you must go back into the camps and find us four people, the most honest of the camps. Two women and two men to help us. This is one of the instructions by our Creator Sun. I'd suggest your mother for one of the women and my grandma for the other one, I know for sure those two rate the highest in honesty. And for the two men, my suggestion is your father and one of my very close friends that didn't go against me before my journey to Creator Sun's homeland."

The girl didn't argue any, she too knew that these four people were very high in their honesty. Back to the camps she went, half running and half walking. Direct to her tipi she went, and without hesitation she told her parents of Scarface's message from Creator Sun. She was told by Scarface to also bring their tanned robes with them, as that was important too. While her parents were getting ready, she hurried to the other two, Scarface's grandma and his best friend who stuck with him always. After these two heard the message, they didn't lose any time. In just a little while, all was ready and they had all come to the Chief's tipi which was towards the west side of the center of this encampment. All had covered themselves with their robes, from head to foot, and then all went out to where Scarface was waiting for them.

The morning was still very early as all got to the place. Scarface told them what was to be done, and their own parts that they had to do. He told the two women, the girl's mother and his own grandma, that their part was to be with the girl at all times through this religious observance to our Creator Sun. Not to let her out of their sight until the time comes. He told the two men not to leave him alone, that one or both must keep their eyes on him both night and day. The two women and the two men were to keep the girl and Scarface from breaking any of the very strict restrictions of Creator Sun, they were to ensure all of the don'ts of this observance.

The girl's mother and Scarface's grandma got all of their instructions of what had to be done throughout this religious observance of the Honor Lodge to Creator Sun. They must stay with the girl every moment of both night and day until the right time came. It was likewise for the two men.

The first restriction was to keep the tanned buffalo robe over their body at all times throughout this very holy ceremony, all of them. Scarface had over his body his own special tanned buffalo robe, which was given to him by his new father, Creator Sun, who adopted him as his own son because of Ibi-so-waus-sin, or Morning Star. Morning Star, from the very beginning of their acquaintance took to Scarface like he was his own big brother. It was soon after this that Scarface was given the tanned buffalo robe by Creator Sun to always wear around him a special robe to keep him from any harm. This special robe was painted black on the left side, with yellow emblems of stars all over straight down the center, from the neck part to the tail end.

The right side of this special robe was painted with the red earth paint all over with black emblems of stars in all of the field of black.

The next restriction that was very important to do at all times was to be sure to pray before every detail of this holy ceremony was carried out and to be very sure to use the pipe for these prayers after the pipe was lit and smoking. To be sure all things that were to be used were blessed with prayers and held over the smoking sweet grass. This blessing of each part and the articles that were to be used was a must, and as a restriction by Creator Sun, and this too was to be done throughout this holy ceremony.

The girl and her mother and father, Scarface's grandma, and his very dear closest friend were the only five that seen Scarface thoroughly that morning, and right away they all noticed his big ugly scar was gone. This proved to them Scarface had really found Creator Sun, for Creator Sun would be the only one to have the power to remove such a scar as he had on his face. Scarface didn't know the five people were sizing him up. Actually, the girl's mother and father weren't supposed to see Scarface at all, but it really wasn't any of the restrictions or anything too important, but because Scarface was going to be their son-in-law after this very holy ceremony. That is, if Scarface came out of it alive.

After these five people had talked with Scarface in the quaking aspen patch and had received their instructions for this holy ceremony, the two ladies were to go back into camp and find four other women to help them during this entire religious ceremony. The four women must be perfectly honest in every way, honest thoughts in their minds, must be known by only their husbands, or, if single, they must still be virgins.

The Chief and Scarface's very good friend must also go find the most honest men, four of them, to help with all of the special chores that had to be done during this several days ceremony.

The girl stayed with Scarface and her mother. Scarface's grandma went back into camp after she and the girl's mother had talked of several honest women to see. It took mostly all day to find the ones that were fit for this trial of honesty.

On the men's side, the Chief stayed by Scarface, while Scarface's best friend went back into camps to select the most honest of the men in the camps. This was after the Chief and Scarface's best friend had talked about the many men that were up to the standards of honesty. He too took all day to find the almost perfect four to do the work that had to be done during the next several days.

It was almost dark when the five men came to the place where Scarface was waiting, among the patch of quaking aspens. It was this selection of the women and men that brought the attention to the whole camp at this time of the coming very religious ceremony. Everyone wanted to take an active role in it now. There were many volunteers for the many small chores that were to be done. But all were told that they would be called on whenever the need arises.

All together now there were seven women, including the girl, and there were seven men, including Scarface. Fourteen of them to maintain the very religious ceremony through its several days. Immediately, Scarface went to work on them, teaching each one what had to be done. Each one had to learn their part in the next three days so each one would know exactly what was to be done. This was very, very important, there was no rehearsing, but all had to be done perfectly during the ceremony. This made it very important to learn everything that had to be done perfectly by heart and to do it right the first time, there wouldn't be any redoing it again. Three days to learn by their hearts what was to be done, and in the most perfect way that it had to be done.

Just before the Honor Lodge was set up the first morning, there was also a last supper too for Scarface and the girl with their followers that's quite like the Bible or Jesus' Last Supper. The Indian last supper was for only the four days it took to make the Honor Lodge.

By the end of the fourth day, all of the men and women that were selected to help had learned their parts, and to perfection. This was due to the almighty powers of the supernatural spirits of the Almighty Creator Sun and those of Scarface too, that he attained during his journey to the land of Creator Sun.

On this last day of teaching what had to be done during the next several days, the five men and five women went back into the camps to tell all of the people what their parts might be. All of the men trekked into the woods near the rivers where the rabbit willow grew, and each man cut a willow, a full-grown willow. There were 560 of these willow trees brought out for the making of the four holy sweat huts to be used the next morning by those fourteen people, the seven women and the seven men, including Scarface and the girl. It wasn't any trouble to find all these men to help and there were plenty more men around for the other chores to be done towards the Honor Lodge.

Four sweat huts or arbors were erected to hold all of the seven men and seven women in each, and it took 140 willows for one of the large arbors for those sweat huts. Four sweat huts erected, two of them were erected direct east of the camps in an east-west row. One arbor closer to camps and one arbor east of that one, and not far apart. Always these sweat huts are erected near some sort of water where the sweat bather can go and wash off. Two of these sweat huts are erected directly west of the camps in the same fashion as the east-side ones, east-west of each other and near some kind of water for washing the sweat off. All of these four sweat huts are erected the day before the beginning of the holy ceremony, because they are to be used for the coming morning just as the sun comes into view on the horizon.

Everyone had learned their personal parts thoroughly, as that fourth day came to an end. The fourteen of them went to bed among the quaking aspen with the birds. The coming morning was the beginning of one of the most highly religious ceremonies that ever came into existence among the Natives of these now American continents.

The next morning was a very big important part for Scarface, and during the night he couldn't sleep much at all. Anyway, he had to watch out for the right time he was told to get up and begin that first day of the most highly religious holy ceremony to ever be conducted here in the Americas.

Creator Sun had told Scarface to watch for the rising of Morning Star or Ibi-so-waus-sin at dawn of that first historical religious morning. As Ibi-so-waus-sin or Morning Star came into view on the eastern horizon, the first fire for the first sweat arbor or sweat hut was to be lighted. This was a set time so the rocks for that first sweat would get red-hot and ready to move into the hut about the time the Creator Sun come peeking over the hills in the east or just before it comes peeking above the horizon. Creator Sun also warned Scarface to be on the alert for the mischievious Boh-tsi-bi-so-waus-sin, Imitation Morning Star, that he might try to mix things up for Scarface or the true Morning Star, Ibi-so-waus-sin.

Scarface must've fallen asleep for a while after the mid-part of the night. He woke up with a start as he looked towards the horizon for Ibi-so-waus-sin, the star that was to appear and let him know the time he was to light up the first fire for that first sweat hut. This was also a very important role for Ibi-so-waus-sin, Morning Star, to appear for the very beginning of this Great Honoring Lodge for his father, Creator Sun. Both him and Scarface didn't want anything to mar this religious beginning in any way, and especially for them. Morning Star, Ibi-so-waus-sin, was given a place for eternity, to show himself where his father, Creator Sun, had given him to appear as a time for that beginning of a great religious system and to appear to all of his brothers and sisters of this Mother Earth.

Scarface was about half awake from his sleep, temporarily forgetting the warning Creator Sun had told him about—Imitation Morning Star, Boh-tsi-bi-so-waus-sin, that he might try something to destroy or try to mar this great beginning of the religious system. Scarface immediately looked towards the eastern horizon, where the star already had appeared, and thought he had woken up late for the rising of his brother, Ibi-so-waus-sin. In his mind he was thinking, "Oh, no, how could I have missed this only morning I was to do something great for my people?" All of a sudden, that warning of Imitation Morning Star, Boh-tsi-bi-so-waus-sin, came to his mind. He gave that star in the eastern horizon a second look. It was identical in every way to Morning Star. "No wonder it almost fooled me," Scarface thought. After he had gathered his wits and was fully awake, he realized that the star he was looking at was just a bit too early for the beginning of the coming dawn. He seen the lay of the stars as they appeared, and he knew it was some time before Ibi-so-waus-sin would be coming up in the eastern horizon and the beginning of the Honor Lodge for Creator Sun, a great religious system. Scarface stayed awake and very alert right to dawn and the rising of Ibi-so-waus-sin, the Morning Star. A great guiding star for the beginning of a Native religious system of faith to Creator Sun.

As Morning Star appeared just above the eastern hills, Scarface gave the word to one of his servants to go and light up the fire for the first sweat hut.

The rest of the men and women got up too to do their personal parts of this first great day.

The Chief and Scarface's closest friend were his personal valets, while the other four men were more of servants for the duration of this Honor Lodge. The girl, too, took her mother and Scarface's grandma as her personal maids of honor, and the other four were her servants for the duration of this religious ceremony.

Almost sunrise. Scarface and four of the men got ready, taking their buckskin garments off, all naked except for the robes over them. All of the women took their buckskin dresses off, they too were naked except for the tanned buffalo robes covering them. Just before the sun appeared on the horizon, two of Scarface's servants began to fork the twelve stones into the pit within the sweat hut. The hut was covered thickly with robes that the women of the camp had brought so the steam from the water that was hand-sprinkled on those red-hot rocks couldn't escape. The more water sprinkled on those hot rocks, the hotter the inside of this sweat hut would get. This sweat in these sweat huts was the truest way to get baptized, and this was the way all Natives of these Americas were baptized into the Native religion from several thousand years back.

The men and the women went inside of the sweat hut, Scarface was the first to go in, and the Chief was second. Scarface sat at the head of this small enclosure, opposite the doorway. The Chief sat to Scarface's right side, and his best friend sat to his left. All of the men sat on the right side of the hut, and all of the women sat to the left. It was a tight squeeze in there with twelve people in the small enclosure. Two of Scarface's servants stayed outside to do what had to be done, while the rest were having their sweat inside.

The top edge of the sun came into view on the eastern horizon. And as it did, Scarface called to the two men on the outside to close the entrance that faced east. The rays had came on in to the inside of the sweat hut, and now the sweat was on, with Creator Sun taking an active part.

In those earlier days, several thousand years ago, all sweat bathing was done in the early morning. The doorway of these huts was closed just as the suns rays came in to the sweat hut and were plainly visible to the people that are taking the sweat. This was letting Creator Sun in to take a sweat with his children of Mother Earth, and open invitation as the sweat bathers wait for the first of the sun's ray to come into the sweat hut and then close the doorway.

As all were waiting for the sun to rise, Scarface smoked and prayed to Creator Sun so nothing would go wrong throughout this Honor Lodge ceremony. Four puffs of the pipe, then it's passed on to the next man. He does his prayers and he passes the pipe on. The pipe goes on to the very last one of the men, and just about that time, the tobacco runs out or is smoked out. The pipe is cleaned out and refilled with tobacco and it's ready for the next smoke. Reverence, veneration, worship, and devotion to Creator Sun was the life of these first great people of these Americas many thousands of years ago, a great love for one another and a bigger love for Creator Sun.

A certain number of songs are sung in this sweat hut, mixed with many prayers, and this takes probably two three hours of the modern time, but them people went by the sun as it went from east to west in the sky. About midway to between sunrise and midday, the group came out of the first sweat hut. Each sweat hut was opened for air four times during the sweat. The fourth time the doorway was opened, those inside must then come on out and take a dip in the nearby water hole to wash off the sweat. Scarface and his group of men and women went on to the second of the sweat huts to take more sweat. The second of the sweat huts was all ready to go into, so all of them came from the pool of water right on to the second of the sweat huts.

With all of the available help from this camp, it wasn't any problem to have a lot of extra help from the men and women. Although the two men servants of Scarface were to take care of all four sweat huts, they had many volunteers from the men and women of the camp to do much of the work that had to be done throughout this Honor Lodge ceremony.

Four more times the door of the second sweat hut was opened for air, while the singing and praying went on. At each opening of the doorway, the pipe was lit for the men sweat bathers. Each man took four puffs, prayed as he took those four puffs, and then passed it on to the man next to him. Of course, Scarface was always the first to smoke some of the pipe and pray, then he passed it on to the Chief. After the last man took his four puffs, he passed it to the men outside.

As the pipe laid idle outside, it had a special place on top of the sweat hut. The pipe laid across the front of the sweat hut just over the doorway and back of it. The pipe was laid a certain way, not just any old way. It was laid on the top of the sweat hut with the bowl towards the south and the mouth end to the north. The tobacco within the tobacco pouch, made of tanned hide, a cleaning stick for the pipe stem and bowl, the flint and striker with the softened dried bark of a tree, and always a flint knife to go along with these articles. All of these were laid in order on top of the sweat hut as the sweating goes on.

About in the middle of the top of the sweat hut, a buffalo bull skull was placed. Whatever it may be called—Observance to Creator Sun, Honoring Creator Sun Lodge, or Medicine Lodge—the buffalo had a great part in these religious lodges. The flesh was food, the hide was used to cover the sweat huts, the fresh rawhide was stripped to tie the poles of the holy lodge in place. The hide was also tanned and used as a robe that covered the ones that are taking an active part within the lodge itself. Most of all, the buffalo tongue was used as the host for the Honoring Lodge.

It's now about midday of this sweat bathing, and the men on the outside of this sweat hut are just opening the doorway. All of the men and women on the inside are coming out from that sweat hut and going on into the pool of water. Dipping and washing the sweat off of themselves, they all come on out of the pool of water. In a procession, all of them make their way to the west side of this very large encampment, to the two other sweat huts there. Not hesitating too much, the twelve people go right on into the third sweat hut.

The third sweat was just like the first ones, singing and praying and the smoking of the pipe as the doorway was opened each time and right when the hut is first entered the praying and singing begins. The hut is closed the first time as the singing goes on and the praying too. At the first opening of the doorway the pipe is lit and passed on into the men inside, first to Scarface and next to the Chief then on down to the last man at the doorway, who takes his four puffs and passes it out to the men there. The pipe is placed into the rightful place again after it's been cleaned and refilled with tobacco and is ready for another round of smoke.

Again the last opening of the sweat hut, the fourth time, the sweat bathers come on out and to the nearby pool of water they all go to wash off the sweat. As soon as they had their dip in the water, all of them go on to the fourth sweat hut, the last one. The sun is almost down, not too long before the sun goes down behind those hills.

Again those songs and the praying goes on, opening the doorway and the smoking. It was now the third time the doorway to this fourth sweat lodge was opened for air and smoking of the pipe. Right after the smoking was done, the doorway again was closed. The two men on the outside of this sweat hut were now very watchful towards the western skies for the setting sun. It had been a while since the doorway was closed, and the sun was on the hills of the western horizon. Slowly, slowly, that sun sank behind those western hills and soon it was out of sight. The two men on the outside of this sweat hut immediately took the big buffalo robe that made up the door for this sweat hut, the sun had set behind those hills and Scarface and the rest of them must now come on out of the sweat hut. This was the fourth and final sweat hut of this day, and the beginning of this Great Honoring Lodge for Creator Sun. But the work had only begun now, and they were slowly coming to the harder part of this Honor Lodge for Scarface and the girl.

Immediately after their dip in the cool pool of water, all fourteen of them slowly were taken in procession towards the center of the encampment and there, towards the west side of this center, stood a tipi already up and standing there. It was ready for occupancy and all was ready on the inside too, with bedding and all that was needed in furnishings for living, including food. Scarface, the girl, and the other twelve people, six men and six women, were taken into this center tipi. It was theirs for the duration of this Honor Lodge ceremony. Whatever was going to take place during the entire ceremony took place from this tipi.

Since that night Scarface arrived in the quaking aspen patch, brought there by Creator Sun, he had regular meals that were brought from the camps by the girl mostly, and from the others of his group that wanted to bring him food. This day was different from the other days. All day he and the others had been sweat bathing, there wasn't any time to eat, all that they had during the day was water. Everybody was now very hungry.

A big meal was waiting for them in this center tipi, and Scarface knew this would be his last big meal for the next four days and his last drink of water. He had one important chore to do, and that was for all fourteen of them. The girl too knew this was her last big meal for the next four days and her last drink of water. Both ate a hearty meal and drank much water.

The group sat for a while after the big meal. This meal was the last evening meal or last supper for the next several days until this great ceremony was completed. Soon after it got dark, all of them got ready and began to sing and pray again. Many of the elders of the camps, other than Scarface's group, came in to help with the holy singing and praying. This went on until about the mid-part of the night.

It was now time for the group to go into the woods to select a tree with good, sturdy, long forks on it. This had to be done in the dark of the night, and mystic power had to be used. This was a very important tree, it was the sacrificial tree, it would hold a human sacrifice up in it. With his power that he had achieved from his journey to find Creator Sun, it was no problem for Scarface.

The group came to the woods. There were many followers from the camps to give their hands wherever it was necessary, but the main ones were the fourteen people—Scarface, the girl, and the six women and six men that they had selected at the beginning of this holy ceremony. They all stopped at the edge of the woods, and there Scarface sang some songs and prayed for help from his father, Creator Sun, to assist him in finding and selecting a good tree for that sacrifice the next morning. His prayers were heard, he led the way into the woods and right to a very nice tree with high forks, straight and not too big at the butt end. This was a very important thing for Scarface.

From the very beginning of his return and his contact with the girl and the rest of the group, everything they done was according to the ways Creator Sun wanted it. There was no hurrying, things had to be done in a humble way and very reverently. Most everything was done in kind of a slow-motion way.

It was almost pitch dark, especially in the woods, not a speck of light to see even a foot away from where one stood. But Scarface found the tree in that pitch darkness of the night. It was just like a made-to-order tree, as they would see the next morning.

The six men began to cut the tree down with their stone axes. It took a little time to down it, even with the help of the other men that had come along to help in any way they could, even if it was late at night. Men and women alike came along with the group for the cutting of this very special tree, and in pitch darkness too.

Scarface had warned the men that the special center tree wasn't to touch the ground after it was cut down. So the six men, with the help from other men, brought this center tree down very slowly and laid it on some blocks that were brought there. Those blocks were old stumps of trees, and with the roots all rotted out, those stumps were easy to kick over. After the tree was laid down on those blocks of wood, Scarface, his tobacco pouch always available at his side, filled his pipe and smoked, praying as he done this. Four puffs, then it was passed on to the next man until all of his six servants had taken four puffs apiece and had prayed with the pipe. While they were doing this, several of the other men trimmed the tree so that only the fork was left on this sacred tree.

Now it was time to pick the tree up and take it out of the woods. With Scarface in the front end of that center tree, and the rest of the six servants and other men strung along the length of the tree, the center tree was picked up and onto the shoulders of the men it went. It was quite a procession coming out through the woods that time of the night. Scarface was in the lead of this procession, and just back of the men carrying the tree came the girl and her six servants. They were to help too, but there wasn't any room for any more help, so they just followed close behind with the girl in the lead of her servants. The six women and the rest of those people that had come out to help them were in the back of her and her group.

The whole procession went about a fourth of the way and then they stopped for a smoke and prayers. Immediately after the smoking and praying, they went on. Two of the girl's servants carried the two stumps. Four times the tree was laid down, but the fourth time they had brought it to where it was going to be used. At each stop the smoking of the pipe and praying went on. The Great Center Tree for the sacrifice the next morning was laid on those same stump blocks the two women were carrying from the woods. All of the people went on to their tipis to rest for awhile.

Scarface went on to that center tipi, his servants and the girl too. Morning wasn't too far off. Everyone had a little rest before daylight came.

While that tree was being chopped down by the men, some of the women had gathered birch branches, a couple of small armfulls of them. It was the ones that they were able to get at during the darkness. These too had a lot to do with the coming sacrifice this next morning.

Just as the eastern horizon began to get gray, the servants of Scarface were already out in the center of the camp near the Great Center Tree they had brought in during the night. They had already dug the ground for that Great Center Tree, deep enough so it wouldn't fall over after it was tamped down. Some of the girl's servants too had already started tying the birch branches securely between the forks of this Great Center Tree.

There was plenty of help from the other people of this whole encampment, even at this time of the morning when it was just lighting up in the east. A hole was dug deep into the ground squarely in the center of the other twelve post holes in a big circle, just so far apart. This large hole in the ground was for the Great Sacrificial Center Tree, the center for this highest of Native rituals that was being conducted for the first time, by one of the greatest persons that ever came into being, Scarface, the only person from Mother Earth to ever truly come in personal contact with our truest Creator of this whole universe.

Singing and praying had been going on before the eastern horizon had gotten gray. One of the most important restrictions had already been going since the mid-part of the night—no drinking water and no eating of anything for both Scarface and the girl. Their followers, the six men and six women, were devoted to them and were just as reverent as they were, so these six men and six women probably went along with Scarface and the girl in not drinking or eating too, These six men and six women were rightfully disciples of Scarface and the girl. No drinking of any liquid, water, or berry juice, and no eating of anything for the next four days.

Each day of these past few days that already went by, Scarface encouraged his group to be sure to follow all instructions as Creator Sun wanted it. He didn't want anything to mar this great beginning of a very true system of reverence to Creator Sun. The Great Lodge was for observing him, the Honor Lodge, Medicine Lodge, or the Tabernacle of Creator Sun, whatever was befitting to call it.

This was a great day, it was the first day of the great sacrifice, Scarface was to give his life and body for the love of this girl that Creator Sun had selected for his own, a virgin girl from this great body of Mother Earth. In other words, Scarface was sacrificing himself to own this girl. According to Creator Sun, all of this must be done before he relinquishes his ownership of the girl to Scarface. Scarface and the girl must suffer for that want of each other. This was a divorce for the girl from Creator Sun, and also a direct permission from Creator Sun for the two to get together as man and wife. After this great ritual, there wouldn't be anything to bind the girl to Creator Sun. Scarface and the girl would have one another, if Scarface came out of this alive. The sacrifice of Scarface to Creator Sun on this Great Center Tree would be the center of things for the coming four days.

Everything was prepared. Some of it was done the day before and some of it was still being done through the night. All things of importance to this great ritual were ready for this morning. It was getting light enough to see around you now, and many people had already began to gather near the center of this encampment. Some were just curious and most came to observe this great day of a human sacrifice.

Everybody in these camps had found out about what was going on and what was to go on. All of the men and older boys and the women and older girls were all so interested in this great ritual that all wanted an active part in it, so anyone called to do something towards this ceremony didn't hesitate to do so. Everyone was just so happy to help in a small way.

During the day before, when Scarface and his group were sweat bathing, many of the men of the camps went out to hunt buffalo, and by evening had all returned with each a big load of fresh buffalo meat. Some brought in the fresh hide of the buffalo, which was very important to this Honor Lodge. Some brought those entrails of the buffalo, the delicacy of the animal. But most important for the people was the bringing in of the buffalo tongue, which was the host for this great ritual.

During the night, several women were told to make sarvis berry (June-berry) soup. Four of these women were given the tongue of a bull buffalo to make that berry soup with, four very large bull buffalo tongues. All of this was done through the night, and by this morning everything was ready. The berry soup and the four tongues of the bull buffalo were cooked nice and tender and were already brought out to the center where things were taking place.

Long before sunup, two men of the followers of Scarface and two women of the girl's had gone to the east side of the center, and there they stripped the green rawhides of the freshly killed buffalo, enough for the tying of Scarface to the forks of that Great Sacrificial Center Tree.

It was still some time before the sun would be coming up over the eastern horizon. Scarface and the girl came out with the girl's father, the Chief of this camp, leading them. The girl was behind Scarface, and behind her came the girl's mother, and behind her came the grandma of Scarface, with the others following closely behind in single file procession and walking along in a solemn, humble, and reverent walk. Coming about a quarter of the way from the center tipi to the tree, the procession stopped, and again that smoking of the holy pipe, singing and praying for an interval, then on their way again only to stop halfway to that tree. The holy pipe was lighted up again, with the usual singing and praying. Again they all got into motion, walking ever so slowly and solemnly. About three-quarters of the way they again stopped to light up the holy pipe, where more praying and singing was done. At this third stop many of the people, men and women alike, even whole families, came to get a personal blessing from Scarface and the girl. All had realized, all had found out the truth of this great beginning of this religion to honor Creator Sun, and all knew by now that Scarface and the girl had been with Creator Sun personally. All of these people that were coming before Scarface and the girl were getting their faces painted with that same dark earth paint that the two used all over their bodies, and even their hair was smeared with the paste of this dark red earth paint.

It took some time to go through all of the people that came before them, to pray for each of them and then anoint them with the dark red earth paint, it was just their faces mostly and hands too. After all of the people had came by them, the group continued its way, the final few steps to that center and by that Great Sacrificial Center Tree. The people knew that to be with Creator Sun personally, like Scarface and the Chief's daughter, these two had to be almighty powerful with the supernatural spirits. So their special blessings for each of the people and their anointing of the sacred dark red earth paint were very holy, because whatever Scarface and the girl had or touched personally was naturally blessed by Creator Sun.

The time had now come to get underway with the most important part of this very holy ritual. Scarface stood between these forks of this Great Center Tree, the girl beside him and the rest of the group of twelve people, six men and six women, in a half-circle around them from the north to west and to the south of them. The multitude of the people of the camps around them were listening and looking on. The soups of the berries and the bull buffalo tongues were brought to the area where Scarface and the girl stood. One of the women had brought a stretched dried rawhide to be used as a table or cutting board. She laid it near the rawhide pots of berry soups. Four strips of the freshly stripped green rawhide of the buffalo were laid over the forks of this tree, one to each of the forks and two other strips at the crouch of the fork where the birch bundle had already been tied with other strips of the same rawhide. These bundled birch branches were for his footrest, with their sharp spurs protruding from each of the small birch branches tied in a bundle. This Sacrificial Center Tree was slowly getting readied. But some things must be done before the actual sacrifice of Scarface. One of the main things was that soup.

First was the eating of the soup and the buffalo tongues. Creator Sun told Scarface, "The four buffalo bull tongues are to represent my body with the strength of buffalo bulls and the increasing of the buffalo herds. The blood is the blood I gave to people to have a strong life that will withstand any ruggedness. Buffalos are known to have a smooth life, a life without sickness and for bearing many little ones. The sarvis berries are to sweeten that smooth life as you live it here on Mother Earth, as she had produced it, and that you may never see any kind of bitterness as long as your lives go on. Several times in between these annual Honor Lodges each year, human beings must eat these foods of Creator Sun to remember me by and worship me. Pray to me before you eat this food and always eat with me. Break a piece off of the tongue, take a berry or a drop of the blood soup, and pray with this food as you hold it up towards the Sun and hold it towards the Mother Earth. After you pray with this food, the piece you hold in your hand must then be buried in the ground where you may be sitting. This is to share with Creator Sun, Mother Earth, and our son, Ibi-so-waus-sin, Morning Star."

The berry soups with the bull buffalo tongues were set before Scarface and the girl. The people quieted down, waiting for the next doing, whatever it might be. Scarface and the girl were in the middle of this huge crowd, their servants around them. Scarface was heard by all of the people in this crowd as he spoke as loud as he could. First he told why this was happening, the life he had when that big ugly scar was on his face and the harassment he got from his fellow young men, the asking of this young girl for marriage and her answer to him, his life that followed after his asking, and his near death adventure of his quest to find Creator Sun. He told of the tortures of it, giving up to die at the shores of the big water with no end, the big white birds that took pity on him and brought him to the land of Creator Sun, his adventures of his first step on that land of mystery, the land of Creator Sun. He told of his visit with the family and how it slowly lead to this observance to Creator Sun, Mother Earth, and Morning Star. This was to be done each year as long as there was a sun, an earth, and a morning star to observe. Scarface confessed all sins and wrongs that he committed to this age he now was living, which wasn't very much, if any.

It was the girl's turn to confess before this huge crowd, and she too spoke as loud as she could so she could be heard by all of the people. There wasn't too much she could say about her life. Almost everyone in this huge camp knew her from almost her infancy to her present age. She was known as a cross woman, which she wasn't, but she had to keep to herself because of her commitment to Creator Sun, and she was still a virgin. So her confession wasn't too long.

Then came the six men. Each of them came to this center and by this holy soup of tongue, blood, and berries, each confessed their wrongs, their sins. After them, the six women servants of the girl came one by one beside her and confessed aloud so all could hear each of them tell of their wrongdoings and sins, if any. Others of this crowd came to confess before this huge crowd, to let these other people know of their honesty. All of these people spoke with their loudest voice to be heard during their confession.

After all of those that wanted to confess had done so, the ritual went on to the next phase.

A piece of bull buffalo tongue and a small horn spoonful of the soup with a few of the sarvis berries in it were taken out of the rawhide pot. With these in his right hand, Scarface first held them up towards the sun and blessed them with a long prayer. Then he held them down to the earth, again with a long blessing and prayers. At the end of this blessing and praying, he stuck the piece of tongue and the soup into the ground, saying at the same time, "This is yours, eat with me and the people all over, my Creator Sun, my Mother Earth, and my brother, Morning Star, and the rest of the stars and all of nature that surrounds us in every place of the ground and above, for all things have that life that we are given by our Father, Mother, and brothers. Creator Sun, Mother Earth, and our brothers, Morning Star and the rest of the stars."

The girl too done the same with that food, blessing it then offering it to Creator Sun, Mother Earth, and Morning Star, all of the stars and the whole of all nature with life. And into the ground she planted it.

Now it was time for these servants to do their part in this early-morning ritual. Four of the women came forward to the rawhide pots of soup with the bull buffalo tongues. The first of these women dipped into the first soup with a long wood fork made of birch branch and pulled out one tongue. She laid it on the stretched dried rawhide that was there for this purpose, kneeling down beside it. A knife was given her and she talked as loud as she could to be heard by all as she confessed her sins, these were very honest women and without hardly any kind of sin to confess. At the end of her confession, she said, "This gives me the right to cut this tongue and blood berry soup." The tongue was cut into many, many small pieces.

The next woman came to the pot of soup with the holy contents, and she too confessed after dipping another tongue out and holding her flint knife towards the sun as the confession was told. She too repeated what the first woman had said about her right to cut this tongue, and for the people to partake of it and the blood berry soup.

After the four women had done their confessing and the cutting of the blessed tongue and the blood berry soup, the girl's mother and Scarface's grandma began to dish out the soup of blood from the cow buffalos and the four bull buffalo tongues mixed with the sweet sarvis berries. All of the people of this big encampment, including all of the children, from babies on up to the very old people got some of the four bull buffalo tongues in their soup of buffalo blood and sarvis berries. This tongue with the blood and sarvis berries was the host food, the body and the blood of Creator Sun, Mother Earth, and Morning Star, mixed with the sweetness of the life of nature, the sarvis berries.

After everybody had gotten their pieces of the tongue and the blood berry soup, most of the men left the center and went to their tipis. This was from all around the camps, about four men from each clan to help erect this Great Sacrificial Center Tree, the Native Cross. They used two tipi poles tied together at the small end, which worked like long arms to help hold and steady the tree at its top. These two tipi poles were tied just wide enough apart so a branch about eight or ten inches could be held between them as the rawhide rope that holds the two together holds the tree there.

In that era, when this Native Tabernacle, Honor Lodge, Creator Sun's Lodge, or Medicine Lodge was made, the camping utensils were very primitive. Buckets for water were a dried rawhide shaped into a bucket with a hoop of a willow dried around the open end of it, or they were made from the buffalo's belly, known as tripe. On this belly part was another small sack that was used for their water. They also used a wooden bucket, which was a hollowed-out part of a large tree. The rawhide bucket and the wooden bucket were also used as cooking pots. They weren't set directly over the fire, they were set alongside of the fireplace, and heated rocks from this fire were put in the pots to cook whatever was being cooked, mainly meat or entrails of the animal, berry soup at times. Sometimes when they were on a move and things had to be hurried a little, they used a square-cut rawhide fresh from a fresh kill, about two feet square. Four pegs were driven into the ground near the fireplace, and the pegs were about a foot and half apart. The corners of this rawhide were tied over the pegs, which made a bowl. Water was put into this bowl of rawhide, and the meat or whatever was going to be cooked. Heated rocks in the fire done the rest.

Plates were made from weaving smaller branches in a square shape or round shape, and only meat or other food in chunks were dished in these plates. A flat rock was used as a plate, or a flat, dried, and cut-square rawhide was used for a plate. Cups and bowls were made from hollowed-out wood. At times a small, hollowed-out rock was used as bowl, and mostly all of the larger buffalo horns were cut and shaped to hold liquids. The smaller buffalo horns were shaped to be used as spoons or dippers. Forked branches from the trees were cut, sharpened, and used for forks. All of the primitive knives were of the Native flint, an extra-hard stone that held its edge always, very sharp, sharp enough to cut the tough buffalo skin. The spears that were used in the *pis-kuns* to finish off the buffalo were also of flint. Stone mauls or large stone hammers were also used for finishing off the buffalo in the *pis-kun*.

At this time, when several men went to their tipis to set the two tied poles, Scarface was readied too. In between the forks he was taken, and there he was lifted by his servants with help from the other menfolks. Resting his feet on the bundled birch branches, his ankles then were tied to the legs of the branches at the crotch of this Great Sacrificial Center Tree. These two branches, the forks of the tree, were longer than his body, so his wrists were tied higher than his head on these branches. The ankles and the wrists were tied with the stripped green rawhide. After he was tied securely, he was briefly left dangling. At this time, as much as she hated to do this to the man she was going to marry if he came out of this alive, she put a crown of juniper branches on his head. If you have never felt juniper branches around your head with them sharp needles on them, try them sometime and see how they would feel on one's head, especially on the bare part. Sage was also tied at the tips of those forks, and tied to dangle down from that bundle of birch branches near his feet.

All the time, as these things were being done to him, Scarface never stopped humming his power songs that he had achieved during his journey to that mystic land of Creator Sun. He was praying for the strength he needed for his personal sacrifice to Creator Sun, that he might come through it strongly and alive.

It was now time to erect the Sacrificial Center Tree with Scarface tied to it. Those men that had gone to their tipis after the two poles tied together were now slowly coming towards the center where all of the activity was taking place, and from all around the camp they were coming and singing a song to slowly march by until they had come to this center where the tree was to be erected. Soon as they stopped as close as they could, the servants of Scarface and other men that were to help began to slowly raise the Great Sacrificial Center Tree.

Everyone that stood around and near this center was singing now as Scarface was slowly raised higher and higher, dangling from the forks of the tree. This Sacrificial Center Tree was always raised towards the east from where the sun rises, this was the symbolic gesture of giving Scarface's life and body to the sun. It was raised towards the east while the sun is coming up towards the west, to meet one another.

When it got too high for hands and arms, the tree was taken over by those men that held the tied-together tipi poles. They steadied the tree as it was being raised vertically, and held it there. The butt end of this tree was already in the hole that was dug for it, and now the tree was to be turned so Scarface would be facing directly south, facing the sun at its hottest during the middays to come these next four days of his sacrifice. Maneuvering the tree around, they got it in the right position, and there the hole was filled with dirt and tamped around the butt end of this center tree. When the men got through with it, it was very solid, nothing could take it down.

Scarface was now up there in that Sacrificial Center Tree, the truest tree of a human sacrifice. Scarface would be left up in that Sacrificial Center Tree for the next four days without food or water, not to be taken down for any reason, not even for urination. He was to suffer for breaking a bond between the girl and Creator Sun. Suffering for sin.

The girl, too, must suffer for that same sin. Soon after the center tree was set, she was led to that center tipi that was theirs these past few days. This morning, before Scarface was offered to the sun and long before sunrise, just at the graying of dawn, she was taken out to urinate and her tongue was dabbed with a soft-tanned buckskin soaked in fresh water. She will be treated this way for the next four days and nights. Only twice a day she will be taken out by her mother and Scarface's grandma to urinate—once in the morning, long before the sun rises, and as she's returned to the tipi at those same times, her tongue will be dabbed with a water-soaked buckskin. No eating and no taking of water until Scarface is taken down from the Sacrificial Center Tree, dead or alive. That was their payment for the sin against Creator Sun. She also had to keep that heavy robe on and over her head, no matter how hot it would be on the outside. At certain intervals, the burning of sweet grass in this tipi was to be done through the days and nights.

Their servants or disciples were very devoted to them. Soon after Scarface was left up in that tree and the girl had been taken to the center tipi, these servants of Scarface painted themselves with white earth paint all over their bodies and smeared a paste of the same stuff on their hair, just a breechclout to cover their privates and nothing else. These servants of Scarface began to do the sun dance for him as he stood up there in the fork of this Sacrificial Center Tree. They were making power for him so he wouldn't give up his life altogether. They too went without eating food or drinking water those next four days, they were so devoted to Scarface. Others of the men of the camps took turns to sing for these dancers both night and day. While two watched over the girl at all times, her other servants came out to the center to help all they could in whatever was to be done. These women were also very devoted to the girl. They didn't want to eat or drink for those next four days either.

The power dancers for Scarface danced throughout the day and night, all of them dancing in one place and mostly facing the sun during the daytime. They were all around the Sacrificial Center Tree, in a circle around it, and they danced very hard.

It was like one of these marathon dances of this modern age, these men danced and danced. There were times when one would fall down from weakness, lack of food, lack of water. The other sun dancers would revive him with their powers without touching him, only dancing around him in their power dance until he gets back up again to continue his dance.

Other men of the camps also came out to dance for the four days, those that had their faith in Scarface and were devoted to him and the girl. Other women came to help in any way they could for those four days.

As those sun dancers danced on the following days, men from all around the camps went and cut small quaking aspen trees, this was to put all around the Honor Lodge as a shelter for its arena, while other men put up the twelve posts in a circle around this Sacrificial Center Tree. On those twelve posts a crossbeam was put into its forks too, until the beams were almost all the way around. There was no crossbeam across the front, the east side of this circular set posts. It was left open from the ground up.

Other men cut rafter poles to reach from the outside circle of crossbeams that laid on those circle of posts. They were only cut and laid all around the outside of these posts of twelve, for further use.

For Scarface, this was the first of the four mornings and there were three more mornings to come. If at any time he must urinate or if his bowels had to be eased, Scarface must do it from up there in that Sacrificial Center Tree. He must do it without the aid of his hands, as they were tied to the forks of this Center Tree with rawhide strips, his ankles too were tied somewhat apart.

In the next four days, the sun shown brightly and got very hot. It was exceptionally hot. Scarface had to stand there and take it up there in the tree. As each day went by, those green rawhide strips began to dry around his wrists and ankles, and as those green rawhide strips dried, they began to stiffen and started to cut into his flesh on his wrists and ankles. The juniper branch crown too began to dry out, and those needles got sharper—or so it seemed to Scarface. They were cutting into his forehead and, to make it much worse, those green rawhides began to smell from the heat and then all that fresh flesh and blood that was on those strips of rawhide. But there wasn't any way out for Scarface, he was suffering for the sin taking the girl from Creator Sun. He couldn't holler "Enough!" He had to stay with it to the end, stay alive or die. His devoted followers, the six men, were doing all they could to encourage him in the days and nights that followed. They all continued dancing the sun dance for him, a power dance for him and for his encouragement that he wasn't alone to suffer.

The girl too was suffering, she had to stay in that center tipi all day long and all night long. If she wanted to move or change positions while she was sitting, or if she was laying down in bed at nights, she had to call on the servants to move her about in the position she wanted. She wasn't free to move in any way while Scarface was up there in that Great Center Tree. Just twice a day she was allowed to go out and urinate, once at dawn before the sunrise and once again just before dark after the sun had set. No water, except those dabs. No food until after those four days. To make it much worse for her, she had to keep that heavy buffalo robe over her body and head throughout the hottest days of this holy ceremony. And at nights she was covered up even thicker with more heavy buffalo robes. There is no comfort in anything when you are going through a sacrifice or self-torture for our Creator Sun that made you and all of the whole universe with all of nature as it is, even these days.

All around the camps, holy bundles were being unwrapped. This was to help Scarface and the girl through this critical time, these last four days by the keepers of these holy bundles. Most generally, the holy earth paint to each holy bundle, the sweet grass, and all the basic articles this holy bundle originated from were all very holy because they were given by holy spirits

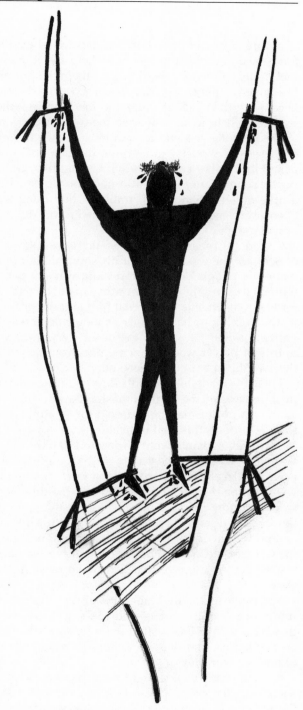

*Creator Sun's Great Sacrificial Tree,*
*the Indian Cross*

of nature. Many of these holy bundles were being honored and being served food for all around the camps to help the two. Many people were getting their faces painted for them, to give them the power they needed at this time. Everyone in this camp was concerned over the two, Scarface and the girl, because of their lack of water and food through these very hot days, and all wanted to help in some way so the two could overcome this sacrifice.

The first day, second day, and most of the third day, the people in the circle of these twelve posts, and around the Center Tree where Scarface was being baked in that hot sun up in that Center Tree, could hear him humming his power songs. Later in the afternoon of this third day, Scarface began to get a little quieter than usual, until his humming was altogether quiet. He'd been overcome with the lack of water and the lack of food through these very hot days.

Creator Sun seen to it that it would be exceptionally hot during this sacrifice of Scarface, he was paying for his sins and that of the girl too. But also, this made the people of this camp more wary of Scarface and the girl, and so with all their might and power they made holy for Scarface to give the power for life, to overcome this ordeal him and the girl were in. In those very days it was nothing to have power as long as one was brave enough to bear the hardships that goes with the quest for power, which was just you alone. Spirits of power wouldn't come near you if there was anyone else around, they would be scared of those people instead.

This also made his servants dance that much harder in their sun dancing, their power dancing for their master that was up in that Center Tree. Probably all of this power making did do a lot for him, give him just enough power to pull through this trial of his life.

Scarface's servants were so devoted to him, they inflicted wounds to their body and skin with the points of sharp flint to lose blood like Scarface was up in the Tree. Those hard, drying rawhides that tied his wrists and ankles were cutting deeper into his skin and making more blood bleed from those wounds, more pain for him. Seeing that agony of pain on his face was all those faithful servants could bear, so by inflicting wounds on their own arms and body, they too would have that pain. They danced on by him all around the Center Tree, all in white earth paint, which made the blood all the more visible, standing out as it oozed down over this white earth paint on their skin.

Scarface was totally limber, his arms were taut as his wrists were tied to those forks and his ankles tied to the forks of the tree. If it hadn't been for that, he would of fallen off of the tree. As his head bobbed around, knocking on one branch and then the other, his head began bleeding from the crown of juniper branches.

At long last, this last night went by with Scarface half dangling from the Sacrificial Center Tree from lack of food and water. He was still breathing the breath of life, but very little. That very hot sun was almost too hot for him.

Dawn finally came this morning of the fifth day. Although the girl was very weak from her ordeal, she managed to get about and go with her servants to the Sacrificial Center Tree. Single file they went there and very solemnly, with the help from the other people of this camp, Scarface was cut down off of his perch on that Sacrificial Center Tree, all bloody. The girl was below at the foot of this tree to receive him as he was brought down to ground level with the help of her mother and Scarface's grandma. The other servants were there too to help her and Scarface's servants, the men that danced the sun dance or power dance for Scarface. They had enough strength to help with their master as Scarface was taken to that center tipi and put inside, on the bed of soft-tanned buffalo robes. All of the Native power doctors (which our white or non-Indians call witch doctors) huddled around Scarface, and with their strange powers soon brought Scarface back around from his almost fatal sacrifice. Each one doctored by his or her own special singer and drummer all in rhythm with one another.

Each Native doctor had his or her own special way to administer the medicine. Each Native doctor had been given power by one of the lives of Mother Nature. As I have mentioned before in this story, all things of this Mother Earth have lives—be it a rock, tree, lake, river, mountain, high hill, butte, all of the animals, birds, serpents, and even the many different kinds of insect, the stars, moon, clouds, thunder, lightning, wind, and all others. All of these have power that they bestow on those that seek from them. This is a known fact among the Natives all over this world. Many of these Natives still use that power for healing others, or it could be used for hurting others too.

Just before the taking down of Scarface from that Sacrificial Center Tree, all of the men got ready with their two poles tied together all around the camps, all of them had gone back to their tipis while Scarface was being taken down from the Sacrificial Center Tree and in pairs stood by the inner circle of tipis with their tipi poles all facing to the center.

As soon as Scarface was taken off of the Center Tree and brought to the center tipi, all of these men that stood around the camps on the inside circle with their tipi poles began to sing, and at the same time started to advance toward the center. Four times they stopped while an elder prayed. The fourth stop they were all at the center, and immediately after another prayer by an elder, the erection to complete this Honor Lodge for Creator Sun was underway. With all of the men involved, it didn't take very long. All there was to complete it was to put the rafters from the outside beams to the fork of the Sacrificial Center Tree—eleven rafters, beginning from the beam above the first panel south of the entrance (there wasn't a beam over the entrance, it was open and there wasn't going to be a rafter there either), so they worked from that first rafter on the right of the entrance as it was facing eastward, to the right, or clockwise, until the eleven rafters were up.

While Scarface was up in that Sacrificial Center Tree, and in between the time he was tied up there and the time he was taken down from there, all of the men had gone out into the quaking aspen patches to cut a small tree with all the leaves still on it and bring it to this center where the Honor Lodge was. The small quaking aspen trees were stacked all around the circle of twelve posts around the Center Tree. They were there for this morning's use as the completion of the rafters was done. Those small quaking aspen trees were all stood up around this lodge, leaned against the beam with the butt ends on the ground. They were quite thick when they were all put up clear around this Honor Lodge. The entrance was left open for Creator Sun from the ground up to the very Holy Center Tree, that he may enter this Honor Lodge for him as soon as he came into view along the eastern horizon and stay in it all day long. It was erected according to his own specifications that he sent with Scarface.

The explanation or the interpretation of this Honor Lodge came to me from my elders, particularly from my grandma, Catches Last Bullchild. She told me the lodge stood for the world as we see it from a standing point of view. Looking all around us, we see trees, hills, the mountains, and above us we see the big blue sky. And most of all—we don't only see him, but we feel its warmth, the heat of him, which makes everyone glad or happy—is Creator Sun above us.

The twelve posts set up in a circle are the symbol for the twelve moons of each year. The twelve servants of the girl and Scarface, six men and six women, are also symbols for the twelve moons. There are eleven rafters to reach from the outside circle to the center or Center Tree, the Sacrificial Center Tree. These eleven rafters are the symbol of the ten main servants of Scarface and the girl, five of Scarface's and five of the girl's, which makes ten, and the eleventh of the rafters is the girl's, because Scarface was up in that crotch personally. And eleven of these rafters also represent the dome of the sky or that which is above and over us. These eleven rafters represent the dome of the sky and the girl with ten of the servants, because those servants were constantly over the girl and Scarface while going through this great holy ceremony of the Honor Lodge. The girl represented Mother Earth, and during the ceremony Scarface represented our Creator Sun. They were so very devoted to the two. And of course that Great Center Tree represents Creator Sun, the center to all life. Scarface gave his body to Creator Sun, tied to the forks of this Great Center Tree, to bake directly under the heat of the sun for those four days of sacrifice.

All of the rafters and crossbeams are tied with the green rawhide of the buffalo stripped into many pieces to go all around this Honor Lodge. This stripped green rawhide of the buffalo represents the first contact made with the strange land of Creator Sun, (long before Scarface ever found it with help from the swans), when a woman was taken to that very strange land. She was the one that brought back the first holy pipe bundle that was known by the Plains Natives as the Ancient Pipe. Because of her loneliness after she got a glimpse of the land below her, her own land and her people, she was brought back down by her man and with that gift of the Ancient Pipe Bundle on her back, and she was let down to Mother Earth with a long striped green rawhide of the buffalo hide.

For many years after this first Honor Lodge was erected for Creator Sun, a human sacrifice was the thing. A person would make a vow, probably in the late fall. This person was so very serious about another life, maybe someone who was sick or badly hurt, who was going to die for sure, and on her or his deathbed. This was a very serious vow, and generally it couldn't be made for anything less than life or death. A person that makes this vow to sacrifice themselves is putting his own body in place of the very loved one. On that Great Center Tree, under the direct heat of the hot sun, one could easily die from lack of water and food, or the loss of blood from the rawhides as they dry in that heat and cut into the flesh. It was asking to save one human body with the giving of a stronger body on the Center Tree, a trade of love for life, a payment for the sick one's sins. That was the vow to sacrifice oneself on this Sacrificial Center Tree.

This human sacrifice went on for many years, until approximately 170 years ago, when the first of the non-Indian missionaries began to come among the many different tribes of Natives. These missionaries told the Natives that this wasn't the true way of religion, and taught their own way. The sacrificing of a human life was at an end. The Native still erected the Honor Lodge to Creator Sun, but in place of the human sacrifice, goods of the cloth material were tied in the forks of that Great Center Tree. From that time on, and still in some of the Native reservations in both Canada and the United States, this Honor Lodge to Creator Sun is observed, and that Sacrificial Center Tree is made very colorful by the hanging of many different colors of cloth goods.

According to the unwritten Native history, never was there a life lost through this sacrifice to Creator Sun.

According to written history of the non-Indian, this stopping of the Native religion in their way was very contrary to the coming to this land of Natives. Those first comers of the non-Indian say that they came for the freedom of religion. But they stopped our way and in place taught us a foreign religion that even now some of us Natives don't really understand, because it's still foreign to us people. Us Natives of these Americas had the truest faith that everyone followed in these lands. We weren't only believers in the sun, but we knew for a fact that it was true to worship the sun, he was our true Maker. He must've made the God that's trying its best to take our Creator Sun's place. Even now, that God takes the glory that our Creator Sun does for all people. That God that the white people try to shove on to us is a selfish God, and only whiteman's God. My Creator Sun is all colors, all nationalities, and helps everyone in this body of Mother Earth, not just certain ones. Creator Sun provides for all, it brings up all food, it gives us breath and life from all of its elements.

At the head of the inside of this Honor Lodge, opposite the entrance there is small closet-like structure, approximately six by six feet, built for the sun worshippers and the religious rituals. It's a place to re-do the earth paint, or it could easily be an altar for the religious men. At times when those sun dancers get a little weak from lack of food and water or are feeling a little sick, this little structure is always open to them. Some people also use this little structure to seek those supernatural spirits that those high religious men might've left behind in them, or the spirits might linger on in them for a while. (But this is when everyone has moved from this particular campsite and no one is around there any longer.) This little structure was a little partition to that farthest wall from the entrance, directly on the west side, inside of this circular Honor Lodge. It was also made for Creator Sun, that his image will sleep there after it had set in the west.

Scarface had been taken down from the Sacrificial Center Tree, and brought in to the center tipi. Creator Sun's Honor Lodge was up and erected to completion. Now a big holy marriage will come between Scarface and the girl.

Both Scarface and the girl were now in the center tipi, and were coming out of their ordeal as good as could be expected. It made Scarface feel much better, and fast, because he knew the girl was his own and this was the day the wedding was to begin. Weak, but feeling much better now, him and the girl called for a survival feast. They had both survived their payment for their sins, and were both so anxious to complete their marriage now. Everyone in the encampment ate with them during their survival feast. Everyone was glad for them to be alive after their ordeal.

Wedding preparations for them were already underway. It was still the same morning, right after the sunrise Scarface had been taken down from the Sacrificial Center Tree as limp as could be. But Natives were very powerful, he not only regained conciousness but was already strong enough to go on with his wedding to the girl.

The high religious men and women were specially invited to come to this center tipi. From the day Scarface was brought down from Creator Sun's land of mystery, he hadn't had the chance to touch this girl he wanted so much. The two of them were still restricted until after the holy wedding took place.

All of those that wanted to attend this holy wedding were all gathered at this center tipi or near there. Those elders of this camp decided to reenact the part where the girl received Scarface at the foot of the Sacrificial Center Tree, this truly was the beginning of taking a bridegroom and a bride. The elders of the camp decided this was a true way for a man and woman to get bonded together as a man and wife, and this was going to be the way it was going to be done whenever a wedding between a man and woman was to take place, from this day on to ever.

As Scarface and the girl got ready, out to the Sacrificial Center Tree they were taken. On each side of Scarface were the Chief and his best friend, in the lead of the others, and always so solemn as they all walked out to that Center Tree. The girl, with her mother on her right side and Scarface's grandma on her left side, were walking along in their solemn way. Behind her, the people of the camps were slowly walking too. Again those four stops were made, and at each stop that holy pipe and prayers were said by the elders again, praying for good luck and a good marriage between the girl and Scarface. At the foot of the Sacrificial Center Tree the last stop was made. The sun was in the western skies at this time, so with Scarface and the girl facing the sun, one of the elders bonded the two together with a long blessing. And at the last of his blessings, he told Scarface and the girl to always honor Creator Sun throughout their lives.

They were brought back to the center tipi and they still couldn't touch each other. They were told that this holy marriage was to be completed before they could touch one another. This was probably the hardest part of the sacrifices. The six men and six women also moved into this center tipi with the two. Neither Scarface nor the girl could go out alone just yet, their servants were always right there to be with them. Those servants were along with them when they went out to the bushes to relieve themselves, and they both couldn't go at the same time. There wasn't any chance for Scarface and the girl to be alone at any time.

At night, the two were made to sleep together, and in those days, mostly all of the Natives slept bare naked. Their servants, the women and the men, slept around their bed and at even the slightest movement by the two, the servants jumped to their sides to find out what was wanted. Throughout the night, the fire in this tipi burned brightly and there wasn't a thing Scarface and the girl could do about this. No matter how much they wanted one another, this was their holy matrimonial marriage, a very holy time of being bonded together. The twelve servants were making sure of this holy bond for four days and nights again, they were to insure the procedure of it. So for the next four days and nights, Scarface and his new wife suffered again for the want of one another. That was the holy bonding of the two, to be with one another for four days and nights and not be able to be as a man and wife because someone was there at all times until after those four days and nights.

It finally came to an end of the fourth night, the last night of their holy marriage. A big sweat bath was ready for the two and some of their servants to the south of the camps. This was a baptismal sweat for both of them, to cleanse their bodies off, sweat off the sins they suffered for during this long holy ceremony, a payment for sins and complying with Creator Sun's orders and the erection of the Honor Lodge for him.

Right after the big sweat, a big marriage feast was all ready for them and all of the people too. The whole camp was invited to eat with them. Scarface and the girl were given the center tipi to live in as their own. Many dogs went with this tipi as gifts to them and many, many gifts from all of the people were brought to this tipi. The Chief of this camp relinquished his chieftainship to Scarface. Scarface and his bride became great leaders of their people, both in their religion and socially. Both were very compassionate to all of the people about them.

The Honor Lodge for Creator Sun became known to many people in these days as the Medicine Lodge. It really doesn't have anything to do with medicine, but again it was translated wrong. Many people are confused by our Native words. Many people translate "holy" as "medicine," instead of the right translation, "holy." It's confusing because, in such things as Native doctoring, those Native doctors combine the medicine with their holy doctoring gear. Holy doctoring gear is the things that one achieves during a quest for supernatural powers. With these and the medicine, a sick one can be healed almost miraculously overnight. So many people confuse holy with medicine.

From the day Scarface was brought to his Native land by Creator Sun among the quaking aspen patches, to the completion of his holy matrimonial marriage to the girl, the Chief's daughter, it took a half of a moon—or, in our count, fifteen days—for the Honor Lodge to be completed.

After these fifteen days of worship to Creator Sun, fun had to be mixed with the holiness. While some of the clans moved away from this camp, some of the livelier people got a-going with some social activity. All of the modern social dancing was in those days unheard of. The social doings and dancing were of the clan type, where only clan members took part, or society members in their own society dancing. Among other dances were the fly dance, the dancing done after the lowly house fly, and the bull tail dance, done after the way a buffalo bull holds its tail when on a run or when disturbed by something, and also the way the bull swings it. Each of these bull tail dancers have a dried bull's tail that is fixed on a belt that is tied around their waists as the dance is in progress. The bull dance is done after the buffalo bull when it's mating during the mating season. The dog's dance is done as a dog when it runs about, jumping and barking. The dove dance was done after the dove when it's hopping around on the ground looking for food. These members of the dove society were food getters of those times.

Many of these social dances were held for a few days after the main event of the Honor Lodge to Creator Sun, while each day many moved on to wherever they were headed for, and the camps dwindled down to nothing.

The day after the Honor Lodge is completed, it was an annual thing for the head Chief of the whole tribe to invite all of the sub-Chiefs, Chiefs of small groups, and also the Chiefs of the many clans of the tribe. In this Chief's meeting, the Chief of the many separate groups or clans decide with their head Chief where their winter was going to be spent, and the many places where each Chief might move to. In this way, the head Chief knows just about where each group is at a certain time, and all of those Chiefs know ahead of time where each group will be so the others will not move near that particular area, because of hunting and preparing for the coming winter as each group stocks up on drying meat and other kinds of food, root medicine, and herbs and barks of the many different growths.

I particularly know the Piegans, but I think all of the many different tribes were the same way. The Piegans had a very large hunting area, consisting of many millions, maybe billions of acres. And so, the Piegans had many places to move to and about, each clan and group chose their way to go each year after the big encampment of Honoring the Sun. As each group moved from the big encampment of Honoring the Sun Lodge, they generally stuck to the routes taken in the previous years. None was in a particular hurry, in these days all the traveling and moving about was done on foot with the dogs doing much of the work and belongings loaded on the dog travois. A travois was called that by the first French trappers that came among the plains Natives and seen these V-shaped carriers. These were fastened on a horse and the horse pulls this along with the wider part of the V dragging on the ground. Tied in the middle of these V-shaped poles was a rack to carry a load. The load was tied down with a tanned rawhide rope. It also carried the smaller children. This was the larger type for the horses that came into Native hands in approximately the last half of the 1700s. It was closer to the 1800s when those Spanish strays slowly made their way northward, and eventually the many Northern tribes began to use horses for moving and for faster transportation.

The dog travois was made according the size of each dog. From our beginning, in our Native legends of old, the dog was known to have been with people and it done work for the people. Mostly all of those dogs of the earlier days were very well trained by their masters and could do almost anything for them.

Many more holy pipe bundles came into existence after that first Honor Lodge to Creator Sun. Some of them were very true, and a lot of them were just made up by people that were jealous over many things and really couldn't go out to achieve their own.

Fighting was unheard of until after horses came into the Native life. Life was love. All Natives loved life of all things—animals, fowls, even insects, the strange lives of the flowers, weeds, trees, rocks, any kind of water, lake or river, the mountains, wind, thunder, lightning, stars, moon, and, most of all, Morning Star, Mother Earth, and Creator Sun.

All Natives loved their brothers and sisters of other tribes in those dog days. Communication just took too long between those many tribes of Natives, and our foot traveling was just too slow. Native tribes met very seldom, and they met with their love for one another and never a hard feeling between any of them. There wasn't any reason to be mad at one another. Camping together whenever a meeting happened and departing from one another with gifts for one another, maybe never to meet again for many years to come.

In both the Christian church and the Native religion, we are told about the creation of earth and universe, and in both they are corresponding. We were taught that man was made from the mud and the woman was made from the man's rib. These are the same between the Church and the Native ways. The life of the biblical characters of the whiteman's Bible and those of the Native legends are very much the same. Faith was just about the same, and their ways of living are about the same. The Bible tells of the Moses that went up in the mountains to see that God of the whiteman, and spent forty days up in the mountains. Here among the Natives, a Native went to the strange land of the Creator Sun, staying with them for a moon and half a moon, which totals to forty-five days. Our tribe of the Piegans (or the Blackfeet, as we were named by the Lewis and Clark expedition) not only believe in our faith, but we do know it really exists. Creator Sun is above us, looks down at us every day, it's our true Creator, because it gives us breath and provides food for us as it grows all from its power of elements.

The whiteman was given to build a tabernacle, not these fancy churches they have in these days. The Native was also given to erect a tabernacle, from the growth of Mother Earth—using the trees mostly, their trunks and leaves and a few birch branches and also the rawhide of the buffalo. (In these later years, cow or cattle rawhide took its place.) We Natives still make our Honor Lodges, Native Churches, Sun Lodges, Observance Lodge, or Medicine Lodge the way our Creator Sun wanted us to build them for him. This Native Tabernacle hasn't changed.

Many of us Natives observe the growth of the whiteman's way. It seems to us that the whiteman is trying to outdo each other by building their churches so expensive and so fancy when truthfully, this Creator's Tabernacle was to be just a plain, temporary place of worship, just for that particular year, and the Creator takes it back after its use for that year. We leave them intact as we build them for Creator Sun, and he takes back through the years that follow. They slowly deteriorate in his own elements of weather and eventually turn back into dust, back to Mother Earth's body where it came from in the first place.

A high religious man conducts of the Honor Lodge, a man that had erected an Honor Lodge for our Creator Sun before. These high religious people change almost from year to year. Among the whiteman's way, some or mostly all professionally taught teachers of the many churches hold that position until they die or retire. There is some that quit that preaching if it isn't profitable. In most cases of the whiteman's way, it has to be money-making for them or it's no go.

The many churches I've gone to, including the Catholic church, in every service the money has to be collected, which they call offerings. A mediator is involved in all of these collections or offerings in the churches, but no one has ever seen anyone from their God's Land come and get that collection for him. Where does that collected money go to? Many places I've overheard the preacher say it's for the needy. I've been needy many times and went to a church to get help. There were some churches that told me I was too lazy, that I must work to make my living. So where does this collected money really go?

Among us natives, we offer too to Creator Sun. We do not have a mediator between Creator Sun and the people that offer him things. Offerings to him go directly to him, all Native offerings are tied up in some tree and offered to Creator Sun through prayers. Like the Native Tabernacles, those offerings slowly deteriorate in the weather and eventually return back into dust, back into Mother Earth's body. To me this is a very true way to offer to Creator Sun, our maker of human beings.

In baptisms of the churches, water is used. Water is poured on the person getting baptized or he is dunked in a tank of water, or it might be a deep hole in some creek or river, while the preacher says a prayer. This is the way of the many churches.

The Native is baptized by sweating for several hours in one of their huts that they make in mostly all of the reservations. Naturally, the Native does things the hard way, the true way we were all given many thousands of years ago.

Some churches burn incense while the service goes on from palm leaves or others of the trees or plants, which is all right. The Native still burns the sweet grass, cedar leaf, sweet pine needle, sage of the prairies, juniper needles, and the pine moss. These were given by Creator Sun to use as incense, and the Native still uses them widely. These are somewhat harder to get, but the Native still travels for miles to get these, as they are very necessary to us. Like I said, the Native way of religion isn't easy.

Many churches of the whiteman break the bread and a little wine in a special service of communion for their host. The Native still uses the tongue of the cattle that took the place of the buffalo tongue as their host at the religious gatherings, and also the blood berry soup that goes with it. This too was the given way, to use natural things of nature. This was our host, the blood of Creator Sun and his body from the things he put on Mother Earth to multiply. Creator Sun gave us things that are a little hard to take, but nevertheless we have to take them for his sake because we love him. The compassion he gave to all of us is the true reason we do the things he wants us to do.

Many thousands of years ago, we were all given this gift of Tabernacles to worship our Creator Sun. But again, many thousands of years back, we divided our beliefs—first into two separate ways, then in time into many ways through the churches. According to my research of the past, I find that us Natives still hold the truest way of that giving of faith. These others, as much as I hate to say, they went that way for the belief in profit or money-making and forgot the true Creator Sun. We have much proof of this, just observe the ways of both the Native and the whiteman.

From time beginning, the Native was taught to revere the maker of people through prayers as a pipe is being smoked. This pipe for smoking was given to the very first people in that beginning to use for prayers, and in time, the others of the incense were given along with the holy bundles of the many holy pipes. We had pure tobacco in those earlier days, one didn't get cancer from it or any other sickness or disease. The smoke that rises into the air is the one that carries our messages of prayers to Creator Sun, it's what he told us. So! In these days, the Native still uses the smoke of the incense or pipe smoke to convey their prayers to Creator Sun.

These are a few comparisons of the Native faith and the Christian faith as seen in these days, there are many more that differ and many that correspond to one another.

The Native lived a serene life before the coming of whiteman. History has it in writing just the opposite from our true ways of life. History has the Native as being war-mongers, barbarians, bloodthirsty people, cruel, brutal, filthy, dirty, lousy with human ticks, savages, and murderers.

None of these were true. Just read the history, wherever it might be a little truly written. We were always just too devoted to Creator Sun and always so very compassionate to others, even to the first comers of the non-Indians. If the Native was so mean, ready to kill on sight, like written history has us, we would've killed off all those non-Indians that were landing their ships along our coasts in those early days. Instead, they were met with welcome by those Natives of those days. You say you might've sneaked to land from those ships or swim to shore unnoticed? No chance, not by an Indian. We lived like the wild, as our Creator Sun had taught us. We had very keen hearing and an eagle eyesight, no chance for that. So this alone proves that we loved and welcomed anyone, even the non-Indian that came in those times.

The Native of the land had no expenses to pay. We didn't have to buy food, we didn't buy clothing, nor all the things that go with daily living. We didn't know anything of rent, we had our portable homes, our tipis. We traveled slow because we had to walk to wherever we were going, only our faithful dogs to carry some of our burdens, but all things were fine until our white friends brought to us their ways of destruction, their disease, their rotten food which we aren't quite used to yet, their killings, their thievery, robbery, and their cunning. This put an end to our once beautiful serene life, and today we are struggling to survive that onslaught of the whiteman, as they have never given up trying to fully conquer the continents. The Native can only pray to our Creator Sun for deliverance from this wicked onslaught and robbery of our lands and now the waters.